£16

China's
Transformations

China's Transformations

The Stories beyond the Headlines

Edited by
Lionel M. Jensen and
Timothy B. Weston

ROWMAN & LITTLEFIELD PUBLISHERS, INC.
Lanham • Boulder • New York • Toronto • Plymouth, UK

ROWMAN & LITTLEFIELD PUBLISHERS, INC.

Published in the United States of America
by Rowman & Littlefield Publishers, Inc.
A wholly owned subsidiary of The Rowman & Littlefield Publishing Group, Inc.
4501 Forbes Boulevard, Suite 200, Lanham, Maryland 20706
www.rowmanlittlefield.com

Estover Road, Plymouth PL6 7PY, United Kingdom

British Library Cataloguing in Publication Information Available

Library of Congress Cataloging-in-Publication Data

China's transformations : the stories beyond the headlines / edited by Lionel M.
    Jensen and Timothy B. Weston.
        p. cm.
    "Successor volume to 'China beyond the headlines'"—data view p.
    Includes bibliographical references and index.
    ISBN-13: 978-0-7425-3862-7 (cloth : alk. paper)
    ISBN-10: 0-7425-3862-1 (cloth : alk. paper)
    ISBN-13: 978-0-7425-3863-4 (pbk. : alk. paper)
    ISBN-10: 0-7425-3863-X (pbk. : alk. paper)
    1. China—Social conditions—1976-2000. 2. China—Economic conditions—
1976-2000. 3. China—Social conditions—2000- 4. China—Economic
conditions—2000- 5. China—Relations—United States. 6. United States—
Relations—China. I. Jensen, Lionel M. II. Weston, Timothy B., 1964-

HN733.5.C442 2006
306.0951—dc22
                                                                    2006019299

Printed in the United States of America

♾™ The paper used in this publication meets the minimum requirements of
American National Standard for Information Sciences—Permanence of Paper
for Printed Library Materials, ANSI/NISO Z39.48-1992.

In remembrance of Liu Binyan, a man of conscience and unstinting courage, whose life offers inspiration for the hard work ahead for China and the world.

Black Map

in the end, cold crows piece together
the night: a black map
I've come home—the way back
longer than the wrong road
long as a life

bring the heart of winter
when spring water and horse pills
become the words of night
when memory barks
a rainbow haunts the black market

my father's life-spark small as a pea
I am his echo
turning the corner of encounters
a former lover hides in a wind
swirling with letters

Beijing, let me
toast your lamplights
let my white hair lead
the way through the black map
as though a storm were taking you to fly

I wait in line until the small window
shuts: O the bright moon
I've come home—reunions
are less than goodbyes
only one less

Bei Dao

Contents

Chronology

1949	Founding of the People's Republic of China (PRC); Mao Zedong (1893–1976) becomes leader of China
	Nationalist Party (Guomindang) retreats to Taiwan, establishing the Republic of China (ROC)
1950–1953	Land reform
1951–1953	Three-Anti and Five-Anti movements
1955	Socialist upsurge in the Chinese countryside
1956	Collectivization
1957	Hundred Flowers Campaign
1958–1961	Great Leap Forward ("Three Hard Years")
1966–1976	Great Proletarian Cultural Revolution
1972	Sino-U.S. Communiqué (Shanghai Communiqué): official affirmation of the One-China policy
1975	Four Modernizations (agriculture, national defense, science and industry, and technology) is proclaimed by Zhou Enlai (1899–1976)
1976	Zhou Enlai and Mao Zedong die
1978	Beginning of the Deng Xiaoping (1904–1997) era; Deng becomes "paramount leader" and restarts the Four Modernizations
1978–1979	Democracy Wall movement
1979	Deng Xiaoping visits the United States
	Deng proclaims the Four Cardinal Principles: keeping to the socialist road, upholding the dictatorship of the proletariat, upholding the leadership of the Chinese

Communist Party (CCP), and upholding Marxism-Leninism–Mao Zedong Thought

United States and China establish diplomatic relations (normalization)

Democracy activist Wei Jingsheng is sentenced to fifteen years in prison for his authorship of the manifesto "The Fifth Modernization: Democracy"

1980   Gengshen democratic reforms

International Monetary Fund (IMF) admits China as a member

1982   The China National Offshore Oil Corporation (CNOOC) is founded

1983–1984   Anti–Spiritual Pollution Campaign

1984   China is given membership in the International Atomic Energy Agency

1985   Hong Kong defeats China in a soccer match, provoking a violent riot

Students rally in opposition to Japanese influence in China and in favor of open door policy

1986   Anti–Bourgeois Liberalization Campaign (crackdown on cultural liberalism and influence from the West)

1986–1987   Widespread Chinese student demonstrations in support of democracy

1987   Fang Lizhi and Liu Binyan (1925–2005) are expelled from the CCP

1989   Millions protest in support of democracy, resulting in Beijing (Tiananmen Square) massacre

National campaign (*yanda*, or "strike hard") against pornography

1990   Promulgation of the Basic Law of the Hong Kong Special Administrative Region (SAR)

Asian Games are held in Beijing

1991   U.S.-led coalition launches Operation Desert Storm to liberate Kuwait

Massive floods in China's East and Southeast displace more than 206 million people

1992   Deng Xiaoping's Southern Tour reaffirms the Chinese government's commitment to capitalism

1994   Publication of the first two volumes of *The Selected Works of Deng Xiaoping*

Announcement of "socialism with Chinese characteristics"

1995   Taiwan's president Lee Teng-hui visits the United States, jeopardizing U.S.-China relations

Third summit meeting between the United States and China yields pledge for constructive partnership

China's National People's Congress adopts the country's first banking law, the Law of the People's Republic of China on the People's Bank of China

1996   China conducts an underground nuclear test

1997   Deng Xiaoping dies; Jiang Zemin becomes president

Return of Hong Kong to Chinese sovereignty

1999   Portuguese entrepôt of Macao returns to Chinese sovereignty

Falun Gong movement stages a meditation vigil outside Zhongnan hai involving ten thousand practitioners

Government crackdown on Falun Gong

Fiftieth anniversary of the founding of the PRC

NATO forces destroy the Chinese embassy in Belgrade, killing three "journalists"

U.S. Congressional Report reveals Chinese theft of U.S. nuclear secrets

2000   Original projected date for realization of the Four Modernizations (revised in 1994 to 2047)

Twenty thousand molybdenum mine workers riot in Liaoning province because of summary dismissal without wages

George W. Bush elected president of the United States

Democratic Progressive Party candidate Chen Shui-bian is elected president of Taiwan and signals ambivalence toward the One-China policy

2001   Publication of *The Tiananmen Papers*

Beijing selected by the International Olympic Committee (IOC) as host city for the 2008 Olympics

Collision of a U.S. reconnaissance aircraft and a Chinese fighter plane over the South China Sea results in crash of Chinese fighter plane, and national anti-U.S. protests ensue; Chinese government conveys protesting students by bus to the U.S. embassy for demonstrations

September 11 destruction of the World Trade Center in New York City and attack on the Pentagon

2002   China is officially admitted into the World Trade Organization (WTO)

United States promulgates its National Security Strategy (Bush Doctrine) justifying preventive war

United States launches Operation Enduring Freedom, in Afghanistan

Promulgation of Jiang Zemin's Three Represents theory, in which the CCP represents the advanced productive forces (businesspeople), the advanced cultural forces (intellectuals), and the masses (workers and peasants)

The CCP announces that businesspeople may be admitted to membership in the party

2003   Sudden outbreak of severe acute respiratory syndrome (SARS); Chinese government intentionally misrepresents the extent of the problem, provoking international protest

Onset of avian influenza (H5N1; bird flu)

United States declares war on Iraq and begins Operation Iraqi Freedom

More than 500,000 Hong Kong citizens march in pro-democracy demonstration

China's first successful manned spaceflight

2004   George W. Bush reelected president of the United States

One hundred sixty-six miners die in an explosion at Chenjiashan coal mine in Shaanxi province

Revelation of U.S. torture of prisoners at Abu Ghraib prison and at the U.S. Special Detention Facility at Guantánamo Bay, Cuba

2005   Protests break out in Beijing following revelation that Japanese textbooks misrepresented the Japanese invasion and occupation of China

China National Offshore Oil Corporation (CNOOC) makes a $18.5 billion bid to acquire U.S.-based Union Oil Company of California (UNOCAL)

U.S. House of Representatives, citing national security, votes 333–92 to block CNOOC purchase of UNOCAL

China hosts the opposition leaders of Taiwan

China's National People's Congress passes Anti-Secession Law authorizing military force to defend China's sovereignty

China's second successful manned spaceflight

Beijing-based Lenovo Group acquires IBM's personal computer (PC) unit, becoming the world's third-largest PC maker

Tennis Master Cup held in Shangahi's Qi Zhong stadium

In Hong Kong, 250,000 protest against Chief Executive Donald Tsang and for democracy

Chinese paramilitaries open fire on peasant protesters in Dongzhou village, killing twenty

2006   Security forces repress antigovernment protests in Panlong,
            Guangdong

            Information Office of the State Council announces new
            measures to control the Internet, instant messaging, and
            cellular phones

            Government announces new law imposing financial
            penalties on domestic news organizations that report
            on national emergencies without permission

            Xinhua, China's official news agency, proclaims new regu-
            lations obliging the foreign media to obtain govern-
            ment approval to distribute news, pictures and graphics
            within China

            Communication Administration Bureau of Beijing an-
            nounces the shutdown of Century China, the most in-
            fluential independent website in China

            Hu Jintao orders the unionization of all Wal-Mart stores in
            China under the aegis of the All China Federation of
            Trade Unions

            Nationwide crackdown on corruption results in detention
            of high-ranking CCP officials in Beijing, Fujian, Hunan,
            Shanghai, and Tianjin

            Arrest of prominent civil rights lawyers Gao Zhisheng and
            Guo Feixiong by Chinese security authorities

            Zhao Yan, a *New York Times* researcher, is sentenced to
            three years' imprisonment for "fraud"

            Ching Cheong, a correspondent for the *Straits Times*, is
            tried and sentenced to five years for "spying"

            North Korea claims to detonate a nuclear device (of inde-
            terminate size) in Gilju, Hamgyong Province

            The initial public offering (IPO) of Industrial and Com-
            mercial Bank of China stock sets a world record in ex-
            cess of $19 billion

            Chinese government announces the drafting of a new la-
            bor law that protects workers' rights, guarantees collec-
            tive bargaining, and cracks down on sweatshops

            More than one hundred Chinese intellectuals sign a let-
            ter protesting the government shutdown of Century
            China

            "Chinese Blogger Conference 2006" is held in Hangzhou

            The Forum on China–Africa Cooperation is convened in
            Beijing; China pledges to double its aid to Africa and
            provide $5 billion in loans and credits as part of a new
            strategic partnership

2007	Projected date for first Chinese astronaut spacewalk
	Projected date of review of Hong Kong's Basic Law; possible beginning of universal suffrage
2008	Beijing scheduled to host the games of the XXIX Olympiad
2012	Date of projected completion of China's national space station

Table of Equivalent Measures and Administrative Units

EQUIVALENT MEASURES

renminbi (RMB; literally, "people's money"): national currency of China
7.91 Chinese dollars (yuan, ¥) = US$1
7.78 Hong Kong dollars = US$1
New Taiwan dollar (NT): national currency of Taiwan
33.1NT = US$1

centimeter	.39 inch
gram	.035 ounce
kilogram	2.2 pounds
square kilometer	.38 square mile
meter	3.28 feet
square meter	10.76 square feet
cubic meter	35.31 cubic feet
microgram	.000001 gram
milligram	.001 gram, .015 grains
millimeter	.001 meter, .100 centimeter
mu	.269 hectare, .667 acre

ADMINISTRATIVE UNITS

There are three larger levels of administrative organization in China. As the United States has fifty states, China has twenty-three provinces; however, below this level the unit designations are more complex. China also has municipalities, such as Beijing, as well as autonomous regions (ARs; Tibet, Mongolia, Ningxia Huizu, Xinjiang Uygur, and Guangxi Zhuang). Under these are prefectures, counties, county towns or county seats, towns, and villages.

List of Figures and Maps

FIGURES

MAPS

A Note on Romanization and Chinese Pronunciation

In a book that tries to make more familiar a China in the throes of an accelerated cultural, economic, political, and social transformation, it is surely unfair of the authors to begin with a tour of the unfamiliar, specifically, a brief discussion of the alphabetic representation of the sounds of Chinese language. However, this is precisely what we must do, for any effort to know more about the contemporary phenomena of China requires that we draw closer to the texture of the place by becoming conversant with a number of its more significant expressions and terms.

In the technical parlance of the Modern Language Association (MLA; a U.S.-based professional organization), Chinese is one of a number of "less-commonly taught languages." But with considerably more than a quarter of the world population now speaking Chinese, it is wise to give some thought to the status of Chinese as one of the world's most widely used languages. It also pays to remember that language in China is very complex, with a welter of dialects so distinct and different as to resemble languages themselves. Indeed, Robert Ramsey, a linguist who has written on Chinese, claims that China has more than fifty languages!

Most readers of this book will know that the written Chinese language consists of *sinographs*, more popularly called "characters," of which in the more-complete Chinese lexicons there are more than fifty thousand. Literacy in Chinese—itself a contentious, because political, topic—requires a minimum active understanding of several thousand such sinographs: approximately three thousand for basic literacy, and six thousand for advanced literacy. To reproduce the sinographic forms Chinese people generally use for such terms as *Internet, economic growth, political reform, capitalism,* and a host of others would be of little value for most of our readers, because the written language is by itself unintelligible. Thus, it is customary for authors of general texts such as this one to provide the *Romanized*, or phonetic, spelling of the sinographs. The objective in this instance is to offer access to the sounds of Chinese, but it is very important to recall in each of these cases that these are only the Western-style letters that represent the sound of the sinographs and that there are several systems by means of which these sounds have been represented, the first efforts having been made in 1605 by the Jesuit missionary Matteo Ricci in his work *Xizi qiji* [*The wonder of Western script*]. Such a phonetic imprint is better than nothing, but it is still not Chinese.

Students have long questioned this phonetic spelling because of the odd-looking words it yields (e.g., *Xizi qiji*) and because there are other Romanization systems that increase their confusion. The purpose of our discussion here is to attempt to allay this customary confusion while explaining the reasoning behind Romanization and trying to assist with pronunciation. Since 1980, the sounds of Chinese have been increasingly represented in the United States via the Romanization system called *pinyin*, literally, "phonetic spelling." Owing to what we might consider a disregard for Western alphabet values, pinyin produces words like *zheng* that look very curious to the untrained eye and occasion the following reaction: How do you pronounce *zh* or *ng*?

To account for the odd appearance of this popular phonetic spelling, or rather this system known as pinyin, and to understand how it came to be favored, requires a sensitivity to politics. One must know that pinyin grew from an earlier system of Romanization called *Latinxua* (Latinization) that was produced in the 1930s in Soviet Asia and incorporated in China as *sin wenz* (new writing) and which was subsequently adopted for use in the Communist base areas of Gansu, Ningxia, and Shanxi in the Chinese Northwest in the 1940s. A few years after the Chinese Revolution, the Chinese government formed a committee to conduct scientific research aimed at standardizing the national language. From 1952 to 1958 this research was the foundation of a national policy of language reform, which generated serious discussion about the abandonment of sinographs in favor of a purely alphabetized form of Chinese. In the end this did not occur, but a systematic simplification of the written language was realized and yielded an official promulgation of pinyin as the nation's Romanization system and of the northern dialect peculiar to Beijing as the standard spoken language of China, or *putonghua*. And because *putonghua* was the common parlance of the North and quite dissimilar from the speech of so many other regions, this decision complicated matters even further, while giving an illusion of linguistic identity. For the purpose of drawing closer to the sounds of Chinese, we take advantage of this illusion throughout the book and provide the pinyin for critical terms. Lastly, the reader must remember that the greater ease of reading and writing pinyin is belied by its deficiency in representing the four tones of *putonghua*, which given the preponderant number of homophones in Chinese is a source of greater ambiguity. (In the complete pinyin system, tones are indicated above the main vowel in each syllable, but this feature has been omitted because of publishing considerations.)

Here are a few pronunciation tips, ones that you would do well to commit to memory so that the chances of your getting at an accurate expression are enhanced. We urge you to spend a few moments here at the start just trying out the sounds of these strange, transliterated words, as such effort will enrich your aptitude for the sounds of the street in China.

DISTINCTIVE VOWELS

a is pronounced like a blend of the *a* in *father* and the *a* in *at*

ai is pronounced like the *ai* in *aisle*

ao is pronounced like the *ow* in *now*

e is pronounced like the *u* in *but* when used in words like *fen*, but like the *e* in *when* in words like *wen*

eng is pronounced like the *ung* in *dung*

i is pronounced like the *ee* in *bee*, except following *ch*, *sh*, and *zh* when it sounds like the *r* of *sure*

ian is pronounced like *yen*

iu is pronounced like *yo*

ou is pronounced like *oh*

u is pronounced like the *oo* in *zoo*

ui is pronounced like *way*

ü is pronounced *yew*

CHALLENGING INITIAL CONSONANTS

c is pronounced like the *ts* in *nits*, so that *cao* sounds like *tsau*

j is pronounced much like the English *j*, so that *jin* sounds like *gin*

q is pronounced like *ch*, but with lots of air, so that *qi* sounds like *chee*

x is pronounced like *sh* but also like *sy*, so that *xiang* sounds like *sheeang*

zh is pronounced like the *dg* in *judge*, so that *zheng* sounds like *jung*, and *zhou* like *joe*

z is pronounced like the *dz* in *adze*, so that *zeng* sounds like *dzung*

Preface and Acknowledgments

It has been over six years since the publication of *China beyond the Headlines* (2000), an experiment in public dialogue the success of which was displayed in the book's ongoing popularity. This work acquired an audience of general readers, faculty, and undergraduate students that sustained several printings and a partial revision. It became a popular text in courses on modern Chinese history and Chinese politics because it offered accessible, interpretative snapshots of a place that increasing numbers of U.S. citizens wanted to understand. But rather than expand and update an already popular text, we take pleasure here in returning to the diverse and rapidly developing topic of contemporary China in the interest of producing a different book governed by the same principles. *China's Transformations: The Stories beyond the Headlines* is the fortunate consequence of our reengagement with both the prominent and the obscure dimensions of the Chinese everyday.

In *China beyond the Headlines*, we as academics were concerned with establishing a dialogue with the general public, in particular U.S. readers (although one of the pleasant surprises of the first book was its popularity in China). To this end, we asked all our contributors to write for the educated but unknowing reader and to be candid about the circumstances of their profession as expert on a region of the world that was once a curiosity but has now become the focus of political attention and economic value. Contributors responded by providing access to complex topics not commonly represented in the increasing volume of media attention on China. A candid assessment of "interest" was expected, and as a result, contributors resisted the temptation to embrace conventional accounts of Chinese economic triumphalism and political repression. In assembling this entirely new volume of readings, we wanted to return to certain topics from the first book, while also expanding our range of coverage to include areas that may have been beyond the headlines in 2000 but are front-page news now: environmental degradation, epidemiological distress, the sex trade, popular film, children's literature, Falun Gong, fiscal crises, public opinion surveys, the Internet revolution, and expanding, intensified labor violence. We found, not entirely to our amazement, that many of the stories we had followed had changed.

The journalistic conceit of *China beyond the Headlines* ensured the revelatory, reportorial quality of some of the contributions, such as those on China's nascent ultranationalism; the counter-hegemonic popular culture of the Uighurs; ethnic, cultural, and religious pluralism; unemployment and labor unrest; and the regional, rural immiseration brought on by the marketization of the Chinese national economy. However, that first volume still lacked an authentic journalistic perspective on the politics of representation, the making of news in China, and the reporting of that news in the West. In this follow-on to *China beyond the Headlines*, the reader has the advantage of two such journalistic voices, Martin Fackler's and John Gittings's, while Xiao Qiang's chapter on the Internet in China addresses journalistic issues from a third perspective. These chapters permit us to understand better the grand complexity of how the story, any story, gets out of China and before the eyes of the interested Western reader, as well as something about information dissemination in China itself.

Even as this ground-level window is opened through the journalist's commentary on the shifting contours of contemporary Chinese life, the news of China moves within the country and gets around the globe faster than it can appear in the press. Since the publication of our first book, the rapid acceleration of and access to information technology has brought knowledge of China's daily life into Western homes as never before while expanding, quite unpredictably, avenues of popular cultural awareness. In *China's Transformations*, we wish to apply this baseline knowledge to the advantage of acquiring a more nuanced understanding of China's complexity in a contemporary political context in which domestic developments have global implications.

During the final editing and revising of *China beyond the Headlines* in the fall of 1999 and winter of 2000, we were mindful of the accelerating pace of material change in contemporary China, and we attempted to include as much reportage as we could. However in the intervening period, China has changed at a preternatural rate, with a dizzying speed unsettling for native and foreigner alike. This second engagement with current Chinese life and reflective commentary on topics both familiar and unfamiliar is offered here through the fresh perspective provided by over half a decade of global political transformation, with the hope that readers will obtain an understanding of China complex enough to prepare them for responsible engagement with the dawning twenty-first century.

Unlike the first book, which was largely the product of a symposium on contemporary Chinese politics, *China's Transformations* collects a commissioned set of chapters drawn from a number of the same contributors but now focused on different topics. We have gathered these chapters under two distinct headings: front stage (*qiantai*) and back stage (*houtai*), which are literal translations of the Chinese terms for public and private behavior. The front-stage chapters cover more familiar ground for the general reader and those things that have been in the news with greater frequency, but this section also contains a few chapters that reflect what is on the front stage, meaning what defines the explicit everyday of the Chinese. The back-stage section consists of chapters on topics less familiar to the general reader but critical to a description of present-day life in China.

A markedly different international context now governs our perceptions. The contrasting effects produced by the changed circumstances of China and the United States are striking: the world and the United States have, for the most part, moved beyond the sense that China poses an imminent threat to world stability; and it is the United States that registers polarizing reactions in world politics. Arguably, the United States is now an international pariah: it is the only major national power other than Australia that is not a signatory of the Kyoto Protocol; it is the only developed country that practices capital punishment; it is the only developed country that considers itself not bound by the Geneva Conventions and that is opposed to the international movement to ban landmines; and it is the world's largest debtor nation. In short, the United States, more than China, is one of the greatest threats to world peace. Such is the uneasy context of our mutual apprehension in this moment of contemporary stocktaking.

In the oft-cited revolutionary changes of China's economy, citizens of the United States, as well as people all over the world, sense the emergence of something altogether new, different, and in many ways challenging. Bill Gates, in an address before the 2005 World Economic Forum in Davos, Switzerland, warned that the countries in attendance should be particularly mindful of the meteoric rise of the Chinese economy and see in it the passing of the global economic torch from the United States and Europe. Just ponder a few of these recent figures: China's gross domestic product (GDP) has grown to more than US$2.2 trillion; it has received $520 billion in total foreign direct investment ($53.5 billion in 2003 alone); in 2005 its exports were worth $768 billion; it is now the world's third-largest foreign trader after the United States and Germany (in the first half of 2005 alone, China enjoyed a $166 billion trade surplus with the United States), and as of late 2006 China owned $1 trillion in foreign currency reserves, which makes it second in the world only to Japan; and in 2004 it had 397 million fixed phone lines. More than 90 million Chinese access the Internet through personal computers, more than 100 million access it through cell phones (over 400 million of which are in use) and text messaging; and 400 million Chinese homes had cable television at the close of 2005. Other dramatic indicators of the heat and speed of China's economy include the average number of sales of cell phones per month (2 million) and the annual rate of growth in sales of automobiles (40–50 percent, with an 11 percent growth in the last quarter of 2005). China uses 7 percent of the world's oil, 25 percent of its aluminum, 31 percent of its coal, 30 percent of its iron-ore output, and 27 percent of its steel products. It is the world's largest consumer of the necessities of industrial production.

A measure of the scope of this last statistic is that the Chinese government could not obtain sufficient steel for the construction of the new National Stadium, the primary site for the 2008 Olympic Games, so it reduced steel use by 40 percent in the stadium's construction. However, it is important to keep in mind that China, with about 20 percent of the world's population, is running a substantial trade surplus, meaning it produces considerably more than it consumes. How then would you characterize the United States, with less than 5 percent of the world's population but which consumes 26 percent of the world's oil supply and had a trade deficit (by consuming more than it produced) in 2006 of around $776 billion? The United States is certainly on the international stage the world's most gluttonous nation, with China not far behind, and the consequences for our global future will be harrowing. Yet there is good reason to believe that the competitive drive of these two grand, national powers may lead to greater cooperation than conflict, in no small measure because the planet cannot long sustain the damage wrought by their pursuit of their national agendas. It is encouraging to observe recent changes in U.S. federal funding favoring school programs focused on Chinese—more than 2,400 primary and secondary schools have applied for such funding—and to hope that an inevitable cultural confluence might trump competition. Understanding is the key, and the interval before us will reveal the depth of our courage to obtain it. It is our hope that *China's Transformations* may prove valuable in promoting that understanding.

Lastly, in an experiment with the accelerating development of the relations between information technology and the printed word, we have created a hyperlink for *China's Transformations* at www.nd.edu/~eall that contains additional links to articles, images, maps, and a video archive, and that permits readers to expand their frame of reference while obtaining a critical perspective of the constantly changing situation in China. Moreover, as an actively maintained Internet site, this site offers space for reader commentary on the book and interchange with the editors; we invite you to engage us by this means.

ACKNOWLEDGMENTS

Institutional support from the University of Notre Dame proved crucial to this book's final production. Specifically deserving of recognition is the College of Arts and Letters' Institute for Scholarship in the Liberal Arts and the Liu Family Endowment for Asian Studies and Development, as well as the International Scholars Program at the Helen Kellogg Institute for International Studies, the underwriting of which was essential in the production of the index and the maps. We are also in debt to Dr. Ali Mohsin Qazilbash, who helped with manuscript editing, final review of the collected chapters, and preparation of the index. Two inspired and intrepid undergraduate students, Jacqueline Collins and Constance Chen, undertook the task of completing the index. We, along with our readers, are immensely grateful for their industry.

Over the last several years we have benefited from timely and intelligent exchanges with our students at the University of Colorado, Boulder, the University of Colorado, Denver, and the University of Notre Dame, as well as from the high quality of coverage of current events in China available through select newspapers, magazines, and Internet sites. We have also benefited from our numerous exchanges with colleagues, in particular, R. Scott Appleby, Susan D. Blum, Bei Dao, Jay Dautcher, Michael C. Davis, Paul Festa, Thomas Gold, Howard Goldblatt, Peter Gries, Lee Haiyan, Victoria Tin-bor Hui, John Kamm and Irene Chan Kamm, Faye and Terry Kleeman, Martin Lee, Sylvia Lin, Perry Link, Liu Binyan, Christine Loh, Jim McAdams, Donald Munro, Dian Murray, Jonathan Noble, Tim Oakes, Henry Rosemont, Orville Schell, David Shambaugh, Ed Shaughnessy, Jonathan Spence, Hoyt Tillman, Jeff Wasserstrom, and Christopher Welna. Generous thanks are also due Peter Jaynes and Tong Lam for their photographs, and Philip Schwartzberg for his finely textured maps. Over the long course of this work's realization we were the supreme beneficiaries of an insightful and imaginative editor, Susan McEachern, whose devotion to this collection of morally engaged, plainly written chapters has proved critical to its successful publication.

As this book was going to press we witnessed the passing of our exemplary teacher, Frederic E. Wakeman Jr., who inspired us to think about China in all its richness and vastness, and as a civilization and nation in constant transformation. We are eternally grateful for his instruction and offer as a symbol of our gratitude this work of our hands, inspired by his example. May his memory be a blessing.

Foreword

Culture Matters—A Report from the Field of U.S.-China Relations

Jonathan S. Noble

The expression *China's transformations* can mean many things, but for most Western readers it will perhaps call forth images of a global economic juggernaut with vast reserves of cheap labor generating a dizzying array of products that have filled store shelves the world over. This is, of course, a prominent dimension of the transformation, and yet there is so much more beyond the headlines that accounts for the commanding global presence of the Chinese. The chapters that follow will draw out less-well-represented stories—the Internet revolution in China, the rise of public opinion surveys, the ominous inflation of labor unrest, unregulated development schemes and the water crisis, the epidemic of sex tourism, Chinese foodways, and current reading habits in China—so that the reader may draw closer to the complex texture of the everyday. And it is this complexity the authors wish to convey.

Complexity is not a quality common to the political and media portraits of "China on the rise" that flood the bandwidth of popular consciousness, and this is largely the consequence of how the subject of China is framed. It is the matter of framing, specifically one in which culture is ignored in the interest of political prejudice, that concerns me as I reflect on how the U.S. government and its policymakers frame, and thereby map out, U.S.-China relations. My recent experience as a fellow in the National Committee on United States–China Relations (NCUSCR) Public Intellectuals Program (PIP) inspired the writing of this foreword, especially in my thinking about the stories beyond the headlines, because so often it is the headlines about China that we explore for keys to current and future events. I would now like to take you behind the scenes of the perceptions and policy of official Washington, D.C.

One of the avowed missions of the PIP is to enhance dialogue between scholars on China and those officials actively involved in designing U.S. policy. To this end, NCUSCR arranges meetings between top government officials and scholars with an eye to establishing grounds for better-informed policy. These meetings provide an insider's view of certain attitudes and practices pervasive inside the Washington Beltway but uncommon among scholars. The second mission of the PIP is promoting the active participation of China scholars in broader education initiatives about China, including public outreach in local communities. The experiences in Washington of the PIP scholars reveal how much still needs to be done in terms of understanding the full complexity of U.S.-China relations, both within policy-making circles and within local communities throughout the country. What must be better understood and what this book addresses is culture, because in this understanding the exaggerated differences between China and the United States become points of complement rather than conflict.

POLITICS 101: TAKING STOCK

Until fairly recently, relations between the United States and China have been characterized by polarity. This was a historical legacy of the long era of the Cold War. But under the administrations of Bill Clinton and George W. Bush, China has been embraced as a "strategic partner." Today this partnership is more dynamic than ever, although certainly not free from volatile domestic politics in both countries. Despite the complexity of U.S.-China relations, simple models still tend to dominate in the U.S. political establishment as well as in media conglomerates, which increasingly are in mutual rather than antagonistic relationships. What this means is that without more cultural information to complicate the data processed by policymakers, the older models of scarcity and challenge-response will endure as the foundation of political analysis of China.

The Bush administration hinted at its China policy in a speech by Robert Zoellick, former deputy secretary of state, at the NCUSCR gala in New York City on September 21, 2005.[1] In addressing the question of how China would use its influence, Zoellick repeatedly called attention to the reasons why China should become a "responsible stakeholder" in the international system. One need not be a linguist or a cultural anthropologist to realize that this statement begs a number of important questions. Who defines what it means to be a responsible stakeholder? The United States? And what does *responsible stakeholder* mean? According to the *Wall Street Journal*, an official translation of the term *stakeholder* in Chinese was slow to appear.[2] The ambiguity of the term brought Chinese delegations to Washington's think tanks, sparked debate among leading Chinese scholars, and animated Internet chat-room discussions. Does the use of such a term reflect the current U.S. policy, known as "ambiguous diplomacy?" Was its use intended to inspire constructive bilateral discussions? Or more cynically, does its use stem from the U.S. superpower's tendency of assuming that the rest of the world speaks English and embraces the political argot of the United States?

According to Zoellick, if China wishes to be a "responsible stakeholder," it must refrain from mercantilist policies that lock up energy sources, increase transparency about its defense spending, crack down on theft of intellectual property and counterfeiting, cooperate in the global fight against terrorism, work with multilateral diplomacy in Asia, and strengthen the rule of law and develop democratic institutions at home. Zoellick's speech was peppered with remarks that hinted at the possibility of conflict unless China changes its ways: "But China does not want a conflict with the United States"; "There is a cauldron of anxiety about China"; "Many countries hope China will pursue a 'peaceful rise,' but none will bet their future on it"; "Some say America's commitment to democracy precludes long-term cooperation with China"; "China needs a peaceful political transition . . . China needs to reform its judiciary." Although Zoellick's remarks emphasize, on the surface, the need for international cooperation, what is given the most weight is how China should behave, rather than how the two countries might truly cooperate to address major global concerns and ensure mutual prosperity.

If George W. Bush's recent visit to Beijing on November 20, 2005, is any indicator, the paternalistic approach his administration has adopted toward China is not working. During that visit, Bush's calls for political liberalization, human rights concessions, and religious freedoms were effectively rebuffed. The most credible result of Bush's ninety-minute meeting with Hu Jintao was a preliminary US$4 billion deal for China to purchase seventy Boeing aircraft, a revelation of China's growing economic might and not a contribution toward the reduction of what turned out to be a $200 billion trade deficit with China in 2005.[3]

Stakeholder, a relatively new term in the language of U.S. politics, carries specific cultural connotations, especially found in the expressions *stakeholder capitalism* and *stakeholder society*. Therefore, urging China to accept its new role as a "responsible stakeholder" also demands that China accept the term's assumptions of betting on a future political outcome. To assume that China can embrace the conditions of its role as a stakeholder in this instance is not so different from expecting U.S. leaders to follow the moral dictates of the Confucian ideal of the *junzi* (superior person). The compliance of U.S. leaders would not only revolve around finding an apt translation for *junzi* (gentleman, Confucian scholar, prince, moral paragon?), but more importantly, it would require acquiescence to the challenge of adapting U.S.

political traditions to an age-old Chinese cultural rubric. Language and, especially, the cultures within which language is embedded are critical to informing the metaphors and paradigms that in turn shape national perceptions and political policies.

Cultural matters, whether implicit or explicit, play an active role in managing U.S.-China relations. Culture, in this context, is not a painting that is hung on the wall as a passive object of appreciation. Rather, culture actively negotiates the terms upon which an observed reality is interpreted. "Culture matters," a notion that emerged during my observations of the relationship between Beltway politics and U.S.-China relations, first refers to the idea that culture, though often represented as abstractly complex and inconsequential, if not superfluous, is critical to a fruitful understanding of political strategies, policies, and relationships. Here, cultural matters are embedded within political rhetoric and used to frame political viewpoints. "Culture matters" also refers to the idea that culture can play a more important role in fostering a mutually beneficial relationship between the United States and China, which will be critical to the future of our planet.

Coverage of China in the U.S. media has increased so dramatically in recent years that news about China is commonplace in major U.S. newspapers and news shows. The breadth of coverage has kept pace, with pieces not merely on Chinese Communist Party (CCP) leadership, policy, and hot-button topics (e.g., economic growth, international trade, and human rights) but on popular culture as well.[4] Western media reports, however, tend to treat cultural issues as secondary—rarely do we see pieces that attempt to highlight the interplay between cultural and political issues, or how the interpretation of hot-button topics is informed by cultural matters. Therefore, policymakers, the media establishment, and the public are not encouraged to think about how specific cultural contexts frame international policy debates, domestic issues in China, or public perceptions.

A number of the Pentagon's declarations, official comments, and reports in 2005 bolstered the "China threat" theory, in which China is seen as a future military adversary of the United States. The Pentagon's *The Military Power of the People's Republic of China*, published in July 2005, emphasized how China's military buildup threatens the global order. In a speech he delivered on June 4 in Singapore, U.S. secretary of defense Donald Rumsfeld specifically questioned China's continued investment in and expansion of its military.[5] Although keeping tabs on the militaries of other nations throughout the world is part of most nations' national security, the policy and analysis of military capability tends to reduce the complexity of international relations in favor of characterizing a nation and its people by the number and range of its missiles rather than by the more abstract nexus of cultural and historical practices that form a more complete and sophisticated understanding.

With the Pentagon's promotion of a more belligerent characterization of China as a military threat, the circulation of images of China needs more than ever to be informed by sincere efforts at cultural understanding that include dissolving a Cold War–inspired polarity between friend and foe constructed along ideological lines and dissolving the neorationalist duality between "hard fact" (e.g., missile counting) and "soft culture." The continued prevalence of these polarities shapes and perpetuates the militarized environment and ideology we find ourselves in today in the United States.

THE POLITICS OF PANDA-HUGGING: ENDLESS COLD WAR?

During the PIP conference, many fellows contemplated why such a program had been inaugurated at this particular historical juncture. During the four days of meetings, it became increasingly clear, to me in any case, that a deep anxiety about China's rise pervaded the policy establishment. This anxiety seemed created less by China's actions than by an invasive, Washington-centered ideological orientation reminiscent of the Cold War. This emergent, neo–Cold War, ideological environment appears to be conditioned by insular fear—and it is precisely this fear that inspires the use of dismissive epithets relative to any individual's China-based sympathies.

The practice of assigning any of an assortment of sobriquets to signify an individual's position on China is thriving in Washingtonian circles, as PIP participants learned very quickly. In this unique political space, cultural complexity is forfeited in the name of political expediency. "Panda huggers" argue for the importance of constructively engaging China for the purpose of global stability, while "dragon slayers" believe that China is a direct economic and security threat to the United States and thus must be contained. "Panda hedgers" is a more recent term that is gaining currency in part due to its resonance with the Bush administration's policy of creative ambiguity. "Panda hedgers," according to Ian Bremmer, a senior fellow at the World Policy Institute, "argue privately that China need not be actively engaged or forcefully contained" because China's current economic reforms will ultimately necessitate greater political reforms.[6] The circulation of these particular stereotypes (each bearing racial and imperialistic overtones) is symptomatic of a Cold War–inspired ideology that many believe is an artifact of the recent past.

As with most political terms of derogation, "panda hugger" is part of a rhetorical strategy and is embedded within a particular ideology that tends to discredit and denigrate. It is a clever term, because it appears to signify positive attributes of caring and affection, and so upon first utterance it may not strike those so labeled as overtly offensive. However, it is precisely the term's seemingly affectionate quality that makes it insidious: it reeks of intolerance and ideological manipulation. Such dismissive epithets as this one do not foster reasonable public debate about U.S.-China relations; if we are to work toward encouraging reasoned public discourse about China, then these labels must be met by resolute rejection.

I also learned that "panda huggers" are members of the "red team." No, the "red team" is not "red" due to its affiliation with the Republican Party. Rather, Washington nomenclature dictates that the "red team" consists of those who support engagement policies with China. *Red* also has an unfortunate association with Communism, which as the purveyors of the "red-team" label would emphasize, is still the dominant political ideology in China. The "blue team," which has nothing to do with the Democratic Party, refers to the pro-containment faction, also known as "dragon slayers." "Dragon slayers" also tend to be vociferous in making Taiwan independence a key issue in U.S.-China relations. Although the teams are marked by otherwise symbolically neutral colors, the connotations become immediately clear: red—Communist; blue—patriotic. The language here does not just disempower but engenders a distinct political morality. The absolute and morally valenced political dichotomy established by these terms is not so different from the coded use of language in China in the early 1950s when landowners were typified as "immoral" and "unpatriotic," or of language use in subsequent years when counterrevolutionaries were "black elements" and "ox ghosts and snake demons." The "blue team" and its ideological use of similar terms resonates with "Red" China's past tyrannical labeling practices.

INFORMING PUBLIC PERCEPTIONS:
WHOSE CHINA FOR WHOM?

The question regarding who is forming public perception in the United States about China is critical. In addition to the important role the broadcast media play, a number of recently published books for general audiences about China's rise purport to promote public education. Ted Fishman's account of China's impact on an endless range of aspects of the daily life of Americans (e.g., fuel costs, pollution, commodity prices, and unemployment) in *China Inc.: How the Rise of the Next Superpower Challenges America and the World* is less a call for the need to understand China and improve U.S.-China relations than a portrayal of China as a competitor and potential "national security threat."[7] Whereas during the Cold War, China was primarily an external foreign policy concern, it has now entered the discussion on numerous issues related to domestic matters such as jobs (outsourcing and intellectual property rights), energy (China's consumption and acquisition), the U.S. federal deficit (the trade imbalance and China's exchange rate), and interest rates (China's financing of U.S. debt). The way China is represented and understood will inevitably play an increasingly important role in U.S. domestic politics. And it is precisely this discourse on the "rise of China" that fuels anxiety about China in the United States.

Given the growing political currency of China in U.S. domestic politics, it is not surprising that books packaged for the general public may be informed by distinct ideological agendas. Indeed, a pronounced partisanship is standard in the trade-book culture wars of the United States. For example, Ethan Gutmann's *Losing the New China: A Story of American Commerce, Desire, and Betrayal* on the surface criticizes the U.S. business community for not doing enough to promote U.S. interests and values in China. However, it more artfully indoctrinates the reader with insidious propaganda characteristic of political ideology from within the Beltway, marked particularly by unreflective ethnocentrism and intolerance.[8] At the same time, however, there are political currents within the U.S. Congress that complement the efforts of the PIP and the contributors to this volume, who seek to overcome the rude limitations of instinctive criticism of the unfamiliar in favor of a more responsible engagement with China. It is this alternative conception of the role of China and of the responsibility of the United States to be better informed about its strategic partner that deserves more coverage.

ENGAGING CULTURE AS A CRITICAL ISSUE FOR U.S.-CHINA RELATIONS

In the United States today, the study of China is inescapably political. By this I mean that the political significance of China for the United States affects the public role of the China scholar. In such a politicized policy environment, China scholars must prepare themselves for how their scholarship may be exploited by proponents of the "red team" or the "blue team." More to the point, China scholars must make a concerted effort to combat this specious, destructive dichotomy that, without their consent and participation, frames their scholarly endeavors. Ezra Vogel outlines the current role of China public intellectuals:

> When extreme views begin to influence public discourse, we public intellectuals have a responsibility to stretch beyond our narrow specialty to counter extremism, providing better information and perspective . . . Our primary commitment is to truth and better public understanding.[9]

In such a climate, it is even more important for scholars to be actively engaged rather than reactive in terms of public education about China.

The United States–China Cultural Engagement Act of 2005, proposed by Senators Joseph Lieberman (D-Conn.) and Lamar Alexander (R-Tenn.), demonstrates the awareness of certain public officials that education must also play a critical role in improving U.S.-China relations. While appealing to patriotism, the act aims to enhance the teaching of Chinese language and culture in the United States from the elementary-school level to the university, in addition to instituting exchange programs that would promote greater cultural understanding and cooperation. It also supports U.S. commercial activity in China. Senator Lieberman introduced the bill to the Senate on May 25, 2005, commenting:

> Engaging China as an ally in international affairs and as partner in building economic prosperity is of the utmost importance to the United States. Only if we succeed in fostering this relationship can we have a future that is as bright as our past . . . The rise of China comes with a whole set of challenges. But the ability to talk and understand each other should not be among them. The United States–China Cultural Engagement Act sets forth a strategy for achieving that level of understanding and cooperation with China.[10]

If the United States has spent more than $333 billion on the Iraq War (as of October 2006), which China is generously (and strategically) helping to underwrite, one would think Congress could approve the expenditure of $1.3 billion on a five-year program such as this that through bilateral exchange would also promote among Chinese the American way of life. The act has faced resistance from members of the "blue team," however, perhaps worried that its execution may result in more "panda huggers." Opponents of the act also cite China's human rights violations, World Trade Organization (WTO) violations, currency manipulation, and mercantilist energy acquisition, among other issues, as matters that must be reconciled before the bill can be passed.

The "blue team," aligned with the U.S. Department of Defense (DOD), must find something suspicious in China's global ambitions. Therefore, tactics aimed at vilifying China in order to justify military expenditures to defend the United States against a Chinese military threat are critical to the "blue-team" strategy. However, these are tactics that make little sense to the "reality-based community," because they are advanced in the face of no credible Chinese threat. According to one Pentagon consultant on missile technology, who insisted on anonymity, "U.S. superpower dominance relies upon the United States' ability to identify an enemy. This is a tacit assumption in the Pentagon. China is this enemy, although we really know China is not." Lieberman and Alexander's cultural engagement act, therefore, would undermine the DOD strategy of making China an enemy, even if China is just a so-called imaginary enemy. On the practical side, just as a medical researcher requires the existence of a disease in order to secure research funds, an identified enemy makes it much easier for the DOD and defense contractors to acquire funding.

To combat this kind of fantasizing requires genuine engagement, something that is not possible without a keen understanding of language and culture, one that is not driven by political bias. The study of language and culture must contribute to the reframing of the policy debate. Indeed, this has been the most repeated object lesson of the U.S. occupation of Iraq: that the government, specifically the DOD, did not pay sufficient attention to Iraqi culture and society in the first phases of the war. Rather than passively accepting the ideological polarity of "us versus them," the study of language, and especially of literature and culture, teaches us how political imperatives are formed out of cultural differences. Chinese literature and culture classes teach us not simply about the Other but more importantly about the ways in which constructions of the Other are contingent upon different worldviews or ideologies. These worldviews and ideologies are in turn connected to power building. The development of a network of power in turn facilitates empire building. The recognition that culture matters generates greater knowledge about ideology, power, and empire, and this knowledge encourages the public to focus on cooperating on transnational interests, such as the environment, disease control, and human rights, rather than on competition between ideologically generated empires.

WHY CULTURE MATTERS IN THE POLITICS OF U.S. PUBLIC OPINION

A belief that culture matters will contribute to forging greater understanding, while repelling the specter of xenophobia, dispelling the fear that is exploited to justify chauvinistic policy making, and strengthening a sense of security for ourselves and our families in the United States. Bridges can be built not just between the governments of the United States and China but, more importantly, between institutions and individuals associated with major policy issues. From a more rational basis of political reasoning, the United States and China alike may demonstrate leadership on the critical problems of an increasingly interconnected and complex contemporary world.

"China's rise in world affairs is one of the four principal trends that define the new global order,"[11] according to David Shambaugh, the other trends being U.S. military supremacy, the European Union's increasing economic prominence, and technological and economic globalization. Consequently, it is in the world's interest to see that China's rise makes the world a better place. Shambaugh astutely observes that the United States and Europe adopt different foreign policy approaches to China. "Unlike analysts in the United States," states Shambaugh, "who focus on China's external posture, European analysts focus primarily on China's internal scene."[12]

The U.S.-studied "external posture" includes concerns about military, energy, and trade, whereas the European emphasis is on the "internal scene," a reference to China's domestic transitions and reforms such as public welfare and the growth of civil society and the public sphere. Europe seems to be outperforming the United States in cultural matters.[13]

Could the U.S. burden as a military superpower inherently delimit and marginalize cultural matters? For a "blue team" so concerned about China's rise as a military superpower, it should not be forgotten that the United States is China's aspirational peer, and as such, that the United States sets the standards for acceptable superpower behavior, from empire-building tactics to cultural matters. In *Democracy Matters: Winning the Fight against Imperialism*, Cornel West argues that democracy must depend more upon ideas, values, and understanding than upon commerce and the military:

> Let us not be deceived: the great dramatic battle of the twenty-first century is the dismantling of empire and the deepening of democracy. This is as much or more a colossal fight over visions and ideas as a catastrophic struggle over profits and missiles . . . This is why what we think, how we care, and the way we fight means so much in democracy matters.[14]

The policy making behind U.S.-China relations must move beyond "profits and missiles," for only then will it be possible to discuss "democracy matters." Despite the anxiety of U.S. leadership at the phenomenon of China's rise, this dramatic transformation can be beneficial for China scholars. When I started to learn Chinese in 1990, China's rise had not registered on the U.S. public psyche. Now enrollment in Chinese language, literature, and culture classes at U.S. universities is skyrocketing. Pedagogues who can teach about China are suddenly in higher demand. Yet it is important not to lose sight of the true academic and intellectual mission—which is not just specialized research but demonstration of a serious commitment to educating the general public about cultural matters.

How can the idea that culture matters be addressed in the United States? Cultural exchanges between the United States and China in a wide array of areas can be increased, not just for elite performance groups but also, for example, between local sports teams and high-school bands. Educational exchange opportunities must be facilitated, but not just for the elite students of premiere schools in China and top prep schools in the United States. In addition, it is necessary to establish enduring exchange programs between public schools throughout the United States and China.

Tourism with an educational and cultural focus can be increased, not just for U.S. travelers going to China but for Chinese tourists coming to the United States. The barriers to Chinese tourists visiting the United States need to be dismantled, as many European countries have started to do.

Grassroots relationships can be forged between communities in the United States and China that share common interests. Incentives can be made available to U.S. and Chinese corporate entities to encourage partnerships and mutual cooperation, and in this way a cultural revolution at home may bring about policy change that overcomes epithets and creates favorable conditions for fruitful engagement—a novel U.S.-China politics for the twenty-first century.

Beijing is certainly not any less ideological than Washington, D.C. We must also not discount the ways in which China's transformations, including the modernization of its military, are affecting the lives of people throughout the entire world. However, when you read the headlines, it is important to be mindful and critical of the politics that motivate certain representations of China. As Robert Zoellick rightly noted, the United States and China share "many common interests and opportunities for cooperation." The adoption of English as the common denominator of global communication has also come with a heavy cost—a disincentive among English speakers to learn how other languages inform different cultural views and perceptions. China's rise is promoting, on an unparalleled and massive scale, a tide of Chinese-language learning around the world. Thus, China's rise is also engendering an unprecedented opportunity to pursue a future of cultural cooperation that is mediated by a capacity to understand cultural pluralism and thereby advance intercultural understanding. And this, in the end, is why culture *matters*.

NOTES

I would like to express my appreciation to the National Committee on United States–China Relations (NCUSCR) for organizing its inaugural Public Intellectuals Program (PIP). During the five-day Fellows Conference in Washington, D.C., the committee organized meetings with Washington's foreign policy establishment, including senior representatives from Capitol Hill, the Office of the Vice President, the National Security Council, the National Intelligence Council, the Brookings Institution, the Carnegie Endowment for International Peace, the Heritage Foundation, the Department of Commerce, the Congressional-Executive Commission on China, the United States–China Economic and Security Review Commission, and the Department of State. Ensuing collegial discussions between the committee's executive staff, advisory committee members, and members of the program inspired the writing of this piece. I accept full responsibility, however, for the ideas expressed within, which are not necessarily endorsed by the committee or the PIP. I would also like to express my appreciation to Lionel Jensen for his energetic editorial assistance and admirable commitment to broadening all of our intellectual horizons. Readers interested in learning more about NCUSCR, its policy publications, and its programs, specifically the PIP, are encouraged to consult the committee's website at www .ncuscr.org.

1. Robert B. Zoellick, "Whither China: From Membership to Responsibility " (speech, National Committee on United States–China Relations, New York, September 21, 2005), www.state.gov/s/d/rem/53682.htm (December 10, 2005). Zoellick left the State Department in July 2006 to join the investment firm of Goldman Sachs.

2. The linguistic bafflement in China over the term is discussed in Neil King Jr. and Jason Dean, "Untranslatable Word in U.S. Speech Leaves Beijing Baffled—Zoellick Challenges China to Become 'Stakeholder'; What Does That Mean?" *Wall Street Journal*, December 7, 2005, A1.

3. David E. Sanger and Joseph Kahn, "Chinese Leader Gives Bush a Mixed Message," *New York Times*, November 21, 2005. This amount represented a 25 percent increase in the trade deficit over 2004 and constituted 30 percent of the total U.S. foreign trade deficit.

4. News stories on popular culture tend to focus on popular culture's challenge to "official" cultural production. Few stories highlight the critical interdependence between different forms of cultural production, which is unfortunate because then the media reinforces the fallacy that "popular art" and "government-endorsed" art are inherently at odds.

5. The Pentagon's shift toward highlighting China as a potential military threat in 2005 is discussed in Michael T. Klare, "Revving Up the China Threat," *The Nation*, October 24, 2005.

6. Ian Bremmer, "The Panda Hedgers," *International Herald Tribune*, October 5, 2005.

7. Ted C. Fishman, *China Inc.: How the Rise of the Next Superpower Challenges America and the World* (New York: Scribners, 2005).

8. Ethan Gutmann, *Losing the New China: A Story of American Commerce, Desire, and Betrayal* (San Francisco: Encounter Books, 2004). I must point out that Gutmann's book was in part facilitated by the Project for the New American Century, "a nonprofit educational organization dedicated to a few fundamental propositions: that American leadership is good both for America and for the world; and that such leadership requires military strength, diplomatic energy and commitment to moral principle" (www.newamericancentury.org). The publisher of Gutmann's books, Encounter Books, is largely funded by neoconservative foundations.

9. Ezra Vogel, "U.S. Public Intellectuals and China: Some Historical Highlights" (paper, National Committee on United States–China Relations Public Intellectuals Program Fellows Conference, Washington, D.C., September 22, 2005).

10. *Congressional Record* 151, no. 71 (May 25, 2005): S5926, http://usinfo.state.gov/eap/Archive/2005/May/27-16802.html (October 27, 2005).

11. David Shambaugh, "The New Strategic Triangle: U.S. and European Reactions to China's Rise," *Washington Quarterly* 28, no. 3 (2005): 7–25.

12. Shambaugh, "The New Strategic Triangle," 14–15.

13. European countries in recent years have established official cultural exchange events. The Year of France in China, held from October 2004 to July 2005, included more than two hundred activities such as music, dances, dramas, movies, and art. The French Culture Center in Beijing was also unveiled in October 2004. The Year 2006 of Italy in China, which will highlight cultural and artistic exchange, is simi-

larly intended to promote mutual understanding between the Chinese and Italian peoples.

14. Cornel West, *Democracy Matters: Winning the Fight against Imperialism* (New York: Penguin, 2004). West's ideas and their pithy encapsulation in the titles of his books, including *Race Matters*, clearly provided inspiration for this essay.

SUGGESTED READINGS

Ian Bremmer, "The Panda Hedgers," *International Herald Tribune*, October 5, 2005.

Congressional Record 151, no. 71 (May 25, 2005): S5926, http://usinfo.state.gov/eap/Archive/2005/May/27-16802.html (October 27, 2005).

Ted C. Fishman, *China Inc.: How the Rise of the Next Superpower Challenges America and the World* (New York: Scribners, 2005).

Thomas L. Friedman, "Joined at the Hip," *New York Times*, July 20, 2005, A23.

Neil King and Jason Dean, "Untranslatable Word in U.S. Speech Leaves Beijing Baffled—Zoellick Challenges China to Become 'Stakeholder'; What Does That Mean?" *Wall Street Journal*, December 7, 2005, A1.

Michael T. Klare, "Revving Up the China Threat," *The Nation*, October 24, 2005.

David M. Lampton, *Same Bed Different Dreams: Managing U.S.-China Relations 1989–2000* (Berkeley: University of California Press, 2001).

Richard Madsen, *China and the American Dream: A Moral Inquiry* (Berkeley: University of California Press, 1995).

David E. Sanger and Joseph Kahn, "Chinese Leader Gives Bush a Mixed Message," *New York Times*, November 21, 2005.

David Shambaugh, "The New Strategic Triangle: U.S. and European Reactions to China's Rise," *Washington Quarterly* 28, no. 3 (2005): 7–25.

Ezra F. Vogel, "U.S. Public Intellectuals and China: Some Historical Highlights." Paper read at the National Committee on United States–China Relations Public Intellectuals Program Fellows Conference, Washington, D.C., September 22, 2005.

Cornel West, *Democracy Matters: Winning the Fight against Imperialism* (New York: Penguin, 2004).

Robert B. Zoellick, "Whither China: From Membership to Responsibility?" Speech to the Committee on United States–China Relations, New York, September 21, 2005, www.state.gov/s/d/rem/53682.htm (December 10, 2005).

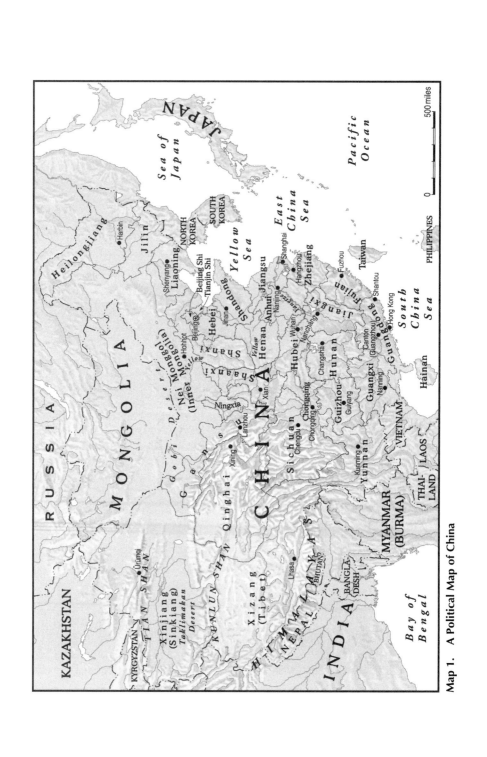

Map 1. A Political Map of China

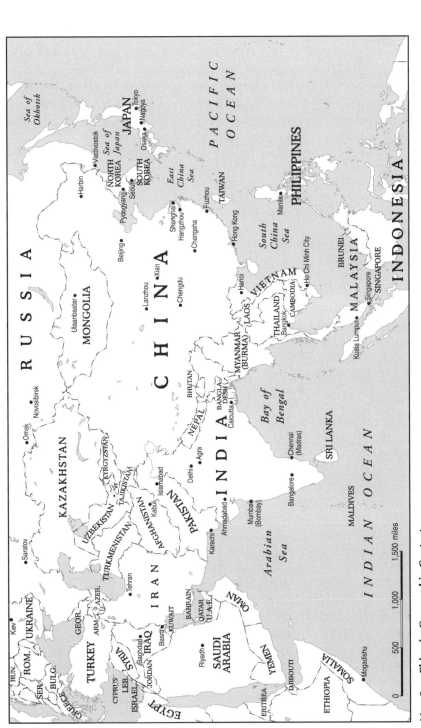

Map 2. China in Geographic Context

Introduction

The New China, a Different United States

Lionel M. Jensen and Timothy B. Weston

For more than three centuries China, whether as a civilization, an empire, a market, a fertile ground for Christian missionaries, or a pilgrimage destination, has been a storied presence in the Western imagination. It has always loomed large, in fact very large, both literally and figuratively. Yet its physical size and its stature in the Western imagination acted as a barrier to understanding and an invitation to mythologize. The West "encountered" it through economic and military expansion, and so China, with a civilization as grand as any made by Western hands, became part of our modern cultural consciousness as a testament to European accomplishment. China and its civilization helped define the West's image of the West's own superiority. But for the past two decades and especially since 2000, China has made history with an expansionist economic force that has transformed contemporary consciousness. With sustained economic growth in excess of 9 percent per year for nearly a quarter of a century—the greatest ever recorded for a major economy—China has offered evidence, by all measures, of its superiority. And it has expanded, in concert with other Asian economies, to forge a new global power and lay legitimate claim for the twenty-first century as the Asian, if not the Chinese, century, something explicitly confirmed in the theme of the 2005 *Fortune* Global Forum (hosted by Beijing), "China and the New Asian Century."

Today, China is "an action painter on a world canvas";[1] its progress is an epic event of contemporary times, not a consequence of others' history, and this event is something that involves all of the world, and most particularly the United States. It is with this knowledge that we have returned to explore China's transformations, presenting in this introduction several timely topics—democracy, the environment, the international economy, the media,

1

the Olympics, and sexuality—that will focus reader attention for the inquiry that follows and emphasize the growing similarities between China and the United States.

To write about China's transformations today in the context of "the stories beyond the headlines" is largely self-defeating, because there is so much that is actually in the headlines. And that's the problem. Coverage of China and popular interest in it have grown so substantially that today news about and from China is extensive in the business, news, and sports pages. Every day there are articles and opinion pieces on China in the pages of most metropolitan newspapers in the United States. The volume and diversity of U.S. reportage from China is impressive. Moreover, those print and broadcast media with bureaus in China generate reports that are quickly appropriated by other news outlets in the United States for republication. Even local dailies like the *South Bend Tribune* or the *Boulder Daily Camera* now regularly weigh in on the subject of today's China. With so much information, it is no wonder that everybody has an opinion about China and that, more importantly, they assume their opinion is reliable. A probable reason for this easy dogmatism is that U.S. citizens believe they know a great deal about China, and what they do not know from the media, they glean from their own imaginations as informed by images from the Internet, films, postcards, television programs, and tourist trips.

In a change from the recent past, the headlines about China now commonly highlight economics, the media, and popular taste more than politics and human rights. Indeed, much of the coverage, usually delivered with an air of playfulness or narcissistic commercial acclaim, is focused more on the China of its postmodern coast and capitals—Shanghai, Guangzhou—than on its political center, Beijing. This offering from a recent "Life" section of *USA Today* is emblematic of the popular press's celebration of a China that with each day becomes more like us:

> Over the city's fabled art deco banking strip, called the Bund, Chinese yuppies and expat dealmakers fiddle with their Blackberrys over foie gras brûlé with pistachio coulis in the hushed recesses of the city's latest dining sensation: the Jean Georges restaurant . . . China's richest, hippest, most sophisticated metropolis, it seems, has been Shanghaied by the West . . . In the past decade alone, a forest of space-age skyscrapers—nearly 3,000 over 18 stories tall—has sprouted along the banks of the Huangpu River in a scene straight out of *The Jetsons* . . . With a staggering 2,000 more in planning or under construction, residents struggle with an ongoing sense of disorientation. Not so, however, the willowy fashionistas in their Gucci and Prada (or knockoffs, at least) who strut along Nanjing Road, Shanghai's Fifth Avenue, or sip mocha lattes in one of Starbucks' ubiquitous cafes, prompting the nickname People's Republic of Starbucks . . . Most ironic of all, the room where Mao founded the Chinese Communist Party in 1921 now anchors a yuppified entertainment complex of

restored traditional houses called Xintiandi. It was designed by American architects.[2]

For many U.S. sojourners in China, Shanghai is "New York City on steroids" (see figure I.1). And for the increasing number of world travelers who count Shanghai among their most desired destinations, this popularly represented China is a very familiar place—chiefly because it is so much like home.

This sense of the familiar, along with the lure of the exotic, has contributed to a growing excitement among U.S. undergraduates for study in China. Over the last five years there has been a dramatic increase in the number of students studying in China for a semester or a year at any of an escalating number of Chinese universities in partnership with U.S. universities, from Sichuan, Yunnan, and Guangdong to Shanghai and Beijing. This development is part of an internationalization of undergraduate programs across the United States, but it also reflects the enterprising spirit of Chinese institutions that can reap substantial rewards from foreign academic exchange. Thus, there are many more ways than before to get to China, but the range of experience, and correspondingly of perception, is not necessarily wide, because most students choose to study in Beijing, Shanghai, or the more-developed coastal cities. In the classrooms of a growing number of U.S. primary and secondary schools, the call of China is loud. Today, in

Figure I.1.   The bustle of Shanghai often takes place under thick blankets of smog. (Photo: Peter H. Jaynes)

response to federally funded challenges, high schools and junior high schools are scrambling to provide Chinese-language instruction.[3]

Because outlets of the official Chinese press such as the Xinhua News Agency and *China Daily*, which tend to groom their reportage of the "Chinese miracle" for internal propaganda purposes and for Western tastes, are our principal sources of information about China, it is no surprise that the China we know is so familiar and also so impressive. In this introduction we will follow a few of the more prominent recent headlines from China long enough to reveal how the stories they tell say much about how China has changed but more about how the context of international politics has changed for both the United States and China. A startling result of this review will be a growing sense of the ways in which each country is becoming more like the other, something we believe is an ominous development for the contemporary world.

The increased awareness of China conveyed through these observations is an appropriate reflection of the prominent place of China in the world, specifically in the world of U.S. consumption. The daily architecture of U.S. domestic life is forged from Chinese exports, a development particularly of the last five years as China's steady economic expansion enabled the United States to avoid substantive recession following the rapid devaluation of its stock market in 2001. And in the United States there is no doubt that middle-class homes are in thrall to Chinese products: 80 percent of Wal-Mart's suppliers are Chinese, and in 2004 Wal-Mart, the world's largest corporation, imported more than US$18 billion of Chinese products—and not simply toys but also microwave ovens, computers, DVD players, telephones, mobile phones, fax machines, and copiers, as well as shoes, textiles, and furniture. Indeed, Wal-Mart is China's seventh-largest trading partner. As China welcomes $520 billion in foreign direct investment (in excess of 40 percent of China's GDP), it is clear that popular awareness of China's global prominence is complemented by the strategic recognition of corporate investors and captains of industry that China itself is a desired site for potential profit making. The prospect of 1.4 billion Chinese consumers is entirely too intoxicating, particularly as China's taste for Western goods grows.[4]

Since 2000 the landscape of world politics has changed dramatically for both China and the United States. China has joined the World Trade Organization (WTO); it is a strategic partner in alliance with the United States in an expanding global "war on terror"; it has conducted two successful manned spaceflights; it has won the right to host the 2008 Olympic Games, which are expected to be the most expensive and elaborate ever; it is one of the world's largest polluters of air and water; and it has taken more than 300 million people out of absolute poverty (defined by an income of a dollar per day), though it still has one of the world's largest populations of people in poverty. China remains manufacturer to the world, but it is now a far more sophisticated manufacturer, whose contributions to the global economy are staggeringly diverse. It has (as of 2003) a new Communist leadership, but one no less bent on the repression of dissent, the control of information, and the repression of religion than its predecessor; and it is a dominant regional power with an effective diplomatic presence, as demonstrated by its prominent role in sporadic, six-party negotiations with North Korea over nuclear weapons and by its expanding foreign investment in Africa, Cuba, Israel, Latin America, and Russia.

The United States, on the other hand, is in a largely ignored economic crisis with spiraling budget deficits and the largest trade imbalance in its history. Of the share of its deficit that is held by foreign countries, approximately 48 percent is assumed by the governments of China and Japan. At last count, China held more than $300 billion in U.S. debt. The United States is also at war and engaged in a very costly occupation of Iraq, the invasion of which was opposed by Europe and the United Nations and deemed "illegal" by the secretary-general of the United Nations, and its illegal incarceration of "enemy combatants" at Guantanamo, its torture of prisoners at Abu Ghraib, and its illegal, secretive transporting of foreign prisoners to third countries for questioning and torture have made it an international pariah for human rights violations. Further, it is the world's largest producer of carbon dioxide (CO_2) emissions (25 percent versus 16 percent for China) and one of only two advanced industrial nations in the world not to have approved or acceded to the Kyoto Protocol.

Civil liberties in the United States have been compromised by the USA PATRIOT Act and in particular by recent revelations about the National Security Agency's wiretapping of private citizens' telephones; the independence of the U.S. media has been undermined. The Bush administration, by all accounts, has pursued the most secretive governing strategy of any administration in recent history, and investigative journalism, once a staple of the print media, is now so rare that it makes headlines when it occurs (as when columnist Seymour Hersh reported on torture in Iraq and the "stovepiping" of U.S. intelligence before the war with Iraq[5] (stovepiping is the conscious manipulation of intelligence for favored, predetermined, strategic-policy objectives), thus breaking a story that drew national and international attention for a few months then receded, though it reemerged in late 2005 as the U.S. Senate voted 90–9 against torture). Most media information is processed by the Bush administration in accord with its political objectives, not altogether different from the way such information is processed in China. With respect to media and politics, then, the current leadership of the United States and of China are becoming more, not less, alike.

The economic entanglement of the United States and China is commonly portrayed as a product of globalization. Although trade driven by the

United States' escalating demand for cheap manufactured goods and China's overabundant and cheap labor supply creates conditions of mutual dependence, as we noted in *China beyond the Headlines*, this economic relationship is now distorted by a dramatic global financial phenomenon: U.S. fiscal insolvency. Today, the U.S. foreign trade deficit with China is but one aspect of the United States' economic dependence on the world's largest manufacturer. The more important aspect of this strained relationship is the Chinese ownership of huge amounts of U.S. national debt, something China, along with Japan, has purchased with singular enthusiasm since the occupation of Iraq, in part to ensure the economic viability of the world's largest economy and as well to purchase a means of future foreign policy persuasion. In 2004 China purchased over $200 billion in U.S. Treasuries, while amassing more than $650 billion in foreign reserves, and in the following year it bought over $300 billion in dollar assets.[6]

Thus, as the United States pursues an expensive policy of preventive war and unilateralism, one that ensures a dramatic expansion of its investment in defense, it becomes more indebted to and dependent upon the opportunistic kindness of its Asian trading partners. This indebtedness, which permits the United States to underwrite its military adventures and allows its citizens to maintain a style of life few elsewhere in the world can afford, also has complex implications for the politics of China and especially the United States, including, in the latter's case, its security agreements with its Asian Pacific allies—most importantly Taiwan. With all those billions of U.S. dollars in Chinese banks, will the United States' disposition to intervene in defense of Taiwan be weakened?

However, U.S. attention to the irony or hypocrisy of this current circumstance is diverted by the public relations efforts of the White House and the media, both of which miss few opportunities to advertise the geopolitical status of the United States as the world's only superpower. In such a thick culture of overwhelming national pride and self-congratulation, it is difficult to see, much less to comprehend, the strategic consequences of U.S. indebtedness, which is why the novel quality of our current relationship with China must not go unremarked. The extraordinary economic dependencies of the United States, moreover, blind it to the fact that fear is an implicit bond of this economic complex. It is the greater global insolvency of current approaches to energy production and economic growth that makes one wonder how much longer the United States can attend to the changing dynamic of U.S.-China relations while losing sight of the larger picture of adverse global consequences (see Afterword). It is the long-established predation of large, developed economies on the oppressed labor of the world's poor that is the crux of globalization, and that is what is at work behind the outsourcing of U.S. and other countries' jobs to Asia and their tremendous investment in China. Questioning this model of development, or the recent history of progress in China, to an extent sufficient to cast in relief its unsustainability and devastating environmental destruction is deemed unpatriotic. On both sides of the Pacific, diverse critics of the neoliberal economic paradigm risk being branded as unpatriotic, and yet in the eyes of these critics, a reckoning of cost and consequence, long and short term, is imminent.

Such an accounting of the cost of this relationship has grown difficult for U.S. citizens and even for scholars of China like ourselves: we have been told that "the world changed forever" on September 11, 2001. Thereafter, our relations with other nations have been reshaped by an aggressive, neoconservative agenda of "us versus them." In this context, it has been very difficult to accord China the prominent political attention it previously commanded, even as it receives kudos for its economic transformation and its commitment to stand with the United States in an escalating "war on terror." The occupation of Iraq, coupled with the rush by Iran and North Korea to produce nuclear weapons, and the intensifying conflict between Israel and Hezbollah in Lebanon, has consumed the attention of U.S. foreign policy, while diverting the substantive, analytic focus of the media away from the domestic and foreign politics of Asia.

Our first attempt to represent the China beyond the headlines was grounded in paradox—that is, in the well-worn commonplace that a little knowledge can prove very harmful. With an increasing volume of public attention trained on China, and a narrowing window of media representation of U.S. politics, we wondered why the chief consequence of this information glut was U.S. misapprehension of the Chinese. The misapprehension persists, but with the declining intensity in journalistic coverage in late spring 2005 of the Iraq War and a return to special reports on the economic and potential military gigantism of China in the *Atlantic Monthly*, *Time*, and *Newsweek*, Western ambivalence about the "rise of China" is again apparent in the headlines, and our prospects for better understanding of China's complexity are enhanced.

THE NEW MEDIA:
INFORMATION EXPLODING AND MANIPULATED

Headlines are not what they were six years ago: newspaper readership in the United States has declined substantially alongside a voluminous increase in popular reliance on cable television and digital media. In China, by contrast, the official number of newspapers is at more than 2,700—twice as many as there were twenty years ago. Nevertheless, the demand for information is insatiable in the era of the World Wide Web, where even in China's Internet portal–restricted environment one can obtain information twenty-four hours a day, seven days a week. The number of the world's new weblogs, or blogs, grows by 10,000 each day. There are now more than 100 million blogs worldwide and (at the time of this writing) more than 36.82 million in China. For today's Chinese there is a glut of information, much of which is officially manipulated, but a great deal of which is simply beyond the reach of the government. Headlines, and even our figurative division in *China beyond the Headlines* of newspapers' front-page contents into "above the fold" and "below the fold," are, in the digital age, archaic, precious, almost obsolete. Yet it is more than just technology that distinguishes China in its information technology (IT) revolution. China has substantially widened access to and speeded the delivery of information, and this is why blogs and online forums, governed by an argot of indirect expression, meaningful abbreviation, and allusion, have filled the expanding virtual space on the other side of the nation's *da huoqiang* (Great Firewall). In just a few short years, China has leapfrogged the United States in the production of broadband capacity and now ranks second in the world in this category, after South Korea.

In excess of 100 million Chinese use the Internet (13 million of these are youths [mostly males] playing games at sites like ganggang.com or at 17173.com), and the volume of domestic online traffic has increased exponentially in terms of access and commerce. For example, it is estimated that the Chinese online video game market generates as much as $800 million annually. Intel Corporation's number-two market is China, and it has twenty venture capital investments and more than three thousand employees there. Computer literacy, educated workers, and engineering have transformed China from what was ten years ago a mere computer parts assembly site into a site for contemporary IT design (China graduates more engineers—300,000 per year—than the United States). Fifty percent of the country's expanding personal computer (PC) production is in the hands of domestic manufacturers like Lenovo, Fandu, and Tongfang. And with Lenovo's acquisition in May 2005 of IBM's PC division, China has made a bid to dominate the domestic market while inserting itself aggressively into the current of international IT sales.

With the expansion of advanced industrial technology and correspondingly wider access by mobile phone and computer to the Internet, we cannot help but wonder if these trends will favor the generation of greater human freedoms (a question taken up in chapter 6). Out of an instinct to preserve its monopoly on political power, the Chinese Communist Party (CCP) has encouraged the expansion of the World Wide Web, but it has found that limiting the number of Internet service providers (ISPs) and placing restrictions on Internet content providers (ICPs) do not permit it to repress what is posted and provides no effective restraint against cellular telephone text messaging, for anyone can purchase a prepaid phone card and use it to make calls that cannot be traced.

This lesson was learned the hard way in a sudden eruption of nationalistic, anti-Japanese protests in April 2005 when thousands of text messages from multiple sites and authors called on Chinese citizens in Beijing and Shanghai to demonstrate against a Japanese revision of history textbooks covering the Second World War. Thousands of protesters were in the streets of Beijing on April 9 and a week later in Shanghai, despite a government demand that students remain on campus and not demonstrate, and another twenty thousand people protested before the Japanese embassy on April 15.

In a distinctive twist on the transnational flows of global capitalism, UT-STARCOM, an IT company founded by Chinese graduates of U.S. universities and based in Alameda, California, is listed on NASDAQ and generates $2 billion in annual sales, most of it in China. As well, China's principal Internet portals, Sohu.com and Sina.com, are the startup products of Chinese graduates of Stanford University who returned to China to provide apolitical, self-censoring sites that claim to be an "ethnically-centered resource about the Chinese community that provides information, supports social activities, and fosters business transactions."[7] There is now a loosened constraint in China from which anyone with nerve or ambition can break free; however, most Internet users are content to shop and surf and to take advantage of the increasing transparency of pricing. Sure, people "game the system," but there is now in China a special Internet police force, and it rarely seems worth the effort to transcend these loosened constraints, especially when violators like Liu Di, the "Stainless Steel Mouse," can be held in China's notorious Qincheng prison for a year without being formally charged, simply for posting political satire or calling for the release of other cyberdissidents. This is a very fluid situation, politically speaking, and it is likely to remain so for some time, with the government becoming more systematic in its censoring of Internet trafficking, and with users developing more ingenious mechanisms to overcome China's *da huoqiang*.

Media and politics are converging in similar ways in the United States and China, one consequence of which is the difficulty of obtaining reliable information about the most troubling issues of the day. It is the potential damage to state propaganda posed by unvarnished information that makes the expansion of netizen culture so problematic for the Chinese government, as was memorably demonstrated in early 2006 when the CCP disavowed the killing of twenty villagers in Dongzhou at the hands of police and public security officials but within two days the information was globally available on the Internet. A conclusion about the virtues of propaganda and the need to limit public access to information has been reached by the Bush administration in the United States, which in renaming its environmental protection initiatives "Clear Skies" and "Healthy Forests" has attempted to persuade the public to accept proposals that would otherwise be rejected out of hand. The United

States under this administration has certainly discovered the advantage of propaganda, producing it by design from an informational overload of print and broadcast journalism. In China, "red envelope journalism," in which newspaper and television reporters who generate favorable copy on a business or industry are given cash supplements in red envelopes, has been a problem for more than a decade, but it has only been in the past year that U.S. citizens have learned of a similar practice by their government. In several celebrated cases since 2004, agencies of the Bush administration were shown to have paid syndicated columnists such as Armstrong Williams, Maggie Gallagher, and Michael McManus to offer advice and to write editorials and commentary in endorsement of controversial parts of the administration's domestic agenda regarding education and marriage.

Misrepresentation is also a signature communication strategy of the current U.S. administration. This strategy was most dramatically displayed in the Comprehensive Report of the Special Advisor to the Director of Central Intelligence on Iraq's Weapons of Mass Destruction, which found that there was no credible evidence of weapons of mass destruction (WMD) in Iraq, the principal rationale for declaring war. There have been other techniques by means of which this administration has erased the boundary between fact and fiction, including its clever production of ninety-second video news releases packaged in a television news format with reporters in the field doing stories on a new Medicare prescription drug law, the No Child Left Behind Act, government efforts to enforce airline security, the fall of Baghdad, and the importance of open markets for today's farmers. Numerous local television stations simply aired these segments without acknowledging that they had been produced by the very government agencies whose work was touted in the reports. Following an inquiry into this deceptive practice, the U.S. General Accountability Office ruled that such use of "federal funds for propaganda" was illegal.

In this respect—legally binding oversight—the governments of China and the United States still remain distinct from one another, the latter displaying comparative transparency, even as both attempt to limit press freedoms through legal action, and in the case of Zhao Yan, a *New York Times* reporter in China, through detention without a hearing. By August 2006, as hundreds of thousands of Chinese were displaced by massive flooding and the most destructive typhoon in fifty years, the Chinese government had announced the drafting its Law on Response to Contingencies that would impose fines of ¥50,000 to ¥100,000 for unauthorized reporting on "sudden incidents" (natural disasters, outbreaks of disease, and social disturbances).[8] Bad news, of which there will be plenty in the course of China's rapid modernization, is at least impolitic and at most threatening to the status quo.

In a fashion reminiscent of CCP practice, the Bush administration has also moved to repress publication of government documents. On April 15,

2005, the U.S. State Department announced that it would no longer publish its annual report on international terrorism (no doubt because there were more terrorist attacks in 2004 than in any year since 1985 when *Patterns of Global Terrorism* was first published). In January of 2003, the U.S. Department of Labor ceased reporting the statistics on mass layoffs (the summary firing of at least fifty people) by U.S. companies. Previously, such a report was issued monthly by the U.S. Bureau of Labor Statistics. The final report was issued in December of 2002 and stated that U.S. employers had initiated 2,150 mass layoffs in November that affected 240,000 workers. Between January and November of 2002, 17,799 mass layoffs were recorded, resulting in the firing of nearly 2 million workers. In February 2003, the U.S. Office of Management and Budget announced the discontinuation of publication of the annual *Budget Information for States*, the primary federal document that reported the amount of federal money each state was to receive. The fiscal 2004 document was not published.

ECONOMIC GIGANTISM:
CHINA, THE WTO, AND U.S. DEBT

Since the publication of *China beyond the Headlines*, the United States has authorized permanent normal trade relations with China (PNTR), thus terminating a practice begun in the Carter administration of conducting an annual debate on most favored nation trading status, a debate joined to an evaluation of China's human rights record. Human rights in China are still monitored by the U.S. State Department and the Central Intelligence Agency as well as by nongovernmental organizations (NGOs), most significantly the Dui Hua Foundation, which has become the principal conduit for communication to the United States about political prisoners and religious detainees. Economics is no longer explicitly tethered to the treatment of Chinese prisoners, because the United States presumes that improved material prosperity in China brings greater prospects for democratization and because pronounced public emphasis on China's deficiencies in this regard will harm U.S. opportunities for trade and investment, not to mention U.S. efforts to cooperate with the Chinese on thorny issues such as North Korea, Iran, and the global "war on terror."

More significant for U.S.-China relations than the establishment of PNTR was China's admission into the WTO. At Doha, Qatar, in November 2001 — following fifteen years of talks with member nations that began as the General Agreement on Tariffs and Trade (GATT) and became the WTO—China was granted membership in the WTO by a unanimous vote of the WTO's 142 members.[9] This event proved especially meaningful to China and the Chinese, not as an economic windfall but as a unique symbol of global embrace. The WTO accession signaled political acceptance of China as one of the world's great powers. Such economic greatness could not be gainsaid at the point of admission, and was dramatically confirmed in the next three years as the U.S. trade deficit with China grew from $50 billion to an all-time high in 2005 of $201.5 billion. At the same time, the WTO accession brought greater economic and political pressures on China's government. An economy of freer global trade with its promise of massive export of cheaply produced Chinese goods has meant greater promise of foreign direct investment and heightened international supervision over and interference with the market Leninism favored by the CCP.

These economic achievements account for much of the popular Western focus on China. Yet scholars are increasingly suspicious of such lavish triumphalism, particularly in light of the CCP's Faustian bargain in which economic prosperity is offered in exchange for political freedom. Still, the statistical data continue to advertise the success of these policy choices and to invite additional foreign investment as China's GDP grew at 10 percent per year between 2003 and 2005, while expanding 10.3 percent and 11.3 percent in the first two quarters of 2006. With its legitimacy tenuously balanced on the peak of an ascending graph of steady economic growth, the CCP may be inclined to doctor the figures to make them statistically confirm the fact of China's growth. And because the U.S. print and broadcast media are highly dependent on official information from China, scholars, as well as the general reading public seeking a balanced view, should pay close attention to stories that cut across the grain by portraying the darker side of China's economic takeoff (see chapter 3). Some scholars have challenged the conventional trumpeting of China's economic expansion by arguing that the compound rate of growth in China's per capita gross domestic product (GDP) over the last twenty-five years, 6.1 percent, was markedly less than that of Japan (8.8 percent; 1950–1973), and South Korea (7.6 percent; 1962–1990). Moreover, China's current per capita GDP is approximately equivalent to that of South Korea in 1982, of Taiwan in 1976, and of Japan in 1961. In light of these comparisons, coupled with ratings provider Standard & Poor's determination that Chinese banks have issued more than $650 billion in nonperforming loans, we might ask instead, "Why is China growing so slowly?"[10]

Although we can debate the pace of China's economic expansion, it is evident that a great many Chinese, mostly residents of China's larger cities, have grown very wealthy in recent years. And those who have not are equally eager to attain such prosperity. A singular measure of the affluence of urban Chinese is the price and availability of upscale real estate, such as in the Shanghai housing complex Rainbow City (similar to the complex shown in figure I.2), built by Hong Kong developer Shui On Properties.

Figure I.2. Upper-story view from a contemporary Beijing apartment high-rise. (Photo: Tong Lam)

In October 2003, all 816 apartments of this complex were sold in three days, mostly to local Chinese. In Shanghai, a nearly complete luxury residential complex in the city's Xintiandi district—which, ironically, encompasses the site where the CCP was founded in 1921—where apartments cost $325 per square foot, had a waiting list of 2,200 prospective buyers. There is money to be made and money to spend, at the same time that parts of the Chinese hinterland (see chapter 12) suffer crushing poverty and hopelessness. While it is certainly less pronounced in the United States and other developed countries, a growing economic disparity is today common in Chinese and Western societies (see figure I.3).

THE PERSISTENCE OF EXCEPTIONALISM: ECOLOGY

U.S. and Chinese *exceptionalism*—a sense of uniqueness and special destiny, which are the products, proudly held, of distinct national and historical experiences and achievements—has blinded both nations to their significantly transformed roles in world politics. The post–September 11 jingoism of the United States and in the case of China a renascent nationalism (see chapter 5) have fed in either country an intensification of national identity

Figure I.3.   New China towers over the old below. (Photo: Peter H. Jaynes)

so visceral at times that questioning the very wisdom of such political passion is regarded as unpatriotic.

We have been struck—sometimes it seems serendipitously—by the resemblances of China and the United States, but particularly by both nations' habit of exempting themselves from judgment according to international standards. This exceptionalism has proved costly. And as national governments tend to make decisions on the basis of the temperament of their leaders rather than as a consequence of experience or history, U.S. and Chinese exceptionalism undoubtedly will continue to come at a high price for each nation and for the larger world that must endure the consequences of their actions. Now that China is the undisputed manufacturer to the world and the United States is the world's sole superpower and largest debtor—much of whose fiscal stability depends upon strategic Chinese holders of U.S. debt—it is more essential than ever for these two great nations to arrive at a recognition of their conjoined fates. By understanding more about China and the Chinese, who already know a very great deal about the United States, we Americans are more likely to find shared political ground with the Chinese. Mutual respect would seem the least these two nations should require of each other as globalization has brought them so much closer.

This, it must be stressed, is not the inevitable consequence of media convergence or global advertising fusion. Our two nations are drawn closer by these phenomena, but is this closeness sufficient for us to see each other more clearly? Ideology in either case negates the advantage offered by our greater resemblance, a resemblance that is most pronounced with respect to our mutual destruction of the natural environment and the customs of international diplomacy.

Attention to the matter of environmental destruction in China, a subject about which most informed U.S. citizens are aware, reveals that the politics of ecology is very complicated and surprising. The air quality of two-thirds of China's cities is below World Health Organization (WHO) standards; this is not astonishing, considering that six of the most polluted cities in the world are in China. By far China has the largest rates of airborne carbon monoxide, and the State Environmental Protection Agency (SEPA) estimates that living in China's most-polluted cities is a pulmonary disaster equivalent to smoking two packs of cigarettes a day. The pollutants in many Chinese rivers are so great that people get skin diseases from contact. A 2005 *New York Times* report on the Huai River basin in Anhui province reveals that the river is a fount of pathology, its riverbed strewn with garbage, dead fish, detergent scum, and human and animal waste. Many of the peasants who depend on the river are suffering from rare cancers, yet they are just some of the many Chinese who endure the consequences of the nation's intensifying environmental pollution. China may have the worst air and water pollution in the world, and although its government may be disinclined by nature to permit popular dissent, environmental protest in China has become one of the areas of real progress in popular activism.

The struggle for human rights in China, instinctively associated in the Western media with the heroic activity of dissidents, is today being waged on the battleground of the environment. It has developed into a fight for the elemental freedom to breathe clean air and to drink clean water, and for just compensation after loss. The prospects for environmental activism in China, within existent political constraints, have expanded dramatically in the last decade. Officially there are about two thousand environmental NGOs in China, and according to recent testimony before the U.S. Congress by Elizabeth C. Economy, director of Asia Studies at the Council on

Foreign Relations, there are as many as two thousand more such organizations that exist either unofficially or as for-profit entities. In addition, Economy claimed that

> through environmental websites such as Green Web, newspapers such as *China Environmental News, China Green Times, Southern Weekend,* and *21st Century Business Herald,* as well as television programs such as "The Time for Environment," Chinese environmental activists reach millions of Chinese daily.[11]

Economy added that

> one potentially harmful change to environmental outreach is the decision by the Chinese government that government bureaus are not required to purchase newspapers such as *China Green Times.* This has sharply limited the income and circulation of such environmental papers.

Stories about the popular shift toward environmental activism in China have been carried by the *Washington Post,* the *New York Times,* the *Christian Science Monitor,* and the *Wall Street Journal,* where one learns that in 2003 a number of Chinese environmental NGOs availed themselves of the Internet to organize a campaign against the construction of thirteen hydroelectric projects on the Salween River in southwestern China.

It is important to point out in this context that China, unlike the United States, is one of the 154 nations that accepted or approved the Kyoto Protocol on climate change. The Chinese government has also made an explicit international commitment to host an environmentally responsible, or "green," Olympics (see chapter 2), and it would appear that SEPA is willing to defend that rhetoric through interventionist action in aggressively enforcing "green" laws by closing down twenty-two construction projects worth more than $14 billion in thirteen provinces.[12] However, even as SEPA asserts political clout in alignment with scientific experts and provincial activists, the pathological toxicity of the Chinese working environment is so great that violent social unrest has outpaced ecological reform, particularly in those circumstances in which officials direct local land-use for profit.

This land-use has become a common problem in rural China, where the expansion of township and village enterprises (TVEs) offers the multiple advantages of profit for local government officials and industrial investors and greater employment for a large, underemployed rural workforce, which is increasingly concerned about its political incapacity to resist the fouling of the environment. Indeed, environmental activism, or at its most basic, the violent struggle against oppressive local power and corruption that contravene agreements to protect quality of life, became one of the most salient political forces in China in 2005, and as the year came to a close there was widespread anger and further disillusionment with the government when some one hundred metric tons of benzene and other toxic substances were discharged into the Songhua river following a November 13 explosion at the state-owned Jilin Petrochemical Company, located 165 miles upstream from the city of Harbin (pop. 4 million). Benzene poisoning causes anemia, cancer, blood disorders, and kidney and liver damage. But in a throwback to the Chinese government's self-defeating denial of the SARS (severe acute respiratory syndrome) epidemic two years earlier and reflecting Chinese officials' penchant for hiding the truth from the people—even those most directly affected by disasters—local leaders for days reflexively covered up the fact that the Jilin explosion had polluted the river, even though they had been told of the chemical spill eight hours after it occurred and had already taken steps to shut off water supplies to people in the region. Once news of the eighty-kilometer toxic slick moving toward Harbin finally got out and the government cut water supplies to the city, widespread panic caused city residents to make a run on bottled water and other necessities, and the city's train station and airport quickly became crowded with people desperate to escape a disaster whose full implications they still could not know.

The local in this case quickly became global—cities in Russia were also endangered by the toxic spill, and the disaster quickly made headline news around the world. The disaster provided a forum for domestic political activists in China, both those focused on the environment and those concerned with other issues. Critics such as Beijing University media professor Jiao Guobiao were quick to accuse local government officials in the area hit by the disaster of acting "more like local Mafiosi than the government of a modern society" and blamed the cover-up on China's lack of press freedom. "If the press had real freedom," Jiao said, "the local authorities wouldn't be able to cover up what happened, even if they wanted to."[13]

Much as Hurricane Katrina's devastation a few months earlier had exposed the U.S. government's failure to prepare adequately for disaster and an unequal distribution of resources in the United States, the toxic spill into the Songhua river starkly revealed who has power in China and who does not, and made clear where the CCP's priorities—or at least those of its local bosses—lie. Concern for the welfare of the people takes a back seat to Chinese officials' desire to protect their own positions and to maximize the climate in China for foreign investment. Both because of its disastrous health and financial consequences and because it received so much international attention, the Songhua river pollution scandal will surely further stoke Chinese environmentalists' demands that the CCP find a way to balance its goal of rapid economic progress with the equally important goal of safe and clean development.

Ecology is one avenue of democratic expression; a more prominent, because intrinsically interesting, path is sexual liberation.

CHINA'S SEXUAL REVOLUTION

In contemporary China, as in the broad stream of global media in which the country wades, sex has a distinct and expanding currency. All of the nation's urban centers have hostess bars, massage parlors, "barber shops," karaoke lounges, and singles' bars, while out in the rural points of transit between Yunnan and Myanmar, or in the exotic sites of tourism in minority nationality autonomous regions (see chapter 11), commercial sex availability is public and polymorphous. Cash is king, and sex is its servant—an attitude bound up with local politics. In 1999 the mayor of Shenyang in northeastern China Mu Suixin encouraged the development of prostitution in order to combat unemployment among laid-off workers of state-owned enterprises (SOEs) and among the migrant labor force of an economically depressed countryside. His 30 percent tax on Shenyang's new sex trade was a boon to the city's economy (luxuriously fed by the profits of the city's more than five thousand "places of entertainment") and inspired other mayors and regional officials to mimic the practice.

In some locales, such as the hyper-urbanized enclaves of the south and southeast coast (Hainan, Guangzhou, Hong Kong, Xiamen, Shanghai, Shenzhen, and other special economic zones [SEZs]) and the northern capital, Beijing, sex is both inescapable and profitable. A cultural revolution in the explicitness and availability of sexual commodities is visible everywhere: risqué clothing styles, brazenly displayed tattoos, pinup calendars, women's fashion magazines, supermodel contests, pornographic books and magazines and videotapes, adult-theme stores, notices for private clinics treating sexually transmitted diseases (STDs), national anti-HIV/AIDS campaigns, prostitution, sex slavery, condom promotion, and breast enhancement advertisements, along with a proliferation of visual images of the body, scantily clad and unclad, are strewn throughout the commercial beckoning of the new urban Chinese streetscape.

The most commonly discussed and the most salient of these indices of behavioral change is the astonishing growth in prostitution in the era since the economic reforms of the 1980s. According to the WHO, China has the largest commercial sex workforce in the world, with an estimated 10 million men and women so employed—more than 300,000 in the city of Beijing alone. Yet commercial sex availability is not simply an urban phenomenon, and its rapid expansion cannot simply be explained as a sudden escalation of public desire. The burgeoning market for commercial sex is evident in the plurality of its offerings, as displayed in the voluminous records of police blotters. There have been hundreds of thousands of arrests of men and women in official "strike hard" anti-vice campaigns, numerous national scandals concerning children in the sex trade, solicitations of underage sex (fourteen years of age and younger), involuntary sexual servitude, and kidnapping of girls for sale into the sex trade or marriage.

Recently, Yunnan's provincial government uncovered a prostitution ring operating in Kunming that was composed of high-school girls, some as young as thirteen, many of whom had been introduced to the flesh trade by older teenagers. The girls admitted that they prostituted themselves voluntarily because of the glamour and the inordinate compensation in wealth and power they received from their clients. However, we learn from the research of Pan Suiming, a scholar who has conducted fieldwork among urban prostitutes, that the work may seem glamorous but it is certainly not easy and often not as remunerative as one might presume by looking at the figures indicating that commercial sex work generates between 6–12 percent of China's annual GDP.[14]

Escort services and the like have recently become more common manifestations of sex work, because the government's Regulations on the Management of Places of Entertainment restricts what would otherwise be an unabashed traffic in flesh. These escort, or "leisure," services have sprung up so that enterprising women can find work as "swim companions" or "theater companions." Private agencies in larger cities offer employment for forty to seventy dollars a month to women who will work as housekeepers, yet the women (and girls) who answer such ads have often been coerced into commercial sex trafficking. In this light, it makes little sense to assess the Chinese sexual revolution in terms of sex or individual empowerment. Rather, it is better to recognize China's sex industry as a capitalist enterprise consequent upon economic scarcity and social jeopardy than to see it merely as a series of personal choices. And given the mutual entailment of commercial sex and official sponsorship of the entertainment industry through hotels, restaurants, and so forth, it is unlikely that national campaigns to prosecute prostitutes and their clients will turn back the tide of sex for sale in which many Chinese cities are awash.

Today sex and sexuality are boldly displayed on billboards and in magazines, on film and television, and in forms of dress, but because they are still not easily spoken of, sex and sexuality stand on the edge of Chinese social life. But a more liberal sexual attitude is found among high-school and college-age youths (as documented in the nation's Sex Civilization Survey in 1997). In 2000 the UN Educational, Scientific and Cultural Organization (UNESCO) reported that studies conducted in Beijing and Shanghai disclosed that 50–85 percent of women interviewed at premarital checkups had experienced sexual intercourse. The sexual liberation of Chinese youths is stridently proclaimed in the pulp fiction read by China's Generation X and Generation Y adults (see chapter 8). Works such as Wei Hui's *Shanghai baobei* [*Shanghai baby*], Hong Ying's *Luowudai* [*Summer of betrayal*], and Mian

Mian's *La la la* are populated with pseudobiographical female figures of prominent sexual bearing and interests whose self-gratification is paramount and whose identity is indissociable from sex. Of course, this addictive, fictional conjuncture of sex and commerce may not represent the actual lives of its readers, but the salience of the effects of this literature is gauged by its overweening popularity.

DEMOCRACY?

Another area of demonstrable change, at least within some regions of China, is the government's promotion of local democratic elections. In 1998 the National People's Congress announced that village committees were required by law to be democratically elected and that these elections must take place every three years. Because the village committee is required to be elected by direct, competitive procedure, village heads may also be democratically elected; however, township and county officials are not elected but appointed. Popular sovereignty is therefore only apparent, and representation is made more problematic by election laws requiring that delegate representation of urban populations (roughly 30 percent of the total) be four times greater than that of equivalent rural populations. Moreover, even with the increased involvement in village elections of NGOs like the Carter Center, the Ford Foundation, and the International Republican Institution, observers report that only 10 percent of these elections may be certified as democratic.

Yet if the practice of democracy means simply greater inclusiveness, then the opening by provincial people's congresses of legislative hearings to the public (as was done in the fall of 1999 in Guangzhou) stands as a significant democratic gesture. And by the same token, there is a modicum of democracy in former president Jiang Zemin's Three Represents theory—announced in 2000 and ceaselessly promulgated in government statements concerning politics or economy—which maintains that the CCP represents the advanced productive forces (businesspeople), the advanced cultural forces (intellectuals), and the masses (workers and peasants). And if the practice of democracy means accountability and a margin of transparency within bureaucracy, then democratic methods are now being tested at the lower levels of the People's Liberation Army (PLA), where vacant positions are announced, standards for appointments have been published, public recommendations have been written, open examinations have been held, and candidates for military office have been made public.

Between 1997 and 2003, political reflection among the Chinese leadership and by academics in the Chinese Academy of Social Sciences negotiated a number of positions on political reform that border on advocacy of democracy and free elections, while also revealing the difficulties for intellectuals (see chapter 13) and party members who wish to advance themes suitable to resolving the political crisis China faces. Such conceptual negotiation at the center includes emphasis on the establishment of the rule of law but falls short of the legal enshrinement of popular representation, as has been called for by alternative, preliminary party organizations such as the China Democracy Party (CDP), which in 1998 boldly proclaimed that "government must be established through the conscious approval of the public [and] through free, impartial, and direct democratic elections."[15] Within two years, however, the CDP had been repressed; there is but one party in China.

At present, it is too soon to tell if these phenomena are best read as the tremors of shifting political ground, and little else, or whether they signal a deliberate movement toward establishing widespread franchise. These tremors represent most likely the urgings of a new generation of party leaders concerned with addressing the widening political chasm between a sovereign government and its people. It is also unclear if suffrage is actually desired by most Chinese, or if they believe it to be a political experiment they are capable of undertaking. To be sure, the Chinese lack any sufficient, real practice in democracy, but it is also evident that in the United States, democratic practice has been flawed in recent state and national elections. In the fall of 2004 the Carter Center, for example, asserted that it could not certify U.S. national elections as they are presently conducted.

Some in China, as well as some of the authors of this volume, including Timothy B. Weston (see chapter 3), caution that the prosperity of the present under authoritarianism should be contrasted with the possible chaos consequent upon the dismantling of the party-state in favor of an unknown form of political order that might, but would not necessarily, ensure more pluralistic representation. According to this reasoning, it is presumed that continued life under the aegis of the CCP is the better of the two alternatives. However, the warrant for the reasonableness of this commonly repeated scenario stands outside consideration of an obvious fact borne in mind by this book's editors and most of its contributors—that the party itself is largely responsible for the chaos of Chinese daily life.

The undecided quality of government commitment to pluralistic representation has proven troubling in circumstances of unexpected popular protest, most notably in spring 2001 and spring 2005, when spontaneous nationalistic demonstrations by students and young professionals against the United States and Japan, respectively, broke out in China's major urban centers. These events, though lasting no more than a few weeks, drew international attention largely because of the specific targets of this public outrage. Another reason for the media-worthiness of these demonstrations was uncertainty surrounding the government's role in fomenting them and how, once begun, the government responded to the protests. Protest is permitted under the 1982 Chinese Constitution (provided the protestors have requested permission from the Public Security Bureau); consequently, repression of spontaneous demonstration is costly to the government. Yet popular agitation against the United States or Japan, if permitted or even encouraged initially then discouraged, might revert to protest against the CCP. It seems, then, that the government's ongoing internal debate over democracy and control demonstrates that the party-state has yet to find a reliable method of encouraging democracy that would not also entail its own dissolution.

It is this conundrum that helps us account for the curious way in which the Chinese government has meddled in the democratic activities of Hong Kong and Taiwan these last few years. In the spring of 2004 upon his return from Washington, D.C., where he had testified before a U.S. Senate subcommittee on East Asia and the Pacific, the celebrated Hong Kong democracy activist Martin Lee was met at Hong Kong International Airport by two sharply divided camps of the island's citizens: advocates of universal suffrage in the 2007 election on the one side, and on the other a group of limited-democracy, pro-Beijing enthusiasts. The latter questioned Lee's patriotism, calling him a traitor and even casting aspersions on his identity as Chinese—an example of Beijing's growing influence over public opinion and of the new cult of authenticity among younger Chinese. Lee's critics complained that the democracy movement had gone too far and that its persistent call for suffrage was destructive of Hong Kong's business climate and its political stability. According to the reasoning of the pro-Beijing patriots, what is Chinese is not democratic but autocratic and culturally eternal.

Just as Beijing has provoked resentment and dissent in appointing the government of Hong Kong, the United States faced similar reactions in 2004 to its appointment of an Iraqi Governing Council and its tinkering with Iraqi national elections, and like Chinese authorities, it has defensively challenged criticism by appeals to patriotism at home. Both provide examples of occupation (one light-handed, the other draconian) and of direction of domestic politics in the name of democracy but with an obvious strain and a definite cost. For the United States, that cost has been borne by Iraqi citizens and U.S. troops under the weight of an expanding insurgency, whereas for China the cost has been an escalating number of protests: 58,000 in 2003, 74,000 in 2004, and 87,000 in 2005, up from a mere 8,700 in 1993 (according to Ministry of Public Security statistics). For both the United States and China, there is much more going on in the way of popular resistance than is reported by news agencies.

CHINA IN THE GLOBAL LANDSCAPE:
THE 2008 OLYMPICS

Arguably the most salient feature of China's transformations in the stories beyond the headlines today is the multiple contexts of its international recognition. While this recognition is significant for a China historically misjudged and underappreciated, more important is the stature the nation has obtained in the eyes of the world through its admission into the WTO and by the International Olympic Committee (IOC) selection of Beijing as the site for the 2008 Summer Olympics.

There was pandemonium in Beijing at the official announcement on July 13, 2001, that Beijing had received fifty-six votes and had been selected to host the 2008 summer games. This represented a critically important landmark in a series of events in which China's pride as a nation on par with the other prominent nations of the world had been incontrovertibly established: the return of Hong Kong (1997), the return of Macao (1999), the spring 2000 U.S. congressional vote granting PNTR to China, and the admission of China into the WTO. As a Beijing university teacher put it in the first moments following the IOC decision, "The world has recognized us," and in saying this the teacher echoed Mao's oft-repeated proclamation at the founding of the People's Republic of China (PRC) that "the Chinese people have stood up."

After the failure of China's 1993 bid to host the 2000 Olympic Games, most Chinese concluded that the West, led by the United States, was opposed to Beijing's being an Olympics host site. Critics of the Chinese bid alleged in 2001, as they had in 1993, that of all the finalists China least exemplified the defining charter of the international Olympic movement, which calls for the democratic honoring of diversity and brotherhood in sport. In international competitions in the late 1990s, a great number of Chinese athletes were found in flagrant violation of amateur athletics rules, particularly involving the use of performance-enhancing drugs. In fact, in a surprise announcement just days before the opening of the 2000 games in Sydney, forty athletes and officials were dismissed from the Chinese national team (including all but one of the fabled world-record-setting runners trained by Ma Junren), after testing positive for erthyropoietin (EPO), a banned substance capable of accelerating the production of red blood cells.

Most if not all of these issues were raised in the world media and were vociferously emphasized by Tibetans in Moscow for the IOC vote, and by human rights groups in Hong Kong and the United States. Moreover, some IOC members and a few journalists cited the example of South Africa in support of rejecting the Chinese bid for the 2008 games. When South Africa made a bid to host the games in the 1980s, the IOC had insisted that South Africa could not be considered as long as apartheid was a foundation of the state. China, these critics pointed out, was an authoritarian state that practiced human slavery as well, though certainly not on the order or in the manner of 1980s South Africa. What was appropriate for South Africa, a rogue nation, was therefore appropriate for China, another rogue nation.[16]

This would be a cynical gloss of the IOC decision and of the Chinese bid. A hopeful reading has it that the hosting of the Olympic Games permits the IOC and the CCP alike to reform themselves in spectacular, very public ways that may very well precipitate even greater fundamental changes. Mindful of the challenges China faces—challenges that are unlikely to be resolved but made more prominent—the Chinese government has cast its cash ($23 billion at last count) like a feverish roll of dice toward the transformation of virtually every aspect of Beijing's urban infrastructure so that national pride in the achievements of "socialism with Chinese characteristics" might be brilliantly displayed on the international stage. At the same time, China's hosting of the upcoming Olympic Games will bring greater international scrutiny to that country's many massive problems. This prospect makes China's leaders wary and is already resulting in a determined propaganda campaign designed to portray China as a modern and just society working rationally to resolve its entangled challenges. It is inevitable that China will continue to be affected by this more complete integration into the world represented by the Olympics; however, the costs of such integration, of resolving the exigencies of nation and world, may well be more prohibitive than either party or people can fathom. In the last two years especially, China's global integration has announced both peril and promise in the fields of epidemiology, diplomacy, and spaceflight, all of which deserve at least cursory review.

EPIDEMIOLOGY, SPACEFLIGHT, AND DIPLOMACY

Since 2003 China has been in U.S. national headlines for one of the most frightening adverse consequences of globalization: rapidly communicable disease. In the winter and spring of 2003, politics and the Chinese economy gave way to epidemiology following the outbreak of a mysterious and deadly respiratory ailment that began in southern China and soon compassed the globe, with quite a number of the afflicted in Canada and the United States. SARS (severe acute respiratory syndrome) was determined to have crossed from infected animals to humans in southern Chinese markets, where there is a marked gustatory predilection for the consumption of civet cats. SARS, unlike HIV/AIDS, posed an immediate public health threat, one that extended far beyond China's borders and that as a consequence brought intense direct pressure to bear on the government. By the end of 2003, global mortality figures had reached nearly eight hundred out of fewer than nine thousand cases, with the disease striking hardest in Beijing, Hong Kong, Taiwan, and Canada (indeed, the largest number of fatalities occurred in Toronto and Beijing).

At virtually the same time as the SARS epidemic was being contained in China, Taiwan, Europe, Canada, and the United States, H5N1 avian influenza, a highly pathogenic, rapidly mutating virus more commonly identified as bird flu, seized headlines out of Hong Kong and China. Like terrorism, a deadly enemy known only by its effects, bird flu incited global alarm as news reports announced the death of two members of a family who had traveled in South China just days before the onset of the virus. In the last two years there has been a steady increase in the number of documented outbreaks of avian flu, which have occurred in Egypt, Indonesia, the Netherlands, sub-Saharan Africa, Thailand, and in the northern region of Vietnam. By 2005 bird flu had come to occupy the attention of most all developed and developing nations, so much so that President Bush made this concern central to a public address to the nation in the fall. The increasingly likely prospect of the successful mutation of H5N1 into a virus transmissible from human to human has caused international anxiety, especially following a revelation by the Chinese government in early August 2006 that a soldier who the government had originally claimed died of SARS in 2005 actually died of avian influenza in 2003. Mounting international concern exacerbated by unreliable reporting, the documented spread of animal infection to Africa, Asia, Europe, the Near East, and the Pacific, and the ambiguity of bird flu's transmission has inspired governments to develop specific plans to address a potential pandemic: programs for quarantine, acceleration of the development of a bird flu vaccine, and purchases of Tamiflu, at present the only known antiviral treatment for this virus.[17]

Another uncustomary appearance in world headlines occurred in fall 2003 when Chinese politics and science joined in advocacy of the nation's space-age modernity by making China the third country to propel a human being into interplanetary space. International attention turned to China's first manned spaceflight, by Yang Liwei aboard a Russian *Soyuz*-type craft named *Shenzhou V*. With his successful navigation of fourteen orbits around the Earth, Yang secured China's place behind Russia and the United States in the space-travel pantheon. At the same time and to the astonishment of the Chinese press, Yang disclosed that, contrary to popular opinion, the Great Wall of China is not visible from space. Yang's successful mission was followed barely two years later, on October 18, 2005, by a second manned flight of 115 hours and 32 minutes by astronauts Fei Junlong and Nie Haisheng in *Shenzhou VI*. There was more symbolism than science in these events, but the nationalistic significance of this novel dimension of China's technological development signaled that China was now one of the global political and technological elite.[18]

Since 2000 and especially following the breakdown of trilateral talks between the United States and North Korea and South Korea in the winter of 2001, China has also been an effective agent of diplomatic change. Over this interval, the Chinese government has tolerated an increasingly large encampment of North Korean refugees (by some accounts as many as 150,000) in the Dongbei region on its northeastern border, seeing to it that they receive sufficient resources to survive. At the same time, North Korean refugees have been able to seek asylum in China, and in a number of cases they have been repatriated to South Korea via circuitous travels from Beijing through the Philippines, Singapore, and other transit points. Moreover, between 2003 and 2006 as the United States floundered in its dealings with the North Koreans and Kim Jong-il restarted his nation's nuclear weapons production, China assumed a prominent and very critical place at the negotiating table with North Korea and the United States in six-party talks on nuclear disengagement. Indeed, the Chinese have been singularly successful in ensuring North Korean participation in the talks. China has also become a global exemplar by increasingly investing in third-world development (although mainly for the purpose of securing economic or political advantage) while assuming a prominent role in the Group of 20 (G20) and in this capacity advocating less-restrictive global trade.

In today's international climate, alongside the bellicosity and aggressiveness of the United States, China can groom an international image of cooperation and constructive leadership. Still, all too often the attention China commands among U.S. citizens is a product of the negative aspects of its society and government: China is Communist; the CCP is evil; China has a dangerously large population; China is an expansionist power; it is one of the world's largest polluters; it has unfair labor practices; it is a shameless violator of elemental human rights; it unfairly freezes the exchange rate on its currency; it unfairly limits foreign access to its domestic markets; it floods the world's markets with cheap textiles; and on and on.

Such oft-repeated contrasts tend to make China our unfavorable Other, as we can see from the spectrum of topics and issues of contemporary moment for both Chinese and U.S. citizens such as are addressed in the following chapters: labor strife, ethnic and religious pluralism, human rights violations, nationalism, the plight of rural and urban Chinese women, popular protest among China's minority peoples, sexual revolution, economic development that disregards justice and safety, ecological adversity, postmodern literature and art, official corruption, the future of democracy, and the constructive and destructive consequences of globalization. Even today, as the U.S. economy continues its recovery from a post–September 11 recession with modest projected annual growth of 3 to 4 percent, China's economy grew exponentially at 9.2 percent in the spring quarter of 2004, and yet the May 3, 2004, issue of *Business Week* featured the title "China: Headed for a Crisis?" on its cover page.

The United States is simultaneously appreciative and apprehensive of China's towering economic achievement and rapid emergence as a world power. Its hot-cold interpretive predilection is the natural expression of anxiety over Beijing's rapidly growing political muscle and China's overheated economy, with which regional and international commerce is significantly intertwined. But when faced with the tendency to either sweepingly praise or blame China without due attention to the many ways it and the United States are becoming more alike and in which they share intertwined challenges, observers should become suspicious. This alternating current of judgment also conveys much about the prominence of China in U.S. everyday life. Nevertheless, the politics and economy of the present have changed, we hope, in such a way as to mitigate any instinctive judgment of China as adversary or ally. China is too important and complex to be treated in a simplistic fashion. Thus, we ask the reader to examine contemporary circumstances with a willingness to reconceive the model of U.S.-China relations, an undertaking that we believe is vitally important even though we remain uncertain as to what, exactly, that model should be. The stories beyond the headlines reveal the frontlines of the present century's reckoning—China on the rise and the United States adrift—as these two great global powers negotiate their fates economically and politically. Negotiations will be inevitable, and it is incumbent on the United States and China to conduct the future drama of these encounters with reason and understanding. It is in an effort to increase understanding that the chapters here are collected and presented.

NOTES

1. Joseph R. Levenson, *Revolutionism and Cosmopolitanism: The Western Stage and the Chinese Stages* (Berkeley: University of California Press, 1971), 2.

2. Veronica Gould Stoddart, "Shanghai Sizzle," *USA Today*, October 29, 2004, D1.

3. Gretchen Ruethling, "Classes in Chinese Grow as the Language Rides a Wave of Popularity," *New York Times*, October 15, 2005, A12. There are three thousand public-school students studying Chinese in Chicago at twenty-five elementary and secondary schools. In 2005 the U.S. Department of Defense gave a $700,000 grant to public schools in Portland, Oregon, in order to increase the number of students studying Chinese in that city's innovative Chinese immersion program. And in May 2005, Senators Joseph Lieberman (D-Conn.) and Lamar Alexander (R-Tenn.) introduced a bill to spend $1.3 billon over five years on Chinese-language programs in schools and on cultural exchanges to improve ties between the United States and China. By 2007, the U.S.-based Educational Testing Service will introduce its Advanced Placement Test for

Chinese; the Chinese government has invested $1.35 million to underwrite development of curricula and examinations for these classes. Even more impressive in this regard has been the official Chinese government sponsored effort to establish Confucius Institutes (*Kongzi xueyuan*) throughout the world. These institutes, formed in partnership with universities, high schools, and urban communities, provide the resources for teaching Chinese language and culture while facilitating exchange between host institutions abroad and Chinese universities. The China National Office for Teaching Chinese as a Foreign Language, known as Hanban, initiated the Confucius Institute project in 2004 and since then has supported the establishment of forty (of a planned one hundred) institutes worldwide.

4. Annual 2005 figures for Chinese car sales confirmed that General Motors vehicles, in particular the Buick Excelle sedan, outsold all other automobile manufacturers' products. Volkswagen placed second. See *Detroit News*, January 7, 2006.

5. Seymour Hersh, *Chain of Command: The Road from 9/11 to Abu Ghraib* (New York: HarperCollins, 2004).

6. Edmund L. Andrews, "Bush's Choice: Anger China or Congress over Currency," *New York Times*, May 17, 2005, C1; Paul Krugman, "The Chinese Connection," *New York Times*, May 20, 2005, A25.

7. This is an excerpt from the mission statement of Sina.com, accessed from its homepage in summer of 2005.

8. David Fullbrook, "The Return of China's Censors," *Asia Times*, July 12, 2006, www.atimes.com/atimes/China/HG12Ad01.html. In elaborating on the Orwellian language of "sudden incidents," Wang Yongqing, vice minister of the Legislative Affairs Office of the State Council (the CCP's cabinet), claimed that the new law was aimed at improving reporting by, according to Fullbrook, "ordering officials to release information quickly while ensuring that journalists reported accurately."

9. In all of the media hysteria and domestic Chinese political spin of the WTO accession, it proved difficult to remember that, several days later, the member nations of the WTO also approved the admission of Taiwan, Republic of China.

10. Martin Wolf, "Why Is China Growing So Slowly?" *Foreign Policy*, January/ February 2005, 50–51.

11. Elizabeth Economy, "China's Environmental Movement" (testimony, Congressional Executive Commission on China Roundtable, "Environmental NGOs in China: Encouraging Action and Addressing Public Grievances," Washington, D.C., February 7, 2005).

12. Robert Marquand, "China Enforcing Green Laws, Suddenly," *Christian Science Monitor*.

13. Radio Free Asia, "China's Harbin Slammed for Toxic Spill 'Cover-up,'" November 29, 2005.

14. Pan Suiming, *Shengcun yu tiyan: dui yige dixia "hongdeng qu" de zhui zong kaocha* [*Subsistence and experience: An investigation into an underground "red light district"*] (Beijing: Zhongguo renmin daxue xing shehuixue yanjiusuo, 2000). According to Pan, a woman working an average "barbershop" solicitation post everyday will be engaged by one client every four days.

15. "Zhongguo minzhudang Zhejiang choubei weiyuanhui chengli gongkai xuanyan [Open declaration of the establishment of the Zhejiang Preparatory Committee of the China Democracy Party]," June 25, 1998, as quoted in Jan van der

Made, *Nipped in the Bud: The Suppression of the CDP* (New York: Human Rights Watch, 2000), 26–27.

16. George Orwell once wrote in a savage critique of socialism that "some brothers are more equal than others." Here lies the difference between the South African and the Chinese bids. International commerce is the foundation of this inequality: many foreign corporations (U.S. and European) were divesting their holdings in South Africa at the time of that nation's bid, while today such corporations are investing in China with legendary largesse. Corporate Olympic sponsors certainly must savor the prospect for an even deeper exploration of a market with which they have become familiar in the ten years since the last IOC consideration of Beijing's eligibility. And the Olympics and the multinational committee that governs it, as the world learned in 1999–2000 IOC bribery scandals, are about money, both legal and illegal.

17. According to the WHO's avian influenza website, since 2003 there have been 235 confirmed human cases of H5N1, of which 137 were fatal. Indonesia (44 cases) and Vietnam (42) have reported the most cases and the most fatalities. China has reported 20 cases of bird flu and 13 fatalities; however, health ministry authorities there have not been especially forthcoming or ingenuous in communications concerning incidences of the disease, thus causing many to worry that the disease may be more widespread. For the WHO's current inventory of cases, see www.who.int/csr/disease/avian_influenza/country/cases_table_2006_08_08/en/index.html. See also a special report on bird flu, "What You Need to Know," Guardian Unlimited, www.guardian.co.uk/birdflu/0,,1131431,00.html. GlaxoSmithKline, a British pharmaceutics manufacturer announced in summer 2006 that it had developed and successfully tested, an H5N1 pandemic flu vaccine. See Mark Tran, "Vaccine Maker Announces Avian Flu Breakthrough," Guardian Unlimited, http://www.guardian.co.uk/birdflu/story/0,,1830402,00.html.

18. The *Shenzhou V* and *VI* flights were a source of profound nationalistic pride but also represented the first stages in a far more ambitious national program of space exploration, including a space walk in 2007 and the construction of an orbiting space station by 2012.

SUGGESTED READINGS

Thomas P. Bernstein and Xiaobo Lü, *Taxation without Representation in Contemporary Rural China* (Cambridge: Cambridge University Press, 2003).

Stephen Bocking, *Nature's Experts: Science, Politics, and the Environment* (New Brunswick, NJ: Rutgers University Press, 2004).

Edward L. Davis, ed., *Encyclopedia of Contemporary Chinese Culture* (New York: Routledge, 2005).

Larry Diamond and Ramon Myers, eds., *Elections and Democracy in Greater China* (New York: Oxford University Press, 2001).

Stephanie Donald and Robert Benewick, *The State of China Atlas: Mapping the World's Fastest Growing Economy* (Berkeley: University of California Press, 2005).

Daniel B. Fewsmith and Joseph Wright, *The Promise of the Revolution: Stories of Fulfillment and Struggle in China's Hinterland* (Lanham, MD: Rowman & Littlefield, 2003).

Peter H. Gries and Stanley Rosen, eds., *State and Society in 21st-Century China* (New York: Routledge/Curzon, 2004).

Chalmers A. Johnson, *The Sorrows of Empire: Militarism, Secrecy, and the End of the Republic* (New York: Metropolitan Books, 2004).

Ian Johnson, *Wild Grass: Three Stories of Change in Modern China* (New York: Vintage Books, 2005).

Liu Dalin, Man Lun Ng, Li Pingzhou, and Edwin J. Haeberle, eds., *Sexual Behavior in Modern China* (New York: Continuum Books, 1997).

James McGregor, *One Billion Customers: Lessons from the Front Lines of Doing Business in China* (New York: Wall Street Journal Books, 2005).

Pál Nyíri and Joana Breidenbach, eds., *China Inside Out: Contemporary Chinese Nationalism and Transnationalism* (Budapest: Central European Press, 2005).

Randall Peerenboom, *China's Long March toward the Rule of Law* (Cambridge: Cambridge University Press, 2002).

Elizabeth J. Perry and Mark Selden, eds., *Chinese Society: Change, Conflict and Resistance*, 2nd ed. (New York: Routledge/Curzon, 2003).

Project Censored, *Censored 2006: The Top 25 Censored Stories*, ed. Peter Phillips (New York: Seven Stories Press, 2006).

Tyrell White, ed., *China Briefing: The Continuing Transformation* (Armonk, NY: M.E. Sharpe, 2001).

Online Sources

China Daily, www.chinadaily.com
China Digital Times, www.chinadigitaltimes.net
China HIV/AIDS Information Network (CHAIN), www.chain.net.cn
Guardian Unlimited, www.guardian.co.uk
People's Daily Online, http://english.peopledaily.com.cn
Radio Free Asia, www.rfa.org/english
Xinhua News Online, www.chinaview.cn/index.htm

I

FRONT STAGE

When I first arrived in China in 1980, the average Chinese produced three hundred dollars' worth of goods a year. The country's prime atmospheric was still fear—of the authorities, teachers, and each other. I had watched that society die as affluence and access to information transformed the Chinese and had begun to alter, albeit more slowly, the party, too. By the time I left China in 2005, the gross domestic product had increased a whopping six-fold over 1980. But fear had not been replaced by freedom. Instead a restless unease coursed through society. The Chinese word for it was *fuzao*, an apprehension tinged with a titillating sense of opportunity. No wonder so many of my classmates worried about the future.

John Pomfret, 2006

1

Trouble-Makers or Truth-Sayers?

The Peculiar Status of
Foreign Correspondents in China

Martin Fackler

Asked what it was like to work as a foreign journalist in China, I often recall Christmas Day 2000. That's when a fire swept through a nightclub in the central city of Luoyang, killing 309 revelers at a Christmas party. It was the first big disaster I covered in China as a reporter for the Associated Press (AP). Reporting on tragedies is tough anywhere, because it requires you to do unnatural things, like try to question grieving relatives as their loved ones' remains are still being sought in the wreckage. But in Luoyang, this was the least of my difficulties. Over a twenty-four-hour period, I was surrounded by a mob, hunted by police, and forced to flee on a road possibly infested by highway robbers. These experiences, while extreme, were not entirely atypical for foreign journalists in China. Partly, they reflected the chaotic contradictions of a country where a vestigial totalitarian state presided over a greed-fueled free-for-all. But they also highlighted something in China that is much less known: the peculiar status of foreign journalists there. This status is important because it influences how journalists work in and perceive China, and this, in turn, colors the outside world's perception of China as well. Yet it rarely gets explicit mention even in press reports.

First, a word about this peculiar status: foreign reporters are alien observers in any country, almost by definition. But in China, this marginality was in my experience pushed to an extreme. The root cause was the constant surveillance, occasional harassment, and at times even blatant attempts at intimidation by the government, and particularly its security agencies. Technically, journalists were allowed to work freely (with a few notable exceptions) so long as they did not, according to Article 14 of Government Regulations on Foreign Journalists, "endanger China's national security, unity or community and public interests." In reality, government officials tried to obstruct us without regard for any press freedoms. All this helped create a highly adversarial relationship between the foreign press corps and official-dom. But the constant government pressure also had an unintended consequence. It defined our interaction with ordinary Chinese. It gave us an ambivalent and contradictory image in the eyes of the people whose stories we were trying to tell. We could be shunned as foreign provocateurs, as the government-run domestic media tried tirelessly to paint us. But we could just as easily find ourselves embraced almost as if we were agents of truth, channels to a world beyond the regime's control, and with the power to expose cover-ups and lies. It was not uncommon in the course of a single conversation to be accused of slandering China and then to be thanked for contradicting the official version of reality.

But when there was a groundswell of popular anger at the government, as happened in Luoyang while I was stationed in China, the latter image of the foreign press corps as agents of truth prevailed, to the point that ordinary Chinese sought us out. Our status beyond the control of the government or the CCP gave us a special credibility in the public eye. Our ability to influence public opinion in the outside world (something increasingly accessible within China via the Internet) meant we were seen as a check of sorts on officials who otherwise had few formal limits. Popular disgust at the lapdog domestic news media also brought us a steady stream of complaints and tips from disgruntled citizens, supplying some of our best story ideas.

The downside, of course, was the hassle of the police following our activities, invading our privacy and intimidating our sources and even friends. Foreign journalists are probably freer now to do their jobs than at possibly any time since China reopened its doors to foreign news agencies in the late 1970s following the Cultural Revolution. AP reporters who were in China right after the Beijing bureau was opened around 1979 say that their every activity was closely scrutinized, often by government minders, who were a frequent presence. Contact with average Chinese was tough, not just because of the minders but also because of the separation created by yawning cultural and economic gaps. Nowadays, the Chinese police have grown more selective in their monitoring, relying on electronic surveillance and showing an interest only in reporting activities that involve politically sensitive topics. Increasingly, wealth and overseas travel also have made it easier for reporters to have normal, even frank conversations with local residents and to enjoy entirely unmonitored friendships.

But correspondents still run up against China's vast and not always well-coordinated security apparatus probably more than any other foreign civilians do. In Luoyang, for instance, police detained my photographer and chased me out of town. Even on a daily basis, we faced constant surveillance of the sort usually reserved for diplomats and other foreign government agents. Our offices, homes, phones, and even possibly our vehicles were bugged. In Shanghai, the showpiece of China's new openness, the phone lines of several foreign-media bureaus were routed through a special government switchboard to facilitate eavesdropping. (This made the bugging less annoying than in Beijing, where phone lines had an odd tendency to snap, crackle, and hiss.) In Beijing, depending on the political season, plainclothes agents tailed us on foot or in one or more vehicles. These cars were sometimes easy to spot because of the bicycle in the back seat, for use in case we darted down a narrow *hutong,* or alleyway. Surveillance was stepped up around sensitive dates. Every year before the June 4 anniversary of the 1989 Tiananmen massacre, a half-dozen cars would appear outside the Jianguomenwai foreign compound in Beijing, where many foreign news bureaus were located. Once, at least two vehicles and a bicycle shadowed me as I walked from the compound back home, four blocks away. But the burden was most onerous on our Chinese acquaintances, who did not have foreign passports to shield them. Chinese staff, all hired through official agencies, were required to report on our activities. People we called about stories and even our friends received demands to inform on us or warnings against consorting with foreign journalists.

In 2002 I wrote a critical story about police in a northern Shanghai district shutting down schools for migrant children and denying thousands of impoverished primary students an education. Within a few days of the story's appearance, my bureau received phone calls from men ordering us to stop "unauthorized reporting." They hung up without identifying themselves. Then one morning I came into the bureau to find our file cabinets unlocked, my computer turned on, and the bureau safe broken open. Nothing was missing, not even the blank checks, bank documents, or other valuables that had been sitting in plain view in the safe. We reported a break-in to the building management but were told cryptically they were "only responsible for what happened in the hallways"—not in tenants' offices. The bureau was in a modern Hong Kong tower, and the management would undoubtedly have been more helpful had this been an ordinary burglary. But their odd evasiveness carried an implicit message: "There was nothing we could do to prevent it. Internal security agencies operate above the law." A week or so later, we got another call: "We've been inside your computers." Click.

Behind the ham-fisted intimidation seemed to lie an uncertainty over how to deal with us. Despite a growing openness in business, tourism, and other areas, Beijing liked to keep a firm grip on information media. This was probably due to the leadership's anxiety about holding together a nation of 1.3 billion people going through rapid social upheaval. At the same time, China has been slow to adopt more sophisticated, and less confrontational, techniques of press manipulation. At least one of my colleagues called the result the worst public relations operation outside of North Korea.

Local authorities proved a determined opponent in Luoyang. On the morning of December 26, 2000, I was the first reporter in the Beijing bureau, as my three colleagues snatched some extra time with their families— a rare luxury in the foreign news services' busy China bureaus, even at Christmas. Then a short, one-paragraph, English-language item popped up on the terminal that displayed stories from the Chinese government's official Xinhua News Agency. The tone was as matter of fact as a weather forecast: 309 people had died the previous night in a fire in a nightclub in Luoyang. Investigation under way. End of item. No other details.

It has to be a mistake, I thought. True, Xinhua was the voice of the government, and its stories were closer to official press releases than anything approximating journalism. But despite its authoritative tones, Xinhua could also be sloppy. For all I knew, that 309 could have been a typographical error for 39. Worse, the item ran only in English, so there was no way to check it against a Chinese original. English-only was the Xinhua News Agency's way of saying a story was solely for overseas use and off limits to the domestic press. This use of language helped construct separate news domains: a domestic, Chinese-language domain constrained by strict limits set by the government, and a freer, foreign domain that was out of the reach of most Chinese. Those Chinese with sufficient English-language skills could access it via the Internet, but the Chinese government tried to restrict this access by blocking the websites of many overseas news agencies, including my own at the time, the AP.

Since the story had been effectively forbidden to the domestic news domain, I couldn't rely on local newspaper and television reports for confirmation, much less additional leads. I typed out a quick story based on the Xinhua item, adding a dose of skepticism about the casualty figure, and put an "Urgent" tag on the top to alert editors to breaking news. Within minutes, the story was transmitted via the AP's computers to news organizations and websites worldwide.

Then a colleague who had just walked in and I started working the phones. First we called directory service in Luoyang to get the phone numbers of every government agency or social service that might be able to confirm that something had happened and supply details. (Directory service is itself an interesting example of how China's opening is working at cross-purposes with government control. Just a few years ago, even getting these phone numbers would have been a challenge. Now all we had to do was call an operator.) We worked our way down an internal checklist, dialing police, fire departments, hospitals, city hall.

One of the surest ways to put Chinese government officials on edge is to cold-call them in foreign-accented Chinese and start asking nosey questions about deadly disasters in their jurisdiction. The favorite deflecting tactic is to claim they're *bu qingchu* (not clear) about anything you ask them, even their own names. Persistence on the reporter's part prompts a more drastic defensive maneuver: hanging up. The frustration mounted as we failed to make headway. I caught half a conversation as my colleague questioned someone at a Luoyang fire department:

"Do you know about the fire at a disco in your district last night?" he asked.

"You're not clear, huh? We hear three hundred and nine people died. Did you hear about that?" he pressed again.

"You're not clear. We've been told the disco was in your district . . . You're not clear. How can you not be clear? Aren't you the fire department? If you're not clear, who is? You're still not clear. Can you tell me who is clear? Hello? Hello?"

One of the fundamental challenges of working in China was the Herculean effort required to unearth even the simplest facts, the sort that would be considered reasonable public knowledge in a more open society: when, where, how many hurt or killed, or even just whether something happened at all. Most officials refused to disclose anything. You ran up against a wall of silence.

There were several factors at work. For one, sharing information, particularly of an even remotely sensitive nature, ran against Chinese officials' political survival instincts. It wasn't that long ago that people were verbally or physically abused during "struggle sessions," or worse, just for uttering the wrong propaganda line. The days of the Red Guards (the late 1960s) were over, of course, but on paper this remained a one-party system, and the government and the party both remained fond of demanding at least lip service to official views of reality. Party members have confided to me that they still faced a career-damaging reprimand or even arrest for mouthing off in public on sensitive topics. In this environment, silence remained the safest option. Our information-gathering difficulties were compounded by a lack of any sense of the public's having a right to know—a problem probably rooted in the lack of civil society. There was also China's strongly technocratic political culture rooted in a long history of administration by powerful, highly educated bureaucrats who served the emperor, not the general population.

We foreign journalists faced an additional hurdle. Reporting what the government didn't want us to report meant we were viewed with great suspicion, as foreign agents or at least as troublemakers. Foreign academics and businessmen might get a kinder reception from local officials (though whether this yielded significantly more information or not was open to doubt). And the difference in attitude could be stark. If we called the same local officials, we stood a good chance of being accused of "illegal reporting" and slandering China.

Another aspect to the information problem was our lack of routine access to officials. In other countries where I've worked, it's common for government agencies of any size to at least have press officers, whose job it is to field media queries, even if only to brush them off. In China, many agencies did have Foreign Affairs offices, whose purpose it was to deal with foreigners of all stripes, not just journalists. These offices usually had no specialized knowledge in dealing with the press or in other aspects of public relations. We called them routinely with requests, but they were slow on their feet and not very forthcoming. They were likely to request a faxed list of questions and then take days to tell you they couldn't discuss it.

In a crisis, the only way to find something out was to randomly call local police precincts, emergency rooms, or the like in hopes of finding someone willing to talk. The latter could be hard to come by. But China is a verbally expressive culture, and sometimes you got lucky.

I found that official in Luoyang after about a dozen phone calls.

We'd pinpointed the fire to Luoyang's Old City district. As I would soon learn, this was a run-down neighborhood of narrow alleys and low, gray-brick shops and houses built in imperial times, a century or more ago. I called the local police substation. An older man answered.

"Three hundred and nine? No way. I was just there. They've found maybe eighty bodies at most," he replied to the first question. Bingo!

He went on to confirm the time of the fire and added that the disco was on top of a four-story shopping center near a major thoroughfare. That was all he knew, but that was a lot. At the very least, we had corroborated that something had indeed happened in Luoyang. We sent out a revised version of the story, still giving the Xinhua News Agency figure but in the second paragraph adding the lower figure for bodies recovered. (Later in the day we succeeded in confirming that Xinhua's death figure was correct.)

This phone call also confirmed that the incident was newsworthy enough to merit traveling to Luoyang to report firsthand. But that presented a whole new host of problems.

Chinese authorities consistently threw another obstacle in our way: restrictions on movement. Under the regulations governing our accreditation as overseas journalists, we were prohibited from traveling outside the four major cities of Beijing, Shanghai, Guangzhou, and Shenzhen. (I'd heard we could also go to Tianjin, though I never tried.) The bureaus of foreign news agencies were restricted to these four cities probably because the cities were seen as China's portals to the world and thus required at least the appearance of openness. Legally, to go anywhere else required permission from the local Foreign Affairs Office, more affectionately known among journalists by its Chinese shorthand term, the *waiban*. What this meant in practice was that every trip started with a battery of faxes sent to the *waiban* in the area you wanted to visit. The procedure was complicated by there being separate *waiban* at every level of government, from Beijing down to the level of rural, state-owned factories and hospitals. The trick was to find the right *waiban* willing to take responsibility for your visit—no mean feat. Arranging a trip this way could take weeks or longer. A visit to the western province of Ningxia Huizu once took me almost a year to set up. Depending on the region and the proposed topic, local officials could prove enormously helpful. But denials were also routine, particularly for anything that might result in potentially negative reporting. Regions that knew they were sitting on sensitive stories simply issued blanket refusals.

A fire that had killed 309 people would qualify as a sensitive story, so official permission was out of the question. At the same time, our profession, and our editors in New York, demanded that we get to the scene to find out what was happening. One of the first rules of journalism is to try to get as close to the news as possible, either by seeing events for yourself or talking to people who have direct knowledge. This is often the only way to perform one of the first duties of a journalist: to circumvent official versions of events and to present, as best you can, what really happened.

That meant a difficult choice: Should my bureau send reporters to Luoyang without permission? This option carried its own risks. The biggest was detention by police. Traveling without permission was prohibited. Police in Luoyang were certain to be on the look-out for foreigners. Many local governments seemed to devote more resources to suppressing news of accidents than helping victims.

Traveling without permission in China was a bit like starring in a spy thriller. You found yourself ducking to hide from passing police cars, looking over your shoulder for "tails," and speaking cryptically into pay phones (cell phones, of course, being bugged). You couldn't let down your guard the entire trip, even in your own hotel room at night. That's because foreigners had to show passports or government-issued residence cards at check-in. These documents clearly displayed your occupation, which clerks were required to note. Police looking for foreign reporters needed only comb hotel registries. This might lead to a particularly dreaded moment: the late-night pounding on the hotel door. I had colleagues who had been pulled from the shower at 10:00 p.m. and interrogated in nothing but a bath towel.

Detention could then mean waiting long hours in a police station, sitting through interrogation, and writing a "self-criticism" confessing your crimes. (These confessions usually ended up an exercise in absurdity: "I apologize for talking to a Chinese person without permission from the Communist Party, protector of the Chinese people.") Then they'd put you on a plane back to Beijing or Shanghai, often with a warning never to report in that region again. It was obvious, though, that not all local officials were happy about having to treat us this way. Many were very polite and friendly and made it clear they were just following orders. Often they sent us off at the airport with a verbal invitation to come back anytime for recreational travel.

"We have great sights. You just can't report on them," an official once told me apologetically.

This was what I had to look forward to on the morning of December 27 as I sat nervously on a flight from Beijing to Zhengzhou, Henan province's capital, this being the province in which Luoyang was located. Mixed feelings of dread and excitement robbed whatever appetite I might have had for the airline-issued meal, a box of chicken and rice. At the exit gate, I scanned the waiting crowd, looking for anyone who resembled plainclothes police—men with flattop haircuts, leather jackets, and an arrogant demeanor. Unfortunately, this was a popular look in the provinces. I ended up keeping tabs on several possible tails, suddenly changing directions to see who followed.

Once in Zhengzhou, I jumped in a random taxi, negotiated a price for the three-hour trip to Luoyang and then watched out the back window. As we pulled onto a brand-new four-lane highway, it was clear no one was following. We were often the only car visible on the road, which had frequent tollbooths that made it too expensive for most locals to use. Beyond the guardrails, villagers still lived in caves cut into hills of the butter-colored deposit of wind-blown sediment known as loess. Henan is a densely populated heartland province of farms but also smokestack industries—kind of the Ohio of China. As we sped past empty December fields, gray smog hung so thick we never saw blue sky. After a time, the haze turned a grimy yellow, probably from the sulfur emitted by coal-burning stoves in urban homes. That's how I knew we had reached Luoyang's outskirts.

I asked the driver about hotels. "Most foreigners frequent the Peony, which has a pool and nice restaurants," he said. Tempting luxuries, I thought, but that would be the first place police would check. "How about something cheaper, without so many foreigners?" I asked. After a couple more suggestions, a promising candidate came up: the Financial Center Hotel. Foreigners rarely stay at such local, mid-level business hotels. I called an AP photographer who had arrived in Luoyang a few hours earlier. By coincidence he'd already checked into the same hotel. Amazingly, we'd somehow acquired the same paranoid logic.

It was getting dark. The photographer had already located the fire site, but police had closed off major roads to it. He said someone had told him city officials had taken over a small hotel to process missing-person claims and post the names of identified dead. After some searching, we found it at about 10 p.m. It was a typical, low-end hotel in a provincial city: a single-story structure in a brick-walled compound. We decided to come back first thing the next day.

After an uneventful night in rooms that smelled of stale cigarette smoke, we hurried to the makeshift command center. I stood outside the compound's walls in the cold morning air, careful not to be visible from the hotel's grimy, metal-framed windows, and the official eyes within. People had gathered in knots, crying in stoic silence or talking angrily. I timidly approached one group and told them I was a journalist from the United States. Word rippled through the other groups: "A foreign reporter." To my surprise, they gathered around, eager to talk. They said they were angry that the local media had only just begun to report the fire and weren't giving many details. They also shared what they had learned so far. They told me the stairwells at the disco had all been locked that night so no one could sneak in without paying a cover charge. The only way in or out was a single elevator. One woman told me children were among the dead, including her friend's three teenaged children. They accused local officials of trying to cover up as much as they could for fear of being held responsible by Beijing for the disco's flagrant safety violations. "Chinese newspapers won't report what really happened here," they said.

Their testimony grew more heated when they started describing how the city was handling disposal of the bodies. Most of the victims had died of smoke inhalation, leaving their bodies intact. On learning this, the relatives of the victims had been mildly relieved, thinking they could at least hold proper funerals. But now city officials had told them the city would cremate the bodies without turning them over. Worse, the cremations would be rushed through over the next couple of days. The city officials said they were doing this for reasons of public health, but the relatives of the victims called it a callous effort to destroy evidence and shirk responsibility for the tragedy.

As we were speaking, word came that a spontaneous protest was forming a few blocks away. The demonstrators proved easy to find. Traffic had quickly backed up, and a line of honking cars led us to some three hundred men and women, many middle-aged or older, marching in a disorganized mass down a main road. There were no organized chants or placards, but looks of icy determination and random shouts of outrage created an air of tension. The group stayed close together, as if seeking safety in numbers from the police who were just starting to arrive.

As the only two non-Chinese there, my photographer and I quickly drew attention. (As far as I know, a Chinese photographer for Agence France-Presse was the only other employee of a foreign news agency who made it to Luoyang.) Some marchers asked who we were. When I told them, we were pulled into the center of the crowd. The entire column halted, and for several minutes all heads were turned toward us.

Again, they competed to tell us their stories. They offered the same complaints as the people at the hotel. They were afraid no one in government would ever be held responsible, and demanded the punishment of officials who had let the disco operate. And they were disgusted that their own media wouldn't tell the truth. Word was circulating that the shopping center that housed the disco had been allowed to operate despite several previous

safety violations, they told me. (This was later verified by state media re-
ports.) "What else could be behind that but official corruption?" they asked.
The crowd said to us over and over, "Tell the world what happened here.
Don't let them get away with it."

By this time, dozens of police had gathered on the crowd's edge. I noticed
some had cameras, which they used to snap photos of the photographer
and me as we spoke with the crowd. But they made no effort to intervene.
This was in line with how I'd seen Chinese police handle other demonstrations by ordinary citizens voicing common complaints, like anger at layoffs
or official corruption. In these situations, the police acted with restraint,
sticking to the sidelines as long as order was maintained. (But it was a different story for protests deemed more politically threatening, like the lone
banner-carrier who still appears on Tiananmen Square on June 4 to mark
the massacre, or demonstrations by the outlawed Falun Gong religious
group. These were and are quickly and ruthlessly suppressed.)

As the crowd started to march again, the photographer and I conferred.
The police were sure to grab us as soon as we left the crowd, he said. We
made a decision to split up. I'd make a run for it to check out the fire site
and file a story. He'd keep an eye on the demonstrators, who offered a more
compelling subject matter for photographs.

After a few minutes, I saw my chance. A narrow alley opened, with no police near. I ducked into a crouch and ran, turning the first corner to get out
of sight. I didn't stop until I had popped out on another busy street, where
I flagged down a cab.

Once I was sure I'd escaped, I asked the driver if he'd heard of the fire. He
had, because reports were starting to appear in the state-run media. He offered to get me close to the site via smaller side roads. (Some Chinese were
so disillusioned with their own leadership, they seemed not only willing
but eager to help us defy official obstacles, like the police roadblocks in this
case.) We were soon winding through the labyrinth of Luoyang's Old City,
navigating dusty alleys between single-story shops and gray, windowless
walls.

The shopping center that had held the disco was easy to find: a tall, glass
building standing above the ancient district's curving tile roofs. There were
few obvious signs of damage, besides some broken windows. Outside, hel-
meted workers were carrying charred debris into wheelbarrows. Several police milled about. I watched from a doorway, uncertain what to do next.
Then my cell phone rang.

It was the photographer. He was in police custody, he said. Dozens of officers had broken up the demonstration and grabbed him right after my dis-
appearance. He was sitting in a station, but the police hadn't even bothered
to take away his cell phone. (China's security apparatus was like that: brutally efficient one moment, surprisingly lax the next. I knew an outspoken

critic of official health policy who said the police carefully monitored her phone calls and visitors but failed to check her mail, allowing her to keep communicating with the outside world.)

The photographer assumed he'd be interrogated, but at that moment he was sitting alone in an office, sipping tea they had given him. We kept the call short to avoid provoking the police into taking the phone away. He said he'd call again once he knew when he'd be released or what they would do with him.

I called the AP Beijing bureau to report his detention and my where-abouts. This was a precautionary measure, so they'd know where to pick up the trail in case they lost contact with both of us. I also described the protest and fire site for an update of the story. (The AP will typically update major stories several times during the day to meet the various deadlines of the thousands of news outlets that use its service.) It was getting late, so I went back to the hotel to log on to my laptop, update the story again, and wait until the photographer called.

That call came sooner than expected. I'd gotten in the room, poured a cup of tea, and had just pulled out the laptop when the cell phone rang again. It was the photographer. "You're released already?" I asked. "No, I called to warn you," he said. "They're on their way to the hotel. Get out of there."

The next five minutes were the longest of my life. After throwing every-thing into my daypack, I rushed downstairs. Then I did something that in hindsight appears incredibly foolish: I went to the front desk and checked out. It was a decision made in the fog of panic, but the room was on my personal credit card and I didn't want them to take the liberty of padding my bill. The paperwork at the front desk seemed to take an eternity. The clerk asked, "Did you use the minibar?" "No." "Charge dinner tonight at the hotel restaurant?" "No, I haven't eaten yet." "Long-distance calls?" I was afraid to ask the clerk to hurry, for fear of alerting someone. I fidgeted, glancing at the hotel entrance every few seconds. "Thank you, please sign here." Then I bolted safely into the nearest taxi. I had the driver circle about as I tried to figure out what to do next.

We drove down the thoroughfare that the marchers had blocked hours earlier. At the end, in front of a large, fenced compound housing the Lu-oyang City People's Government, a few dozen protesters who had appar-ently regrouped stood yelling at the closed gates. It was too risky to join them now. Later as I hid in the back corner of a small restaurant wolfing down a quick dinner, the phone rang. "They just came back, and they're re-ally pissed you weren't there," the photographer said. "You'd better not stick around where they can find you." Sounded like good advice. That was the last time I spoke with the photographer before his release the following day. They finally took his phone and the memory cards from his digital camera. But he did a noble thing. Before handing over the memory cards, he erased them so they couldn't be used to identify the protesters who'd spoken to us. That infuriated the officers, who yelled at him and kept him in the station until late that night. They let him sleep in his hotel room, but with officers watching his door.

The next morning, they grilled him for several more hours before loading him on a plane to Beijing. While this sort of experience was unpleasant and even frightening, it rarely involved threats of violence or imprisonment. (Indeed, I recall only one instance of police violence against a Western journalist when I was in China. This occurred when a photographer for Agence France-Presse was roughed up outside a concert hall in Beijing for taking "unauthorized" photos of a crowd lined up to see a performance by the Three Tenors.) In the Luoyang incident, as the photographer faced interrogation, I was high-tailing it out of Luoyang. No hotel in the city would be safe now. I flagged down the first taxi I saw. "Take me to Zhengzhou," I said. The driver seemed to hesitate. He named a price much higher than what it had cost me to get to Luoyang the day before. At first I thought he'd sensed my urgency and was taking advantage of it. But after we were on the highway, he told me the reason he had been reluctant to go: bandits.

It sounded like something out of the Dark Ages, but it was true: at night, robbers came out to prey on travelers using this brand-new highway, and did so by setting up roadblocks to stop vehicles, then robbing their occupants at gunpoint, as I later learned from a Chinese press report on one such gang's arrest. My driver's fear seemed to be shared by other drivers on the highway that night. Our taxi was soon part of an impromptu convoy, as the drivers of other cars banded together out of an instinctive urge to find safety in numbers. Then I had one of those Twilight Zone experiences that seem so ordinary in China but that can really only happen in a country like this, where pell-mell economic development could create startling clashes of the ancient and the modern. As our convoy roared through the Henan night, and as I scanned the darkening horizon for scimitar-waving raiders on horseback, my cell phone rang again. It was a voice I didn't recognize.

"My name is Eli Fachler. I'm calling from Jerusalem. I saw your story on the Internet, and our family names are almost the same. I wonder if we're related." A man I'd never met had hunted down my cell-phone number by calling the AP bureau, first in Jerusalem and then Beijing. And as we speculated whether we were long-lost cousins, it struck me: Here I was, in an ancient country, at the mercy of medieval highway robbers, fleeing agents of one of the world's last states that still at least claimed to revere Lenin and Marx—and all while cruising down a four-lane freeway and chatting about genealogy on my cell phone with someone on the other side of the planet. Eli Fachler and I never figured out if we were relatives, but such jarring juxtapositions of the ancient and the modern were what made working in China so worthwhile.

Yet very little of this, including my run-ins with the local authorities, made it into the fire-related stories I filed out of Luoyang. It was simply too personal, too dependent on the firsthand experiences of the reporter, to appear in a straight news story on a breaking event. Our profession teaches us that journalists aren't the news, so we tend not to mention our own experiences in reporting stories. The most I was able to do was to squeeze some of the taxi ride into a more colorful feature story I did a week or so later about the resurgence of criminal gangs in China, as an illustration of how even modern highways in China were at risk. But capturing all China's contradictions and complexities would remain one of the biggest challenges during my work there.

So what did make it into the Luoyang fire stories? In the United States, the tragedy was a top item in the AP's domestic news service for about four days, a pretty good run for an overseas event not involving U.S. citizens. It may have gotten added attention because of timing: hundreds had been killed on Christmas Day. Our stories ranged from six hundred to eight hundred words each, typical for a story of this sort because of tight space on the international pages of U.S. newspapers.

Reading back over those stories, I see two distinct phases. The first was during the first day and a half before we could get going on the ground in Luoyang. Our goal then was to piece together as complete a picture of events as possible, based on scant and sometimes contradictory information. The presentation was straightforward and neutral, with an emphasis on stating the sources of our information—mostly the Xinhua News Agency and other Chinese media, especially toward the end of the second day as more details started to trickle out. Our stories had very little firsthand information, reflecting how little progress we were able to make via the telephone because of official stonewalling. As a result, the stories tended to reflect the government's version of events. The first paragraph of a story I wrote the night of December 27, after my having just arrived in Luoyang but before going out to gather information on my own the next morning, was typical: "Investigators questioned managers of a shopping center Wednesday where a Christmas fire killed 309 people, and Premier Zhu Rongji demanded 'severe punishment' for anyone found responsible."

Once I was in Luoyang, the stories changed dramatically. Details of the fire scene and of the city's makeshift command center started appearing, as did testimony by the victims' relatives. Having firsthand information meant I was able to deviate from the official accounts, offering a very different picture of the fire than what was appearing in the state-run media. The focus of the stories also shifted to the protests, which were completely ignored by China's domestic press. The protests gave me a way to highlight the larger political significance of these events, in this case, public discontent with government cover-ups and official indifference. This was apparent in the top paragraph of the story I filed out of Luoyang the night of December 28: "Angered by revelations of years of safety violations at a shopping center that caught fire on Christmas, the relatives of hundreds who perished in the blaze marched Thursday to demand better public safety and complain of callous treatment by authorities."

At the same time, there were common elements running through all the stories. One was a consistent tone of skepticism and distrust toward the Chinese government. Chinese officials ended up getting painted as the bad guys, even more so than the sloppy welders eventually found guilty of sparking the fire. And it wasn't just the Luoyang coverage. I saw it over and over again during my time in China, in the reports of most major, English-language news organizations.

This critical tone had many causes. It was absorbed from the Chinese people themselves, who as they showed in Luoyang could be very skeptical of their own government when given a chance to speak their minds. Another factor may have been an accumulated moral repugnance toward all the arrests, beatings, and jailings that the regime had meted out to its critics and opponents, and on which we as journalists often reported.

But a big part of it was also the government's clumsy and brutal handling of the journalists themselves. This was apparently intended to force us to toe the line, but it had the opposite effect.

One way official treatment influenced the attitudes of foreign journalists was by making us into a closer-knit group than we otherwise would have been. Overseas reporters consorted together much more in China than in other countries where I've worked. Of course, we were competitors, and we kept plenty of secrets from each other. But as foreign reporters, we also had a lot in common. Most of us had been hired in part because of our ability to speak Chinese, a skill acquired either by growing up ethnically Chinese or by studying in a university language program. (In my case, I'd majored in Asian studies as an undergraduate and had earned a master's degree in East Asian history before becoming a reporter. I also speak Japanese, and my first job for the AP was in Tokyo. Since leaving China in 2003 following a two-and-a-half-year stint there, I worked in Tokyo again, this time for the *Wall Street Journal*. A typical stretch in China for a foreign reporter is longer: four to six years.)

This shared background of experience drew the foreign press club in China together. So did a sense of "us versus them" caused by official Chinese government harassment. This meant that all we had to do was look in the rearview mirror to see who "they" were. This sense of camaraderie was further nurtured by yet another restriction imposed upon foreign journalists, and one that I haven't mentioned yet: we could not live where we wished. In Beijing, where about 90 percent of accredited foreign journalists in China are based, foreign reporters until very recently were required to live in government-run diplomatic compounds guarded by uniformed soldiers. These restrictions have been eased in the past couple of years, but journalists are still limited to living in the city's eastern Chaoyang district, where the embassies are located. The government undoubtedly does this to facilitate monitoring. But this enforced proximity encouraged journalists (and others in the compounds, including diplomats) to swap information, share gripes, and form similarly unflattering opinions of the regime that had imposed these restrictions in the first place.

It was also easy for us to paint the government as the bad guy when officials refused to talk. We couldn't tell their side of the story if they refused to give it to us. The regime's critics and opponents, by contrast, were far more accessible and willing to talk. Many even sought out the foreign press. This helped get their voices into foreign news reports. We reporters also felt a natural sympathy for many of them. They approached us despite the risk of harsh punishment. Many were ordinary Chinese with nowhere else to take their grievances. Serving as a voice for the voiceless was deeply satisfying to us; it got to the core of why many of us had become journalists in the first place.

There was even a sense of duty or obligation among some foreign journalists to report these kinds of stories, because of the shortcomings of China's own press. As we saw in Luoyang, the wholly state-controlled media routinely ignored disgruntled citizens and legitimate criticisms—not to mention the state's victims. So if foreign reporters didn't report on these, no one would. (We can, however, get a glimpse of what Chinese journalists would be capable of if unleashed. A handful of Chinese publications do test the boundaries of the permissible, most notably Guangdong province–owned *Southern Weekend*, with its long, investigative pieces and eye for detail, and the business magazine *Caijing*'s cutting probes into irregularities in stock markets and corporate accounting. But publications like these remain the exception, even as mounting commercial pressures edge other media outlets toward serving readers as well as the CCP.)

Chronic adversity between the foreign press and Chinese authorities may also be at least partially a result of what remains the biggest and most vivid news event in recent Chinese history: the 1989 Tiananmen massacre. Of course, foreign journalists and Chinese officials were at loggerheads before then. But there was a different perspective to coverage in the 1980s, one that was willing to see positive attributes in Deng Xiaoping and other leaders. This generosity disappeared as journalists and the world watched Chinese tanks crush demonstrators in support of democracy. The tight-knit nature of the foreign press corps then made it easier to pass this new disillusionment down to succeeding generations of journalists.

The ghosts of June 4 seemed to haunt even relatively minor demonstrations in China, like the one I saw in Luoyang. We reporters never knew if we were witnessing a flash in the pan or the outbreak of China's next great uprising. This was always a possibility; China's problems were so numerous and massive that the country could feel like a huge tinderbox. The Tiananmen massacre also seemed to lurk behind authorities' efforts to drive us away, as if the only lesson they had drawn from the crackdown was the need to keep future protests hidden from the eyes of the world. June 4 even seemed to overshadow our interactions with ordinary Chinese. Many seemed secretly eager to discuss June 4 and would suddenly raise it in private conversations. Some wanted to tell us we reporters were too sympathetic to the 1989 protesters, who they said would have led China into chaos. Others praised us for not letting the regime cover up the protesters' deaths.

Whatever its origins, the mutual distrust between the Chinese government and the foreign press has been self-perpetuating, a sort of negative feedback loop. The government saw foreign journalists as overly critical and as slandering a country they didn't fully understand, while the reporters in turn saw the government as keeping them from fulfilling the task they had, as agents of the truth, come to China to do. In the future, Chinese government officials may figure out more sophisticated ways to deal with the foreign press. It's not hard to imagine them emulating the public relations strategies of governments and private corporations in the West (see chapter 10) and trying to "spin" foreign reporters in a more positive way. Unfortunately, the current policy of harassment has only made the foreign press more skeptical and cynical. The result: an almost structural inability of the two to see eye to eye. This may change if China, under President Hu Jintao and the new generation of leaders, shifts toward a more technocratic and less repressive style of rule. In this case, China would probably become more of an economic story and less of a political one in the eyes of the foreign press. However for this to happen, any government change would have to include an easing of the pressures now faced by foreign reporters. At present, these still remain as constant, nagging reminders of the regime's true nature.

SUGGESTED READINGS

John Gittings, *The Changing Face of China: From Mao to Market* (New York: Oxford University Press, 2005).
Peter Hessler, *River Town: Two Years on the Yangtze* (New York: HarperCollins, 2001).
Ian Johnson, *Wild Grass: Three Stories of Change in Modern China* (New York: Pantheon, 2004).
Nicholas Kristof and Sheryl Wudunn, *China Wakes: The Struggle for the Soul of a Rising Power* (New York: Crown, 1994).

Komori Yoshihisa, *Pekin houdou 700 nichi: Fushigi no kuni no shimbun tokuhain* [*A foreign correspondent in wonderland*] (Tokyo: PHP, 2000). This is a Japanese journalist's account of working in China.

Shimizu Yoshikazu, *Chuugoku noumin no hanran: Shouryuu no akiresuken* [*Chinese rural uprisings: the Achilles heel of the dragon*] (Tokyo: Kodansha, 2002). This is an excellent book by a Japanese journalist on reporting in China.

Online Sources

www.nanfangdaily.com.cn/zm. This newspaper's weekly publication *Nanfang zhoumo* [*Southern Weekend*] offers the best Chinese-language journalism in China.

2

The Political Roots of China's Environmental Degradation

Judith Shapiro

Both Chinese and Western coverage of China's environmental problems is extensive and dramatic; it depicts the high cost of unchecked economic growth being paid with unlivable landscapes, parched cities, pollution-choked skies, and exhausted energy supplies. It shows how China's leaders are starting to have doubts about the sustainability of a Western-style development model with its high energy demands, automobile-centered transport, and meat-oriented diet. However, the news rarely addresses the fact that environmental issues are, at heart, political problems created by human beings. The real environmental story is one of struggle over access to and control of resources and of competing understandings of how to interact with the nonhuman environment. Also, it includes analysis of the political structures that govern these struggles. In China, discussion of such topics is largely forbidden because so many political issues are off limits. This is especially true for issues such as the behavior of leaders, the ineffective governance of existing political structures, corruption, the lack of rule of law, and the relationship between continued, red-hot economic growth (see figure 2.1) and the political legitimacy of government leadership.

In this chapter, I will examine these connections while exploring the link between human suffering and the degradation of the environment during the Mao years, the dynamics of which continue to affect China even today. This chapter then concludes with a look at how Beijing's handling of the 2008 "green" Olympics may illuminate a connection between human rights and the environment. I will also explore the connection between environmental protection and political freedoms such as freedom of speech, freedom of association, freedom of access to information, and other intel-

50

Figure 2.1. Construction and modernization, two sides of China's transformation. (Photo: Peter H. Jaynes)

lectual freedoms, which ironically are explicitly guaranteed in China's constitution. Article 35 of the constitution, for example, states: "Citizens of the People's Republic of China enjoy freedom of speech, of the press, of assembly, of association, of procession and of demonstration." Other clauses guarantee freedom of religion, freedom to vote and run for election, freedom from unreasonable searches and seizures, and other basic rights. The situation in practice is, of course, quite different, as has become increasingly evident with respect to mounting popular concern over ecological adversity. The struggle for human rights in China, instinctively associated in the Western media with the heroic activity of dissidents, is waged in part on the grounds of the environment. It has developed into a battle for the elemental freedom to breathe clean air and to drink clean water and for just compensation for loss.

The following story illustrates this point quite well. In March 2001, the farmers of Gaoyuan township, a region upriver from the Three Gorges dam, chose eight representatives to travel to Beijing to present a petition protesting local officials' embezzlement of resettlement funds. All along the upper Chang (Yangtze) river, China's most ambitious effort to conquer nature was causing hardship. Some of those forced to leave their homes to make way for the dam never saw the compensation they had been promised in terms of better housing, cash payments, and new jobs; others who were relocated to higher ground found infertile slopes unsuitable for planting; still others sent to faraway provinces felt unwelcome there and homesick. In many cases, those whose homes were to be flooded by the construction of the Three Gorges dam simply had nowhere to go.

In Gaoyuan, local police detained most of the eight representatives before they could depart on their mission. The three who did travel to Beijing were traced to their hotel and arrested before presenting their petition. After a rigged trial, the leader, He Kechang, a sixty-three-year-old farmer, was sentenced to four years for "disturbing public order . . . leaking state secrets, and maintaining illicit relations with a foreign country" (doubtless a reference to the foreign journalists who were covering the story). The others also received prison sentences in local jails. These representatives and farmers were exercising free speech, but in doing so, they were denied due process and liberty.

Political repression associated with legitimate complaints against government failure in the Three Gorges dam project clearly points up the intersection of human rights and environmental issues. As an engineering project, the Three Gorges dam has caused the world's largest forced resettlement. By the dam wall's completion in 2006, nearly 2 million people had been relocated. Yet the individuals most affected had little say in the decision to build the dam and little influence on the disposition of their fates. From the beginning, information about the dam and its impact was suppressed. Debate on the issue, not only among potential relocatees but also within the top government leadership, was curtailed; the prominent anti-dam activist Dai Qing, a former member of the National People's Congress, spent a year in prison for her outspokenness concerning the dam and other examples of political repression. Even today, few in the region are fully informed about the dam's risks, which include possible structural problems, military vulnerability, riverine ecosystem destruction, the extinction of rare species like the Chang river dolphin, heavy-metal contamination from submerged factories, sewage accumulation, inundation of archaeological treasures such as the artifacts of the ancient Dai people, eradication of sociocultural traditions, and the despoliation of a landscape that for millennia painters have depicted as a symbol of China's natural beauty.

The Three Gorges dam project is only the most obvious arena in which concerns about environmental degradation and political repression have come together in contemporary China. Far more broad-ranging and subtle are the effects on environmental protection of China's limits on freedom of association and suppression of intellectual freedom. The discussion begins, however, with some background on the relationship between these issues as they have been treated in other parts of the world.

THE ENVIRONMENT AND HUMAN RIGHTS: THE GLOBAL CONNECTION

Until recently, social activists in developed Western countries have tended to address environmental degradation and human rights violations as separate, even conflicting problems. Some environmentalists have blamed the planet's ills on human folly and excess, even as they worried that the basic global structures that sustain all living creatures were at risk of collapse. They sought to broaden interpretations of international legal instruments like the United Nation's Universal Declaration of Human Rights (UDHR)—a powerful tool for advocacy and accountability—to include environmental concerns. But human rights advocates resisted such interpretations, fearing that their own legal weapons would be weakened. They emphasized that their mandate was a well-defined focus on civil and political rights, and they sometimes dismissed environmentalists as caring more about nature than about people. As an analyst of the UDHR has written, "Perhaps, looking back at the UDHR after half a century, the only significant lack is in the area of the environment."[1]

Today, formerly sharp divisions between these issues have become blurred. Environmentalists from the developed world are coming to understand that they cannot protect the natural world by building fences around it, since environmental issues cannot be divorced from human development. At the same time, human rights activists have become increasingly interested in concepts like environmental justice, which encapsulates the problems of unequal distribution of environmental harms and unequal access to resources. The unsafe labor conditions that often accompany suppression of workers' rights to organize, particularly in the developing world, have also focused attention on a "race to the bottom" for the world's poorest people. This has been especially evident as of late in China's coal industry, which is largely unregulated and the most dangerous in the world. The anti-globalization movement, noted for its inclusiveness, has further broken down barriers among environmental, human rights, and labor organizations: "Turtles and Teamsters, Together at Last" was a dominant slogan of the 1999 World Trade Organization (WTO) protests in Seattle, Washington. However in the developed world, despite conceptual effort and programs intended to break down barriers, much work remains to be done to resolve the strategic, conceptual, and cultural differences among these groups of activists.

In less-developed nations, activists rarely dwell on such distinctions. On the ground, it is often evident that environmental issues are linked to human rights, public accountability, and civic justice. In Indonesia and Myanmar, for example, where the state and multinational corporations routinely violate human rights in their pursuit of oil, gas, gold, timber, and other natural resources, grassroots activist groups take on environmental and human rights issues equally. Clear examples include Unocal Corporation's Yadana natural-gas pipeline case, in which it is alleged that conscripted laborers are being forced to deforest the route through southern Myanmar to Thailand; and Freeport-McMoran's gold-mining operation in Indonesia's Irian Jaya, in which protest against toxic contamination from mine tailings has led to alleged murders of activists by government military units. The death of Nigeria's Ken Saro-wiwa, executed by the government for exposing the environmental devastation caused by Shell Oil's offshore drilling, the mysterious murder of Brazil's anti-logging activist Chico Mendes, and recently, the death of Dorothy Stang, a seventy-three-year-old American nun murdered in Brazil in 2005 for her efforts to protect the landless poor and the rainforest, have become poignant symbols of the human dangers of environmental work. In Mexico, environmental activists Rodolfo Montiel Flores and Teodoro Cabrera Garcia were jailed because of their opposition to logging in environmentally sensitive areas, and in Russia, Alexander Nikitin was imprisoned for his work to publicize nuclear contamination.

In China, environmental activists dare not publicly link their work to human rights; they must work carefully, and within government-approved parameters. Human rights activists can function only underground or in exile. However, China is no exception to the principle that the two issues often go hand in hand. Environmental degradation is closely linked to political repression, just as environmental protection and intellectual and political freedoms are ineluctably tied. The resolution of China's environmental problems will depend on increased political participation and public debate, an impartial legal system open to all, and unrestricted freedom to create civic groups that are unafraid to monitor and challenge the government. China's prospects for achieving sustainable development may rest upon Chinese citizens' exercise of the full panoply of human rights—such as freedom of association, publishing, and speech—that are particularly relevant to this difficult task. Despite these challenges, the prospects for environmental activism in China have expanded dramatically in the last decade; officially, there are about two thousand environmental nongovernmental groups (NGOs) in China, and as many as two thousand more may exist unofficially or as for-profit entities. In recent years, a number of these groups availed themselves of the Internet to organize a remarkable campaign against the construction of thirteen hydroelectric projects on the Salween River in southwestern China, resulting in a cessation of construction and additional environmental review.

CONTEMPORARY CHINA

Today, scientists and engineers are heavily represented among China's "pragmatic" new leadership. President Hu Jintao, for example, has a background in hydraulic engineering. There is impressive public commitment to "sustainable development," a phrase prominent in national policy planning documents and speeches.[2] To its credit, China has ratified important international environmental treaties, most recently the Kyoto Protocol on climate change (unlike the United States); established an elaborate environmental protection bureaucracy, with the ministerial-level State Environmental Protection Administration (SEPA) at the top; and has passed some of the most stringent environmental laws in the world. China is taking its terrible environmental problems seriously, with major efforts to close polluting factories, set higher fuel-efficiency standards, reforest deserts, ban logging near flood-prone rivers, implement water conservation measures, and experiment with modern, market-based, emissions-trading techniques. Yet despite China's apparently serious commitment to environmental goals, political repression continues to hinder China's efforts to carve out a more sustainable future. Government regulatory agencies control NGOs by requiring them to meet onerous registration criteria, censor newspaper and book publishers, and limit legal avenues for the redress of environmental injustice.

Critics of the Chinese government's continuing propensity for massive projects have been silenced; even as the Three Gorges dam is completed, work gets under way on the great South–North water transfer scheme, a massive project to pipe and pump Chang river water to the parched Huang (Yellow) river in the North, where a rapidly declining water table has created a water crisis in Beijing. There has been little discussion of the environmental implications of this huge project, although two of the three planned routes are already under construction. There is similarly little debate about the potential impact of China's ambitious plans to "open up the West" to development (see chapter 12), where the fragile ecosystems of some of China's less-populated regions will now be deeply affected by new roads, railways, and infrastructure projects. The environmental agency SEPA was included in planning meetings only after protests from leading environmentalists. Even now, environmental considerations remain marginalized in China as local leaders focus on economic growth.

FREEDOM OF ASSOCIATION AND POLITICAL PARTICIPATION

Every Chinese NGO must register with the Ministry of Civil Affairs through the sponsorship of an approved government agency, which then becomes responsible for supervising the NGO's activities and is jokingly known as its "mother-in-law." The approval process is so arduous that many groups are discouraged from forming independent organizations, and several

well-known groups like Liao Xiaoyi's Global Village of Beijing have resorted to registering as for-profit institutions, even though this means they
must pay tax. Although environmental NGOs thrive, their activities remain
sharply circumscribed, and they generally avoid confronting the government. Agitating to protect Tibetan antelopes carries little political risk, for
example, but suing a local Environmental Protection Bureau for permitting
a polluting factory to reopen could cost an NGO its right to exist. Planting
trees, picking up garbage, promoting recycling, organizing educational
programs, bird-watching, and producing environmental television for children are considered acceptable activities; organizing public demonstrations about environmental issues or taking on party officials who are cir-
cumventing logging bans is usually not. (The rare exception is a young
photographer-writer couple, Xi Zhinong and Shi Lihong, who defied the
odds to confront loggers in Yunnan province and have become environmental heroes and media figures.) The U.S. embassy in Beijing summarizes the NGOs' tricky situation:

> Most knowledgeable experts summarize the current situation for NGOs in
> China as one of legal uncertainty—there is no smooth or transparent registra-
> tion system, nor any legally guaranteed "right" to exist. On the other hand,
> even NGOs that have been unable to register admit that Chinese authorities of-
> ten do not restrict them from carrying out their work.[3]

In spite of the many challenges to their existence, including enormous difficulty in raising funds, the environmental NGOs in China are flourishing.
Moreover, college student groups, often organized under the umbrella of
the Communist Youth League, are encouraged to put on exhibitions, plant
trees, educate local farmers about excessive pesticide and fertilizer use, and
publish environmental newsletters. The above-mentioned campaign to protect the Tibetan antelope has become a major cause among college students
and has helped them to build a nationwide Internet network of environmental youth groups, thereby using electronic forums to avoid the risk of
gathering in groups without official sanction.

Aside from membership in these groups, public participation in environmental matters is often limited to use of complaint lines run by the local
environmental bureaucracy because these are officially sanctioned and pose
little threat to the government's perceived need to control public order. Although most people choose to express their dissatisfaction through approved channels, public protests about pollution have become more frequent in China. Such demonstrations break out when polluting factories
with close ties to local government officials or even to local Environmental
Protection Bureau officials are permitted to poison a community's air or
water with impunity, or when these factories are permitted to reopen in violation of the law.

In the village of Huaxi in southeastern China's Zhejiang province in spring of 2005, for example, as many as fifty thousand peasants, tired of unresponsive politicians and corrupt factory owners, rioted over a period of several days, destroying police cars and repulsing the three thousand police officers sent in to quell the disturbance. The peasants (many of them elderly) had collected funds to secure legal representation and had filed official complaints with officials in Zhejiang and Beijing for more than two years, asserting that the emissions from two local factories had fouled the air, water, and surrounding farmland, which was incapable of sustaining crops. President Hu Jintao's "people first" platform was challenged by the protestors, who held the government accountable for its promises to monitor the factories and restrict their pollution, and who in the end took matters into their own hands. However, as one China specialist recently observed, "Even factories that are closed down because of excessive pollution often reopen in another locale or operate at night, safe in the knowledge that the environmental inspectors are unlikely to return any time soon."[4] It is just this sort of recurrent flouting of law and community consensus that is behind the growing volatility of the environmental debate in rural regions.

This persistent abuse of rural lands and disregard for the human costs of development seems to have reached a breaking point in other locales, most notably in Dongzhou province, also in southeastern China, where on December 6, 2005, paramilitary police and government anti-riot units fired upon thousands of village residents protesting the construction of a power plant on lands improperly confiscated from them. According to village eyewitnesses, as many as twenty residents were killed, while the government's official statement reported that three people had died. It was the deadliest use of force by the party-state since the Tiananmen massacre. Popular unrest launched out of prolonged frustration, yet legitimized under the official guise of a new, state-driven populism, might be regarded as proto-democratic. Nonetheless, the response of the government in such circumstances precisely indicates the limits of an ecologically engaged, local defense of life and property.

In rare cases, pollution victims have been able to bring class-action lawsuits. The Beijing-based Center for Legal Assistance to the Victims of Pollution marshals media attention and provides lawyers to help Chinese citizens fight industrial pollution, a confrontational approach so unusual that it has attracted coverage in both the Chinese and Western press. However, the legal system in China is usually closed to such groups, in part because of the difficulty of proving responsibility and demonstrating damages, and in part because the lawyers themselves risk intimidation or worse.

There is one further avenue for political participation: victims of injustice may present their petition to higher authorities, a time-honored practice in China. Citizens who are harmed through the failure of their local leaders to implement the law, or through their local leaders' active involvement in polluting enterprises or unfair development schemes, may appeal to leaders higher in the administrative bureaucracy by traveling to their offices to present a letter detailing their case, as the Gaoyuan villagers attempted to do in the case of the Three Gorges dam corruption. Yet as those villagers experienced, those who try to present petitions risk being set upon by police in the pay of corrupt local officials, or even by thugs hired by developers. Even if the petitioners are not beaten, they may be sent away without a hearing.[5] There are, however, numerous stories of redress achieved when a tale of injustice captures the attention of a higher official.

FREEDOM OF INFORMATION

Lack of information undermines debate about an economic and political system that rewards short-term gains and does little to deter environmental degradation. Firewalls restrict Internet access to foreign websites, often including those of environmental NGOs and government organizations. The reports of organizations such as the World Resources Institute, Worldwatch Institute, and Resources for the Future could help China make better development decisions; for example, they could encourage the Chinese leadership to rethink their embrace of the private automobile. Better access to global research on the environment and development might also rebut the pernicious notion that China, following a Western model, will be able to develop first and clean up later—an approach that remains popular among officials and policymakers. Although Chinese university students have ways to circumvent the government's Internet firewalls, their wish to avoid political trouble acts as a significant deterrent to their intellectual curiosity.

Without an open airing of information, environmental burdens will more easily be placed disproportionately on those least able to bear them. In one industry in which this is already a problem, computer recycling, China has become an international dumping ground for toxic waste. Today, desperately poor villages in the country's Southeast and hinterlands compete for the right to dismantle the developed world's surplus technology, and information about the resulting negative health effects of pollution from lead, mercury, and other poisonous metals is suppressed. Similarly, poor environmental safeguards are common when workers have little knowledge of the health impacts of the chemicals that they handle and breathe. Two dramatic examples of the impact of information suppression are the SARS (severe acute respiratory syndrome) and HIV/AIDS epidemics, both of which spread widely in China, the government first calling HIV/AIDS a "foreigners' disease" (see chapter 11), then later denying the existence of SARS in China, and in both cases censoring information about the causes of the epidemics. While these diseases may be environmental problems only in the broadest sense of the term, they have undoubtedly deprived many Chinese citizens of the right to health, and in many cases, of the most fundamental human right of all, the right to life. As two Hong Kong legal scholars wrote in a paper on human rights and SARS, "A variety of rights, including the right to transparency in governance, the right to information and the right to health are clearly implicated."[6]

Despite the relative lack of press freedom in China, environmental journalism does offer bright spots in a tightly controlled arena. A 1999 Friends of Nature survey identified forty-seven thousand news articles about environmental issues, culled from seventy-five newspapers. China's energetic environmental journalism reflects intense public interest in environmental issues, born in part from China's extremely heavy pollution and its daily health impact (sixteen of the world's twenty most polluted cities are in China, and many Chinese citizens suffer from lung disease or cancer). The relative freedom that journalists enjoy to write about environmental issues is also an indication of government support for environmental goals.

THE MAO YEARS (1949–1976): A CONTEXT

The current situation is in some ways an extension of patterns established during the Mao period, thus demonstrating the powerful pull of habits of mind and behavior despite economic and environmental consequences. Chairman Mao was an equal-opportunity violator of human rights and a destroyer of nature. For him, the struggle against people and the struggle against nature were conjoined. He wrote, famously, "To struggle against the Heavens is endless joy; to struggle against the earth is endless joy; to struggle against people is endless joy." The conquest of class enemies and the war against the physical world were hallmarks of his era.

Unfortunately, as we now know all too well, the dictatorship of the proletariat and the leadership of the CCP failed to create the promised socialist paradise in which the mountains would bow their heads and rocks produce grain. Rather, Mao broke the Chinese people and destroyed nature. Tellingly, the worst of the human suffering of this era paralleled the severest environmental damage. And projects like the Three Gorges dam demonstrate the continued validity of the fatal triangle of utopian socialist aspiration, repressive politics, and destructive ideology, as first evidenced in the postrevolution experiments in social transformation.

Beginning with the anti-rightist movement (1957), the link between political repression and environmental degradation in Mao-era China was starkly evident. During this national campaign, China silenced outspoken intellectuals such as Beijing University president Ma Yinchu, who warned about overpopulation, and Huang Wanli, a hydro-engineer who fought against huge, Soviet-style dams. Had Ma Yinchu's warnings been heeded, China's draconian one-child family policy might have been unnecessary and China's huge population might not now be placing such extreme pressures on nature by depleting natural resources, taxing the water supply, expanding into the final refuges of animal and plant species, and dumping more waste into the air and water than can effectively be treated. Had Huang Wanli's views about the dangers of damming the main watercourse of a major river prevailed, the Sanmenxia dam would not have been built on the Huang river, only to silt up quickly and become all but useless for flood control or hydropower. Huang Wanli's subsequent struggle against the Three Gorges dam, even as he was undergoing reform through labor, demonstrates not only the depth of his commitment to reason but also the stubborn indifference of China's leaders to their own historical mistakes.

By the Great Leap Forward (1958–1960), few clear-thinking people dared to point out that deep-plowing and close-planting schemes were at best a waste of energy and at worst a destruction of fertile land. Competitive boasting about agricultural production made such a mockery of statistics that high-level leaders had little reliable information about the rural food situation. Few risked their future to speak out as China's forests fueled "backyard furnaces" designed to help China catch up with Britain in industrial output. Journalists could do little but report the ever-growing weight of useless lumps of "steel" even as they smelted their own pots and pans. The great famine that resulted from the Great Leap's excesses was an ecological collapse as well as a catastrophe of human suffering.

During the Cultural Revolution (1966–1976), state-led forcible relocations were carried out on an unprecedented scale as the renunciation of science in favor of passion brought Maoist revolution and the nation to grief. Peasants were made to leave ancestral homes to make way for new dams such as the Gezhouba (a Chang river precursor of the Three Gorges dam, approved in 1970 by Mao, hastily begun to celebrate his birthday and completed after great difficulties some nineteen years later); workers were sent involuntarily from coastal areas to the mountainous interior in an effort to build a "Third Front" and shield defense industries from possible Soviet attack. Twenty million former Red Guards and other "educated youths" were forced to move to the countryside, some two million of them to frontier areas to prepare for war while transforming nature and themselves. These relocations resulted in both acute suffering of people and severe destruction of nature. The homesickness of the educated young people is legendary; they had to petition and demonstrate in order to be permitted to return to the cities, and even today they consider themselves China's forgotten generation, many of them unable to compensate for their loss of educational opportunities and find a niche in China's credentials-oriented new society.

Less well known is the suffering of the farmers relocated for hydroelectric projects and that of the young soldiers and factory workers sent to establish the industrial Third Front in China's mountains and caves. They too were abruptly uprooted and forced to eke out livelihoods in inhospitable ecosystems that were barren, hilly, and too remote to be suitable for development.

Intellectual freedom, particularly freedom of expression, remained sharply circumscribed during this time. As young people were brought in to level the Xishuangbanna rainforests in an effort to "break through the bourgeois superstition" that the area was too far north for rubber plantations, forestry officials who knew the value of this biodiversity treasure chest that was being summarily destroyed by revolutionary intervention were themselves in reeducation camps, engaging in formal self-criticism because of their respect for "reactionary" foreign science. Similarly, when the "grain first" movement reached its high point of frenzy, geographers and agronomists who understood that the local mountainsides were too steep to sustain terraces had to participate in leveling trees and cutting into the earth, a deforestation resulting in topsoil loss, erosion, siltation of rivers, and changes in rainfall patterns. In Sichuan province, the accelerated habitat loss associated with inappropriate terracing contributed to the decline of wild pandas and other rare species. And Tibetan herders, forced to grow wheat instead of barley, had little choice but to comply, even though they knew that winter hailstorms would destroy the crops.

Maoist thought was believed capable of overturning the laws of science. The unleashed labor power of China's masses would expose "bourgeois superstition" about what was and was not possible. "Red science" would triumph over "bourgeois science" or "reactionary science." Hydro-engineer Huang Wanli protested, albeit futilely, that the sun would not revolve around the earth just because the party ordered it to. Songs and poems promoted the notion that Maoism could "make the mountains bow their heads, make the rivers flow uphill" in a great war on nature. "Foolish old men" would remove mountains with their bare hands and inspire the girl farmers of Dazhai commune to scrabble at the frozen earth with their fingertips day and night. "Red engineers" were praised for designing steel factories and dams while construction was under way, and trained engineers criticized themselves for doubting the infinite creativity of the masses. Lakes were filled in without the use of concrete cores in dikes; dams were built even if the structures could not be built, according to "bourgeois" specifications. Mao's former secretary Li Rui, purged in 1959 for attempting to tell Mao that the Great Leap was a disaster, wrote that one of the most important lessons of this tragedy was the danger of ignoring the laws of nature. Indeed, so distinctive was the notion that Maoism was more powerful than science that it sets the period off from other examples of great human suffering and environmental destruction. The period represents the very negation of intellectual freedom, a time in which political repression and the requirements of intellectual conformity drove such a deep wedge between thought and correct expression that some of those who lived through it must have doubted their sanity and questioned their own memories of alternative instructions about the workings of the physical world.

Mao died in 1976, and radical Maoism died with him. An era of left-wing excess and political campaigns now seems safely in the past. Intellectual and personal freedoms are far greater today than in the Mao years, for the door to the outside world stands open, property rights are better defined, and Chinese people are free to find jobs of their choice. "Market socialism" is the dominant economic system, and living standards are far higher than at any time in China's history. Nevertheless, China's environmental problems have become even more acute under the onslaught of explosive economic activity. A weak and corrupt framework for implementation of environmental regulations, and widespread cynicism about government-sponsored projects for the public good, are just a few of the Mao-era legacies that complicate government efforts to protect the environment. Today, focus on profits has supplanted the Maoist ideology of nature-conquest as the driving engine of resource depletion and pollution, but the environmental destruction of the Mao period, which left many shaking their heads at its senselessness and profundity, seems mild compared with the consequences of present-day economic growth. The Mao era's most common modes of environmental destruction—infilling of countless lakes, construction (and collapse) of thousands of poorly designed dams, pillaging of forests and ravaging of biodiversity—have been dwarfed by contemporary industrial activities and accidents that are more poisonous still.

Whether China's integration into the world economy will lead to more or less environmental degradation is open to debate. Some Western advocates of economic globalization argue that China's WTO membership will open the door to multinational corporations that adhere to high environmental and labor standards. Others argue the opposite: that an increase in manufacturing and trade and an emphasis on economic growth and consumption at the expense of other values may only cause China's environmental problems to worsen. There are grounds for hope for a better environmental future for China, including the adoption in 2004 of fuel-efficiency standards more stringent than those in the United States, since they are based on individual vehicle weight rather than weight-class averages. This may also help China to deal with its lack of energy security. Unfortunately, such policies may not be enough to keep pace with China's development. Millions of new cars clog China's roadways each year; energy demand is skyrocketing. The city of Shanghai has even seeded summer clouds to induce rain in order to reduce sweltering temperatures, in this way hoping to prevent blackouts from excessive air conditioner use. The sheer number of China's people and their concurrent demands for energy and water may overwhelm the best of policies. China is set soon to overtake the United States in emissions of carbon dioxide, the primary greenhouse gas, despite having made impressive gains in power plant efficiency and having instituted a broad policy of energy reorientation from coal to natural gas. The inadequacy of policy measures alone to set China on a more sustainable course only underlines the importance of the full participation of Chinese civil society in all aspects of environmental protection and conservation. There must be a larger civic commitment to repairing and preserving the environment, something the Chinese government promoted for the 2008 Olympics, the first "green" Olympics.

THE 2008 OLYMPICS: A WINDOW ON THE FUTURE?

The intersection of Chinese environmental and human rights issues is evident in the choices China made for the Beijing 2008 Olympics, which the government promoted as an environmentally friendly, or "green," event. On the one hand, these summer games offer an unprecedented opportunity for China to strengthen and publicize its commitment to environmental goals. The Olympics permitted the country to attract environmentally friendly investment and technology, clean up pernicious problems of air and water pollution in the capital region, and harness the city's and the nation's pride to create a "greener," more livable Beijing. Chinese environmental institutions and organizations, governmental and nongovernmental, have used this international event as a catalyst to garner domestic support for environmental priorities and values. However, China's recent political history and its crisis of values, ideology of modernization, international aspirations, authoritarianism, and profound environmental problems may interact to make the 2008 Beijing Olympics a risky and complex enterprise, which for the informed raises a series of difficult questions.

Will Beijing's cleanup come at the price of other regions' despoliation? Environmental harms may be displaced, and investment in environmental public goods may be concentrated in the capital to the detriment of other regions. For example, although the Capital Iron and Steel Works, located in Beijing at Mao's behest in an era when smokestacks were considered aesthetically pleasing, has at last been relocated outside the city proper and rebuilt with less-antiquated technologies, will the inhabitants of the surrounding regions experience a decline in their air quality (see figure 2.2)?

Has the government's commitment to solving Beijing's environmental problems by 2008 actually hastened other ill-advised infrastructure projects? The great South–North water transfer scheme, for example, was expedited to ensure that Beijing will have plenty of water for the event, despite environmentalists' warnings of inadequate impact assessments.

Figure 2.2.   Apartment buildings next door to a belching smokestack. (Photo: Peter H. Jaynes)

Further, have infrastructure construction and the "greening" of Beijing led to forcible relocations? In Beijing's effort to provide verdant entryways to the city, homes along rail lines have been razed with less than two weeks' notice to residents. (In what may be a worrisome sign that the government is more interested in foreigners' perception of Beijing's "greenness" than in the fact of it, Beijing citizens were mobilized to paint dry grass green to prepare for the Olympic selection committee's visit.) Moreover, the government has a well-established practice of relocating Beijing's huge "floating population" of migrant workers in preparation for international visits and events. No one can deny that new subway lines are a tremendous asset to the city. But will the razing of the city's historic *hutong* (lanes, or alleys) and stone compounds, accomplished by developers at a dizzying pace and with little consideration for the wishes of the displaced, someday be cause for sharp regret?

Finally, before and during the event itself, has civil society experienced a lockdown on free expression as the government tries to present an attractive face to tens of thousands of international journalists, athletes, and tourists? When the UN Fourth World Conference on Women was held in Beijing in 1994, the Chinese government housed NGO representatives in Huairou, a town so distant that representatives were unable to attend the conference's main meetings. The Chinese government's heavy-handed management of this international event therefore raises questions about treatment of the large numbers of foreigners visiting Beijing in 2008. Dissenters and pro-testers who might seek to draw attention to their views are likely to be rounded up and silenced, as typically occurs when Falun Gong practition-ers or Tibet protestors demonstrate in Tiananmen Square.

How China deals with these issues sheds light on whether its government is providing the core intellectual and political freedoms that will permit sound environmental decision making and environmental justice to flour-ish. Although civil freedoms such as freedom of speech, freedom of pub-lishing, freedom of assembly, and freedom of academic exchange cannot guarantee China a more sustainable future, they are necessary precondi-tions for it. It will not be enough for China's central government to rely on slogans and top-down exhortations and decrees; China's people have had enough of slogans, and implementation of environmental regulations re-mains vulnerable to the widespread corruption that dogs the rest of the na-tion's political system. China's efforts to follow a "greener" development path are likely to succeed only if the Chinese people can carve out space for themselves in which to become full partners in environmental issues. They must be able to form civic and scholarly groups, link across borders with the international environmental movement, bring lawsuits without fear of reprisal against corrupt enterprises and governmental agencies, and conduct a full range of grassroots activities beyond the constraints of government su-pervision and censorship. As governments of other countries struggling with environmental degradation have already learned, the Chinese govern-ment has less to fear from this than it seems to think, and much to gain.

NOTES

Some parts of this chapter are adapted from Judith Shapiro, *Mao's War against Nature: Politics and the Environment in Revolutionary China* (Cambridge: Cambridge University Press, 2001), and Judith Shapiro, "Choking Off Debate: How Political Repression Con-tributes to Environmental Degradation," *China Rights Forum* 4 (2000), www.hrichina .org/public/contents/article?revision%5fid=2650&item%5fid=2649 (June 30, 2006).

1. Peter Bailey, "The Creation of the Universal Declaration of Human Rights," www.universalrights.net/main/creation.htm.
2. Former premier Zhu Rongji, for example, spoke at the Johannesburg World Summit on Sustainable Development in September 2002, affirming that

> Sustainable development is a new outlook on development as defined by the UNCED [1992 UN Conference on Environment and Development] in Rio, which represents a radical departure from the traditional concept and model of development. Namely, economic development must contribute to the continuous use of resources and the virtuous cycle of the ecosystem, and must not be achieved by abusing the resources and destroying the eco-system. (www.fmprc.gov.cn/eng/wjdt/zyjh/t25090.htm; July 2004)

3. For the full report, see www.usembassy-china.org.cn/sandt/ngos.htm.
4. Elizabeth Economy, quoted in *Harvard Asia Quarterly* (Winter 2003).
5. This common consequence of exerting one's legal rights is described in Jim Yardley, "Chinese Appeal to Beijing to Resolve Local Complaints," *New York Times*, March 8, 2004, A3.
6. Michael C. Davis and Raj Kumar, "The Scars of SARS—Balancing Human Rights and Public Health Concerns," www.hk-lawyer.com/2003-5/May03-phprac .htm (July 7, 2004).

SUGGESTED READINGS

Dierdre Chetham, *Before the Deluge: The Vanishing World of the Yangtze's Three Gorges* (New York: Palgrave Macmillan, 2002).
Dai Qing, *The River Dragon Has Come! The Three Gorges Dam and the Fate of China's Yangtze River and Its People* (Armonk, NY: M.E. Sharpe, 1998).
Elizabeth C. Economy, *The River Runs Black: The Environmental Challenge to China's Future* (Ithaca, NY: Cornell University Press, 2004).
Richard Louis Edmonds, ed., *Managing the Chinese Environment* (New York: Oxford University Press, 2000).
Judith Shapiro, *Mao's War against Nature: Politics and the Environment in Revolutionary China* (New York: Cambridge University Press, 2001).
Vaclav Smil, *China's Past, China's Future: Energy, Food, Environment* (London: Routledge/Curzon, 2004).
World Bank, *Clear Water, Blue Skies: China's Environment in the New Century* (World Bank: Washington, D.C., 1997).

Online Sources

China Rights Forum, "Human Rights in China," Special issue on the environment, no. 4, 2002, www.hrichina.org
China Watch, www.worldwatch.org/features/chinawatch
Constitution of the People's Republic of China, http://english.peopledaily.com.cn/ constitution/constitution.html
Friends of Nature, www.fon.org.cn/english

Probe International, www.probeinternational.org
Professional Association for China's Environment, *Sinosphere*, www.chinaenvironment
.net
United States Embassy, Beijing, Environment, Science, Technology, and Health Section, www.usembassy-china.org.cn/sandt
Universal Declaration of Human Rights, www.un.org/Overview/rights.htm
Woodrow Wilson Center for International Scholars, *China Environment Forum*, http://wwics.si.edu

3

Fueling China's Capitalist Transformation

The Human Cost

Timothy B. Weston

China's economic rise over the past two and a half decades has been nothing short of spectacular and is among the most important developments in recent world history. China is now an economic giant and a formidable global political power. China's economy has already surpassed Japan's to become the second largest in the world, and it may well overtake the United States as the world's largest economy within the next quarter century. This ongoing Chinese "economic miracle" is inextricably bound up with the country's move from a socialist economy to one that is ever more capitalist in nature, a transformation that began in the 1980s and has accelerated since 2001, the year China became a member of the World Trade Organization (WTO). China's embrace of capitalist-style economics at all levels of society has provided cheer for those in the West and elsewhere who champion the salutary political and social benefits that can be delivered by market economic systems. Indeed, in recent Chinese history, champions of capitalism appear to have found an effective rhetorical weapon to subdue defenders of the socialist planned economy.

But market forces have also unleashed grave social, administrative, and political problems that now threaten to slow or even reverse China's impressive growth rates. The world tends to focus on the upward-trending lines on the charts and graphs that show how much wealth and buying power China is injecting into the global economy; by contrast, negative developments simultaneously unfolding within the Chinese economy generally receive less attention. To be sure, excellent coverage of the tragic side of the Chinese economic story is available—indeed, it would have been impossible to write this chapter without my drawing heavily on mainstream news sources. Nevertheless, most popular writing on Chinese economic development of the past quarter-century focuses primarily on its extraordinary successes. Moreover it tends, quite uncritically, to accept the overall wisdom of the country's abandonment of socialism in favor of capitalism.

In this chapter I cast light on the darker side of China's move away from socialism and in so doing demonstrate a relationship between the market logic that now reigns in Beijing and the extraordinary degree of human suffering apparent in the country today. My purpose is not to deny the many phenomenal successes that have occurred in China over the past quarter-century, nor am I offering any specific predictions about whether the country will be able to complete its perilous journey from planned to free-market economy successfully. Rather, my aim is, first, to call attention to a story that remains largely obscured to most casual observers of China; second, to show the complexity and intertwined nature of the challenges that China faces today; and third, to argue that the troubling subject matter that I discuss should not be understood apart from, or simply as an unfortunate by-product of, the growing emphasis on the free market in China. Instead, such grievous consequences must be understood as an integral part of the story of China's economic transformation. Specifically, I treat this topic by discussing what I consider to be the quintessential symbol of the Chinese government's retreat from socialism, namely, the massive unemployment among and consistent mistreatment of the country's workers, those once known as the "masters of society." In this chapter's first section, I establish the scale and nature of China's unemployment and broader social crisis; in the second section, I focus on the situation that now obtains in China's coal-mining industry in order to illuminate one of the most tragic substories playing out within the larger story of the Chinese economic boom.

JOBLESSNESS, CORRUPTION, AND UNREST

China's unemployment rate today is the highest since the CCP came to power in 1949. The numbers are notoriously difficult to calculate; independent experts place the actual figure at over 20 percent, although the official unemployment rate is around 4 percent. In addition, reliable sources suggest that between 15 million and 25 million people will enter the Chinese job market each year between now and 2020. In urban China today, estimates have it that upwards of 60 million people are unemployed. A high percentage of that figure is made up of people who were once employed by state-owned enterprises (SOEs), which have shed some 25 million workers since 1998 and which will lay off many millions more in the next four years as the government moves to complete privatization. In addition to the huge number of urban jobless, there are vast reservoirs of under- or unemployed people in China's rural areas, some 150 million to 200 million of whom have migrated to China's cities in search of work in recent decades. Experts assert that there are perhaps 200 million unemployed people in China.[1] To put these numbers in perspective: China's population of unemployed is equivalent to roughly half the population of the United States, or to the total number of people in England and France combined.

Not only have tens of millions of people lost the ability to provide for themselves and their families, so too have they lost their identity as productive members of society. These may be boom times in China, but for a huge number of people they will be remembered as the dark years, the time when the bottom fell out of the promise of the 1949 Communist Revolution. Indeed, the society in which socialist egalitarianism reigned only a few decades before is now one of the most unequal in the world. Over the past twenty years, China's inland rural provinces have witnessed worsening poverty, and in 2003 the number of Chinese living in extreme poverty (those who earn less than US$77 per year) actually increased for the first time in a quarter-century. Today peasants earn on average one-sixth of what urbanites earn per year. The poorest 10 percent of the Chinese population owns less than 2 percent of all assets in society, whereas the richest 10 percent owns over 40 percent of all assets.[2]

The vast pool of under- and unemployed people in the Chinese countryside, which is home to between 750 million and 800 million people, has permitted China to transform itself into one of the world's great sweatshops. Each year, lack of opportunity in China's rural zones prompts a fresh tide of men and women to venture to the cities in search of work. These migrants typically find work as domestics, construction workers, sex workers, or in other low-skill occupations. Especially in the southeastern coastal region, many migrants end up as industrial workers, employed either by township and village enterprises (TVEs) or in joint-venture factories set up with a combination of Chinese and foreign capital. A high percentage of the inexpensive goods that consumers purchase in affluent countries are made in Chinese factories staffed by migrant laborers.

Typically far from their native places, unfamiliar with their new surroundings, discriminated against by a household registration system (*hukou*; as noted below, abolished by the CCP in eleven provinces in 2005) that makes it illegal for people to freely leave the countryside and denies them basic welfare benefits if they do so, and ignorant as to their rights under Chinese law, such workers are frequently paid low wages, forced to work extremely long hours, and subjected to unsafe or dehumanizing work conditions. At the same time, however, conditions in some factories employing migrants are actually quite good, and in recent years the Chinese government has made efforts to eliminate the worst abuses in factories that treat their workers poorly. Also very recently, migrant workers, especially in the highly industrialized Pearl River Delta region, where some foreign employ-

Figure 3.1.   Migrants in Chinese cities are often reduced to begging on the streets. It is not uncommon to see adult beggars accompanied by their young children. (Photo: Peter H. Jaynes)

ers (especially U.S. companies) pay higher wages, have begun to demand better wages and working conditions. The majority of migrant laborers who do face dehumanizing work situations tend to endure them silently, however; they know there are no opportunities for them in the countryside and that plenty of other unfortunates would snap up their jobs at a moment's notice (see figure 3.1).

The huge army of rural Chinese who are looking for employment and are willing to work in poor conditions for low wages directly affects urban workers employed in SOEs, the onetime backbone of the country's socialist workforce. Until recently, SOE workers constituted socialist China's "labor aristocracy," in that they were guaranteed lifetime employment, were paid living wages, and were eligible for subsidized housing, medical care, and numerous other substantial benefits. However, the rise of the TVE sector since the beginning of the reform period in 1978, while providing work for millions of poor Chinese from the countryside, has also resulted in stiff competition and declining profits for SOEs, which employ some 40 percent of the country's urban workforce.[3] The CCP, long burdened by the unsustainable costliness of the SOEs, announced at the Fifteenth Party Congress in 1997 that it was going to speed up reform of the public sector of the economy by permitting profitability to play an increasingly more important role in determining how SOEs are run as well as which survive and which do not.

By joining the WTO in 2001, China under the CCP gambled that international competition would do what the CCP had been unable to do—namely, impose market discipline on an economic and social system that had been remarkably successful at resisting the forces that govern economic decision making in most other parts of the world. With the muscle of the WTO behind it, the CCP now hopes it will finally be able to force reluctant officials to privatize or close down jealously protected but hopelessly insolvent SOEs. Over the past decade—before China joined the WTO and even more afterward—the CCP has been seeking to rid itself of a massive financial burden, and now by doing so it hopes to encourage the growth of an internationally competitive, market-driven economy. This expectation is perfectly understandable, given the heightened competition that opening up to the global economy has forced on Chinese businesses and manufacturers, thereby precipitating the selling off of SOEs and permitting unprofitable SOEs to be privatized or simply to declare bankruptcy. Still, millions upon millions of Chinese have lost their jobs as a result.

The loss of gainful employment has been economically and psychologically devastating. (See figure 3.2.) Crime, drug use, prostitution, depression, and suicide are all on the rise in China. Workers laid off by SOEs are legally entitled to apartments, living allowances, and medical reimbursements, but many are never able to collect even a fraction of these benefits. Nor can many of the recently laid off count on having their falls broken by a social safety net, since the nets the government has promised to weave are full of gargantuan holes and are regularly torn to shreds by corrupt officials. This means that millions of middle-aged and older people who once could rely on the "iron rice bowl" will, for the foreseeable future, be faced with a hand-to-mouth existence.

What makes all of this especially galling to those who are suffering is that while so many people are being reduced to penury, the managers of the factories upon which they once depended often make out like bandits. It is common practice for managers to withhold laborers' salaries or medical benefits on the pretext that the company is facing financial difficulties while

Figure 3.2.   Unemployed students hoping to be hired as tutors. (Photo: Peter H. Jaynes)

at the same time skimming large quantities of money for their own use. Managers have also taken to selling off the assets of failing factories. While this would be one way to raise money to pay a factory's workers, unscrupulous managers frequently treat the proceeds as their personal property. Corruption is hurting workers in other ways as well. As I will discuss below, in the name of higher profits, revenue-hungry local officials often look the other way when workers' rights are being violated or when workers' lives are endangered by unsafe work conditions.

Given the dramatic increase in unemployment and corruption, it comes as no surprise that China's dispossessed are crying out for help. Their discontent is recorded in the rapid rise in the number of grievances filed across the country at letters and complaints bureaus, government offices that receive reports of dissatisfaction from those whose complaints have been ignored by their bosses or local officials. Only a tiny percentage of those who file grievances this way ever get their problems resolved by the tired-looking officials sitting in bare rooms behind wooden desks, however, thus leading many filers to lose faith in the system. A seriously ill fifty-year-old man from Liaoyuan in the Northeast is a case in point. Denied benefits promised by the corrupt managers of his company at the time he and two hundred other employees were laid off several years ago, Mr. Zhao sought help from local Communist authorities, only to be imprisoned without trial for eighteen months. As the recently freed Mr. Zhao concluded: "There is no law in

China. Where there is money, there is power, and where there is power, that's where the law is." An associate of Mr. Zhao, Mr. Cui, expressed himself in equally sharp terms: "I thought the party was good, but here it didn't work for the people. I don't believe it anymore." Tens of thousands of angry people, armed with the belief that central government officials will be more responsive than those at the local level, have taken to traveling long distances to Beijing in the hope that someone there will give them a hearing. Indeed, the number of petitioners traveling to Beijing for this reason has grown so large that the central government, in an effort to divert the flood, is now seeking ways to force officials to take greater responsibility at the local level.[4]

An extreme case took place in July 2004, when twenty-three petitioners from the Northeast, most of them laid-off miners, traveled to Beijing and climbed to the top of a building outside China's Supreme Court, threatening to jump off together in a mass-suicide protest if their grievances were not addressed. One of those in the crowd that had gathered below to express sympathy for the desperate protestors told a reporter, "These people are petitioners who have had no redress for their grievances for a very long time. They have no way to go on existing. They have nothing, no money, so they are in despair. They don't want to live."[5] After a five-hour standoff, the potential suicides were talked down and the situation was defused, but the symbolism of the incident and the fact that it was covered by international news agencies certainly caused alarm within the Chinese government.

In fact, angry protests are becoming more frequent in Chinese cities, especially those hit hard by layoffs. The largest demonstrations since the founding of the PRC took place in the northeastern rustbelt cities of Daqing and Liaoyang in 2002. They were sustained over an extended period of time, involved thousands of workers, and united people from different occupational backgrounds. Official Chinese statistics indicate that "3.6 million people took part in 74,000 'mass incidents' in 2004, an increase of more than 20 percent on 2003."[6] In one of these mass incidents, following the brutal beating of a worker by a government official, in October 2004 up to eighty thousand workers and unemployed people were involved in a night of clashes with thousands of police officers in Wangzhou in the province of Sichuan. Rioters smashed windows and set police cars ablaze. To restore order, paramilitary units were called in from nearby cities. The same month in Bengbu in Anhui province, textile workers protested in large numbers in an attempt to win an increase in their poverty-level pensions. Many of the protesters were women, who were joined by thousands of sympathizers who snarled up the city's traffic. Fearing a repeat of the violence in Wangzhou, the authorities decided against sending in the paramilitary on that occasion.[7]

There is also a pattern of chronic disturbance in the countryside; in almost every Chinese village, peasants are protesting something. Anger over the seizure of farmland for development projects is ablaze these days, as is disgust over official corruption and factory pollution. In April 2005 in a particularly dramatic example of this, tens of thousands of peasants clashed with police when authorities sought to dismantle a tent city that protestors had erected at the entrance to an industrial park in Huaxi in Zhejiang province. The tents were occupied by elderly people fed up with years' worth of failed efforts to get local officials to do something about the terrible pollution produced by the factories in the industrial park. Enraged when security personnel smashed their tents and began arresting people, peasants overwhelmed the police, beat those they could, then destroyed all of their buses and cars. Ultimately the authorities backed down, and six of the thirteen factories in the industrial park were ordered to move out of Huaxi for good. As such cases suggest, direct confrontations between security forces and ordinary Chinese people are becoming more violent, and in some cases the people are winning the battles. According to Li Qiang, executive director of New York–based China Labor Watch, whereas "before people felt like they could resolve their problems through the government," they now "no longer have any confidence in the government, so small cases turn into riots."[8]

All of this has definitely gotten the attention of leaders in Beijing; they know that discontented peasants typically overthrew Chinese dynasties in the past, and they now talk about rural unrest as a life or death issue. At the National People's Congress convened in March 2005, top officials agreed that to prevent even more dangerous levels of disillusionment and violence, the CCP must do much more to address the country's growing income gap. In a historic shift in emphasis since the beginning of the reform period, rather than placing economic growth before all else, party leaders embraced President Hu Jintao's ideological campaign to build a "harmonious society" and to focus on "social well-being," a shift meant to focus greater attention on the glaring injustices that are igniting all the protest. Increased government attention to poverty and inequality represents a significant and welcome change in direction for the CCP. Whether the party can solve these problems remains to be seen.

China's tens of millions of dispossessed have to hope that the central government will succeed in making society more just, but for the time being they remain largely powerless to defend themselves. A Chinese lawyer involved with unemployment issues recently described the problem: "The reliable structure of the old society that took care of people from birth to death is gone and now people must defend themselves to survive. But the new society doesn't provide people with individual rights and legal ways to protect themselves."[9] Chinese workers are forbidden to organize independent trade unions. The CCP has consistently blocked such efforts in recent years and has arrested numerous labor organizers. Rather than granting workers autonomy to found independent trade unions, the government demands that they go through the state-run All China Federation of Trade Unions (ACFTU) in order to solve their problems. Many dedicated civil servants staff the ACFTU; however, given its association with the party-state, the official trade union remains hamstrung in its ability to provide the assistance workers desperately need. Fundamentally, the ACFTU has been compromised by the CCP's insistence that it promote political and economic stability above all, and that it manage China's labor environment so as to attract foreign investors. Workers regularly complain that the ACFTU does nothing to protect their interests. China is a member of the International Labor Organization (ILO) but is one of the few nations not to have ratified two core ILO conventions guaranteeing the right of workers to organize and the right of workers to engage in collective bargaining. Some of the consequences of the Chinese government's choices on these issues can be more clearly understood by looking at the tragic situation in the Chinese coal-mining industry.

COAL MINING IN CHINA:
THE MOST DANGEROUS JOB IN THE WORLD?

In Chinese coal mines, the canary's voice is rising loud and clear to announce the deaths of at least 6,000 miners per year. On October 20, 2004, a terrible disaster occurred at the Daping mine in Henan province. A gas explosion killed 148 coal miners that day. On November 11 an explosion at another mine in the same province claimed 33 lives. Two days later, an explosion in Sichuan province killed 13 miners and left 6 others missing. Then on November 28, 2004, 166 coal miners died in an explosion at the Chenjiashan mine in Shaanxi province, the worst such accident in China since 162 miners lost their lives in a coal-mine explosion in Guizhou province in September 2000. Five days before the Chenjiashan blast, the miners had told their bosses that there was a fire burning underground; the workers were then threatened with fines or dismissal unless they went back down the mine. Following this horrendous accident at the Chenjiashan mine, where a gas explosion had already killed 38 miners four years earlier, the *Beijing Review* carried an article of mourning that called for greater attention to safety and supervision in Chinese mines.

A month later on New Year's Day, Premier Wen Jiabao flew to Shaanxi province to visit with the dead miners' bereaved families. Tearfully, Premier Wen stated that the accident was a "lesson paid for with blood" and promised to work for improved mine safety throughout the country. But the explosions and dying did not end. On December 9, 2004, 33 more miners died in a gas explosion at a mine in Shanxi province. Just two months later, on February 15, 2005, an explosion at the Sunjiawan mine in Fuxin in Liaoning province set a grisly new record for the PRC: 216 miners killed in a single day. The fatal accumulation grew by 27 more the following day in an accident in Yunnan province and by another 19 in a mine explosion in Sichuan province on March 17. Then two days later, 70 more miners were killed in yet another mine blast, at the Xishui colliery in Shouzhou city, Shaanxi province. By March 24, 8 more miners had died in an accident in Hunan. Halfway through 2005, 2,672 miners had been killed according to official statistics, a 33 percent rise over the number killed during the same period in 2004.[10]

China is highly reliant on coal as a source of fuel; a whopping two-thirds of the country's total energy supply and nearly 80 percent of its electricity supply is generated by coal (compared to roughly 25 percent in both Japan and the United States). Bottlenecks in the coal-transportation system and poor rail networks exacerbate the problem of supplying the country's essential energy needs, and coal-industry officials report that the existing transportation system is only able to carry 40 percent of the coal that must be shipped. China produces more coal than any other country; about 35 percent of the world's production occurs there. Coal is also a major source of greenhouse gases, and according to a recent report in the *New York Times*, "experts predict that by 2020 China could pass the United States to become the world's biggest source of carbon monoxide" (see chapter 2). In the same article, Zhang Jianyu, program manager for the Beijing Office of Environmental Defense, raised a moral and practical issue that Americans would do well to ponder: "The fundamental problem is that China is following the path of the United States, and probably the world cannot afford a second United States."[11]

Some 80 percent of the world's annual coal-mining deaths occur in China. The fatality rate for Chinese coal miners is one hundred times that for American miners. However, that estimate is based on official Chinese statistics; independent experts believe the actual annual death toll in China is far higher than reported. In 2004, one Chinese official set the figure at roughly twenty thousand dead per year.[12] The squalid and inhumane conditions in Chinese mines, where pit owners frequently treat workers as disposable objects and cover up accidents, are powerfully depicted in the film *Blind Shaft*, a 2003 crime drama that director Li Yang secretly filmed in a coalmine (see chapter 7). Banned in China, *Blind Shaft* is essential viewing for anyone wishing to get a feeling for the bleak, desperate lives of Chinese coal miners.

In China the mortality rate is significantly higher in small, private mines than in large, state-run pits. Of China's roughly twenty-eight thousand mines in operation in early 2005, some twenty-four thousand were small mines. Such mines supply roughly 40 percent of the country's coal needs, and their official fatality rates are seven to eight times higher than those of state-run operations.[13] But state-run mines are also very dangerous. The worst of the recent disasters have been at state-run mines: for example, the Chenjiashan explosion that killed 166 people in November 2004, the Sunjiawan tragedy that claimed 216 lives in February 2005, and a terrible accident in Heilongjiang province in November 2005 that took the lives of 169 miners.

This carnage is directly related to China's economic boom. Following a quarter-century of rapid economic growth, China is now the second-largest energy consumer in the world after the United States (per capita, however, Chinese energy consumption is roughly a quarter of Japanese and German consumption, and about an eighth of U.S. consumption). In the four years between 2000 and 2004, Chinese energy consumption grew by an average of 16 percent, and during that period China alone was responsible for no less than 54 percent of the increase in world energy consumption. The rapid growth in China of highly energy-intensive industrial sectors such as steel, cement, aluminum, and chemicals, and the increased use of electric heaters and blankets, televisions, DVD players, and the like—all signs of growing affluence—help explain China's voracious appetite for energy. So does an explosion in the number of vehicles on Chinese roads. The total number of cars, trucks, and motorcycles in China rose from 6.3 million in 1990 to 36 million in 2003, a nearly sixfold increase in thirteen years. Investment banking and securities firm Goldman Sachs projects the number of vehicles in China will increase to 131.6 million by 2020 and to almost 200 million by 2030, surpassing the absolute number in the United States sometime between 2020 and 2025 (although in terms of the number of cars per capita, China will remain far below the United States).[14]

This remarkable economic growth has stretched China's energy supply thin. Despite record coal production in 2004 (more than 10 percent higher than in 2003) and increased power generation, dozens of Chinese cities in twenty-four provinces experienced brownouts during summer 2004 and many factories were ordered to work nights instead of days, when demands on the energy grid are highest. In a symbolic move, the glittering lights on Shanghai's famous waterfront, the Bund, were darkened for long periods in order to conserve energy. A difficult energy situation is always more dire during the winter months. With the onset of winter in 2004, China experienced a serious coal shortage and its worst electricity shortfall in two decades. *China Daily* reported that Beijing had only 50 percent of the coal it needed for the winter, and the fuel supply figures for other large urban areas in the North were even more sobering. Although summer 2005 was a better one as far as power outages were concerned—thanks to better energy-demand management, rainy weather that kept temperatures lower, and improved coal transport—China continues to face a massive challenge when it comes to meeting its fuel needs.[15]

To meet these needs, the government has committed itself to construction of two new nuclear power plants per year until 2020 and increased purchases of oil. The country's political leadership is also considering plans to end energy subsidies. By forcing consumers to pay market rates for fuel rather than artificially holding down costs, reformers hope to promote greater efficiency and to cut down on energy use.

In 2004 China met 22.3 percent of its energy needs through oil, and today oil is China's second leading source of energy after coal. As recently as 1993 China was self-sufficient in oil. But since then its demand for oil—which in 2003 surpassed Japan's, making China the second-greatest consumer of oil in the world after the United States—has far outpaced its domestic production abilities. Indeed, since the early 1990s China has become one of the world's major oil-importing nations (in 2004 it was the world's third largest after the United States and Japan). Between 2003 and 2004, China's oil imports rose by nearly a third, and today fully half of the oil the country consumes comes from abroad. Experts predict that China will double its oil use and triple its oil imports by 2030. Most of that will come from abroad, since China's accessible domestic supplies are beginning to be tapped out, and those still to be opened will not come close to meeting the country's demand.

China's growing oil consumption is having global economic ramifications and is one of the major causes of the sharp increases in oil prices that the world has experienced in recent years. China's quest to secure oil supplies has also caused political tensions, especially with the United States. A growing U.S. hegemony in the Middle East and especially in Iraq since 2003 has endangered Chinese investments in that country's oil sector made during the Saddam Hussein era. Beijing recognizes that it has become strategically vulnerable as its dependence on foreign oil has increased, and it is seeking to diversify its sources of foreign oil. China is now actively courting regimes around the world, including the governments of Iran, Venezuela, and Sudan, in an attempt to secure access to the oil supplies that they control. This has irritated the United States, which accuses Beijing of seeking to gain access to foreign oil by selling weapons to, and using its seat on the UN Security Council to do favors for, countries whose political leaders the United States opposes. Direct tensions with the United States over access to oil became headline news in summer 2005 when the state-controlled China National Offshore Oil Corporation (CNOOC) offered $18.5 billion to purchase Unocal, a California-based oil company. Alarmed by the prospect of the Chinese government gaining control over American oil supplies and fired by nationalistic rhetoric, the U.S. House of Representatives passed a nonbinding resolution opposing the deal on national security grounds, thereby prompting CNOOC to drop its bid in anger. In light of that episode, China is now more likely to cozy up to oil-rich countries that the United States considers rogue states.

China's drive to acquire more oil is an important story that will continue to play out in coming years. However, since oil will remain both in shorter supply and more expensive than coal for as far as the eye can see into the future, it will be impossible for China to rely too heavily on oil as an alternate fuel source. Indeed, even with rapidly growing oil imports and new sources of energy coming on line, such as hydroelectric power from the massive Three Gorges dam, government officials concede that China will be forced to depend on coal for at least half of its energy needs for another three to five decades. (Experts predict that if China's economic growth stays on course, its demand for energy will double its present level by 2020, and that China will account for 25 percent of the world's increase in electricity generation in the next thirty years.)[16] In other words, China will continue to burn coal because without sufficient electricity, its rapid economic development will stop in its tracks. This is the defining economic and ecological bind of contemporary life in China.

For Chinese miners, this intense demand for coal has brought jobs aplenty, but also extremely dangerous working conditions. Take the fuel shortage of 2004 for example. Faced with the unsavory prospect of profit loss due to inadequate energy to sustain production that summer, the Chinese government called for emergency coal shipments to meet urban needs. At the state-owned Chenjiashan mine in Shaanxi province, a push for maximum output led to promises of hefty bonuses for managers who met or exceeded production targets. The mine was expected to produce 1.8 million metric tons of coal for the year, which it had done by October; ¥400,000 (US$48,300) bonuses were to be given only if the mine produced another 400,000 metric tons by the end of December. Given that incentive, management was unwilling to halt operations when workers reported a fire in the mine in November 2004. A few days later, an explosion ripped through the facility and claimed 166 lives. Said one miner who lost his brother in that accident, "We all needed money and there is a penalty of one hundred yuan [$8.30] for refusing to go down [in the mine]." Small and often illegal mines thrive in this environment of stepped-up pressure to produce ever more energy, and the fact that the price of coal rose by 20 percent in 2003 and by 50 percent in 2004 has certainly provided reason for small-mine owners to open pits even at the risk of prosecution.[17]

Faced with such great demand for coal, local officials who stand to profit personally or whose administrations need the tax revenue generated by the mines have been turning a blind eye to the reopening of small, illegal pits. Stephen Frost, an expert on labor issues at City University in Hong Kong, has stated that the huge demand for energy in China has "created a wonderful opportunity for people to run more illegal mines and more dangerously. People are ignoring licensing, reopening closed mines. Mines are woefully equipped, the workers are not skilled in the least and management is appalling." Speaking to this matter recently, a Chinese coal-industry expert asserted that over 90 percent of China's small mines should be shut down because they cannot meet basic safety standards.[18]

The overall unemployment situation in China and the fact that in many rural areas there is no good work to be found have turned peasants into lambs going to their sacrificial slaughter, especially in these small, private mines. Most of China's miners are uneducated migrants from rural villages, and the majority of the country's largest coal deposits are located in its poorest provinces, where people can scarcely afford to be selective about the work that they take on. Workers laid off from SOEs also provide a significant source of China's mine labor. Joseph Kahn put it well in an article in the *New York Times*: "Becoming a coal miner in China is less a career choice than an act of desperation. It is a job for the poor who calculate that the income, however modest, outweighs the likelihood of injury and the constant specter of death." Miners rarely earn more than $150 a month, says Kahn, but even at that wage scale they "do better than peasants who work the surface of the land." Even more tragic is migrant workers' and mine owners' complicity in avoiding compliance with recommended safety standards. Despite frequently awful working conditions (twelve-hour days, twenty-eight days a month) and living conditions, low wages, and the danger involved, workers desperate to keep their jobs often conspire with mine owners to resist the institution of expensive security measures that might force the pits to close. Under these circumstances of economic desperation, the government often has no good options. In August 2005, for example, after officials shut down dangerous mines in Guangdong province, nearly a thousand miners clashed with police in violent protests against the closures.[19]

Across China, families live in fear that one of their members will be the next to die in a mine accident, and needless to say, those who lose husbands, fathers, sons, or brothers to mine disasters are often left in desperate straits. One miner, a Mr. Liu from Shanxi province, faced with his mother's tearful pleading that he not go down into the same mine where his brother had been killed, told an American reporter, "I lie to her and tell her that I work in a factory now. She could never take it if we told her the truth. But I can't survive without going down." There are currently tens of thousands of mining widows in China, many of them with young children. As Jonathan Watts reported recently in the *Guardian*, "There is widespread anger that miners' lives are being sacrificed for economic growth." One widow with whom Watts spoke told him, "It is said there is blood on every piece of coal in China. My husband used to talk about the danger all the time. But we are very poor. We have children. What else could we do?" Compensation paid to the families of miners killed in the accident at Chenjiashan amounted to ¥71,000 ($8,555), plus an additional ¥20,000 ($2,409) if the miner's body was not recovered. When compared with the ¥400,000 ($48,190) bonus offered to the mine's managers if they exceeded the production target figures by 400,000 metric tons, Watts's statement that "Life is cheap, while coal is increasingly dear" rings painfully true.[20]

The Chinese government understands that the foxes are guarding the henhouse. Thus, especially after the Chenjiashan tragedy, it has sought to limit carnage in the country's mines, decreeing that mine owners in Shanxi province would be required to pay each bereaved family ¥200,000 ($24,096). A report carried by China's official news agency asserted that this sum would be adopted as the new standard in order to "discourage" mine owners "from reaping undeserved profits at the cost of the miner's personal safety." Just two weeks after the Chenjiashan blast, thirty-three miners died in another explosion in Shanxi; consistent with the new compensation rate, the mine owners were required to pay ¥6.6 million ($795,180) to the bereaved families. It remains to be seen how effective the new compensation rate will be in reducing the death rate. Most of China's private mines have little evolved beyond centuries-old models; indeed, mortality rates in such mines recall those of British mines in the third quarter of the nineteenth century.[21]

BETWEEN A ROCK AND A HARD PLACE

China confronts a highly complex situation in terms of labor, safety, and fuel production, and it is one without easy answers. The Chinese economy must continue to grow by more than 7 percent per year into the foreseeable future simply to avoid an increase in an already breathtakingly high and politically explosive rate of unemployment. To maintain that speed of growth, factories need a steady and reliable source of fuel, the vast majority of which will derive from coal for decades to come. Brownouts, such as those that occurred across the country in summer 2004, reduce the likelihood that the healthy portion of China's industrial sector will be able to absorb a sizable number of people from the unemployment lines. Inadequate energy supplies are therefore a major factor now limiting the country's economic growth.[22] Yet the CCP knows that without new jobs, protests and other ways of expressing dissatisfaction will continue.

Faced with these circumstances, the party is desperately searching for a balance between high-speed economic growth, on the one hand, and a more humane social environment on the other. As I've mentioned, the massive revolts erupting across the country have brought greater government attention to the problems of the poor and dispossessed than at any time since the beginning of the reform period, to the extent that President Hu Jintao and Premier Wen Jiabao focused the March 2005 National People's Congress on the theme of building a "harmonious society." According to Hu Jintao, this means a "fight against corruption, for farmers' incomes, for food security, against income disparity, against unemployment, for environmental protection, for stock markets, and for education." Marking a dramatic shift away from the party's priorities under Deng Xiaoping and Jiang Zemin, in March 2005 the CCP's leaders focused their attention on the countryside—promising to eliminate all farm taxes by 2006, to institute new protections against land seizures by local governments, and to plough $660 million into eight hundred farming counties to help pay for education, health care, and science and technology. In addition, the leadership is now dedicated to easing the suffering of the urban unemployed, and it is preparing to spend large sums to erect a social welfare system—though it will be years before such a system can fully meet the needs of those who will rely upon it.

It is clear that the CCP is serious about instituting major changes. In June 2005 the central government announced that peasants across the country would be exempted from agricultural taxes in 2005, and the government was also preparing to annul education fees in the countryside so peasants could afford to send their children to school. In another highly important move, in November 2005 the CCP announced that the household registration system (*hukou*), in place since the 1950s, would be abolished in China's eleven most economically developed coastal provinces, thereby making it possible for people to move from inner provinces to the cities without fear of punishment or loss of privileges. The fact that the party has undertaken this reform over the objections of the police, who oppose it out of fear that social chaos and soaring crime rates will result, indicates that the country's leaders feel an urgent need to alleviate the explosive social tensions in the countryside.[23]

With respect to coal-mine safety, the State Council signaled the seriousness of its intention to stop the slaughter when, following the February 2005 Sunjiawan explosion, it upgraded the State Administration of Work Safety Supervision to ministerial-level status (under a new name, General State Administration of Work Safety Supervision) and allocated millions of yuan to improve mine safety. In July 2005 the government announced further steps, including eight-hour workdays for miners and the requirement that mine owners buy accident insurance for all miners. CCP leaders also stated that the ACFTU would place 100,000 safety supervisors (drawn from among senior miners) in Chinese mines within the next year. This marked a significant recognition on the part of the party that miners themselves needed to be involved in the implementation of safety measures. In the same spirit, in August 2005 officials in Shanxi province announced monetary awards and anonymity for workers who reported hidden dangers in the mines.[24]

These important measures cannot be enacted fast enough, for in the second half of 2005 the death toll in China's coal mines continued to climb at an appalling rate: 19 miners died in an illegal pit in Shanxi on July 2; over 80 died in a mine explosion in Xinjiang on July 12; 123 perished in Guangdong when the Daxing mine flooded on August 7; more than 30 lost their lives in a gas explosion at a mine in Henan on October 3; 16 died in a blast in Shanxi on November 6; at least 14 perished in a Xinjiang accident on November 8; 16 died in a gas explosion at a mine in Inner Mongolia on November 11; and at least 10 more were killed in another mine explosion in Guizhou on November 18. Then on November 27, returning to the massive death tolls with which the year began, a coal-dust explosion at the state-owned Dongfeng mine in Heilongjiang claimed the lives of no fewer than 169 miners; on December 3, 42 miners disappeared and were presumed dead in a mine flood in Henan; and on December 8, 91 miners died and another 12 were presumed dead in a coal-mine explosion in Hebei province. Sadly, this is only a partial list of the accidents that took place during this time.[25] Nor was the first half of 2006 any better. More than five hundred coal miners died in work-related accidents between January 1, 2006, and July 31, 2006.[26]

Embarrassed by the slaughter and by the obvious connection between these disasters and official corruption, on August 22, 2005, after it became known that the vice director of a provincial Bureau of Work Safety had taken ¥100,000 ($12,000) in bribes to issue a safety certificate to the Daxing colliery just two months before a flood there claimed the lives of 123 miners, the central government directed all government officials to immediately withdraw their investments in coal mines (this only pertained to investments in private mines). It further directed the authorities in provinces with particularly bad mine-safety records to close private mines in large numbers. On November 20, 2005, for example, the State Council called on twelve thousand mines across the country to suspend production until they could pass safety inspections. These orders represented a tacit admission by the CCP that conflicts of interest produced by China's lightly regulated path to capitalist development had created a situation in which "terms like 'legal' and 'illegal' when applied to a mining operation . . . mean little more than whether or not the mine's owner has paid off the right authorities."[27]

By the end of October 2005, 4,578 government officials had given up personal investments in coal mines totaling ¥653 million ($80.5 million). Nevertheless, outside observers do not believe the Chinese government has done enough to prevent future conflicts of interest. Li Qiang of China Labor Watch believes government officials will circumvent the government ban on their owning shares in coal mines by demanding bribes from mine owners after pulling out their shares. Making the same point, the *China Labour Bulletin*, an important Hong Kong–based independent organization that monitors labor conditions in China, states that although the government's new policy can stop government officials from investing in coal mines in their own names, it is highly likely that many will circumvent the orders by using the names of others to hide their involvement. And there is still the issue of bribes from mine owners for operating licences and other kickbacks.[28]

Meanwhile Robin Munro, research director at *China Labour Bulletin*, opines that government demands that all mines in provinces with poor safety records be closed down are unrealistic. "It just goes from one extreme to another and pushes prices up because of reduced supplies," says Munro. "We have seen these vicious cycles many times before where more privately-run coal mines spring up and more accidents happen."[29]

Activists concerned about labor conditions and social justice in China applaud any and all efforts by the CCP to reduce poverty and promote mine and workplace safety. Nevertheless, the *China Labour Bulletin*, which frowns on violent protest and promotes using the legal system to fight for workers' rights, insists that even more urgent than new initiatives and promises "is for the Chinese government to begin taking determined steps to actually implement and enforce the country's existing laws and regulations on workplace safety."[30] Making new laws and appointing 100,000 new safety supervisors sounds like it will improve conditions in China's coal mines, these activists concede, but none of it will have any effect if the CCP is ultimately afraid to challenge the vested interests of those in the party and out who have committed crimes. Those people must be punished according to the laws already on the books. Miners can only hope this happens, because the government has denied them the most basic tools to fight for their own safety. Migrant workers are in a particularly bad position, given that the ACFTU generally does not consider their welfare to be its responsibility (although this may change with the lifting of the household registration system), but even workers in SOEs are hard pressed to get significant help from the ACFTU. For this reason, activists concerned about the plight of Chinese workers have called on the CCP to comply with ILO standards, which stipulate that workers be given the right to participate in workplace safety efforts and that they be permitted to form independent trade unions (which have successfully pushed for greater workplace safety in other countries).

The growth of the Chinese economy over the past several decades has produced phenomenal results, lifting hundreds of millions of people out of poverty and producing a globally integrated and (unevenly) modern society. These extraordinary and historic achievements have made China the envy of much of the developing world and have won admirers (while also inspiring no small amount of fear) in industrialized parts of the world. Yet it is a cruel irony that as China has emerged as one of the world's most unregulated capitalist economies, this one-time socialist state's refusal to provide its workers with tools to defend themselves has created an often powerless, deeply demoralized, and impoverished Chinese working class worse off than both its predecessor of the Mao Zedong era and its counterparts in most of the capitalist world. There are no easy answers to the complex web of problems China now faces. All parties, the CCP and Chinese workers, have ample reason to hope that the country can work its way through the tragic contradictions discussed in this chapter. Should this fail to happen, the stability of Chinese society will be in doubt, and the quality of life for many Chinese people will further deteriorate.

NOTES

I wish to thank John Carlson, Peter Gries, Lionel Jensen, and Chris Smith for their helpful comments and suggestions.

1. Robin Munro, "Labor Unrest and Denial of the Right to Organize in China," *China Labour Bulletin*, July 2004; *China Labour Bulletin*, "An Overview of Unemployment in China 2003," July 2004.
2. *Asian Times*, "New Five-Year Plan Called 'Revolutionary,'" October 13, 2005; Tim Luard, "China Rethinks Peasant 'Apartheid,'" BBC News, November 10, 2005.
3. Tim Wright, "The Political Economy of Coal Mine Disasters in China: 'Your Rice Bowl or Your Life,'" *China Quarterly* 179 (September 2004): 637; *China Labour Bulletin*, "An Overview of Unemployment in China 2003."
4. James Kynge, "Power to the People," *Financial Times Weekend*, March 12–13, 2005; Edward Cody, "System No Help to China's Laid-Off Workers," *Washington Post*, January 24, 2005; Florence Chan, "Crying Out for Justice in Beijing," *Asian Times*, December 7, 2004.
5. Radio Free Asia, "Petitioners Attempt Mass Suicide in Beijing," July 12, 2004; Agence France-Press, "Chinese Petitioners Threaten Mass Suicide in Beijing," July 14, 2004.
6. Jonathan Watts, "Protests Surge as Reforms Fail to Match Rising Hopes," *Guardian*, October 11, 2005. On the Daqing and Liaoyang protests, see Timothy B. Weston, "The Iron Man Weeps: Joblessness and Political Legitimacy in the Chinese Rust Belt," in *State and Society in 21st Century China: Crisis, Contention, and Legitimation*, ed. Peter Hays Gries and Stanley Rosen (New York: Routledge, 2004), 67–86.
7. John Chan, "Mass Protests in China Point to Sharp Social Tensions," *World Socialist*, January 1, 2004.
8. Jim Yardley, "Rural Chinese Riot as Police Try to Halt Pollution Protest," *New York Times*, April 14, 2005; Edward Cody, "For Chinese, Peasant Revolt Is Rare Victory," *Washington Post*, June 13, 2005. The Li Qiang quotation is from Kathy Chen, "Chinese Protests Grow More Frequent, Violent," *Wall Street Journal*, May 11, 2004.
9. Quoted in Chen, "Chinese Protests Grow More Frequent."
10. *Shanghai Star*, "Mining, China's Most Dangerous Job," November 18, 2004; *China Labour Bulletin*, "Death Toll of Shaanxi Coal Mine Explosion Rises to 166,"

December 1, 2004; Jonathan Watts, "Blood and Coal: The Human Cost of Cheap Chinese Goods," *Guardian*, March 14, 2005; Eric Baculiano, "China's Mines Putting Profit ahead of Safety," MSNBC, December 1, 2004; Wang Jun, "Another Coalmine Tragedy," *Beijing Review*, December 9, 2004; *China Labour Bulletin*, "Another Mining Disaster: When Will Chinese Miners Be Given the Right to Monitor Their Own Safety?" April 8, 2005; CNN, "China Mine Blast Kills 203," February 15, 2005; *China Labour Bulletin*, "The Disasters Continue: Sixty Miners Killed at Xishui Colliery in Shouzhou," March 21, 2005; *China Labour Bulletin*, "Safety Standards in Chinese Mines? What Are the International Standards?" December 21, 2004; *China Labour Bulletin*, "Sunjiawan Coal Company Backtracks on Compensation Offer to Families," March 9, 2005; *Epoch Times*, "Sixty-nine Die after Another Mine Disaster in China," March 28, 2005; www.chinaview.cn, "Eight Killed, Six Injured in Hunan Coal Mine Explosion," March 24, 2005; Jonathan Watts, "China Shuts 7,000 Pits in Safety Drive," *Guardian*, September 1, 2005.

11. John Ruwitch, "China's Dependence on Dangerous Coal Keeps Growing," *Reuters*, October 16, 2004; Pablo Bustelo, "China and the Geopolitics of Oil in the Asian Pacific Region," May 9, 2005, www.realinstitutoelcano.org/documentos/226.asp (July 7, 2006). Zhang Jianyu is quoted in Jim Yardley, "China's Economic Engine Needs Power (Lots of It)," *New York Times*, March 14, 2004.

12. On the figure of twenty thousand dead per year, see *China Labour Bulletin*, "More than 4,500 Officials Report Shares in Coal Mines with a Total Investment of 650 Million Yuan," November 2005, www.clb.org.hk/public/contents/news?revision%5fid=18706&item%5fid=18700 (July 7, 2006).

13. Hoo Ban Khee, "Heads Roll over Latest Mine Tragedy," The Star Online, February 27, 2005, http://thestar.com.my; Wright, "Political Economy of Coal Mine Disasters," 632.

14. Bustelo, "China and the Geopolitics of Oil."

15. Jonathan Watts, "China Faces Cold Winter as Fuel Grows Scarce," *Guardian*, November 16, 2004; Emma Graham-Harrison, "China Beats the Power Crunch," *Standard*, September 19, 2005.

16. Mary Hennock, "China's Miners Pay for Growth," BBC News, December 12, 2004; Yardley, "China's Economic Engine Needs Power."

17. Elaine Kurtenbach, "Industrial Boom Makes China Mines Deadly," *Washington Post*, December 1, 2004; Alice Yan, "Miners Forced Down Blazing Pit 'To Secure Bonuses for Bosses,'" *South China Morning Post*, December 1, 2004; Wang Jun, "Another Coalmine Tragedy"; Watts, "Blood and Coal"; Baculiano, "China's Mines Putting Profit Ahead of Safety."

18. *China Labour Bulletin*, "Continuing Carnage in China's Coal Mines: Official Responses and Recommendations," September 6, 2003; Kurtenbach, "Industrial Boom Makes China Mines Deadly"; *China Labour Bulletin*, "Safety Standards in Chinese Mines?"

19. Kurtenbach, "Industrial Boom Makes China Mines Deadly"; Terry Cook, "Drive for Coal Produces More Deaths in China's Mines," *World Socialist*, March 16, 2004; Joseph Kahn, "China's Coal Miners Risk Danger for a Better Wage," *New York Times*, January 28, 2003; *China Labour Bulletin*, "Continuing Carnage in China's Coal Mines"; Martin Perry, "China 'Pays' with Death to Fuel Its Economy," China Labor

Watch, www.chinalaborwatch.org; AFX News Limited, "Miners, Police Clash over Forced Closure of Mines in Southern China," August 22, 2005.

20. Mr. Liu is quoted in Kahn, "China's Coal Miners Risk Danger"; Watts, "Blood and Coal."

21. *China Labour Bulletin*, "Safety Standards in Chinese Mines?"; Wright, "Political Economy of Coal Mine Disasters," 632.

23. Watts, "China Faces Cold Winter."

23. Hu Jintao is quoted in Marc Erikson, "'Humdrum' Congress Changes China's Course," *Asian Times*, March 15, 2005; *International Herald Tribune*, "China's Rural Poverty Is Now a State Priority," March 11, 2005; Xinhua News Agency, "Farmers to be Free from Agriculture Taxes," June 29, 2005, www.xinhuanet.com/english; *China Daily*, "Chinese Farmers Remain Marginalized Economically," September 8, 2005; Joseph Kahn, "China to Drop Urbanite-Peasant Legal Differences," *New York Times*, November 3, 2005; Luard, "China Rethinks Peasant 'Apartheid.'"

24. Kynge, "Power to the People"; *China Labour Bulletin*, "Another Mining Disaster"; *China Labour Bulletin*, "New Calls for Coal Mine Safety Regulations amid Further Fatal Accidents," July 6, 2005; Xinhua News Agency, "Coal Mine Workers Encouraged to Report Hidden Danger," August 29, 2005, www.xinhuanet.com/english.

25. *China Labour Bulletin*, "New Calls for Coal Mine Safety Regulations"; Shirley Wu, "Mine Owners Hid 17 Bodies after Blast," *South China Morning Post*, July 15, 2005; *China Labour Bulletin*, "Will a Ban on Officials' Personal Investments in Coal Mining Boost Safety in China's Mines?" http://iso.china-labour.org.hk/public/contents/news?revision_id=17349&item_id=17013 (July 7, 2006); Reuters, "Gas Explosion Kills 34 in Chinese Coal Mine," October 3, 2005; Reuters, "Three China Mine Disasters Kill at Least 57," November 8, 2005; *China Labour Bulletin*, "12,000 Mines Ordered to Suspend Production While 40 Miners Die in Three Recent Coal Mine Disasters," November 2005; Xinhua News Agency, "State-Owned Coal Mines Insured for Work Injuries," October 26, 2005, www.xinhuanet.com/english; Xinhua News Agency, "Death Toll Rises to 161 at State-Owned Coal Mine," November 30, 2005, www.xinhuanet.com/english. On the December 2005 blast in Henan, see www.usmra.com/Chinatable.htm, and United States Mine Rescue Association, "China Mine Disaster Watch," www.usmra.com/Chinatable.htm.

26. This information is readily available from the United States Mine Rescue Association, "China Mine Disaster Watch," www.usmra.com/Chinatable.htm.

27. *China Labour Bulletin*, "More than 4,500 Officials Report Shares"; AFX News Limited, "Miners, Police Clash over Forced Closure"; *China Labour Bulletin*, "12,000 Mines Ordered to Suspend Production." The quotation is from Han Dongfang. See *China Labour Bulletin*, "A Deadly Conflict of Interests," September 15, 2005.

28. *China Labour Bulletin*, "Will a Ban on Officials' Personal Investment in Coal Mining Boost Safety in China's Mines?"

29. Quoted in Chan Siu-sin, "Experts Say Pit Safety Steps Are Not Enough," *South China Morning Post*, October 1, 2005. Also see *China Labour Bulletin*, "More than 4,500 Officials Report Shares."

30. On the *China Labour Bulletin*'s position regarding violent protests versus legal strategies, see Han Dongfang, "Chinese Labour Struggles," *New Left Review* 34 (July–August 2005); *China Labour Bulletin*, "Safety Standards in Chinese Mines?"

SUGGESTED READINGS

Anita Chan, *China's Workers under Assault: The Exploitation of Labor in a Globalizing Economy* (Armonk, NY: East Gate Books, 2001).

Han Dongfang, "Chinese Labour Struggles," *New Left Review* 34 (July–August 2005). This is an interview with Han Dongfang, founder of the *China Labour Bulletin*.

Dorothy J. Solinger, *Contesting Citizenship in Urban China: Peasant Migrants, the State, and the Logic of the Market* (Berkeley: University of California Press, 1999).

Tim Wright, "The Political Economy of Coal Mine Disasters in China: 'Your Rice Bowl or Your Life,'" *China Quarterly*, 179 (September 2004): 629–46.

Online Sources

China Labour Bulletin, www.china-labour.org.hk/public/main
China Labor Watch, www.chinalaborwatch.org
United States Mine Rescue Association, www.usmra.com/Chinatable.htm

Film

Blind Shaft (dir. Li Yang, 2003). This fictional film was produced in mainland China and is available at commercial video outlets in the United States.

4

Qigong, Falun Gong, and the Body Politic in Contemporary China

David Ownby

Few topics in the history of contemporary China demand looking beyond the headlines more than does the spiritual movement Falun Gong.[1] Prior to April 25, 1999, when thousands of Falun Gong practitioners "surrounded" CCP headquarters at Zhongnanhai, a stone's throw from Tiananmen Square, few China watchers in the West had even heard of Falun Gong, and Chinese authorities (who had heard of it) were caught completely off guard. Several months later in a subsequent crackdown, Chinese authorities labeled Falun Gong a dangerous, "heterodox sect" and sought to link it to such notorious cults as Aum Shinrikyo in Japan and the Branch Davidians in the United States. To the angry astonishment of Chinese authorities, Falun Gong practitioners outside China—most of them part of a new Chinese diaspora of recent emigrants from the Chinese mainland—fought back in a very effective media campaign, claiming that Falun Gong was an innocent system of mind and body cultivation and that the Chinese government's campaign of suppression was an infringement on fundamental rights of freedom of speech and freedom of religion.

The resulting war of representations was played out in newspaper headlines and television news stories both in China and in the West,[2] and the topic came to be polemicized to the point that an objective depiction of Falun Gong was (and is) extremely difficult to find. This is unfortunate, as Falun Gong directly relates to many themes that have characterized the post-Mao period: the search for spiritual meaning in the wake of the perceived failure of revolutionary transformation; the growth of semiautonomous social organizations in the relative vacuum created by the retreat of the Chinese state from the front lines of social engagement; the exploitation of new market opportunities created by Deng Xiaoping's economic reforms, as represented by charismatic masters like Falun Gong founder Li Hongzhi who were able to sell their charisma to consumers with more money in their pockets than ever before; and the difficulties experienced by the Chinese state in attempting to maintain control over an increasingly free-wheeling society.

The point of this chapter is to provide the kind of objective overview of Falun Gong that has been lacking by replacing it in the proper historical and cultural context. I bring to this task some years of experience as a historian of Chinese popular religion and of having worked on groups and movements that might be considered historical antecedents of the Falun Gong.[3] My translations of popular religious scriptures, as well as my work on the history of apocalyptic thought and movements in China, proved useful in coming to terms with Li Hongzhi and his writings. The existence of large numbers of Chinese Falun Gong practitioners in North America meant that I could add fieldwork to my documentary study of Li Hongzhi's writings and of other Falun Gong texts.[4] I attended Falun Gong events, circulated questionnaires in order to establish a basic sociological profile of North American practitioners, conducted interviews with practitioners, listened to their exchanges, and even marched with them through the streets of Toronto and Montreal.

I should stress at this point that although I marched with Falun Gong practitioners, I am not a practitioner myself. Indeed, I was raised a Southern Baptist in the heart of America's Bible Belt, and although I no longer consider myself religious, I am not by culture or early education predisposed to adopt Falun Gong beliefs and practices. Paradoxically, however, my early exposure to a Western form of fundamentalism helped in some ways to prepare me for fieldwork among practitioners of an Eastern faith with its own fundamentalist overtones. I can for instance easily recall the emotional urgency of the quest for salvation that was at the heart of the religiosity I remember from my childhood and can readily empathize with people for whom salvation, emancipation, and spiritual release remain compelling concerns—even if they seek salvation in ways that look esoteric at first (or even second) glance. In addition, prolonged exposure during my youth to the often heavy-handed proselytizing of friends, relatives, and neighbors allowed me to shrug off the occasional Falun Gong practitioner who insisted that I could never *really* understand what Master Li said without becoming a practitioner myself (I might add at this point that Falun Gong practitioners are in general less aggressive proselytizers than Southern Baptists). Similarly, having grown up in a culture where many otherwise normal people had seemingly strange beliefs—such as my high-school biology teacher, who refused to teach evolution—I had little trouble dealing with Chinese computer scientists who believe, say, in the possibility of demonic possession.

In any event, my research led to the following conclusions: Falun Gong should be understood as a form of *qigong*—this is a general name, which might be translated as "the discipline of the vital force"—which describes a set of physical and mental disciplines based loosely on traditional Chinese medical and spiritual practices, and often organized around a charismatic master who teaches his followers specific techniques as well as general moral precepts, with the goal of realizing a physical and moral transformation of the follower.[5] Although many *qigong* masters (including Li Hongzhi) claim to locate the source of their powers in ancient Chinese traditions, *qigong* as we understand it today was actually invented in the 1950s by the Chinese state (via the Chinese medical establishment) as an effort to preserve certain elements of traditional Chinese healing practices in the face of rapid Westernization of Chinese medicine. *Qigong* only became a mass movement much later, in the 1980s, partially filling the void created by the failure of Mao Zedong's attempt to create a new Communist Chinese identity through political and cultural revolution. Chinese authorities allowed the *qigong* movement to take wing in part because *qigong*'s celebration of the glories of traditional Chinese medical culture dovetailed with the CCP's celebration of Chinese nationalism (indeed, many high party and government officials were enthusiastic *qigong* supporters and practitioners).

This official support helped to create what may have been one of the largest mass movements in Chinese history; some scholars estimate that as many as 200 million Chinese participated in the *qigong* boom at its peak, seeking health and spiritual meaning in ways that had nothing to do with Chinese Communism. Falun Gong emerged at the end of the boom and came under attack in large measure due to the Chinese state's slow yet frightened recognition that it had helped to create a popular movement that acknowledged sources of authority and power beyond the state's control. And if Falun Gong's rise can be seen as part of a larger search for spiritual meaning, the surprisingly successful resistance of Falun Gong to the Chinese government's campaign of suppression, beginning in the summer of 1999, should be seen as evidence of the emergence of a less passive Chinese people, a Chinese people increasingly willing to stand up to the capricious authoritarianism of the Chinese state.[6]

THE INVENTION OF *QIGONG*

Trying to understand Falun Gong without a basic knowledge of *qigong* is like watching a Hong Kong kung fu movie without the subtitles; you can more or less follow along, but inevitably you miss some details. In many ways, Falun Gong is but a footnote to the larger history of *qigong*, which has yet to be written in English.

Although rare usages of the term exist in ancient texts, *qigong* as I noted above was created in the 1950s by part of the Chinese medical establishment as an effort to maintain traditional Chinese medicine—more specifically, Chinese medical practices involving regular physical gestures (not calisthenics; *qigong* does not particularly target the cardiovascular system) and mental disciplines aimed at achieving physical and mental health.[7] The major objective was to modernize such practices by removing the superstitious and religious packaging that surrounded them in imperial times and to incorporate them into a scientific discourse.

The inventors of *qigong* sought out traditional healing methods as practiced by charismatic masters, often in rural areas, and transplanted these practices to modern hospitals and sanatoriums. The process of transplantation involved the transformation of the original superstitious and "feudal" language employed by traditional practitioners to describe and explain their art into a new, neutral, scientific language. Practices directly linked to religion—prayers, mantras, magic formulas, the invocation of the names of deities—were replaced by an emphasis on meditation and the development of mental discipline. The goal was to separate the wheat from the chaff, to keep what obviously worked and to get rid of what was obviously nonscientific and nonsensical, so that the Chinese people could benefit from traditional wisdom without falling victim to traditional superstitions.

This project received considerable high-level political support from the early 1950s to the onset of the Cultural Revolution in 1966. Indeed, *qigong* became relatively popular among the Chinese governing elite, who sought cures for their aches and pains in sanatoriums that often combined the functions of spa and resort. This elite support also allowed *qigong* to carve out a niche for itself within the Chinese medical establishment. *Qigong* research groups carried out experiments and published their results; *qigong* classes were added to the curricula of certain programs in Chinese medicine. There was, however, no "*qigong* boom" in Mao's China. The *qigong* of the 1950s was the invention of cadres loyal to the Communist state, and *qigong* therapy was embraced by high-level government and CCP officials whose ideological commitment to the regime was beyond question.

Qigong became something very different in post-Mao China.[8] The *qigong* institutions and networks established prior to the Cultural Revolution had been destroyed by the revolutionary iconoclasts who supported the Cultural Revolution and who argued that *qigong* was nothing more than feudal superstition. Indeed, the emergence of charismatic *qigong* masters was an indirect result of this destruction, as those who remained committed to *qigong* were forced to take their enthusiasm directly to the public. A woman named Guo Lin (b. 1909) was one of the first such masters and began teaching *qigong* in public parks in Beijing in the early 1970s.[9] Guo had cured her own uterine cancer through *qigong*, and her passion was thus that of a true believer who had witnessed the power of *qigong* on her own body. Guo Lin's *qigong* was not the same as that invented by the Chinese state in the 1950s. Instead, she had learned certain healing techniques from her grandfather, who had been a Daoist master, and she had adapted these practices to the needs of her diseased body. She referred to her practice as *qigong* because this label was less problematic than anything else she could have chosen. Other masters, emerging at roughly the same time, resembled Guo Lin in that they too came to *qigong* from outside the safe, institutional *qigong* world of the 1950s, having learned their skills from a variety of sources, most of which were related to traditional religious or spiritual practices.

In fact, these masters would quite likely not have been allowed to come to prominence had it not been for the "scientific discovery" in the late 1970s and early 1980s of the material existence of *qi* (traditionally in Chinese culture, the "life force" or "breath" of everything that exists), a discovery that gave an immense boost to the burgeoning world of *qigong* masters and practitioners. In the late 1970s, well-known scientists working at respected Chinese universities and research institutions conducted experiments that purported to demonstrate that the *qi* emitted by *qigong* masters could be measured by scientific instruments.[10] The publication of such results created a sensation: if *qi* was a substance whose existence could be proved through scientific experimentation, then a large part of the objectives of the early *qigong* workers of the 1950s had been realized; once provided with a material base, *qigong* no longer belonged to the world of magic and superstition but rather to that of science and dialectical materialism.

A *qigong* "world" (*qigong jie*) rapidly came into being on the basis of these claims.[11] This world was composed of scientists who continued to conduct experiments on *qi* and *qigong*; journalists who embraced *qigong* and spread the word of *qigong*'s power and benefits to the Chinese public; *qigong* masters, whose numbers increased exponentially in step with the burgeoning general enthusiasm for *qigong*; and—most importantly—CCP and government officials who saw in *qigong* a uniquely powerful Chinese science as well as a practical, economical means to achieve a healthier population (and thus a less-expensive healthcare system). This official support was crucial to the further development of the *qigong* boom and took a variety of forms, including private patronage of particular masters and scientists by powerful members of the ruling elite, as well as broader organizational efforts, such as the establishment of the Chinese Qigong Scientific Research Association in April 1986.

Qigong boomed from the early 1980s on, as tens if not hundreds of millions of Chinese became devoted followers of one school of *qigong* or another, an extraordinary affair in which the Chinese state gave its support to a varied cast of characters pursuing a diversity of ends. Paranormal phenomena, for example, soon came to be linked to *qigong*, and journalists competed to report on youngsters who were able to "read via their ears"—a mysterious feat whereby someone would write Chinese characters on a piece of paper and the gifted youth would read these by wadding up the paper and placing it in his ear. The connection between *qigong* and the paranormal was the notion that through *qigong* practice, human beings could achieve far greater potential than in the past. The *qigong* craze also swept college campuses, and students emerged from their classrooms to literally embrace trees and other plants in the hopes of absorbing "natural" *qi* (they later decided that this was not nice to the trees).

The most important aspect of the *qigong* boom, however, was the formation of large, often nationwide *qigong* organizations, led by charismatic *qigong* masters, many of whom became the equivalent of rock stars.[12] The first master to achieve this status was Yan Xin, a previously unknown Chinese medical practitioner, but he was only one among many.[13] Many of these masters carried out nationwide lecture tours in which thousands of enthusiasts bought tickets for the events, often held in a local arena and lasting for several hours at a time. Many of the *qigong* masters promised to "emit *qi*" in the course of their lectures, a telling indication of the difference between the *qigong* of the 1950s and that of the 1980s: *qigong* in the 1950s had been a therapeutic discipline practiced by the ailing patient under the guidance of a trained professional; *qigong* of the 1980s was a magical power possessed by charismatic heroes whose therapy consisted of directing their personal *qi* indiscriminately toward a mass of followers. Miracle cures—reminiscent of what we know of televangelists in our own culture—were the most spectacular manifestation of *qigong* power. At the same time, many *qigong* masters took advantage of the newly liberated Chinese economy to produce *qigong* books, audio- and videocassettes, and a wide variety of paraphernalia (*qigong* tea, for example), all of which was sold to an eager and undiscriminating public. Journalists helped to feed the craze, some by becoming the biographers of *qigong* masters. Such biographies, printed in runs of tens if not hundreds of thousands, became must reading, in addition to the how-to manuals and the audio- and videocassettes.

According to the estimate I cited above, as many as 200 million people participated in the movement at the height of the *qigong* boom—or almost one-fifth of China's vast population. Such estimates are notoriously difficult to verify, particularly because most groups did not maintain membership lists, and many masters surely inflated the number of their followers in an attempt to enhance their self-importance, but even if the estimate is wrong by an order of magnitude and there were 20 million followers rather than 200 million, the number is still impressive. Many practitioners were followers of the particular *qigong* masters who built nationwide followings and organizations, while others simply moved from group to group, seeking cures for their ailments or the thrill of the collective activity. Most of the activities took place in public parks throughout urban China (although *qigong* was known in rural areas as well), parks being one of the few open urban spaces available in this overcrowded, over-controlled country of 1.2 billion. The *qigong* boom was a mass movement on the scale of the Cultural Revolution (without the overt political overtones) but was largely ignored by observers in the West, many of whom were waiting for another challenge to the state on the part of Western-oriented dissidents (which of course came about in 1989). They did not know what to make of *qigong* masters, who looked like an odd cross between exercise guru Richard Simmons and televangelist Pat Robertson.

LI HONGZHI AND FALUN GONG

Li Hongzhi and Falun Gong appear much less eccentric and esoteric if understood within the context of the larger *qigong* boom. Falun Gong was received as a variety of *qigong* (the *gong* of *Falun Gong* and the *gong* of *qigong* are the same) when Li Hongzhi began to publicize his teachings in 1992. It is true that from the very beginning, Li denounced many other *qigong* masters and claimed that Falun Gong was *qigong* "taken to a higher level." It is also true that other *qigong* schools sought to distance themselves from Falun Gong, particularly after the beginning of the Chinese government's campaign against it. Still, had there been no *qigong* boom, there would have been no Falun Gong. Falun Gong was quickly welcomed into the Chinese Qigong Scientific Research Association, which sponsored and helped to organize many of Li's activities between 1992 and 1994. Among those activities were fifty-four large-scale lectures given throughout China to a total audience of some sixty thousand; Li followed squarely in the footsteps of Yan Xin and other *qigong* masters. Li also published books of his teachings (actually, transcriptions of his lectures), which achieved such success that he was soon able to offer his lectures free of charge—a significant difference from many other *qigong* schools.

Nonetheless, even if Li Hongzhi and Falun Gong owed their initial success to other *qigong* masters and schools who had paved the way, there was, as I've mentioned, something different about Li Hongzhi. Almost from the very outset, Li condemned other branches of *qigong* for their materialism, accusing them of charlatanism and fraud. At a more basic level, he argued that *qigong* as a whole had become obsessed with healing and supernormal powers, at the expense of more important spiritual concerns. Essentially, Li argued that Falun Gong was *qigong* taken to a higher plane, that Falun Gong was what *qigong* *should be*. In other words, Falun Gong could cure disease and confer supernatural powers, but the more important objective was to arrive at a fundamental transformation of one's understanding of the universe and one's role therein, as well as a physical transformation of the practitioner's body. These transformations were to be realized in part through the exercises Li Hongzhi had invented as part of Falun Gong practice (pictures and explanations of these are found in the book *China Falun Gong* and on Falun Gong websites).[14] At the same time, Li accorded far more importance to scripture (i.e., his transcribed writings) than did most other *qigong* masters. Most *qigong* texts either illustrated proper *qigong* technique or offered explanations of the efficacy of the practice. Li Hongzhi's writings were treated as holy: even after the writings became freely available via the Internet, practitioners were forbidden to write on the pages they had themselves printed out on their home computers. It was the reading, rereading, and absorption through memorization of Li's written teachings that made up the core of Falun Gong practice. Falun Gong also stressed Li Hongzhi's miraculous, god-like powers (among other things, he had the ability to ensure the health and welfare of all of his followers throughout the world at all times) in a way that other *qigong* schools rarely did in their own writings—although those masters who performed miracle cures by "emitting *qi*" were not far from claiming god-like powers, and few *qigong* masters refused the adulation visited on them by their followers.

When we examine the contents of Li Hongzhi's teachings, we find an eclectic mix of Buddhism, Daoism, popular religion, and scientism. Li's main religious inspiration is Buddhism (in its folk variety), and he enjoins followers to abandon their "attachments" (generally referred to as "desires" in more orthodox Buddhist texts), be they to meat, alcohol, medicines, material possessions, or other human beings (practitioners are to be compassionate to all but should avoid emotional encumbrances that might detract from the quest for salvation). In his lectures and his writings, Li frequently evokes the traditional Buddhist notion of karma, the idea, linked to that of reincarnation, that one reaps what one sows. From the perspective of karma, the lives we presently lead are the result of our moral behavior in previous lives, and how we live our present lives will similarly determine our future lives.

Li Hongzhi's understanding of karma is, however, "new and improved." For Li, karma has a material basis: it is a black substance, physically present in the body, that can be transformed through suffering and/or through virtuous practice into a white substance ("virtue"). This transformation occurs at the molecular level (in other words, it is more than symbolic), which accounts logically for the improved health claimed by Falun Gong practitioners (some of whom claim to have reversed the aging process). Indeed, the allure of better health has been the chief attraction of Falun Gong for many practitioners, who consider disease a form of karma to be eliminated through suffering and cultivation. This is why most Falun

Gong practitioners prefer to avoid doctors, hospitals, and medication; medicines can of course treat the symptoms of a disease, but they do nothing about its root cause—karma. Some Falun Gong practitioners also claim to have obtained supernormal powers through their practice, but Li Hongzhi insists that such powers are not the goal of cultivation and will cease to function if used for any purpose other than that of benevolent morality.

Li argues furthermore that truth, benevolence, and forbearance, the three cardinal principles of Falun Gong practice, are in fact the forces that make up the physical universe. This is part of Li's self-presentation as a man of science, as is the idea that karma has a material existence. Falun Gong practitioners thus achieve unity with universal, scientific reality by cultivating truth, benevolence, and forbearance in their personal lives. Matter and spirit are one. Li himself claims to have transcended science and to comprehend all of reality from another, higher level; at various points in his writings he speaks of himself as a god or a Buddha possessed of a more complete understanding of our "multileveled" universe than that of ordinary mortals. Still, his writings are full of scientific (or parascientific) references (his reflections on the proper understanding of gravity, for example), which many practitioners take as seriously as the rest of his scriptures. Indeed, many North American Chinese followers of Falun Gong have advanced degrees in the hard sciences, such as physics, and have assured me repeatedly that recent developments in theoretical physics have followed from Li Hongzhi's insights.

Another aspect of Li's teachings concerns the apocalypse—world destruction and renewal. On a number of occasions Li has stated that the world has been destroyed and re-created eighty-one times, and he has claimed that certain signs lead him to believe that another such cycle is imminent. Although such musings appear esoteric to Western readers, Li in fact adopted these ideas wholesale (even the number 81) from traditional strains of Chinese apocalyptic thinking, found especially in popularized versions of Daoism and Buddhism and in the scriptures of certain sectarian groups of the late imperial period. The ideas and symbols are widely known—if not necessarily shared or believed—throughout China, in the same way that the teachings of the biblical Book of Revelations are generally known in the West. My impression is that Li did not stress apocalyptic themes in the period prior to the Chinese government's suppression of Falun Gong, although he certainly made more than passing reference to such themes.

Falun Gong practice is simple, if time-consuming. The exercises are to be performed on a daily basis if possible, alone or with other practitioners. But the exercises themselves are relatively unimportant compared to the reading and rereading of Li Hongzhi's most important work, *Zhuanfalun* [*The re-*

volving law wheel]. *Zhuanfalun* is held to be the source of all truth; many practitioners report having read it initially in a single sitting (Li counsels followers to read the book in such a manner) and having experienced an immediate revelation (often accompanied by physical manifestations—vomiting, diarrhea, a purging of the body). Since 1995, Li has given more lectures abroad than in China (he moved to the United States in 1996 and established permanent residency there in 1998); these lectures are transcribed and made available to followers via the movement's websites. These new scriptures by now constitute an important addition to *Zhuanfalun*, which remains, nonetheless, the Bible of the movement.

Like other *qigong* masters, Li built a nationwide Falun Gong organization of practice centers in China that came to enroll between 2 million and 60 million practitioners, depending on whose estimates one accepts. Li's own lecture tours within China from 1992 to 1994 provided the initial impetus for the creation of the organization, which one might characterize either as centralized or as decentralized. On the one hand, Li attempted to limit the power of local Falun Gong leaders by forbidding them from preaching or teaching Falun Gong doctrine. Local leaders were permitted to do little more than facilitate others' cultivation, provide literature, lead exercise sessions, and organize group activities; Li insisted that the genuine spiritual connection be between individual practitioners and the master, a connection unmediated by any third-party interference. From this perspective, Falun Gong looks to be dangerously centralized.

On the other hand, my impression is that Li Hongzhi never really succeeded in building the sort of organization that would enable him to impose his vision on local groups. Between early 1992 and late 1994, Li had his hands full touring the country, making himself known, and setting up the rudiments of an organization, and he left China in early 1995. Some of his writings from this period do indeed suggest that he was concerned with the quality of the organization he was leaving behind. At the same time, repeated references to problems with local leadership suggest that the problems remained largely unresolved.

I suspect that Li may not be a "nuts and bolts" type leader, that he has in general been more interested in articulating his vision of truth than in perfecting the organizational mechanisms of his movement. Such tendencies were surely accentuated by Li's decision to "go international" from early 1995 on, which removed him physically from the majority of his following, which remained of course in China. After Li had established himself in the United States, Falun Gong websites came to be a major vehicle of Li's vision, but if a website can indeed inform followers of a master's musings, it is not sufficient in and of itself to ensure organizational uniformity.

Moreover, between the summer of 1999 and fall of 2000, Li largely disappeared from circulation altogether in reaction to the beginning of the campaign against Falun Gong in China. Local groups in Canada and in the United States did not know what he expected of them and were delighted when he began to reappear toward the end of 2000. The result has been that Falun Gong groups in North America (to say nothing of groups in China) have been largely left to their own devices, a state of affairs that has encouraged individual responsibility and initiative in all but doctrinal matters. The original Falun Gong organization in China has of course been all but destroyed by the Chinese government's protracted anti–Falun Gong campaign (although underground branches clearly remain). Perhaps the organization in China once had a more centralized cast, but given Li's other preoccupations before leaving China, I tend to doubt it.

Chinese authorities often accuse the Falun Gong of brainwashing and of placing improper pressure on group members—not to visit a doctor when they are ill, for example. In my fieldwork in Canada and the United States, I have in general not found that groups exercise this sort of control over their members, which does not mean that Falun Gong groups in China did not do so (as Chinese government sources insist that they did). Groups in North America do not solicit information about practitioners, do not register members, do not maintain membership lists, and do not demand regular contributions (although local events are financed by voluntary contributions from local practitioners). A spirit of cheery goodwill characterized most of the Falun Gong events that I attended (tainted in recent years by sadness verging on despair as media fatigue makes it harder and harder for the Falun Gong to get their message into the Western media). I never had the sense that those present were constrained to be there, nor do most practitioners seek to cut off their ties with nonpractitioners, although this can happen; much depends on the personality of the practitioner in question. In general, however, Li Hongzhi asks that practitioners remain "within the world" so as to spread the way and to work off their own karma through the suffering that the world imposes. In sum, my fieldwork does not suggest that Falun Gong tends to establish strong "us versus them" distinctions or to encourage separation from an unclean world of nonpractitioners. In other words, I have found little evidence of "brainwashing" or "mind control" among Falun Gong practitioners in North America, although the movement is too decentralized for my limited fieldwork to serve as a definitive judgment on the question. I might add that even if Falun Gong were guilty of the crimes of which it is accused by the Chinese state—which I seriously doubt—the punishment visited upon practitioners in China has vastly exceeded proper boundaries. There is no question that the campaign against Falun Gong has constituted—and continues to constitute—a major human rights concern in the PRC.

FALUN GONG IN THE HEADLINES

Falun Gong made headlines by daring to protest against the Chinese state's refusal to protect practitioners' rights to cultivate. Indeed, the peaceful protest organized by Falun Gong practitioners on April 25, 1999, unleashed the fury of the Chinese state and culminated in the condemnation of *qigong* as a whole, as well as a massive campaign against Falun Gong. How should we understand the origins, unfolding, and implications of these events?

First, we should note that the *qigong* movement as a whole had long had its ups and downs, and its detractors as well as its supporters. It is unlikely that the strange marriage between the control-oriented Chinese authorities and the wild and wonderful world of *qigong* could have long endured, and it was to some extent accidental that Falun Gong was the cause célèbre that brought the *qigong* boom to a crashing end. At the same time, one can identify certain peculiarities that perhaps help to explain the role of Li Hongzhi and Falun Gong in this turn of events.

First, Li Hongzhi had always been less careful than other *qigong* masters to cast his teachings in terms that CCP and government authorities would find palatable. In his pre-crackdown writings, Li Hongzhi appears to be consistently nationalistic, patriotic, and apolitical, but while other *qigong* leaders took care to express themselves in such a way as to avoid conflict with the authorities, Li seems to have worried little about the response his writings might evoke. *Zhuanfalun*, for example, teems with references to spirit possession, world destruction and re-creation, and alien interference in the affairs of mankind—in short, a multitude of references unlikely to please Communist authorities who were happy to back *qigong* as long as it appeared scientific (and of course, there is "science" in Li's writings as well). Nor could Li's depiction of himself as a god have pleased Chinese authorities, who were only too familiar with the dangers of cults like those that had surrounded the late Chairman Mao. Like other *qigong* masters, Li Hongzhi had the backstage support of important high officials, in this case, officials in the Bureau of Public Security. Perhaps Li felt that his contacts were important enough to protect him, perhaps he was naïve, perhaps arrogant, but in any event, his writings are relatively free of the ritual nods to Communist authorities that other masters were careful to make on a regular basis.

Another of Falun Gong's unique features was its propensity to react quickly and vigorously to perceived slights in media portrayals of Falun Gong, a practice that immediately became "political," since most media outlets in China are little more than mouthpieces for the regime. Sources hostile to Falun Gong cite evidence of more than three hundred such reactions, beginning in the summer of 1996, none of which were violent and all of which essentially demanded that incorrect information about Falun Gong be put right or that Falun Gong spokesmen be given equal time to rebut the charges.[15] Falun Gong practitioners now compare their protests to those of Gandhi or Martin Luther King Jr., but China has little tradition of civil rights demonstrations, and an action like that of surrounding the state-run Beijing television station, which Falun Gong practitioners did in May of 1998, was perceived as audacious if not seditious in the Chinese setting (Gandhi and King were similarly perceived in colonial India and in the American South). Falun Gong is not the only organization to take to the streets in post-Mao China; Chinese society in general has become much more openly contentious in the past twenty years, as peasants, workers, and other disgruntled citizens become increasingly willing to take their complaints to the barricades or to the courts. Still, as the charismatic leader of a mass movement commanding millions of followers, Li Hongzhi must have been either naïve in assuming that Falun Gong protests would not elicit an official reaction or arrogant in assuming that his personal power or the weight of his movement was enough to stay the hand of Chinese authorities.

In any event, Falun Gong's relationship with Chinese authorities became troubled fairly early, although other *qigong* groups went through similar periods of difficulty. Falun Gong parted company with the Chinese Qigong Scientific Research Association in the fall of 1994, although this organization had initially accepted and sponsored the Falun Gong. Li's exodus to the United States was yet another sign of the worsening of relations between his movement and Chinese authorities; reportedly, Li had heard rumors that Falun Gong had been compared by certain detractors to the Boxers (a group associated with popular anti-foreign uprisings in the early twentieth century) and had decided that he would be safer elsewhere. Indeed, while Falun Gong seemed to continue to thrive despite Li's absence from China, certain groups and individuals among the authorities continued their efforts to investigate and perhaps close down Falun Gong, efforts that were, more often than not, stymied by Falun Gong supporters among other high officials. The incidents of media "slander" that so angered Falun Gong practitioners were often part of this semiofficial campaign to undermine Falun Gong, and the encirclement of CCP headquarters in April 1999 by Falun Gong practitioners was the movement's response to such tactics, a continuation—in much more spectacular form—of what they had been doing since 1996.

Indeed, the events that immediately preceded April 25 and that constituted the spark that lit the fuse of the larger demonstration were completely in line with the history of Falun Gong reactions to perceived media misrepresentation. Practitioners took exception to an article published in an obscure Tianjin journal on April 11, 1999, and organized a demonstration in which some six thousand practitioners demanded redress. In response, local riot police beat demonstrators and arrested forty-five. Outraged practitioners were further informed that authority for such actions came from Beijing and that if they wanted to continue their protests, they should do so at the capital, located a short train ride away.

Falun Gong called the authorities' bluff. Li Hongzhi himself stopped over in Beijing on the eve of the massive demonstration, en route from the United States to a Falun Gong event in Sydney, Australia, and must surely have given his approval, though it's not known who did the actual organizing. Thousands of Falun Gong practitioners appeared outside Zhongnanhai in the early morning of April 25, waiting quietly and patiently for their demands (essentially, to be left alone to cultivate as they wished and without harassment) to be heard. According to many accounts, Premier Zhu Rongji did emerge from party headquarters and asked for representatives of the group to come inside and make known their demands, which they did. The rest of the crowd remained for some hours before dispersing peacefully, believing that a resolution had been reached.

President Jiang Zemin thought otherwise, however, and began that very evening to mobilize the state apparatus for a massive campaign against Falun Gong. In late May, police in Beijing were ordered to make a list of those who had participated in the demonstration; on June 6, hundreds were interrogated. On June 7, Jiang Zemin made a speech, identifying Falun Gong as "the most serious political conflict since 1989's student movement at Tiananmen Square." On June 10, Jiang authorized the establishment of what came to be called the 610 Office (named for the month and day of its establishment), whose sole mission was the suppression of Falun Gong. On July 20, police launched a nationwide campaign against Falun Gong, ransacking practitioners' homes and confiscating Falun Gong–related materials. On July 22, *Renmin ribao* [*People's Daily*] published an article titled "The Truth about Li Hongzhi," setting the tone for the campaign that was already under way. On July 28, Chinese authorities asked INTERPOL to cooperate in arresting Li Hongzhi and deporting him to China; INTERPOL refused. On October 25, Jiang Zemin gave a speech identifying Falun Gong as an "evil cult"; the speech was carried by all Chinese media on October 26. On October 30, the Standing Committee of the Chinese People's Congress passed legislation bearing the heading "Banning Evil Cults, as well as Preventing and Punishing the Activities of Evil Cults." On the same day, all major media outlets in China published a Supreme Court and Supreme People's Legislative Court document titled "An Explanation on How to Prosecute Criminal Activities of Evil Cults under Existing Law." At the same time that the Chinese state was putting together the legal framework for the prosecution of Falun Gong, the state propaganda machine was churning out hundreds of articles, books, and television reports against Falun Gong. The Chinese public had not witnessed such overkill since the heyday of the Cultural Revolution.

For students of Chinese politics, the campaign against Falun Gong was interesting in that it illustrated—sadly—that the Chinese state retained the capacity and the willpower to carry out such a massive mobilization, even in the context of the more "liberal" post-Mao era. And some of the themes sounded in the propaganda campaign against Falun Gong were interesting as well: for example, some commentators stressed, in a way they rarely had before, the positive contributions of normal institutional religion to the stability of life in socialist China. But the main importance of Jiang Zemin's campaign against Falun Gong has been, for Western observers, to illustrate just how far China still has to go to put its authoritarian past behind it. In other words, the campaign against Falun Gong tells us something about what is *not* new in today's China.

Falun Gong's reaction to the campaign was another story completely. China's leaders surely imagined that it would be relatively easy to bring the movement to its knees. After all, Falun Gong's leader was outside the country, and the movement was fairly decentralized—hardly a match for the "forces of order." But China's leaders were guilty of a serious miscalculation.

Within China, many Falun Gong practitioners simply could not believe what they now read about their cultivation practice in official Chinese government publications (which had, after all, largely supported Falun Gong until that point) and refused to accept the outlawing of the movement. Most believed that the Chinese authorities were uninformed and set out to educate them. They first sought out local officials, and on learning that the local officials were following orders from above, they then set their sights on the capital. Over the course of the fall of 1999 and throughout 2000, small groups of Falun Gong practitioners arrived in Beijing hoping to make an appeal to higher authorities, a right granted by China's constitution. When these appeals fell on deaf ears, the practitioners developed other approaches, including peaceful demonstrations in Tiananmen Square, individually or in groups, seeking in part to convince the public of the righteousness of their cause but also welcoming arrest, because the police were seen as part of the power structure they were hoping to reach.

The existence of a new Chinese diaspora of PRC immigrants in major cities throughout the Western world added a new and completely unexpected twist to the struggle. This was the audience Li Hongzhi had sought out after leaving China in 1995, and by 1999 there were thousands of well-educated, Chinese-speaking Falun Gong practitioners in North America, Europe, and Australia. To the intense dismay of Chinese authorities, these practitioners outside China began to bring pressure on the governments of their host countries to protest China's campaign against Falun Gong. In North America particularly, Falun Gong practitioners succeeded in creating considerable sympathy for the plight of their fellow practitioners in China, playing on the anti-Communist sentiment that continues to resonate in some parts of the continent, as well as on the claim that freedom of speech and freedom of religion are universal values that should be respected universally. The U.S. and Canadian political establishments called repeatedly on China to moderate its anti–Falun Gong campaign, all the while hoping that such criticisms would not harm their countries' commercial relations with China.

The embarrassment and frustration felt by Chinese authorities surely account for the increasingly brutal nature of the campaign within China. As practitioners continued to evade security controls and to reach the capital, central authorities pressured local authorities to increase their efforts, in some instances fining local public-security personnel for every Falun Gong practitioner who arrived in the capital. It is not surprising that local police responded in many instances with what can only be called a reign of terror against local practitioners.[16] Nor is it surprising that jails, detention centers, and labor camps came to be filled to overflowing with Falun Gong practitioners. In the fall of 1999, practitioners in North America began to track the anti–Falun Gong campaign in China and set up websites to disseminate the results of their findings worldwide.[17]

Li Hongzhi was largely silent in the months immediately following the crackdown, but when he reemerged in the fall of 2000, giving speeches as he always had at experience-sharing conferences, largely in North America, his tone had changed considerably. Li understandably felt compelled to explain the disaster that had befallen him and his followers, and he did so by highlighting the apocalyptic messages that, prior to April 1999, had been a relatively minor part of his discourse: the CCP's campaign against Falun Gong was now presented as part of a final "test" leading up to the destruction and renewal of the world. Those practitioners who passed the test—by remaining steadfast in their resolve—would remain part of the elite destined to survive the apocalypse, while those who crumbled in the face of pressure might not. Those who suffered or died for their beliefs, moreover, were offered the promise of instant "consummation" (or enlightenment). Li's speeches during this period are rather dense and lend themselves to different interpretations (Falun Gong practitioners in North America often met to discuss Li's speeches in the hopes of coming to a common understanding), but it seems clear that he encouraged those Falun Gong practitioners who chose martyrdom over prudence. If the Chinese authorities clearly lit the fire, Li Hongzhi just as clearly fanned the flames.

Such flames became all too deadly in 2001, when a number of Falun Gong practitioners apparently set themselves on fire in Tiananmen Square on January 23, resulting in five deaths. This incident remains highly disputed, Falun Gong practitioners and spokesman insisting that the event was staged by Chinese officials (who long refused, for example, to allow Western journalists to interview those who had survived their own attempted self-immolation, although it would seem that such interviews would have been a golden opportunity for China to illustrate that Falun Gong "drives people crazy").[18] Whatever the truth about the incident, it clearly marked an important public relations victory for the Chinese state *within China*, because many Chinese who had remained neutral to that point now came to share the authorities' view that Falun Gong was indeed a dangerous, heterodox sect. Falun Gong practitioners within China did not of course immediately cease their efforts to promote their cause, but my impression is that the fight became an increasingly uphill battle from this point forward. Still, as the wave of Chinese martyrs diminished, practitioners from abroad—both Chinese and foreign—began to make their way to Tiananmen Square, taking advantage of the protection afforded them as residents of foreign countries, and of their greater "journalistic value," to try to keep their cause in the headlines.

Today the campaign of resistance continues to smolder, despite China's public relations victory. Protestors continue to appear in Tiananmen Square and elsewhere. Falun Gong websites report that experience-sharing conferences continue to be held, if sporadically and secretly, within China. Practitioners have also continued their efforts to reveal the truth about their movement and its suppression to ordinary Chinese (who generally have access only to state-controlled media; China has invested millions in firewalls to keep China's rapidly growing cyberworld free of Falun Gong–related information). On a number of occasions, practitioners have broken into local cable-TV networks, or even into state-controlled satellite feeds, to broadcast their version of the story. Outside China, practitioners have continued to appear before international human rights tribunes and have used the courts to attempt to bring Chinese officials to justice. Chinese officials visiting the United States now plan their itineraries carefully to try to avoid being served with legal papers. One imagines that Jiang Zemin's retirement will eventually have an impact on the anti–Falun Gong campaign, because many commentators agree that he was personally responsible for the Chinese authorities' having resorted to such extreme measures. But there is little evidence that the standoff between Chinese authorities and Falun Gong resistance is moving toward resolution.

Li Hongzhi's own statements have become increasingly political and inflammatory, so that even if Chinese authorities were looking for a way to ratchet down hostilities, they could not do so without losing considerable face. To take only a few examples among many, Li began branding CCP authorities as "thugs" as early as 2001 but has broadened his rhetorical attacks to the point that virtually every problem in China is explained in such a manner. In a speech at an experience-sharing conference in Chicago in June 2003, he identified the criminal immorality of the CCP as the cause of the SARS (severe acute respiratory syndrome) virus—an extension from the individual to the political of his theory of karma. A very recent initiative is a

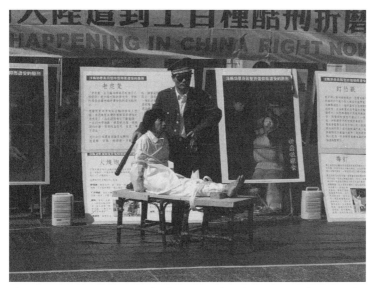

Figure 4.1. Reenactment of Falun Gong imprisonment and torture by the Chinese Public Security Bureau, International Human Rights Day, 2004, Chater Garden, Hong Kong. (Photo: Lionel M. Jensen)

newspaper (in both Web and print editions), the *Epoch Times*, which has clear if unidentified links with Falun Gong. Prominently featured in the *Epoch Times* is "Nine Commentaries on the Chinese Communist Party"—a blanket condemnation of the CCP (and of the Communist movement as a whole) and an invitation to party members to renounce their membership in light of the party's bleak and shameful history. According to the October 27, 2005, Web edition of the *Epoch Times*, 5,171,382 members had done just that. Whatever the value of such claims (and such numbers), it is difficult to treat seriously continued denials that Falun Gong is "not political." On the other hand, the fact that the leadership of Falun Gong is now undeniably political does not mean that the movement had political goals from the outset. Nor does it mean that politics is necessarily at the core of the experience of the average practitioner.

CONCLUSION

It is hard to decide what Falun Gong tells us about today's China. It would be tempting to interpret the *qigong* boom and the emergence of charismatic masters like Li Hongzhi as a grassroots, populist reaction to the failure of China's peasant revolution, a symbol perhaps of the kind of popular dissatisfaction that has brought down many a dynasty (often in the guise of peasant revolts that were fueled by popular religion). At the same time, we should bear in mind that *qigong* and Falun Gong were largely urban phenomena and appealed to members of the intellectual and political elite as well as to workers forced into early retirement. Falun Gong has also "boomed" in Taiwan (eliminating the failure of Mao's revolution as an explanation for the movement's popularity) and among well-educated and relatively privileged Chinese émigrés in North America, Europe, and Australia (most of whom, according to my surveys, discovered Falun Gong after leaving China). Like the new Japanese religious movement Soka Gakkai, Falun Gong has also reached out to foreigners—with some success. It may not be an exaggeration to say that Falun Gong represents the first Chinese religious movement in modern times to have achieved international status.

I find that I am ultimately uncomfortable with explanations of *qigong* and Falun Gong that insist on the "spiritual void" they are filling, as if such spiritual concerns would disappear once China became "normal." I personally do not find Li Hongzhi's teachings compelling, but one cannot spend time with Falun Gong practitioners without coming to appreciate their vitality and their ability to work together.

Indeed, even as Falun Gong recycled traditional beliefs and practices, it showed itself to be open to innovation and flexibility. Li Hongzhi built a nationwide then an international organization (something his "peasant forbearers" had not done), and his disciples pieced the structure together with sophisticated cybertools. Falun Gong activists in the West have not hesitated to make use of Enlightenment discourses on freedom of thought, conscience, and religious belief—arguments that protect and indeed champion the individual—even as their own spiritual beliefs call for the suppression of individual desires. It remains to be seen whether Voltaire and Buddha can make common cause on a long-term basis, but I would argue that Falun Gong practitioners in North America have done as much to advance the cause of civil society in China as have many U.S.-based Chinese democracy advocates. In any event, the effectiveness of the efforts of Falun Gong practitioners outside China to bring their concerns to the public highlights the existence and dynamism of this new Chinese diaspora, created since the 1980s, which is in the course of changing the image of China-towns and Chinese émigrés throughout the Western world. China beyond the headlines is also China beyond China's borders.

NOTES

1. *Falun Gong* might be translated as "the discipline of the law wheel," *fa,* or "law," being the Chinese translation of the Sanskrit term *dharma,* which arrived in China

with Buddhism early in the Christian era. *Law* should be understood as synonymous with *truth* or *way* and not in the sense of a legal code. The wheel is the revolving entity Li Hongzhi claims to install in the abdomens of practitioners so as to cleanse them. Falun Gong is also known as *Falun Dafa*, "the great way of the law wheel." The terms can be used interchangeably because their meanings are all but identical. Practitioners who wish to insist on the difference between Falun Gong and other schools of *qigong* (see below) may use the term *Falun Dafa* because it does not contain the character *gong*.

2. The Center for Studies on New Religions (CESNUR) maintains a very useful compilation of reports on Falun Gong published in major English-language newspapers and magazines throughout the world. See "Texts and Documents" and "New Religious Movements, Case Studies," www.cesnur.org.

3. See David Ownby, "The Heaven and Earth Society as Popular Religion," *Journal of Asian Studies* 54, no. 4 (1995): 1023–46; David Ownby, *Brotherhoods and Secret Societies in Early and Mid-Qing China* (Stanford, CA: Stanford University Press, 1996); David Ownby and Qiao Peihua, eds. and trans., "Scriptures of the Way of the Temple of the Heavenly Immortals," *Chinese Studies in History* 29, no. 4 (1996): 1–101; David Ownby, "Chinese Millenarian Traditions: The Formative Age," *American Historical Review* 104, no. 5 (1999): 1513–30; and David Ownby, "Imperial Fantasies: Chinese Communists and Peasant Rebellions," *Comparative Studies in Society and History* 43, no. 2 (1999): 65–91.

4. Li Hongzhi's writings are readily available on the Internet at www.falundafa .org.

5. The best single-volume treatment of *qigong* is David Palmer, "'La fievre du *qigong*': Guérison, religion et politique en Chine contemporaine" (PhD dissertation, École Pratique des Hautes Études, 2002). Palmer is translating his work for English publication. See also Nancy N. Chen, *Breathing Spaces: Qigong, Psychiatry, and Healing in China* (New York: Columbia University Press, 2003); Zhu Xiaoyang and Benjamin Penny, eds., "The Qigong Boom," *Chinese Sociology and Anthropology* 27, no. 1 (Fall 1994): 1–94; Kunio Miura, "The Revival of Qi: Qigong in Contemporary China," in *Taoist Meditation and Longevity Techniques*, ed. Livia Kohn (Ann Arbor: University of Michigan Press, 1989), 331–58; and Xu Jian, "Body, Discourse, and the Cultural Politics of Contemporary Chinese Qigong," *Journal of Asian Studies* 58, no. 4 (1999): 961–91.

6. This general theme is explored in Ian Johnson's delightful *Wild Grass: Three Stories of Change in Modern China* (New York: Pantheon, 2003). His third story is that of Falun Gong.

7. On the invention of *qigong*, see Palmer, "*La fievre du qigong*," pt. 1, ch. 1.

8. On the *qigong* boom, see Zhu and Penny, "The Qigong Boom"; and Palmer, "*La fievre du qigong*," pt. 2, chs. 2–7.

9. Guo Lin is discussed in Palmer, "*La fievre du qigong*," pt. 2, ch. 2.

10. These experiments are discussed in Palmer, "*La fievre du qigong*," pt. 2, ch. 2.

11. See Palmer, "*La fievre du qigong*," pt. 2, ch. 4.

12. See Palmer, "*La fievre du qigong*," pt. 2, ch. 3.

13. Like Li Hongzhi, Yan Xin now spends most of his time in the United States and has set up a similar network of practice centers and websites. See www .yanxinqigong.net.

14. See Li Hongzhi, *China Falun Gong* (New York: Universe Publishing, 1999), which illustrates the exercises.

15. See Tan Songqiu, Qin Baoqi, and Kong Xiangtao, *Falungong yu minjian mimi jieshe: Xiejiao Falungong neimu de da jiemi* [*Falun Gong and popular secret societies: Exposing the inner secrets of the Falun Gong cult*] (Fuzhou, China: Fujian renmin chubanshe, 1999), 93.

16. Ian Johnson provides a compelling account of this reign of terror in his *Wild Grass*. See particularly pp. 276–92.

17. See for example www.faluninfo.net and www.upholdjustice.org. These websites are set up and maintained by Falun Gong practitioners and thus are not "objective." However, human rights workers with whom I have spoken about these sites and the information provided on them have assured me that they generally accept the validity of the information. One China specialist told me that she had "never found anything in Falun Gong publications that was verifiably false."

18. See www.clearwisdom.net, "Staged Tiananmen Self-Immolation," for Falun Gong's analysis of the immolation.

SUGGESTED READINGS

Nancy Chen, "Urban Experiences and the Practice of Qigong," in *Urban Spaces in Contemporary China*, ed. Deborah Davis, Richard Krauss, Barry Naughton, and Elizabeth Perry (Washington, D.C.: Woodrow Wilson Center, 1995).

"The Effect of Falun Gong on Healing Illnesses and Keeping Fit: A Sampling Survey of Practitioners from Beijing Zizhuyuan Assistance Center" (Beijing, 1998), www.falundafa-pa.net/survey/survey98-2_e.pdf.

David Eisenberg, *Encounters with Qi: Explaining Chinese Medicine* (New York: W. W. Norton, 1985).

"Fitness and Health through Qigong," *Beijing Review*, 32, no. 17 (April 1989).

Barend ter Haar, "Falun Gong: Evaluation and Further References," www.let.leidenuniv.nl/bth/falun.htm.

———, *The White Lotus Teachings in Chinese Religious History* (repr., Honolulu: University of Hawaii Press, 1999).

Human Rights Watch, *Dangerous Meditation: China's Campaign against Falun Gong* (New York: Human Rights Watch, 2002).

Human Rights Watch and the Geneva Initiative on Psychiatry, *Dangerous Minds: Political Psychiatry in China Today and Its Origins in the Mao Era* (New York: Human Rights Watch, 2002).

Kang Xiaoguang, *Falun gong shibian quantoushi* [*A comprehensive view of the Falun Gong incident*] (Hong Kong: Minbao chubanshe, 2000).

Li Hongzhi, *China Falun Gong* (New York: Universe Publishing, 1999).

———, *Zhuan Falun: The Complete Teachings of Falun Gong* (Gloucester, MA: Fair Winds Press, 2001).

———, "Fa-Lecture during the 2003 Lantern Festival at the U.S. West Fa Conference." Lecture given February 15, 2003, www.clearwisdom.net/emh/articles/2003/2/27/32713.html.

———, "Teaching Fa at the 2003 Midwest-U.S. Fa Conference." Lecture given in Chicago, Illinois, June 22, 2003, www.clearwisdom.net/emh/articles/2003/7/8/37905.html.

Nova Religio 6, no. 2 (April 2003). This issue is devoted entirely to Falun Gong.

David Ownby, "Falun Gong as a Cultural Revitalization Movement: An Historian Looks at Contemporary China." Lecture given at Rice University, Houston, TX, October 20, 2000, www.ruf.rice.edu/~tnchina/commentary/ownby1000.html.

———, "The Falun Gong in the New World." *European Journal of East Asian Studies* 2, no. 2 (2003): 303–20.

———, *Falun Gong and China's Future* (Lanham, MD: Rowman & Littlefield, 2007).

David Palmer, *Qigong Fever: Body, Science, and the Politics of Religion in China, 1949–1999* (London: Hurst, 1996).

Benjamin Penny, "Falun Gong: Prophecy and Apocalypse," *East Asian History* 23 (June 2002).

———, "The Life and Times of Li Hongzhi: Falun Gong and Religious Biography," *China Quarterly* 175 (2003): 643–61.

Elizabeth J. Perry, *Challenging the Mandate of Heaven: Social Protest and State Power in China* (Armonk, NY: M. E. Sharpe, 2002).

Danny Schechter, *Falun Gong's Challenge to China* (New York: Akashic, 2000).

James Tong, "An Organizational Analysis of the Falun Gong: Structure, Communications, Financing," *China Quarterly* 171 (2002): 636–60.

John Wong and William T. Liu, *The Mystery of China's Falun Gong: Its Rise and Its Sociological Implications* (Singapore: World Scientific, 1999).

Zhu Xiaoyang and Benjamin Penny, "The Qigong Boom," *Chinese Sociology and Anthropology* 27, no. 1 (Fall 1994).

5

Narratives to Live By

The Century of Humiliation and Chinese National Identity Today

Peter Hays Gries

In August 2004 during the Asian Cup held in China, Chinese soccer fans in Chongqing and Jinan hurled insults at the Japanese team and even besieged their bus. Japanese opinion was outraged, and Prime Minister Junichiro Koizumi publicly called on Chinese fans to shape up. During the cup final in Beijing, Chinese authorities sought both to coerce and to cajole Chinese fans into better behavior. A heavy police presence was stationed both inside and outside Workers Stadium, and entering fans were forced to run a gauntlet between two lines of officers in body armor and riot gear. Inside, the scoreboard flashed the message "Be Civilized Spectators! Show a Civilized Demeanor!" Neither intimidation nor persuasion appeared to have much effect, however, as Chinese fans repeatedly chanted, "Kill! Kill! Kill!" and "May a big sword decapitate the Japanese!" during the game. After the 3–1 loss, Chinese fans pelted the Japanese team bus with bottles.[1]

Eight months later, tens of thousands of young Chinese took to the streets in cities as diverse as Beijing, Guangzhou, Shanghai, and Shenzhen for three successive weekends of anti-Japanese demonstrations, which were precipitated by the publication of a Japanese history textbook that downplayed Japanese atrocities in China during World War II. On April 16, 2005, for instance, thousands of college students and young professionals protested in downtown Shanghai with banners expressing their grievances: "Oppose Japanese Imperialism!" "Oppose Japan Entering the Security Council!" "Boycott Japanese Goods, Revitalize China!" "Oppose Japan's History Textbooks!" "Protect Our Diaoyu Islands!" On their march to the Japanese consulate, the protestors smashed the windows of Japanese stores and restaurants, overturned Japanese cars, and burned Japanese flags and photos, as well as placards of Koizumi. When they arrived at the consulate, they hurled eggs and pelted it with paint bombs.

How should such virulent, anti-Japanese sentiment be understood? Western analysts tend to dismiss Chinese nationalism as mere party propaganda: a top-down attempt by the CCP to bolster its nationalist credentials through appeals to Chinese victimization. This chapter, in contrast, argues that much nationalism in China today is a genuinely popular, bottom-up phenomenon and that it has its origins in contested narratives about China's past encounters with Japanese and Western imperialism. Seeking to read beyond the headlines, I argue that Chinese national identity at the dawn of the twenty-first century cannot be understood apart from evolving and contested narratives of China's national past.

Specifically, recent expressions of anti-Japanese and anti-Western sentiment in China must be understood in the context of Chinese stories about the Century of Humiliation, lasting from the mid-nineteenth to the mid-twentieth century, a period that begins with China's defeat in the First Opium War and the ceding of Hong Kong to the British in 1842. When the Century ends, as we shall see, is less clear. Major wars in the period include the two Opium Wars (1840–1842; 1856–1860), the Sino-Japanese "Jiawu" War (1894–1895), the Boxer Rebellion (1900), the War of Resistance against Japan (1931/1937–1945),[2] and (for some) the Korean War (1950–1953).

THE PAST IN THE PRESENT

What impact does this Century of Humiliation have on Chinese nationalism today? More broadly, what is the relationship between past and present-day nationalisms around the world?

One common view holds that the past determines the present. For instance, the Kosovo war (1999) was frequently depicted as "intractable" because of Muslim-Christian enmity dating back to the Battle of Kosovo in 1389 (610 years earlier!), when Muslim Turks defeated the Christian kingdom of Serbia. In this view, Muslim-Christian conflict today is predetermined by past conflict.

Such *pastism* is also prevalent in studies of China. Alarmist predictions of a "China threat" almost invariably locate that threat's origins in Chinese anger at China's early victimization at the hands of Western imperialists. Nineteenth- and twentieth-century humiliations like the Opium Wars and the Rape of Nanjing, in this view, predetermine Chinese revisionism in the twenty-first century.

Another widespread view maintains precisely the opposite: it is historians and nationalists writing in the present that determine the past. Eric Hobsbawm has argued that national histories are "invented"; nationalist historians render complex pasts into Manichean histories, pitting a good "us" against an evil "them." As Elie Kedourie noted over forty years ago, "Nationalists make use of the past in order to subvert the present."[3] In this view, it is not the Battle of Kosovo itself that has causal weight. Instead, it was the skillful manipulation of the battle by present-day nationalists like Slobodan Milosevic (1941–2006) that best explained the Kosovo conflict.

This *presentism* is also prevalent in contemporary studies of China. Following in Hobsbawm's footsteps, China scholars have largely stressed how Chinese historians invent histories and traditions to serve contemporary ends. Cultural critic Geremie Barmé goes so far as to assert that "every policy shift in recent Chinese history has involved the rehabilitation, re-evaluation and revision of history and historical figures." In his fascinating study of the Boxer Rebellion, historian Paul Cohen similarly highlights Chinese historians who "draw on [the past] to serve the political, ideological, rhetorical, and/or emotional needs of the present." In 1990, for example, *Renmin ribao* [*People's Daily*] sought to combat post–Tiananmen massacre Western sanctions and garner popular nationalist support by commemorating the ninetieth anniversary of the Boxer Rebellion, with articles describing the brutality of the foreign armies that marched on Beijing in 1900.[4]

While there is little doubt that China's rulers have long used the past to serve the present, such presentist approaches often inadvertently downplay the weight of the past in shaping contemporary Chinese nationalism. On the other hand, the determinism of pastist approaches leaves little room for human agency and freewill. Both presentism and pastism thus hobble our capacity to understand the complex interplay of past and present in nationalist practice today.

The concept of *national narratives* can help us overcome this dualism to better understand the role of the past in nationalist politics. Narratives are the stories that we tell about our past. These stories, both personality psychologists and sociologists have argued, infuse our identity with unity, meaning, and purpose.[5] We cannot, therefore, radically change them at will. The idea of "national narratives" applies these ideas about the importance of narratives of the past to present-day identities to one particular social identity: national identity, that aspect of an individual's self-concept that derives from his or her perceived membership in a national group.[6] Nationalism is here understood as a commitment to protect and enhance national identity.

This chapter explores the role that contending narratives about a national past play in the evolution of Chinese national identity today. It begins with the recent rewriting of the Century of Humiliation: the late 1990s reemergence of a *victim narrative* to challenge the Maoist *victor narrative*. It then turns to more-detailed case studies of the endurance of the Mao-era victor narrative in Chinese writings about the Korean War and of the prevalence of the new victim narrative in recent anti-Japanese discourse and practice. Insecurity about growing American power may explain why writings about the United States have clung to the victor narrative, while increasing confidence about a rapidly developing China's ability to take on Japan may explain why popular nationalists in China have embraced a victim narrative about China's past conflicts with Japan. Both state, or official, nationalist propagandists and popular, or mass, nationalists participate in this debate, with the latter leading the way in developing the new victimization storyline. These contending Chinese histories, which often show up in the Chinese headlines, reveal a great deal about what it means to be "Chinese" today.

DEBATING THE CENTURY

Narratives about the Century of Humiliation frame the ways that many Chinese understand themselves today. Most educated, twenty-first-century Chinese are painfully aware of the unequal treaties China signed with the British in 1842 and the Japanese in 1895 (and with other countries during the same period). Unilateral concessions forced on the Chinese such as indemnities, extra-territoriality, and foreign settlements in treaty ports are still perceived as humiliating losses of sovereignty. Other resonant symbols of the period include the ruins of the Old Summer Palace and heroes like Lin Zexu (1785–1850). The stone ruins of the Old Summer Palace outside Beijing, which are all that were left after the palace was looted and burned by Europeans in 1860, are a recurring symbol of this "rape" of China. Lin Zexu, a famous Chinese crusader against opium and British aggression, stands for Chinese courage and virtue.

This Century of Humiliation, I contend, is neither an objective past that works insidiously on the present (pastism) nor a mere invention of present-day nationalist entrepreneurs (presentism). Past and present, instead, exist here in an interactive relationship: they are mutually constituted through constant dialogue about their relationship to one another. The Century is a continuously reworked narrative about China's national past central to the contested and evolving meaning of being "Chinese" today.

The Century, furthermore, is a traumatic and foundational moment because it fundamentally decentered Chinese views of the world. In many Chinese eyes, earlier invaders were Sinicized, and barbarians beyond the border paid humble tribute to "civilization," reinforcing a Sinocentric view of Chinese civilization as universal and superior. "Our ancient neighbors," wrote one young Chinese nationalist in 1996, "found glory in drawing close to Chinese civilization."[7]

China's violent, nineteenth-century encounter with the West was different. The "Western devils" had a civilization of their own that challenged the perceived universality and superiority of Confucian civilization. This traumatic confrontation between East and West fundamentally destabilized Chinese views of the world and China's place within it. "Trauma brings about a lapse or rupture in memory that breaks continuity with the past," writes historian Dominick LaCapra in a discussion of the Holocaust. "It unsettles narcissistic investments and desired self-images."[8] Just as the trauma of the Holocaust led many in the postwar West to question their Enlightenment tradition, the Century has threatened a Chinese identity based upon the idea of a universal and superior civilization. "The Israelis' vision of the Holocaust has shaped their idea of themselves," Tom Segev writes, "just as their changing sense of self has altered their view of the Holocaust and their understanding of its meaning."[9] The same is true of the Chinese and the Century of Humiliation: Chinese visions of the Century have shaped the Chinese sense of self, and this changing self-concept has altered the Chinese view of the Century. Past and present, in other words, exist in a dialectical relationship in which stories about the past both constrain and enable Chinese national identity in the present.

Today, Chinese struggles to come to terms with their traumatic encounter with imperialism are reflected in the emergence of new narratives about the Century. Under Mao, China's modern sufferings were blamed on the feudalism of the Qing dynasty and Western imperialism, and the Maoist account of the Century highlighted the heroism of the anti-feudal, anti-imperialist masses in throwing off their chains and repelling foreign invaders. This victor narrative first served the mobilizational requirements of Communist revolutionaries in the 1930s and 1940s and later the nation-building goals of the PRC in the 1950s, 1960s, and 1970s. New China needed heroes. The title of a 1959 movie about the First Opium War, for instance, was changed from *The Opium War* to *Lin Zexu* (Lin Zexu being the official who is depicted as leading the Chinese resistance against the British) to glorify Chinese heroism.

Over the past decade, however, the Maoist victor narrative has been slowly joined by a victim narrative that blames the West, here including Japan, for China's suffering. Suffering a legitimacy deficit following the Tiananmen massacre in 1989 and the collapse of Communism in the Soviet Union and Eastern Europe, the CCP undertook a Patriotic Education Campaign in the early 1990s. The CCP's own need for nationalism thus created political space for the emergence of popular nationalists. Even more importantly, after almost two decades of "reform and opening," the late-1990s Chinese experienced an unprecedented degree of economic, social, and cultural freedom that many—especially young professionals living in the cities—used to challenge the Maoist victor orthodoxy.

This recent interest in past suffering is actually a renewal of the focus on victimization in pre-Mao, republican-era (1912–1949) writings on the Century.[10] Symptomatic of this shift, the trope of China as a raped woman has reemerged after a Mao-era respite. In republican China, playwrights like Xiao Jun wrote about rape in nationalist plays such as *Village in August*.[11] The rape-of-China theme faded after the Communist victory in 1949, because the Maoist arts stressed heroic victories. Today, rape is back. Chinese-American Iris Chang's 1997 bestseller, *The Rape of Nanking*, which had a major impact on Chinese nationalists, has recently contributed to the transformation of the 1937 massacre into a rape.

Indeed, 1997 was a pivotal year in the reemergence of the Chinese victim narrative. The countdown to Hong Kong's "return to the Motherland" from Britain in the spring and summer of 1997 created a strong desire to "wipe away national humiliation." And in the fall of 1997, sixtieth-anniversary commemorations of the Nanjing Massacre and the Iris Chang sensation directed Chinese attention to their past suffering as never before. Anticipating closure on this humiliation, many Chinese paradoxically reopened a long festering wound. For many Chinese nationalists, this painful encounter with past trauma was expressed in the language of victimization.

China in 1997 may thus prove comparable to Israel in 1961, when Adolf Eichmann's trial precipitated a dramatic shift in Israeli attitudes toward the Holocaust. The repression of Holocaust memories in the name of nation-building (creating a "New Israel") that prevailed in the late 1940s and 1950s gave way to a new identification with victimization in the 1960s. The early postwar Israeli rejection of victimization is reflected in the evolution of Holocaust Day, which was established only in 1953 and became a mandatory national holiday in 1959. Holocaust Day commemorations in the 1950s, furthermore, generally emphasized the "martyrs and heroes" of the ghetto resistance—not the victims of the concentration camps, who would be highlighted in later tributes.[12] China is now undergoing a similar process, as long-suppressed memories of past suffering are resurfacing, and victor narratives of resistance are being challenged by more somber narratives of suffering.

The victor narrative about the Century has not disappeared, however. China-as-victor and China-as-victim narratives coexist in Chinese nationalist discourse today. The publisher's preface to a series of books titled "Do Not Forget the History of National Humiliation" is typical, describing the Century as both a "history of the struggle of the *indomitable* Chinese people against imperialism" and a "tragic history of suffering, beatings, and extraordinary *humiliations* [italics mine]."[13] Many Chinese nationalists, it seems, are eager to capitalize on the moral authority of their past suffering. But there is a downside to the victim narrative: it entails confronting vulnerability and weakness. The enduring need for heroism and a victor narrative serves, it appears, to allay the fears of those who are not yet ready to directly confront the trauma of the Century of Humiliation.

Evolving and contested narratives about the Century of Humiliation, in sum, both reflect and powerfully shape Chinese understandings of what it means to be Chinese today. Because these narratives invoke the people (e.g., Lin Zexu), events (wars, unequal treaties) and symbols (the Summer Palace ruins) of China's modern encounter with Western imperialism, the Chinese continually return to the unresolved trauma of the Century, hoping to master it.

"VICTORY" IN KOREA: HEROISM IN U.S.-CHINA RELATIONS

As Chinese nationalists tell stories about China's past encounters with the United States, they redefine their sense of self. This is particularly evident in recent Chinese writings about the Korean War, which construct a victorious vision of China. To many Chinese, Korea marks the end of the Century of Humiliation and the birth of New China. The perception of victory in Korea is thus central to the self-esteem and self-confidence of many Chinese nationalists today.

Several of the Chinese narratives about Korea to be examined here were written during the Taiwan Straits Crisis (1996), when many Chinese acquired the self-confidence to take on and defeat the United States. Pride and confidence are both positive self-evaluations, differing only in their time frame: pride is directed toward the past, while confidence is directed at the future. Psychologists have demonstrated that when we are proud of our accomplishments, we not only feel good about ourselves, we also gain confidence.[14] Chinese nationalists today similarly draw on proud narratives of past "victories" over the United States in Korea and elsewhere to create the confidence necessary for possible future Sino-American conflicts.

Telling proud stories about past events to bolster confidence in an uncertain future is decidedly not uniquely Chinese. In 2001, U.S. media coverage of September 11 was notable for a relative absence of images of victimization and suffering, such as images widely shown abroad of people who were forced to jump out of the burning towers to their deaths. The U.S. media focused, instead, on symbols of U.S. courage and heroism, such as the New York City Fire Department, New York City mayor Rudolph Giuliani, and the passengers of United Airlines flight 93, who resisted the terrorists and brought down their plane in Pennsylvania before it could hit the White House. Shanghai avant-garde artist Zhou Tiehai's 2002 painting of Giuliani evoked the hero worship reflected in the post–September 11 U.S. media, implicitly comparing it to the Mao worship of China's Cultural Revolution. Americans, it seems, did not wish to dwell on their victimization; they desired, instead, stories of resistance and victory. Similarly, in

2004 the U.S. government was found to be censoring photos of the coffins of dead soldiers being returned from Iraq. Confronting an uncertain war against terrorism, the United States needed heroes, not images of more fallen Americans.

When did China's Century of Humiliation end? Official Chinese sources frequently declare that it ended in 1945, with Chinese participation in the Allied victory over Japan. Many Chinese, however, are haunted by the belief that Japanese and Westerners do not acknowledge China's victor status in World War II, assigning victory instead to the United States and the atomic bombs dropped on Hiroshima and Nagasaki. Victory over the Japanese, seen by many Chinese as "lowly," in any case, is not very gratifying for those Chinese who maintain a Sinocentric view of Asia.

Official sources also declare that the Communist victory in 1949 marked the end of the Century. The civil war between the Communists and Chiang Kai-shek's Nationalist Party was over, foreign influence had been driven from the mainland, and, from an ideological perspective, socialism had defeated capitalism. According to Mao Zedong, "The Chinese people have stood up." To many Chinese, however, China's victories in 1949 were incomplete and unsatisfying. Taiwan and Hong Kong were yet to be returned to Chinese control; the country was not united. And although the United States had backed the Nationalists, the Communist victory over them was not particularly glorious. There was nothing unprecedented about Chinese killing Chinese.

Victory over the United States, however, could be construed as something special. Mao's need to disparage the United States as a "paper tiger" revealed an anxiety about American power—an anxiety that persists today. *The Sino-American Contest* (1996), written by members of a Chinese State Security Bureau think tank, refers to the American military of the 1950s as the "world's number one military power" and asserts that the Chinese people, "relying on their own strength," defeated it.[15] Defeating the champ, it seems, made China the new champion. This argument, notably, completely dismisses North Korean contributions to the Korean War. Chinese nationalism dictates that China win on its own.

Pride in this perceived Chinese victory over the United States can be an important psychological resource that builds self-confidence when tensions with the United States rise. In 1990 the Beijing elite, facing United States–led international sanctions following the Tiananmen massacre, capitalized on the fortieth-anniversary commemorations of the onset of the Korean War to bolster their self-confidence, issuing a barrage of nationalist articles and books on Korea. The role of Korea as a psychological resource is often explicit. In his preface to *A Paean to the War to Resist America and Aid Korea*, for instance, veteran Yang Dezhi is blunt: "The psychological riches that the war has left me are precious. I am confident that China will prosper."[16]

In 1996, following the deployment of two U.S. aircraft carriers near Taiwan, both state and popular nationalists also used the "victory" in Korea to revive what appears to have been a shaken confidence about conflict with the United States. Premier Li Peng warned that if the United States "uses force against China, the outcome has already been proven by past experience." In his preface to *The Sino-American Contest*, former PRC ambassador to the United States Chai Zemin issued a stern warning to the United States: "Do not to forget history." American behavior during the Taiwan Strait Crisis (1996), when the United States sent an aircraft carrier to Taiwan following People's Liberation Army (PLA) missile exercises directed at Taiwan, was to the Chinese "insufferably arrogant and bossy." The political commissar of the Chengdu military region similarly evoked both Korea and Vietnam: "China has dealt with the U.S. on more than one or two occasions. What was the outcome? The United Sates was defeated on every occasion."[17] By evoking glorious "victories" over the United States in the past, these Chinese officials sought to raise confidence that they could deploy to meet present-day challenges.

Unlike the 1990 fortieth-anniversary commemorations of the Korean War, when official nationalism largely fell on deaf ears, popular nationalists did respond to official appeals following the Taiwan Strait Crisis. As did Li Peng and Chai Zemin, they also alluded to Korea to bolster their self-confidence. The cover of the first issue of *Shenzhen Panorama Weekly*, for instance, was a photograph of a Korean War veteran sternly waving his finger. It was accompanied by a large caption, warning: "We have squared off before." In other words, we'll beat you again if we need to. In their 1996 *Surpassing the USA*, popular nationalists Xi Yongjun and Ma Zaizhun explicitly link pride in past victories to confidence in the future: "On the Taiwan question, Americans have forgotten the enormous losses they bitterly suffered on the Korean battlefield and in . . . Vietnam . . . China is strengthening, and the myth of American invincibility has already been shattered."[18]

In the United States by contrast, Korea is often referred to as the "Forgotten War." Although United States–led UN forces successfully repelled an invading North Korean army and saved South Korea, Americans look back on the war not as an unqualified victory but with ambivalence. As the movie and to a lesser extent the subsequent popular television series *M*A*S*H* suggest, many Americans view the war as a dark and senseless tragedy. Indeed, a Korean War Veterans Memorial was dedicated in Washington, D.C., only in 1995. And its somber statues of soldiers slogging through the rain in Korea evoke not glory but the tremendous human cost of war.

There is no equivalent of *M*A*S*H* in China today. Korea was a victory, pure and simple—even though the war was in many ways a disaster for the PRC. Over a million Chinese died—more than ten times the number of UN forces that perished—and the United States by intervening in the Taiwan

Strait reversed its earlier policy, thereby thwarting Communist desires to re-unify China. Yet there is not the slightest hint of ambivalence in China to-day about Korea. "Victory" in Korea continues to be central to how many Chinese understand themselves and their role in the twenty-first century.

THE RAPE OF NANJING: VICTIMIZATION IN SINO-JAPANESE RELATIONS

War is at once the graveyard of peoples and the birthplace of nations. Most nations are born out of the ashes of war; indeed, nations define themselves through conflict with other nations. Stories about the Second World War continue to drive Chinese views of Japan and—more to the point—of themselves. For the first three decades of the PRC under Mao, China's self-image, aggressively projected to the world, was that of a victor. Today, how-ever, most Chinese have come to think about the Second World War in less glorious terms. At the beginning of the twenty-first century, many Chinese focus less on China's heroic resistance during the war and more on Chinese victimization.[19] Symptomatic of this shift is the trope of wartime China as a raped woman, first utilized by nationalist writers during the 1930s but suppressed under Mao, and which is now resurgent.

Why have so many Chinese today come to think about themselves as vic-tims? I ask this question not to cast doubt upon the undeniable suffering of the Chinese people during the Second World War but to better understand the evolution of Chinese national identity today. Public debates between Chinese and Japanese over past wars are not just about the past; they are primarily about what it means to be Chinese or Japanese in the twenty-first century. For many Chinese, painful memories of past trauma have clearly generated a deep anger toward Japan. Few have moved beyond what soci-ologist Thomas Scheff calls "humiliated fury."[20] Japan bashing in China is ascendant and unquestioned.

For instance, during the April 2005 anti-Japanese protests mentioned above, protestors carried defaced images of Japan's prime minister Junichiro Koizumi. One protestor gave him a mustache to make him look like Adolph Hitler. Others went farther, painting a pig's snout and ears onto his face and declaring, "Death to Koizumi the pig!" But the most ominous im-ages evoked a dead Koizumi, with tombstones bearing his name and a photo of a funeral with Koizumi's picture at the center.

Koizumi was also a frequent target of China's cyber-nationalists. Lin Zhibo of the *People's Daily* sought to dehumanize Koizumi on *People's Net* online, comparing him to a dog. Lin cited Koizumi's statement, made while visiting U.S. president George W. Bush at Bush's Crawford, Texas, ranch in 2003, that "If China will not compromise on the Diaoyu Islands issue,

Japan will make China regret it." Lin's reaction was fierce: "These are the threats of a thief or a hoodlum. Spoken at his master's ranch . . . They are like a dog barking and biting."[21] Whether depicting Koizumi as a pig or a dog, such nationalist discourse dehumanized Koizumi and Japan, thus laying the psychological foundation for violence.

Why did Koizumi in particular become the focus of so much Chinese nationalist ire? Part of the answer clearly lies in the realm of power politics: China and Japan are competing for position in the evolving East Asian security order. By refusing to abjectly apologize to China over the Second World War and accept a subordinate status, Koizumi threatened Chinese nationalist visions of China's rise and a Sinocentric East Asia.

But the passion of these anti-Japanese protestors and cyber-nationalists still requires explanation. They are clearly motivated by something more than the instrumental pursuit of China's national interest. I suggest that the reason Prime Minister Koizumi evoked so much hatred was that his regular visits to Yasakuni Shrine, where Japan's war dead are honored, challenged the new Chinese victim narrative about the war. In this Chinese view, Koizumi sought to mitigate Japan's responsibility for World War II. This represented a direct threat to the vision of China as a victim to unmitigated Japan aggression in the war. And because narratives about the past implicate identities in the present, many Chinese and Japanese have become locked into a zero-sum existential conflict that will be difficult to resolve. These identities tend to be absolute, and there is little room for compromise on either side. Sino-Japanese relations in the first decades of the twenty-first century, therefore, are likely to remain rocky at best.

CHINESE NATIONAL IDENTITY IN AN UNCERTAIN WORLD

In October 2005, following the success of China's second manned spaceflight, *Shenzhou VI*, the *People's Daily* declared in a front-page editorial that "the sons and daughters of China all feel an incomparable pride and self-worth." China's official Xinhua News Agency added, "At this moment, history is returning dignity and sanctity to the Chinese nation."[22] The official press declared astronauts Fei Junlong and Nie Haisheng national heroes.

China's propagandists were not alone. The dominant feeling expressed on the Chinese Internet was unquestionably one of pride and joy. Sina.com, China's largest Internet portal, constructed massive sites in both English and Chinese to celebrate the successful mission. Anger could often be found simmering just below the surface, however. As one Sina.com netizen wrote in a poem, "Oh Motherland,"

Remember the . . .
hateful actions of the Western nations and the Eight Nation Force [of 1900] . . .
and the heinous crimes the little Japs committed on our women and children . . .
Who would have thought that a nation that was once beaten is now finally so
strong?
America couldn't imagine it, England couldn't imagine it, and certainly little
bitty Japan couldn't imagine it.[23]

The Century of Humiliation clearly lives on in today's China. The victory in
1945 over "lowly Jap devils" did not satisfy. Although Mao declared, "The
Chinese people have stood up," victory in 1949 over the Nationalist Party
in the civil war and the declaration of "liberation" did not gratify either.
"Victory" over the "American imperialists" in early 1950s Korea, as we have
seen, is a more satisfying story. Yet the anger expressed by many Chinese netizens following the successful *Shenzhou VI* space mission suggests that feelings of humiliation live on.

The past does not, however, predetermine Chinese aggression in the present. Nor is it a mere tool in the hands of present-day Chinese nationalists.
I have argued that the Century of Humiliation is a continually contested
narrative of the past central to the evolution of the very meaning of being
Chinese today. This contest, I have suggested, revolves around two competing narratives. The Mao-era victor narrative highlights the heroism of
China's anti-feudal and anti-imperialist masses during China's CCP-led nationalist triumph. Meanwhile, the past decade has witnessed the reemergence of a victim narrative, directing Chinese attention at past sufferings at
the hands of Western and especially Japanese imperialists. While these two
narratives coexist in current nationalist discourse, there appears to be a distinct empirical pattern: the victor narrative remains more prevalent in nationalist accounts of Sino-American relations, while the victim narrative is
more prevalent in writings about Japan.

What accounts for this difference? One explanation might center upon
the past itself: objectively speaking, the Chinese have suffered more at the
hands of the Japanese than at the hands of the United States. Indeed, many
more Chinese died in the Second World War than in the Korean War.

But the past does not speak for itself. The stories that we choose to tell
about our past reflect our understanding of who we are in the present. I
therefore suggest an alternative explanation: past wars with Japan and the
United States hold very different meanings for Chinese today. The Rape
of Nanjing and other Second World War atrocities must be understood in
the context of a centuries-old Chinese view of the Japanese as subordinate within a Sinocentric world order. Japanese aggression is thus seen as
the treachery of an ungrateful younger brother beating up his older
brother. While Chinese anger at Japan today undeniably has a visceral

component stemming from the brutality of atrocities like the Rape of Nanjing, it also has a higher, or ethical, dimension tied to strong feelings of injustice. Victimization at the hands of "little brother" Japan thus has had profound implications for Chinese understandings of themselves and their place in twenty-first-century East Asia.

Past conflicts with the United States are understood in a very different manner. Although well over ten times as many Chinese as Americans died in Korea, Chinese today do not dwell on their war dead or the sufferings of their families. While many U.S. citizens see the Korean War as a tragedy, most Chinese see the war as an unqualified victory. Why? Many Chinese today see the United States as a formidable, potential foe over issues like Taiwan. When Chinese require confidence about possible future conflicts with the United States, they draw on the psychological resource of past "victories" over the United States, whether in Korea or in Vietnam. It may just be that despite frequent Chinese warnings about the "revival of Japanese militarism," most Chinese citizens no longer fear Japan as they fear the United States. They therefore have the luxury of engaging in a new anti-Japanese "victim-speak" that allows them to express long-repressed anger at past injustices. Confronting what many perceive to be an expanding American hegemony, however, Chinese today have no such luxury in dealing with the United States. A China confronting the United States still requires heroes.

The recent reemergence of the victim narrative about the Century of Humiliation can be regarded with both caution and hope. In the short run, this reencounter with long-suppressed suffering has created substantial anger, an anger that has largely been directed at Japan. Japan-bashing is unquestionably ascendant in China, and the dehumanization central to such discourse lays the psychological foundation for violence. This is dangerous. In the long run, however, squarely confronting and working through the tragedy of China's past encounters with Western and Japanese imperialism could help heal an old wound, enabling the mainland Chinese to develop the self-confidence that they need to attain their goal of becoming a "responsible great power."

The example of the 2004 Asian Cup protests that begins this chapter shows that nationalist sentiment is readily expressed through sports. In light of this, the 2008 Beijing Summer Olympics promise to reveal a great deal about how far many Chinese have come in working through their past victimization at the hands of foreign imperialists. The Olympics are intended to highlight internationalism, and the selection of host countries is generally viewed as a way of affirming that the host country in question is either among or eligible to become one of the world's mature and developed nations. This helps explain Beijing's determined campaign over the course of the 1990s to play host to the Olympics. During that decade, the government was seeking to escape the dark shadow cast by its violent suppression of the

Tiananmen protests and to project itself on the global stage as a responsible, modernizing power. Having finally won the honor of hosting the games, the Chinese government is now working feverishly to build the required facilities and to beautify Beijing in time for this big "coming-out" party. But all of this promises opportunity and risk. Although Beijing constantly exhorts the Chinese people to build a civilized society that they can be proud to show to the world in 2008, it also opens itself to greater scrutiny on the part of foreign journalists, who may be anxious to point out the ways that the Communist government manipulates images to convey impressions of civility and maturity not in accord with the daily realities of Chinese life.

One area that will surely come under close watch is China's attitude toward winning and losing on the playing field. The Olympics are meant to showcase healthy competition, and the host country has a particular duty to set a positive tone in this regard. Will the Chinese display healthy national pride (or disappointment) over the outcomes of competition, or will they display unhealthy pride (or anger), especially when it comes to competition with countries such as Japan, Korea, and the United States? Beijing doubtless intends to do its utmost to prevent unseemly displays of nationalist sentiment, but will it succeed? As this chapter has shown, nationalism can be useful to the Chinese government, but it can also be a threat, for once unleashed, renegade nationalism can be difficult to keep in check. If Chinese nationalist emotion slips out of the government's control in 2008, the Olympics could be an occasion for the expression of internationally divisive sentiments. Nor can Beijing afford to be too heavy-handed in its treatment of vocal Chinese nationalists, without thereby provoking an angry backlash from those same people. The political line Beijing must follow, then, is a very fine one. If the government can persuade the Chinese people to take pride in China's accomplishments (both in hosting the games and in athletic competition) without feeling the need to denigrate Japan and the West, we will know that a self-confident China is ready to play a leadership role in the twenty-first century.

NOTES

1. Jim Yardley, "In Soccer Loss, a Glimpse of China's Rising Ire at Japan," *New York Times*, August 9, 2004.

2. The Japanese invaded and colonized Manchuria following the Mukden Incident in 1931; invasion of China as a whole, however, did not begin until after the Marco Polo Bridge Incident in 1937.

3. See Eric Hobsbawm and Terence Ranger, eds., *The Invention of Tradition* (New York: Cambridge University Press, 1983); Sudipta Kaviraj, "The Imaginary Institution of India," in *Subaltern Studies 7*, ed. Partha Chatterjee and Gyanendra Pandley (New York: Oxford University Press, 1992), 6; and Elie Kedourie, *Nationalism* (Cambridge, MA: Blackwell, 1993), 70.

4. See Geremie Barmé, "History for the Masses," in *Using the Past to Serve the Present: Historiography and Politics in Contemporary China*, ed. Jonathan Unger (Armonk, NY: M. E. Sharpe, 1993), 260; and Paul A. Cohen, *History in Three Keys: The Boxers as Event, Experience, and Myth* (New York: Columbia University Press, 1997), 213, 221.

5. Sociologists Anthony Giddens and Margaret Somers maintain that narratives infuse identities with meaning. Giddens argues that narratives provide the individual with "ontological security": "The reflexive project of the self . . . consists in the sustaining of coherent, yet continually revised, biographical narratives." Somers contrasts "representational narratives" (selective descriptions of events) with more foundational "ontological narratives," which are "the stories that social actors use to make sense of—indeed, to act in—their lives . . . [They] define who we are." The storied nature of social life, in short, infuses our identities with meaning. "Identities," Stuart Hall notes, "are the names we give to the different ways we are positioned by, and position ourselves in, the narratives of the past." See Anthony Giddens, *Modernity and Self-Identity: Self and Society in the Late Modern Age* (Stanford, CA: Stanford University Press, 1991), 5; Margaret R. Somers, "The Narrative Constitution of Identity: A Relational and Network Approach," *Theory and Society* 23 (1994): 618; and Jeffrey Olick and Joyce Robbins, "Social Memory Studies: From 'Collective Memory' to the Historical Sociology of Mnemonic Practices," *Annual Review of Sociology* 24 (1998): 122. For personality psychology approaches, see Dan McAdams, *The Stories We Live By: Personal Myths and the Making of the Self* (New York: Guilford, 1996); and Jefferson A. Singer and Peter Salovey, *The Remembered Self: Emotion and Memory in Personality* (New York: Free Press, 1993). McAdams's title inspired the title for this chapter.

6. This definition draws from Henri Tajfel's description of "social identity." Henri Tajfel, *Human Groups and Social Categories: Studies in Social Psychology* (Cambridge: Cambridge University Press, 1981), 255.

7. Li Fang, "Women zhe yidairen de Meiguo qingjie [Our generation's America complex]," in "Zhongguo ruhe shuobu [How China should say no]," special issue, *Zuojia tiandi* [*Writer's World*] (1996): 23.

8. See Dominick LaCapra, *History and Memory after Auschwitz* (Ithaca, NY: Cornell University Press, 1998), 9.

9. Tom Segev, *The Seventh Million: The Israelis and the Holocaust* (New York: Hill and Wang, 1993), 11.

10. Paul A. Cohen also notes a resonance between republican-era writings and those of the 1990s. See "Remembering and Forgetting: National Humiliation in Twentieth-Century China," *Twentieth-century China* 27, no. 2 (2002): 17.

11. Lydia Liu, "The Female Body and Nationalist Discourse: Manchuria in Xiao Hong's *Field of Life and Death*," in *Body, Subject, and Power in China*, ed. Angela Zito and Tani E. Barlow (Chicago: University of Chicago Press, 1994).

12. See Yael Zerubavel, *Recovered Roots: Collective Memory and the Making of Israeli National Tradition* (Chicago: University of Chicago Press, 1995), 75. My thanks to Paul Cohen for this reference.

13. Jiang Shuyu, preface to *Wuwang guochi lishi congshu* [*Do not forget the national humiliation historical series*], ed. Jiang Shuyu (Beijing: Zhongguo huaqiao chubanshe, 1991), 1.

14. One group of social psychologists found, for instance, that subjects who supported a particular team were more self-confident after a team victory than after a team loss. See Edward R. Hirt et al., "Costs and Benefits of Allegiance: Changes in Fans' Self-ascribed Competencies after Team Victory versus Defeat," *Journal of Personality and Social Psychology* 63, no. 5 (1992). See also J. M. Barbalet, *Emotion, Social Theory, and Social Structure: A Macrosociological Approach* (New York: Cambridge University Press, 1998), 87.

15. Chen Feng, Huang Zhaoyu, and Chai Zemin, *Zhongmei Jiaoliang Daxiexhen* [*The true story of the Sino-American contest*] (Beijing: Zhongguo renshi chubanshe, 1996), 69.

16. Yang Dezhi, preface to *Kangmei Yuanchao De Kaige* [*A paean to the war to resist America and aid Korea*] (Beijing: Zhongguo da baike chuanshu chubanshe, 1990), 3.

17. Chai Zemin, preface to Chen Feng, Huang Zhaoyu, and Chai Zemin, *Zhongmei Jiaoliang Daxiexhen*, i–ii; John W. Garver, *Face Off: China, the United States, and Taiwan's Democratization* (Seattle: University of Washington Press, 1997), 107–8.

18. Xi Yongjun and Ma Zaizhun, *Chaoyue Meiguo: Meiguo shenhua de zhongjie* [*Surpassing America: The end of the American myth*] (Harbin, China: Neimenggu daxue chubanshe, 1996), 232.

19. In a review of fiftieth-anniversary scholarship on the war, Chinese Academy of Social Sciences historian Zeng Jingzhong argues that although it has been long suppressed, research on Japanese violence has become a strength of the field. See Zeng Jingzhong, "1995 Nian kangri Zhanzhengshi yanjiu de jinzhan [1995 developments in research on the war of resistance against Japan]," *Kangri Zhanzheng yanjiu* [*Studies on the War of Resistance against Japan*] 1 (1996): 216. On the Nanjing Massacre in particular, *China Daily* has noted that "In [Mao's] China . . . Not enough was done to study and publicize Japanese war crimes and other atrocities during World War II. Starting from the early 1980s, however . . . The Chinese public has become increasingly aware of the shocking facts of the massacre." See "China Massacre Brought into Focus," October 12, 1998.

20. Thomas J. Scheff, *Bloody Revenge: Emotions, Nationalism, and War* (Boulder, CO: Westview, 1994).

21. Lin Zhibo, "Another Questioning of the 'New Thinking.'" Peoples Net online.

22. *Renmin ribao* [*People's Daily*], "Kexue shensuo de weida lichengbei [A great milestone for scientific exploration]," October 17, 2005, www.people.com.cn/GB/paper464/15938/1409390.html; Jonathan Watts, "China Plans First Space Walk in 2007," *Guardian*, October 18, 2005.

23. See http://news.sina.com.cn/c/2005-10-17/09158027129.shtml.

SUGGESTED READINGS

Benedict Anderson, *Imagined Communities: Reflections on the Origins and Spread of Nationalism* (New York: Verso, 1993).

J. M. Barbalet, *Emotion, Social Theory, and Social Structure: A Macrosociological Approach* (New York: Cambridge University Press, 1998).

Paul A. Cohen, *History in Three Keys: The Boxers as Event, Experience, and Myth* (New York: Columbia University Press, 1997).

Joseph Fewsmith, *China since Tiananmen: The Politics of Transition* (Cambridge: Cambridge University Press, 2001).

Peter Hays Gries, *China's New Nationalism: Pride, Politics, and Diplomacy* (Berkeley: University of California Press, 2004).

Maurice Halbwachs, *The Collective Memory*, trans. Francis J. Ditter and Vida Yazdi Ditter (New York: Harper and Row, 1980).

E. J. Hobsbawm and T. O. Ranger, *The Invention of Tradition* (Cambridge: Cambridge University Press, 1983).

Dominick LaCapra, *History and Memory after Auschwitz* (Ithaca, NY: Cornell University Press, 1998).

Dan McAdams, *The Stories We Live By: Personal Myths and the Making of the Self* (New York: Guilford, 1996).

Thomas J. Scheff, *Bloody Revenge: Emotions, Nationalism, and War* (Boulder, CO: Westview, 1994).

6

The Internet

A Force to Transform Chinese Society?

Xiao Qiang

In November 1992, an oceanographer in Seattle, Washington, called my office at Human Rights in China after finding a bottle that had been drifting across the Pacific Ocean for eleven years. A leaflet inside contained information about Wei Jingsheng, then China's most prominent political prisoner, who had been sentenced to fifteen years in prison in 1979. Until the contents of the bottle arrived on my desk in New York, the world had not heard anything about Wei since his sentencing.

More than a decade later, we need not rely on fortuitous messages in bottles to receive news from inside the PRC. The country's opening to the outside world, the rapid expansion of access to the Internet (*Wangluo*), and reforms in state-owned media reveal there is a greater flow of information within China, and between China and the rest of the world than ever before. Over the past two decades, China's rapid economic growth has made it a significant economic and political power in the international community. China is now a member of the World Trade Organization (WTO) and will host the 2008 Summer Olympic Games. With booming Internet use and an expanding high-tech sector, the Chinese government lauds the country's transformation into an "Information Society."

Despite this remarkable progress, however, the country remains a one-party state, and its leaders are fearful that free speech combined with the free flow of information could destroy their political legitimacy as well as their control over society. Thus, maintaining the status quo and preventing democratic reform is the central agenda of the ruling CCP. Although Wei Jingsheng was eventually released and exiled after international pressure and attention, human rights organizations such as Amnesty International have documented that thousands of political prisoners still languish in

China's jails, including an increasing number of individuals who published material online. The Chinese government views the Internet as vital to economic and technological development, but it is expending significant resources to maintain control over both content and public access to it.

The rise of the Internet has provided PRC citizens with unprecedented opportunities to access a diverse range of information and perspectives. Furthermore, citizens' rising demands for greater freedom of expression, combined with new technologies, are challenging government controls and facilitating conditions for the growth of civil society and the emergence of a free press. This is a critical area of political change with which I have become concerned in the last two years after starting the Berkeley China Internet Project at the Graduate School of Journalism, at the University of California, Berkeley. In the twelve preceding years I had served as executive director of Human Rights in China, but I had decided to assume a new challenge and have been exploring the new digital communication revolution and how it has affected China's ongoing social and political transition. In this chapter, I will share some of my observations on this dynamic point of interchange.

THE DEVELOPING INTERNET AND ONLINE CENSORSHIP

China is undergoing a digital revolution. Internet usage in China has continued to expand exponentially. As of 2005, according to the Ministry of Information Industry, China has more that 100 million Internet users, with 30.1 million using broadband connections. A recent Gallup survey found that 86 percent of Chinese Internet users have college degrees, and of these, 85 percent are male, while 40 percent are in the 21- to 25-age group. A majority of users cited in a survey by the China Internet Network Information Center say that entertainment (37.9 percent) and getting information (37.8 percent) are their primary reasons for going online. The three major Chinese portals, Sina.com, Sohu.com, and Netease.com, target young Internet users by providing news and entertainment, while other online communities such as Tianya.com, instant messenger services such as QQ, online gaming services such as Shengda.com, search engines such as Baidu, and weblog-hosting services such as bokee.com have all also become major draws in attracting younger people to the Internet.

At the same time, other communication technologies are exploding in China. Over the past three years, according to official statistics, the number of cell phone users in the country has increased by 60 million a year, reaching an approximate total of 400 million in 2006. And the cell phone in China, unlike those in the United States that are substantially used for real-time conversations, has become the principal means of accessing the Internet. Although most Internet users in China today live in large cities, there are also 1.8 million Internet cafes, a significant number of which are in middle-sized cities and small towns, and which are becoming ubiquitous throughout China. Because of their very inexpensive fees, these cafes have become a popular place, especially for young people, who use them to get on the Internet for playing online games and using e-mail and chat-room services.

Since 1995 and in order to improve the country's economic competitiveness as a "knowledge-based economy," the PRC government has been the main force promoting the expansion of the Internet and information technology in China. The government acknowledges that China needs the economic benefits the Internet brings; yet authorities fear the political fallout from the free flow of information it seems to facilitate. Because of this, since the Internet first reached the country in the mid-1990s, the government has used an effective, multilayer strategy employing more than thirty thousand people to control online content and monitor online activities at every level of Internet service and content.

Authorities use licensing regulations and financial penalties to punish any companies that fail to comply. This regulation also applies to international Internet companies such as Yahoo! and Microsoft, among others. Eager to expand their Chinese market share, many of these companies are more than keen to collaborate with these censorship mechanisms. This willing collaboration with state censorship has been a source of controversy among netizens both in and beyond China, on the pages of the business section of the *New York Times*, and in the online journalism of *Wired* and the *Free Internet Press*. The arm of the party-state is long and critical to market share: MSN China, a new portal opened in late May 2005, is a joint venture between Microsoft and Shanghai Alliance Investment, a company funded by the Chinese government.

All major Internet service providers (ISPs) and Internet content providers (ICPs) in China are required to hire people who do nothing but watch online information on their websites and are prepared to delete content considered sensitive. In addition to human censors, all website hosting services have also installed keyword filtering software. Posts on politically sensitive topics such as Falun Gong, human rights, democracy, and Taiwan independence are routinely filtered. A list obtained by the Berkeley China Internet Project last year found that over one thousand words, including *dictatorship*, *truth*, and *riot police*, are automatically banned in China's online forums.

The regulation is backed up by real policing power. Since 2000, China's police force has established Internet departments in more than seven hundred cities and provinces. The Chinese Internet police monitor websites and e-mail for "heretical teachings or feudal superstitions" and information "harmful to the dignity or interests of the state." They also have access to software that enables them to detect subversive keywords in e-mails and downloads as well as to trace such messages back to the computers from which they were sent.

In a recent case that shocked many around the world, Chinese journalist Shi Tao was sentenced to ten years in prison for sending an e-mail about news censorship in China to an overseas, pro-democracy website. The catch here—and this is precisely why Shi Tao's arrest was internationally provocative—was that the Chinese Internet police traced the e-mail back to him not through their state-of-the-art surveillance software technology but thanks to the willing collaboration of Yahoo! It is instructive that this California-based company turned the information over to Chinese officials even though that information was stored in a server in Hong Kong, a special administrative region (SAR) purportedly outside the jurisdiction of the mainland police.

Aside from legal regulations, police oversight, and licensing, another key component of the party-state's control is the so-called Great Firewall (*da huoqiang*), a centralized mechanism that controls the nine gateways that connect China with the global Internet and allows the government to block domestic access to individual foreign websites. This Great Firewall mechanism is mainly designed to prevent Chinese Internet users within China from accessing certain undesirable Web content outside China. Typically, such problematic Web content is found on overseas Chinese-language news websites such as offered by the BBC (British Broadcasting Corporation), most Taiwan and Hong Kong news sites, and human rights and religious group websites such as those of Falun Gong. Before the rise of weblogs, or blogs, such online content was typically distributed through a limited number of news hubs, and all the censors needed to do was add these hubs to their list of blocked sites, and then popular access could be controlled or curtailed. According to a Harvard University Berkman Center report from 2003, the Chinese government has blocked access to "thousands of sites offering information about news, health, education, and entertainment." By late September 2005, the government made more explicit its opposition to the growth in surfing for news beyond the reach of the safe harbor of domestically approved websites, launching a "smokeless war" against Internet and media dissent. Scarcely a week before this announcement, a Chinese journalist was sentenced to seven years in prison for "inciting subversion" by submitting articles to overseas websites for online publication. Yet given the rapidly evolving landscape of information technology and popular technical expertise in China, one cannot help but wonder: Can the Internet be controlled?

Even under these restrictive conditions, the development of the Internet has registered significant effects on Chinese society, irrevocably altering the information environment available to Chinese citizens. While government efforts to control the Internet have been largely effective, the flexibility and pervasiveness of new media is enabling more and more censored information to penetrate the Great Firewall. It seems that, just as the original Great Wall of China didn't work in barring foreigners from entry into China, neither will this new technological wall. Those Chinese who can get online are exposed to more diverse and numerous sources of information and have manifold opportunities to communicate and express themselves on social, political, and personal issues. Simultaneously, the interaction between information and communication technology and the traditional media creates a dynamic that is challenging almost all boundaries of the traditional censorship system and as well the official media.

Ever since the founding of the PRC in 1949, control of information has been central to the CCP's governing strategy. As a one-party authoritarian regime, the CCP has made all mass media—from newspapers and magazines to radio stations and TV channels—mouthpieces of the party. As Daniel Lynch, author of *After the Propaganda State*, has noted, the CCP creates and maintains a "symbolic environment" in order to encourage citizens to accept the regime's political legitimacy, thereby preserving a balance between an apparently "open network" and a "closed regime."[1]

But after twenty years of market-oriented economic reform, commercial pressure is a primary factor behind the pluralization of the CCP's "symbolic environment." As a result, the Chinese media have become more diversified and commercialized. While the government's mechanisms to control the media are still firmly in place, they are increasingly challenged by market pressures and a growing sense of independence among the country's media professionals. For example, even the party's most important mouthpiece, *Renmin ribao* [*People's Daily*], has set up a daily tabloid *Jinghua shibao* [*Beijing Times*] as a livelier, market-oriented, profit-generating subsidiary. Because it meets the needs of the market, the *Beijing Times* has quickly became the most active media site in Beijing, as citizens turn there for coverage of breaking local news events. As a result of this new approach, the *Beijing Times* has become one of the most popular newspapers in Beijing, with an estimated circulation of 280,000.

The Internet has accelerated the transformation of China's media landscape and is now helping to promote the growing autonomy and diversity of the traditional media. A recent survey found that one-third of all Chinese college students depend on the Internet for news. As of April 2004, Beijing's online users were estimated at 3.8 million—more than twice as large as the circulation of the capital's three main daily newspapers—the *Beijing Evening News* (circulation 700,000), the *Beijing Youth Daily* (380,000), and the *Beijing Times* (280,000)—put together. And the fastest growing business for Sina.com and other similar ISPs is transmitting text messages, including news flashes to cell phones.

The state media has also been getting online. In 1993, the *Hangzhou Daily* launched the first electronic edition of a Chinese newspaper, and 95,000 of 100,000 Chinese media organizations, including magazines, newspapers, radio stations, and TV channels, were online by the end of 2003, according to mainland scholars' statistics. Because online versions of official publications have a more direct interaction with their readers, rely on breaking news, and are under less-stringent editorial control than their print counterparts, the reporting in Internet publications is often livelier and more independent than in the traditional media.

As Internet users within and outside China develop creative, new methods to circumvent government Internet blockades, PRC citizens have access to increasingly diverse and abundant sources of news from outside the country. While most of the major overseas Chinese-language news sites— including those of the BBC, Voice of America (VOA), and Hong Kong or Taiwan newspapers—are blocked by the government, the content of these publications still enters China through bulletin boards, mass e-mails to individual inboxes, and other online channels. These information conduits, such as alerts from the banned Falun Gong spiritual movement, VOA news updates, and dissident newsletters, reach Chinese readers despite the government's use of advanced filtering technology. Many books banned domestically in China are also available online, such as *The Tiananmen Papers*,[2] Nobel Laureate Gao Xingjian's *Soul Mountain*, and the Bible.

THE INTERNET'S INFLUENCE ON
TRADITIONAL NEWS REPORTING IN CHINA

One prime example of the Internet's influence in China can be seen in the coverage of major events in the traditional Chinese media. When covering a natural disaster, a major industrial accident, or an urgent public health issue, journalists in the traditional media are not allowed to investigate independently and report without official sanction (as made vividly clear in chapter 1). The Internet is helping to change these rules. Journalists are now learning to evade these sanctions by distributing and collecting information online, making it more difficult for propaganda bosses to silence their reports. Ordinary Internet users can also write about events they witness and disseminate their reports online, making the suppression of urgent breaking news virtually impossible. Internet users in China are now much more likely to find out about a breaking story in real time and to question why the official press hasn't covered it. As a result, the Chinese media now feel more pressure from the public and have more space to cover those events.

Commercial news portals such as Sina.com, Sohu.com, and Netease.com have become very popular among readers in China. Although these sites must get their content from official news sources and lack the right to publish political news, their methods of collecting and presenting the news are already changing traditional reporting in China, where editors and reporters otherwise must adhere to strict guidelines about what, how, when, and even if to report on certain events. There are also increasing numbers of *zi meiti* (self-media) sites, run by individuals who use weblog software to gather, organize, and spread news and commentary. The sites, such as no4media.org, blogchina.org, and hundreds of others, rely on their online readers' participation to spread community-related news or to fact-check official media reports.

The hyper-accelerated growth in weblogs that Internet users have witnessed recently could not have been anticipated by the Chinese government. Moreover, even with a list of proscribed terms including *Dalai Lama, democracy, Falun Gong, freedom, independence, Taiwan, Tiananmen Square,* and even as e-mail transmissions disappear unaccountably, Internet inquiries into certain subjects yield no answers, websites are blocked, and popular search engines such as Google are suddenly disabled, the prospects for future expansion of the private sphere of weblogs seem unlimited. In a June 2005 story titled "Microsoft Censors Chinese Blogs," for example, *Wired's* online news reported that MSN Spaces, which offers free weblog space and is connected to Microsoft's new MSN China portal, recorded the creation of 5 million weblogs between May 25 and June 12, 2005. The balance between state control of the Internet and individual freedom of expression is a dynamic one, which in the last few years has tilted toward the latter.

At the onset of the SARS (severe acute respiratory syndrome) epidemic in China in the winter of 2003, the Chinese government attempted to mask the severity of the disease by instituting a reporting ban on domestic media and denying access to international health inspectors. The cover-up provoked widespread international condemnation, which reached the Chinese public through the Internet. During the government cover-up period, e-mail played an important role as a catalyst to spread otherwise censored information. Only a very few technically savvy Chinese Internet users were able to use proxy servers to get around government blockades and to access overseas media such as Hong Kong and Taiwan news sites, VOA, the BBC, and Radio Free Asia. Starting in March 2003—after SARS had spread to Hong Kong and was being widely covered by the press there, and when the World Health Organization (WHO) and international governments and media were beginning to report and protest the apparent cover-up by the Chinese government—this news gradually leaked back to China, particularly through e-mail from abroad.

E-mail also gives Chinese citizens who are determined to expose the truth a technical means to reach out. A critical turning point in SARS coverage in China occurred when Dr. Jiang Yanyong, a retired surgeon of the People's

Liberation Army Hospital no. 301, decided to send an e-mail to Hong Kong describing the epidemic as much more severe than the Chinese government had acknowledged. On April 7, 2003, *Time Asia* used Dr. Yanyong's e-mail report to expose the government's cover-up.

EMERGING PUBLIC OPINION

Before the Internet emerged as a source of information dissemination, the Chinese media were not a forum for public discussion and debate. Now, the Internet facilitates discussion of public affairs, especially through online bulletin boards. About one-fifth of Chinese netizens regularly make use of BBS (bulletin-board systems), the most politically active place in Chinese cyberspace. These BBS can be run by individuals, commercial companies such as Sina.com, or government agencies.

At any given time, there are literally tens of thousands of users active in these BBS and forums, reading news, searching for information, and debating current affairs. Even official websites have BBS, such as the *People's Daily*'s popular BBS, Strong Nation Forum, which has more than 280,000 registered members and more than twelve thousand posts per day. Together with e-mail listservs, chat rooms, instant message services, wireless short-text messaging, and an emerging weblogging community, the BBS provides unprecedented opportunities for Chinese netizens to engage in public affairs. In the past two years, over 300,000 people in China have started their own weblogs, which cover topics ranging from daily personal anecdotes to commentary on current affairs.

Journalists are also helping blur the boundaries between traditional and online media in China by creating their own weblogs. Likewise, some online writers have built a professional reputation and are now working in the traditional media. It has become clear that the power of the Net and its interplay with traditional media is creating public opinion in China.

Public intellectuals have developed a significant presence on the Internet, as it has given a voice to professors, lawyers, journalists, and independent writers concerned about social and public policy issues. Although it can be difficult for these intellectuals to publish in the traditional media, they are able to write and publish on the Net and so become opinion leaders in the virtual public sphere. Some have their own websites or weblogs, while others create professional communities such as China Lawyers Network or Home for Reporters. The Internet has given them a place to gather, debate, communicate, publish, and receive information. Consequently, it has become a place for them collectively to articulate and amplify their opinions on public matters.

A very public and positive example of this development was witnessed in Shenzhen, a special economic zone (SEZ) in China's South about an hour's train ride from Hong Kong. On November 16, 2002, an author using the online name Crazy for You posted a long essay titled "Shenzhen, Who Abandoned You?" on Strong Nation Forum and also on Development Forum, another popular BBS hosted by the government's official Xinhua News Agency website. The article outlined many of the existing problems with Shenzhen city government policy, including inefficiency, mismanagement of the residential certification system, and a poor investment environment. The author, who was clearly very familiar with the inner workings of the Shenzhen city government, wrote a thoughtful and well-documented piece, staying within approved political boundaries. Nevertheless, such an independent and frank critique would not have been published by the official press. After publishing his piece online, the author received a tremendous amount of public support, which the government was unable to ignore or dismiss. The posting generated hundreds of responses. Many readers e-mailed it to friends nationwide, and it soon appeared on many official and semiofficial websites across China. In an unprecedented response, Shenzhen's mayor met the author and publicly responded to his criticisms in the local official press, even putting the issues discussed in the piece on the city's policy reform agenda. This milestone demonstrates the Internet's power to be a positive force in broadening China's public discourse.

INTERNET-FACILITATED SOCIAL AND POLITICAL ACTIVISM

After two and a half decades of market-oriented economic reform, Chinese citizens are becoming increasingly aware of how to protect their economic and social interests by using the language of rights. For example, when facing abuse of power, the media and the victims themselves increasingly use a new term, *weiquan* (defending rights), to challenge the existing system. Another new expression, *zhi qing quan* (right to know), has also entered the public discourse, especially after the SARS outbreak. The momentum of this rising demand for rights in Chinese society is now being aided and accelerated by the rapid spread of the Internet.

During the past five years, the expanded space for discussion of public affairs facilitated by the Internet has thus allowed for the establishment of online communities that challenge government limitations, creating and fostering space for civil activism to push the boundaries of associative and communicative freedoms. While the authorities in China effectively stifle a civil society of independent social organizations, grassroots groups that depart from the official agenda in covering environmental issues, women's rights, homosexuality, and other social issues often rely on the Internet to organize and distribute information.

Under the state censorship system, online discussions are most limited to politically acceptable topics such as legal reform and anticorruption efforts. However within these boundaries, Internet-enabled activism, such as online petitions, have not only expanded traditional media reporting but have also contributed to political results on those issues. On March 17, 2003, Sun Zhigang, a twenty-seven-year-old college graduate who was working for a graphic design company in Guangzhou, was stopped by police. He was detained for not having proper identity papers and died in custody three days later. After the authorities refused to investigate the circumstances of his death, Sun's parents posted background information on his case and a petition letter on the Internet. His case was picked up by a reporter from the *Southern Metropolis News*, one of China's most progressive papers, and then the story hit the Net.

Within two hours of being posted on China's largest news portal, Sina.com, this news item generated four thousand comments from readers. Almost immediately the case was being discussed throughout Chinese cyberspace, from official sites to personal weblogs and e-mail groups. Police brutality is not new in China. International human rights organizations and those advocating legal reforms in China have called for abolishment of the Custody and Repatriation system, an administrative procedure established in 1982 by which the police can detain nonresidents if they do not have a temporary resident permit and return them to their place of origin. It was this inherently arbitrary form of administrative detention under which Sun was held. But the explosive reaction from Internet users to Sun's case was unprecedented. The official media, including China Central Television (CCTV; Zhongyang dianshitai), soon picked up on the public outrage and reported heated debates over treatment of migrants living in the cities and police corruption.

On May 29, in an unprecedented appeal to the National People's Congress, four professors, including two from Beijing University Law School, called on the state prosecutor to investigate Sun's death. Three months later, the government abolished the entire Custody and Repatriation system, and the officials responsible for Sun Zhigang's death were convicted in court.

Not every online uprising wins in this ongoing war. For example, in another prominent case last winter, hundreds of thousands of netizens reacted against a lenient sentence given to a well-connected woman who hit and killed a peasant and injured twelve others with her BMW. Even so, following this explosion of protest on the Internet, the government upheld the verdict, and major Internet portals continued to report the news but banned users' comments.

In another incident, top editors at the *Southern Metropolis News*, including the paper's general manager Yu Huafeng and former editor in chief Cheng

Yizhang, were arrested in April 2004, apparently in retaliation for their aggressive reporting on Sun Zhigang's case, SARS, and other issues. Then on March 16, 2005, the government shut down Shuimu.com, the largest Chinese university Internet forum, and one that occupies a domain at Tsinghua University. The site was closed to users outside the Tsinghua campus by order of the Ministry of Education. This ad hoc constraint aimed at restricting incendiary speech provoked immediate student protest at the university and led to a string of Internet appeals from other BBS calling for a broader public outcry.

In yet another well-publicized example, Internet users initiated a campaign to release a fellow Internet writer, Liu Di, a twenty-two-year-old psychology student whose online name is Stainless Steel Mouse. Liu's thoughtful, insightful, and humorous writing often challenged the political and social system, making her a popular commentator on China's largest online BBS, Xici Hutong, which has 500,000 registered users. In one essay, she commented that the work of the Internet police was actually endangering national security by not allowing people to express themselves.

After she disappeared from Xici Hutong in September 2002, her Internet friends investigated and discovered that she had been arrested on suspicion of "endangering national security." Her arrest triggered a global, grassroots online campaign, and more than two thousand netizens—including many prominent Chinese writers and intellectuals—signed a petition to the national government demanding her release. In a show of solidarity, hundreds of online writers put *Stainless steel* in front of their online names, making Liu a powerful symbol of freedom of expression in China. After more than a year of relentless online campaigning, Liu Di was released on November 28, 2003, days before the visit of Chinese prime minister Wen Jiabao to the United States. In contrast to Wei Jingsheng, who was also sent to prison for his political writings, Liu Di did not have to wait thirteen years for her supporters to send information to the world via a floating bottle. Rather in this particular case, the Internet ignited an immediate, global, grassroots movement (and a fight for freedom of expression) in her name that finally gained her release.

In 2003 there were more than half a dozen of these online movements, most involving protests against police abuse, corruption, crime, and miscarriages of social justice. Not every case had as direct a political result as Sun Zhigang's or Liu Di's, but together they have generated a new form of public opinion in China: *Wangluo yulun* (Internet opinion) became a formal phenomenon and entered Chinese public discourse.

It is important to understand the highly distributed, decentralized nature of these online movements; none have a central leader or organizer. This means that when an issue resonates with millions of Chinese netizens, it is expressed not only on the BBS but also through implicit communication channels including e-mail, instant messages, and wireless short-text messaging services, as well as within the growing weblogging community. Instead of being produced by the official media, these online events, powered by the Internet in a distributive and immediate manner, now actually drive the agenda of the official media.

Such "online uprisings" have had a significant impact on Chinese society because there is still no systematic way for the public to participate in and express themselves on public policy and social issues (this is beginning to change, however; see chapter 10). When online discussions of current events are within the limits of government political tolerance, then the official media are allowed to discuss and report on them. Because the traditional broadcast and print media remain under the tight editorial control of propaganda officials, their reports alone and without the Internet will never be able to generate such debate. Within current political limits, Internet opinion has also reduced the risk to the traditional media of reporting on these issues; sometimes Internet opinion even generates commercial pressure for them to do so.

The most recent and uniquely illustrative case of Internet-enabled protests was the massive anti-Japanese demonstrations in several major Chinese cities—Beijing, Shanghai, and Shenzhen—in spring 2005 (see chapter 5). Even before these protests, however, Chinese cyberspace had been buzzing with anti-Japanese sentiment on popular nationalistic websites. In fact, these nationalistic websites are virtually the only political websites tolerated by the Chinese government. That's well demonstrated by the fact that while popular commercial news portals, such as Sina.com and Sohu.com, are careful to censor their political content on other issues, they frequently post high-profile, anti-Japanese articles and discussions without any fear of repercussions.

Some popular nationalistic websites and online forums have been around since the mid-1990s. However the site Coalition of Patriots, which has gathered tens of millions of online signatures on numerous anti-Japanese petitions, was established in 2002. For the most part, such sites formerly confined their activities to online expressions of anger. But that changed dramatically in early April 2005 in reaction to the news that Japanese history textbooks had misrepresented Japan's military imperialist aggression of the 1930s and 1940s in East Asia. Right after the first public anti-Japanese demonstration in Beijing on April 9, eyewitness accounts, photos, and video clips from the protests spread rapidly through Chinese cyberspace despite a complete blackout of coverage in the official media. Within a week, a protest momentum had developed throughout China's major cities; there were even notices calling for public action posted in the student unions of university campuses in Hong Kong.

At the same time, demands for a boycott of Japanese products, online petitions, and calls for street demonstrations in many cities throughout China were widely distributed by the Internet and cell phones. Many of these messages were extraordinarily detailed, giving logistical information such as protest-march routes and even what slogans to chant. Many of the messages had multiple authors but no clear organizational identity. They were sent out in chain-letter form through e-mail or text messages and were posted online on BBS and chat services. For the most part, this is how the April 16 protest—in which an estimated twenty thousand people participated—was organized, defying calls from Shanghai authorities for students to stay on campus.

From an organizational point of view, the Shanghai demonstration was a decentralized, bottom-up event, organized by taking advantage of the opportunities presented by digital communication technologies. Chinese authorities may have initially given the demonstrators leeway because they wanted them to let out some of their virulent nationalistic fervor. They may also have used this demonstration of Chinese "public opinion" as a lever to support Beijing's diplomatic intent of opposing Japan's bid for a seat on the UN Security Council.

But whatever leeway the anti-Japanese activists were initially given, the success of their technology-enabled protests now poses a serious challenge to the Chinese authorities' traditional mechanisms of social control. That was demonstrated by the failure of efforts by Shanghai authorities to use such technology to dissuade students from attending the march. According to information posted on Chinese BBS and weblogs, Shanghai authorities broadcast text and e-mail messages in the run-up to the April 16 protest reminding people that "demonstrations must be approved ahead of time through proper application procedures." Numerous participants in the April 16 march mentioned having received such messages or seeing them online.

Although the size of these recent anti-Japanese marches may have been exceptional, the government's own statistics show that the number of public protests in China has increased dramatically over the past ten years. According to a report from the Ministry of Public Security, the number of public protests reached 74,000 in 2004—up from 58,000 in 2003, and 8,700 in 1993. Chinese authorities have traditionally used three methods to try to curb such demonstrations. First, all such protests require prior approval from the Public Security Bureau (an approval which is almost never granted). Second, police are sent in to contain the crowds and identify the leaders of those protests that do occur. Finally, the government's tight grip on the traditional media and the flow of information has been used to prevent news of unrest from spreading to other parts of the country. But this last control mechanism has now cracked in the face of the explosion of new forms of information technology outside the government's control, prompting a recent warning from the Ministry of Public Security that it is illegal to use the Internet or text messages to organize protests. On April 25,

2005, the state media reported that police detained a Chinese netizen for trying to organize an anti-Japanese protest in Nanjing in May.

Despite the silence of the official media in reporting the anti-Japanese demonstrations, many BBS and weblogs have engaged in a lively debate about Sino-Japan relations, Chinese nationalism, and the goals and impact of the demonstrators. Many online writers have also criticized the crude form of nationalism seen in the protests and questioned the government's motives in giving anti-Japanese sentiment some political space. By providing its own space for a pluralistic debate on such a heated topic, the Internet allows rational voices to be heard and may ultimately help aid the development of civil society.

Thus far, the Chinese government has managed to use the development of the Internet for its economic benefits, while maintaining a measure of control over online information. However, despite all the state's censorship measures, it is also indisputable that the Internet is expanding the freedom of information and expression in China. Although many of these changes are still incremental, they are nevertheless profound. In the long term, as Internet penetration of Chinese society deepens, and as more radical social and political change emerges in Chinese society, the Internet and other digital communication technologies such as cell phones will definitely play a powerful role, perhaps driving those changes in a positive direction and to a positive result: the peaceful transition to a more open and democratic China.

NOTES

1. Shanthi Kalathil and Taylor C. Boas, *Open Networks, Closed Regimes: The Impact of the Internet on Authoritarian Rule* (Washington, D.C.: Carnegie Endowment for International Peace, 2003), 13–42.

2. *The Tiananmen Papers* was published in 2001. It offers a record of high-level CCP meetings and discussions throughout the spring of 1989 leading up to the decision to use force against the Tiananmen protestors. Immediately following publication of *The Tiananmen Papers*, the Chinese government held a news conference to condemn that publication. The work is proscribed in China.

SUGGESTED READINGS

Shanthi Kalathil and Taylor C. Boas, *Open Networks, Closed Regimes: The Impact of the Internet on Authoritarian Rule* (Washington, D.C.: Carnegie Endowment for International Peace, 2003).

Benjamin L. Liebman, "Watchdog or Demagogue? The Media in the Chinese Legal System," *Columbia Law Review* 105, no. 1 (January 2005), www.columbialawreview .org/pdf/Liebman-Web.pdf.

Jack Linchuan Qiu, "The Internet in China: Technologies of Freedom in a Statist Society," in *The Network Society: A Cross-Cultural Perspective*, ed. Manuel Castells (Cheltenham, UK: Edward Elgar), 99–124. A working paper prepared for the Annenberg Research Seminar on International Communication, October 1, 2003, is available at http://annenberg.usc.edu/international_communication/Papers/JQ_China_and_Internet.pdf.

Xiao Qiang, "The 'Blog' Revolution Sweeps across China," *New Scientist* (November 2004), www.newscientist.com/article.ns?id=dn6707.

———, "The Development and the State Control of the Chinese Internet." Written presentation to the U.S.-China Economic and Security Review Commission, "Hearing on China's State Control Mechanisms and Methods," April 14, 2005, www.uscc.gov/hearings/2005hearings/written_testimonies/05_04_14wrts/qiang_xiao_wrts.htm.

7

The Politics of Filmmaking and Movie Watching

Sylvia Li-chün Lin

The PRC, with its vast population, cheap labor, and emerging role in the global economy, is more than ever the focus of Western attention, and it is regularly in the news. With myriad information coming from different venues, one can hardly be expected to be fully informed. Films, therefore, often become the most approachable medium for getting at China, because their visuality and drama provide an accessibility rarely available in the print or broadcast media. Cinematographic representation inevitably shapes our knowledge and perception of any country, and with one as diverse and complex as China, the attempt to identify the real and the represented is problematic. Especially because cinema for many people is *the* window on China, a number of critical questions must be posed here at the start. What do we actually know about Chinese cinema? How much of what we see is the real China? Why are certain films chosen to be distributed in the United States? What other films are Chinese directors creating, and who else is making movies in China? Why aren't we seeing these movies? The answers to these and related questions are complicated and involve the politics of filmmaking in China and movie watching in the United States, which will be explored through a sequence of reflective responses to particular questions in this chapter.

WHAT IS CHINESE CINEMA?

When asked what they know about Chinese film, most U.S. moviegoers will probably come up with just two names: Gong Li and Zhang Yimou. Some might add Chen Kaige, as well as the titles of a few movies such as *Raise the*

Red Lantern or *Farewell My Concubine*. *Crouching Tiger, Hidden Dragon; Hero;* or *House of Flying Daggers* might also appear on some lists. Such a response is hardly surprising since *Red Sorghum*, directed by Zhang Yimou and starring Gong Li, was the first contemporary Chinese film commercially distributed in the United States (in 1989). But these names and movie titles take us no closer to answering the fundamental question: What in fact *is* Chinese cinema? And the matter gets complicated once we begin looking at the many factors involved in the production of a movie: director, actors and actresses, financing, and audience. In other words, what specifically makes a movie Chinese?

Certainly, the director of the movie and most of the cast members ought to be Chinese, which is generally true in most Chinese films. But one need only look at director Ang Lee, whose cinematic oeuvre includes *Pushing Hands* and *The Wedding Banquet* (both set in the United States), *Crouching Tiger, Hidden Dragon* (set in premodern China), *Sense and Sensibility* (nineteenth-century England), *The Ice Storm* (New England), *The Hulk* (partly animated), and *Brokeback Mountain* (1960s Wyoming) to see that this distinction is not always useful. Some critics suggest that Lee's identity as a Chinese and American director "indicates the dissolution of national boundaries that Hollywood has been so fundamental in maintaining."[1] Or one can look at actress Michelle Yeoh of *Crouching Tiger, Hidden Dragon* and the James Bond thriller *Tomorrow Never Dies* to begin to question this homogeneous image of an all-Chinese film industry. Yeoh was born in Malaysia and educated in England; shall we call her a Chinese actress if she only stars in Chinese movies? And we also need to consider capital investment: in this era of global economic flows, can a movie be considered Chinese if the production costs are largely shouldered by Japanese or French investors? Even within Chinese culture itself, the label "Chinese cinema" seems to be coming more unglued by the day.

And that is at least partly a problem of geopolitics. As film scholar Yingjin Zhang has remarked, "'Chinese cinema' as a general term is often applied to films made in mainland China, Hong Kong, and Taiwan. Yet many Westerners see these regions as three entirely separate and antagonistic 'nations' or 'countries.'"[2] While we need not probe here Western views of Chinese politics, we do need to recognize a possible confusion in nomenclature. Since 1997, Hong Kong has been a part of the PRC, but it retains its unique culture and cinematic history. And in Taiwan, an increasing number of its citizens claim an independent cultural and political status for their island, including even those who favor reunification with the mainland. The burgeoning scholarship on Chinese cinema also contributes to such balkanization by treating Hong Kong, Taiwan, and the PRC separately.

Two edited volumes with similar titles, *New Chinese Cinema: Forms, Identities, Politics*, and *Transnational Chinese Cinemas*, appear to be the only books now available that encompass cinematic production from all three regions (plus overseas Chinese communities in the latter volume). But their titles are revealing in their geopolitical orientation. The PRC, Taiwan, and Hong Kong are covered under the umbrella term "Chinese" in the former book's title, while the latter book's title treats the three regions as separate political entities. Such a division is not without merit; however, it inevitably becomes reductive.

Hence, films from the PRC enjoy a more prominent (albeit ambiguous) status, while the general impression of Hong Kong cinema seldom moves beyond the realm of kung fu movies (director John Woo and action superstar Jackie Chan and their recent forays into Hollywood, in the view of some Chinese, only exacerbate such a biased perception), and Hong Kong directors Stanley Kwan, Wong Kar-wai, the late King Hu, and newcomer Fruit Chan are largely unknown to most people in the United States. By contrast, films from Taiwan receive virtually no attention except in New York and Los Angeles or at international film festivals, even though Taiwanese directors such as Hou Hsiao-hsien, Edward Yang, and Tsai Ming-liang continue to receive rave reviews from film critics. The cause of this lopsided perception likely has as much to do with economics as with politics.

FOR WHOM ARE THE FILMS MADE?

Determining target audiences may be one feasible approach to answering this question. For instance, Bernardo Bertolocci's *The Last Emperor* (1988), while entirely about the last emperor of Qing dynasty China and set on the mainland, should be considered non-Chinese, because the director's primary target audience was not Chinese. But audience is an immensely complicated factor in the Chinese film industry. Beijing-based musician and cultural critic Kaiser Kuo, a Chinese-American columnist for *Time Asia* who also subtitles many Chinese films, put it most poignantly when he pointed out the two less-than-ideal choices for aspiring Chinese directors: go the underground route or cater to mainstream tastes.[3] The former will be a low-budget (usually self-financed) endeavor involving mostly a director's friends and family. It requires a provocative plot and daring language that will guarantee censorship by the government. But that is precisely the point: once the film is banned in China, its director can then go abroad to present the film at various international film festivals from Toronto to Cannes.

[But] this approach has its drawbacks—chiefly, that your bold and groundbreaking masterpiece gets seen by a handful of goateed guys in black turtlenecks, and not by your own countrymen. And unless those trophies you pick up at Cannes or Venice are followed up by serious distribution deals, don't expect you'll be swimming in money.[4]

In this rather cynical view of Chinese directors, Kuo seems to imply that they are materialistic opportunists who know exactly which political buttons to push to get themselves into international filmdom. This is, however, not far from the truth. A case in point is *Frozen*, a movie about a young performance artist who commits suicide by burying himself in ice as his last work of art. Above the title of the film printed on the DVD case are the words "Banned in China," and it is, according to Kuo, "those three words that practically guarantee you heaps of accolades at the international festivals."

It is difficult to ascertain whether the director of *Frozen*, who, according to the promotional blurb on the DVD case, "must hide behind the pseudonym Wu Ming, or 'No Name,'" was indeed striving for international recognition by making a highly controversial movie. A more important and relevant question for us is why filmgoers and critics in the West almost invariably welcome and praise this type of film. What exactly does it say about Americans and their perceptions and expectations of China? There is a polarized view in the West—banned by the Chinese government, good; praised by the Chinese government, bad—and we must confront the fact that film distributors in the United States manipulate this view out of a belief that American audiences are eager to embrace anything condemned by the PRC government.

Kuo calls attention to another problem facing Chinese directors: Does it make sense to make movies that target only a handful of international film judges? What about a domestic audience, or any paying audience, for that matter? To return to my earlier question of what constitutes Chinese cinema, we need to ask whether a film made by a Chinese director that will probably never be seen by a domestic Chinese audience can still be called Chinese. Some critics argue that by garnering international prizes and recognition, a director can then force the Chinese censorship machinery to reevaluate a movie and make concessions. For instance, *To Live* brought Zhang Yimou close to being banned from making films for five years, but the near ban was lifted after the movie had won two foreign-language film awards at Cannes, proof that "international status protects many directors from outright bans."[5] Not everyone is of the same sanguine opinion regarding film awards. Sheldon Hsiao-peng Lu has observed that when Zhang Yimou's *Red Sorghum* won the Golden Bear Award in Berlin in 1988,

It was also the beginning of an end. As some scholars contend, this entrance of Chinese cinema into the global film market marked the end of the short-lived classical phase of New Chinese Cinema, a phase characterized by intellectual elitism, disregard for the film market, idiosyncratic mannerism, and artistic experimentation.[6]

The dynamics between domestic markets, government censorship, artistic performances, and international film critics cannot easily be reduced to a doomsday prediction. If anything, we might actually turn the tables on Lu and make a case for how international awards actually help new, less-well-known directors who would otherwise have to make mainstream films without regard to artistic experimentation.

For those who are less inclined toward the daring, the alternative is to make a mainstream movie that will ensure generally good box-office receipts. But just as for film directors everywhere, it is not easy to gauge popular tastes, raise capital, and cast the most popular stars. To go the mainstream route means to "do it big," including mass advertising, and in the process, creativity can be sacrificed and principles compromised. And as Kuo has also observed, that is not the end of a director's trouble, for if "you're lucky, your movie does some decent box office and you make a neat little pile before the eye-patch-and-parrot guys sink their hooks into it."[7] Despite government efforts, piracy remains a serious problem for which effective solutions have yet to be devised.[8]

Obviously, few domestic viewers in China will manage to see films that are banned there, although underground copies are always available to the artistic few. The general populace is then left with mainstream (*zhuxuanlü*, literally, "main melody") works that meet the approval of the government. A survey from *Film Art* shows that the number-one movie in China in 1998, with a revenue of ¥10 million (about US$1.25 million), was a documentary about former premier Zhou Enlai. The blockbuster hit of 2000, with a box office of over ¥100 million ($12.25 million), was *The Life-and-Death Decision*, an anticorruption movie praised by Premier Jiang Zemin, who "suggested" that everyone should go see this movie. Box-office numbers may not say much about the artistic quality of a movie, but they do indicate trends in popular taste, especially where films are concerned. In the case of China, however, one cannot help but wonder about the felicitous fact that a documentary about Premier Zhou and an anticorruption film topped the charts in 1998 and 2000. To be sure, not all mainstream Chinese films are drearily didactic; for instance, number four in the 2000 top ten list was *Shower* (box office, ¥30 million [$3.70 million]),[9] a comedy set in a traditional bathhouse that deals with conflicts between modern life and cultural heritage. It won several international awards, but the difficulty of ensuring such a happy combination of box-office success and international recognition, though not a problem in the Chinese film industry alone, continues to plague filmmakers in China.

What makes filmmaking in China such an arduous endeavor results in part from the fact that government agencies and regulations have been slow to catch up with the film industry in an economy eager to enter the global market. In the past, the Chinese government maintained a stringent set of regulations concerning filmmaking, the strictest being censorship. Uncertain as to whether a film would eventually receive approval, a film's potential backers were generally reluctant to risk losing their money. Hence directors, except for the most established, were hard-pressed for cash if they were not affiliated with state-owned film companies. In other words, the practice of the market economy became an impediment to less-well-known, nonmainstream directors under the censorship system.

A new set of rules came into effect on January 1, 2004, which the State Administration for Radio, Film and Television (SARFT) hopes will encourage filmmakers to produce more films, in light of a steady decline in audience numbers. According to *China Daily*, an official English-language newspaper, "To get a license to make a new film with an ordinary theme, filmmakers need only submit an outline of the script with their application, instead of the full film script as was previously required."[10] However, close examination of the full script is still required for films dealing with "the military, police, the judiciary, religion, international affairs or Taiwan." Even so, filmmakers now have a better sense of what is permissible, which in turn ought to encourage more investment. A report from the Hong Kong–based *South China Morning Post* cites film-industry experts who believe that more needs to be done to stimulate the industry, because foreign films, especially those from the United States, continue to draw audiences away from domestic films. "Audience numbers have been declining for more than 25 years, with the average person going to the cinema only once every 18 months."[11]

Related to the issue of censorship is the matter of underground films. By definition, underground films are those for which their directors do not receive official approval to film. While these individuals are sometimes prohibited from directing for a certain period of time and are generally categorized as "underground filmmakers," their status can change easily and often, since it is a specific film that designates a director as "underground." Wang Xiaoshuai, for example, repeatedly falls in and out of favor with SARFT.[12] Another director, Zhang Yuan, whose film on homosexuality *East Palace, West Palace* (1996) sent him underground, later made the domestically acclaimed *Seventeen Years* (1999) about a female prisoner furloughed to visit her family during the Lunar New Year Festival, and he was therefore "rehabilitated."

Ironically, the notion of underground films is as much a phenomenon created by Western film-festival organizers and promoters as it is a result of Chinese government censorship. A case in point is Li Yang's *Blind Shaft*, a film about two coal miners plotting the "accidental" deaths of other coal miners in order to claim compensation, which has been widely touted in the West as an underground movie that subverts the Chinese government

Figure 7.1. Two homicidal migrant miners looking for their next victim in Li Yang's *Blind Shaft* (2003).

(see figure 7.1; for a discussion of the dangers of coal mining in China today, see chapter 3). As Jonathan Noble observes,

> Though Li Yang certainly did face certain risks in the production of *Blind Shaft*, personal risks that he faced for breaking the law in China were lessened because of his status as a German citizen. Li Yang's nationality was downplayed, as was his transnational identity and the film's transnational production [e.g., German capital], within the international film circuit.[13]

Li Yang did not get permission to shoot this film, not because the government refused to grant him a license but because he did not apply for one. Obviously he felt that SARFT would either deny him permission or require him to make changes in the film.[14] The distinction between shooting illegally—that is, without a license—and actually being banned in China is more often than not obscured in promotional literature produced by film festivals in the West.

WHO ARE THE FIFTH- AND SIXTH-GENERATION DIRECTORS?

Read film reviews online or in major U.S. newspapers such as the *New York Times*, the *Los Angeles Times*, or the *Chicago Sun-Times* and chances are you will encounter *generational* labels. Exactly what do they signify? What constitutes a generation? The First Generation of Chinese filmmakers was a group of directors active in the 1920s, the era of silent movies, when cinema was introduced in China and the first movies were shown in teahouses (the closest to a theater-like facility at the time). The 1930s and 1940s, the era of sound, marked the directors of the Second Generation, while those working between 1949 and 1966 were identified as the Third Generation. Those who were trained in the 1950s and the 1960s at the Beijing Film Academy and made movies in the late 1970s and early 1980s belonged to the Fourth Generation, while later Beijing Film Academy graduates, such as Zhang Yimou and Chen Kaige, make up the Fifth. Younger filmmakers, active in the 1990s and early 2000s, are the rising stars, the Sixth Generation directors.

Age and subject matter are the two most common yet ultimately inadequate criteria used to distinguish these last two groups of directors. What made Zhang Yimou, Chen Kaige, Tian Zhuangzhuang, and others of the Fifth Generation so prominent was the fact that they belonged to the first group of students admitted into the reopened Beijing Film Academy (it was closed in 1966 on the eve of the Cultural Revolution, when most youths were sent to the countryside for rustication). The experiences of these directors in China's hinterland and their scars from the traumatic ten years of the Cultural Revolution manifested themselves explicitly or implicitly in their films and in their attempt to represent modern Chinese history—a reflection of the desire of these directors to comprehend and reproduce their wasted youth on the screen.

As Ni Zhen's, Zhang Yimou's, and Chen Kaige's teacher at the academy has written,

> So many young men and women, only sixteen or seventeen, whose lives were just beginning, are buried forever under the red soil on the mountain peaks laid bare by hacking and cutting. And those who returned from the red soil have given their lives over to endlessly remembering and talking about it, for each of them is haunted by living spirits they cannot drive away.[15]

If their films seem excessively obsessed with modern Chinese history, particularly the Cultural Revolution, it is because these directors had to come to terms with their own pasts.[16] This is in sharp contrast to the younger group, the Sixth Generation directors, who were mostly born in the 1960s: "The Cultural Revolution was part of their early childhood. Uninterested in the broad sweep of history, the directors concentrate on personal accounts of young people's experience."[17] Their films are generally characterized by descriptions of malcontent over contemporary life and views of urban ills. If generational labels are to make any sense at all, it is this significant difference in subject matter that distinguishes these two groups, while their shared experience as graduates of the Beijing Film Academy stands as a marker of continuity in Chinese cinematic tradition.

Dai Jinhua, China's preeminent cultural and film critic, has complained about an overdetermined use of generational labels. At an Asian film festival in the United States, she wrote, one of the organizers promoted *Postman* as a film by a Sixth Generation director (He Jianjun), saying that it was "'an important mainland Chinese film whose inclusion is a special honor to the film festival.'" Dai continues,

> A *New York Times* review . . . echoed the same note. Except for hollow, flamboyant praise and a plot précis, the only comment on *Postman*'s value was that "it was completely different from the Fifth Generation works." Naturally the "Sixth Generation" will differ from the "Fifth Generation." But, being different does not, in itself, say anything about the Sixth Generation.[18]

Dai's complaint about excessive (and often unwarranted) praise of younger directors by festival organizers points to a blind spot in the reception of Chinese films in the West. Generally speaking, even bad films get a pass in the West, while good ones are praised to the skies. These directors may well be talented and have laudable potential, but should we not allow them room to mature? Should we not concede the possibility that films from first-time directors could very well be merely good?

HOW ARE CHINESE FILMS APPRECIATED IN THE UNITED STATES?

Consider this:

> Simply speaking, after *Yellow Earth* appeared in 1984, no one, no matter with what attitude, could look upon Chinese film as in the past, before *Yellow Earth* was made. Praised or criticized, the film left an indelible imprint, a proof of spiritual extension. The waist-drum dance, filled with national vitality, and the ritual of the rain prayer, loaded with ancient tradition, transmitted a shock, a warning and a distant yet clearly heard clap of thunder to Western film circles, which had constantly evaluated and judged in terms of European cultural criteria. An Oriental culture had produced a film, authentic by all international standards, that was aimed directly at them.[19]

And this:

> One of the challenges of foreign movies is to determine how they would play on their native soil. Here, for example, is "Happy Times," from the sometimes great Chinese director Zhang Yimou. It is about a group of unemployed men who build a fake room in an abandoned factory, move a blind girl into it, tell her it is in a hotel, and become the clients for daily massages, paying her with blank pieces of paper they hope she will mistake for money.
>
> On the basis of that description, you will assume that this movie is cruel and depraved. But turn now to the keywords under "tone" in the movie's listing at allmovie.com, and you will find: "Sweet, Reflective, Light, Humorous, Easygoing, Compassionate, Affectionate" . . . .

. . . When American critics praise the movie (and most of them have), they are making some kind of concession to its Chinese origins. A story that would be unfilmable by Hollywood becomes, in Chinese hands, "often uproariously funny" (*New York Magazine*), "subtle and even humorous" (*Film Journal International*), and "wise, gentle and sad" (*New York Times*).[20]

The first quotation is from an essay written by Ni Zhen in 1985, the second a review by Roger Ebert in 2002. Although the two comments are separated by nearly two decades, they are still illuminating in demonstrating the kind of cultural misunderstandings and appreciation fallacies that are constantly at play between China and the United States. For Ni Zhen and other, likeminded Chinese intellectuals, China is always being judged according to Western standards, and although China has long and impressive traditions, it is forever catching up to but never on a par with the United States. This mixed sense of superiority and inferiority is perhaps not entirely groundless, but one senses in Ni's remarks that too much nationalistic pride has been invested in a movie that was not appreciated by Chinese audiences, at least at first. As Ni Zhen reveals elsewhere in the same essay, *Yellow Earth* met with a worse than lukewarm domestic reception, and a cinema in Beijing even had to apologize to the audience, refund their tickets, and replace *Yellow Earth* with a different film. It was only after *Yellow Earth* won international acclaim that the Chinese warmed up to it, and in retrospect it is considered the film that ushered in a new era in Chinese cinema. One wonders if Ni Zhen would have lauded the movie as a thunderclap had it not won international recognition. As for other films that came after *Yellow Earth*, it is often foreign attention that enhances a movie's domestic recognition, or may even help lift a ban on it.

This is not intended as a criticism of Ni Zhen's somewhat defensive view of Chinese cinema but rather as a way to show the complexities of filmmaking in China and how that filmmaking is intricately intertwined with Chinese nationalism and the West. The West, represented by the United States, often applies, contrary to Ni's claim, a cultural-relativist standard to Chinese films, which is pointed out in Roger Ebert's exasperated response to the words critics used to describe *Happy Times*. Or one can say it is precisely these words, and their condescending overtone, that irritated Ni many years ago. Although appreciation of art is often a matter of personal, subjective taste, we cannot deny a common standard that transcends national, cultural, and geographical boundaries.

While Ebert might appear astute and judicious in his comments about *Happy Times*, he is not completely guiltless of the appreciation fallacy. A quick survey of his reviews of Chinese movies shows his cinematic preference: movies as a window into daily life in China. Here is a line from his review of *The Story of Qiu Ju*: "Along the way we absorb more information about the lives of ordinary people in everyday China than in any other film I've seen." And on *Not One Less*: "For Western viewers, there's almost equal interest at the edges of the screen, in the background, in the locations and incidental details that show daily life in today's China." To be sure, for Western audiences it is difficult to avoid seeing a foreign movie as representative of anything more than just a segment of a culture or a figment of a director's imagination. But one should be aware that there is more to a movie than details of daily life and be mindful of the distinction between *representation* and *representative*.

HOW ARE CHINESE FILMS INTERPRETED?

Given the subjective nature of film appreciation, it is difficult to accept as definitive a single reading of a certain movie, and it is not necessary or feasible to do so. On the other hand, how a foreign film is interpreted and appreciated by a particular culture or society is often indicative as much of a different aesthetics as of the working of cross-cultural politics. In the following section I focus on two films, both of which are available in the United States with English subtitles, to examine how they have been interpreted by scholars and film critics and how these various interpretations reveal types of cultural misunderstandings that are often at play between China and the United States.

Yellow Earth (Dir. Chen Kaige, 1984)

No other film produced in the post–Cultural Revolution era has drawn more attention than *Yellow Earth*.[21] The film features a young People's Liberation Army (PLA) soldier, Gu Qing, who goes to a barren village in northern Shaanxi province to collect folk songs for adoption by PLA soldiers. Gu Qing lodges with a prematurely aged widower, his daughter, Cuiqiao, and son, Hanhan. While helping out with work inside and outside their cave dwelling, Gu Qing preaches the Communist "gospel" that young people in the liberated South are no longer forced into prearranged marriages. When a marriage is proposed for Cuiqiao, she asks Gu Qing, who is now returning to the South, to take her along, but he refuses by saying he will apply for PLA membership on her behalf and come back for her. But when he finally returns, Cuiqiao has apparently already drowned in the raging Yellow River in an attempt to reach the South and escape from her marriage. The film ends in a rain-prayer scene, in which Hanhan runs against the crowd and seemingly toward Gu, who disappears from the horizon.

The consensus among film critics and scholars about *Yellow Earth*'s importance primarily lies in that fact that it is "regarded as a pioneering work in modern Chinese cinema. . . . It focused international attention on the burgeoning Chinese film industry; it influenced other young directors."[22] Despite later enthusiasm among scholars and the movie's cult status in China, *Yellow Earth*'s initial screening in Beijing, as we have seen, was worse than paltry. One must wonder what, in addition to the Silver Leopard the film won at the Locarno Film Festival, caused this sea change. Mary Ann Farquhar believes that domestic audiences' initial lack of response was largely due to the fact that the film does not rely on overt didacticism, which until then was the dominant film language. Ni Zhen, while refuting the idea that *Yellow Earth* is a propaganda movie, focuses on the use of "symbolic, imagistic and metaphoric devices to excavate national history."[23] Following an obliquely similar line of judgment, Farquhar uses the Daoist notion of yin and yang to analyze the film and concludes that it is the Daoist aesthetic (an integral part of traditional Chinese cultural heritage) that "produced a film which is stunningly 'different' from the usual Communist product."[24]

Both Ni Zhen and Mary Ann Farquhar all but ignore the fact that the film is deliberately set in 1939, ten years before the founding of the PRC. Although one would prefer to focus on the aesthetic level, one cannot elide a long tradition of commenting on the present by using the past (*yi gu yu jin*). In other words, perhaps this film has a hidden message about China in 1984, since it is set at a time when Communism held so much promise, a promise that, in retrospect, turned out to be empty (and therefore similar to the promise Gu Qing makes to Cuiqiao?). If indeed, as Bonnie Mc-Dougall detects, there are "deep reflections on Chinese history" in this film and a "search for new meaning in the Chinese national character,"[25] how should we relate such reflections to the film's specific reference to 1939? Granting that the movie, and particularly its ending, is ambiguous, we should not be surprised that some might read it as Communist propaganda. On the other hand, the historical setting and the undisclosed but assumed death of Cuiqiao also encourage the audience to regard the movie as an oblique criticism of the CCP, represented by Gu Qing, who comes back too late and with too little hope for either Cuiqiao or Hanhan. These readings of this pioneering work that ushered in the New Chinese Cinema are inevitably colored by the understanding and prejudices of another culture, and they point to the ambiguities that allow for various interpretations.

Happy Times (Dir. Zhang Yimou, 2003)

Happy Times is ostensibly based on the novella *Shifu, You'll Do Anything for a Laugh* by Mo Yan, whose novel *Red Sorghum* was adapted by Zhang Yimou and established Zhang's reputation in China and overseas. The original story depicts a factory worker who is laid off just before his retirement and hence is deprived of the pension due him. He petitions for help from various officials, but all to no avail. Desperation and the need to survive drive him to convert an abandoned bus into a "love hotel," where lovers are charged a fee to satisfy their need for privacy. By describing the consequences and sufferings of the average Chinese worker in the aftermath of large-scale privatization of state-owned enterprises (SOEs), the story raises a question: How far may an individual go to help himself after being abandoned by his government?

In Zhang Yimou's movie we still have our *shifu*, or master worker, Old Zhao, whose factory is also shut down, but we detect no dire need for self-preservation. Old Zhao's desperate need for money and his subsequent failed attempt to run a love hotel derives from his wish to be married. His love interest, almost as an exchange for marriage, asks him to find her ex-husband's blind daughter a job and therefore remove the girl from her house. To be sure, one should not fault a man in his fifties for his desire to be married to the woman of his choice. However, this shift in focus not only skirts the issues raised in Mo Yan's story but also dilutes the severity of the problems facing laid-off workers in China. That is, one man's desperate attempt at survival in the novella is turned in the movie into a quest for an odious, heartless woman who, at one point in the movie, literally throws a helpless blind girl out on the street.

As Roger Ebert suggests, this plot would never be adopted by Hollywood directors if it were taken out of China and set in, say, New York City; U.S. film reviewers' exuberance over the film is a not uncommon sign of their willful double standard. On the other hand, we can appreciate U.S. critics' predicament in reviewing Chinese films. Western film viewers and scholars of the Chinese cinema have long been plagued by what I call the "national allegory dilemma"—that is, an inability to escape a belief, suggested by the now-famous phrase of Fredric Jameson that "all third-world literature is national allegory."[26] In the context of Chinese cinema, Western viewers seem unable to avoid treating these movies as a sort of comment on or criticism of the state of the PRC (hence, literary or cinematic works banned in China are welcomed in the West). The pitfall of such an attitude is that Western critics deny Chinese directors and filmmakers their creativity and artistic freedom, since these critics want to see every movie as a reflection of Chinese society and are unwilling, it seems, to accept the possibility that a movie can be good in spite of a lack of social criticism. In a word, it is nearly impossible for many Westerners to appreciate art from China for art's sake. "There is a temptation for Western viewers to scrutinize these films with a Chinese censor's eyes, looking for political criticism or social irony in every frame. Of course, what is belligerent folly to the censor is political bravery to us."[27]

That said, anyone self-aware enough to be conscious of such a bias embedded in cross-cultural understanding is bound to find themselves incapable of appreciating *Happy Times*. If we look at the movie not as a representation of social ills in contemporary China but as a film about a group of laid-off workers lying to a blind girl presumably to help her out, even though none of them has the means to do so, we would likely find it morbid and cruel, and not at all "uproariously funny." In addition, when the blind girl leaves the temporary lodging Old Zhao has found for her, we see her walking on a bustling street teeming with motor vehicles and pedestrians, and we are told everything will be fine. How will everything be fine for her, a blind girl with no money, no job, no friends, and no place to live? The movie assaults our sensibilities by disguising its lack of plausibility with a sugary portrayal of interpersonal relations. The only way to consider it a great movie is by treating it as an allegorical representation of Chinese society: the blind girl, like the majority of the Chinese population, is tricked into believing that she is making progress toward her goal—finding her father and recovering her eyesight—only to find it is all a big lie. It is then even more ironic, following this line of argument, when the blind girl tells Old Zhao that the time she spends with him is the happiest of her life. By approaching the film in this manner, we detect the irony in the title, *Happy Times*, because happiness for the girl is nothing but a mirage. Such a reading, however, puts us squarely back in the national allegory dilemma.

China is undergoing rapid changes, while its importance in the world economy continues to grow. The country's admission into the World Trade Organization (WTO) will exert even greater influence and pressure for further changes, signs of which were evident in the revision of rules governing the production and distribution of films in China. Recently, the Chinese film industry has also witnessed a relaxation of censorship and limits on capital investment, as well as expanded foreign investment in films by Chinese directors, most notably Zhang Yimou's *Hero* (see figure 7.2) and Chen Kaige's *The Promise*. The challenge from the West, mainly Hollywood, to make profitable

Figure 7.2.   Maggie Cheung as a daring swordswoman in Zhang Yimou's *Hero* (2002).

movies will probably force Chinese directors to sacrifice some degree of artistic creativity; on the other hand, more changes in SARFT's regulation of the industry are not only possible but foreseeable. Ideally, expanding Sino-U.S. contacts will help U.S. moviegoers improve their sophistication in appreciating Chinese films, and the mystique of China will be lifted in a more positive way as the cachet of Chinese censorship diminishes in the West and more films are screened for their artistic achievement.

NOTES

1. See Wei Ming Dariotis and Eileen Fung, "Breaking the Soy Sauce Jar: Diaspora and Displacement in the Films of Ang Lee," in *Transnational Chinese Cinema: Identity, Nationhood, Gender*, ed. Sheldon Hsiao-peng Lu, (Honolulu: University of Hawaii Press, 1997), 216–17.

2. Yingjin Zhang, *Screening China: Critical Interventions, Cinematic Reconfigurations, and the Transnational Imaginary in Contemporary Chinese Cinema* (Ann Arbor: University of Michigan Press, 2002), 18.

3. Kaiser Kuo, "Zhang Yuan's Third Way," *Chinesecinema* (February 2003). I wish to thank Kaiser for sharing this essay with me.

4. Kuo, "Zhang Yuan's Third Way."

5. Sheila Cornelius, with Ian Haydn Smith, *New Chinese Cinema: Challenging Representations* (London: Wallflower Press, 2002), 48.

6. Sheldon Hsiao-peng Lu, ed. *Transnational Chinese Cinema: Identity, Nationhood, Gender* (Honolulu: University of Hawaii Press, 1997), 8.

7. Kaiser Kuo, "Made in China: Necessary Evil?" *Time Asia*, www.time.com/time/asia/news/printout/0,9788,100067,00.html.

8. Unbeknownst to many U.S. citizens, not only imported but also domestic products are being pirated in China, but a discussion of piracy is beyond the scope of this chapter. Kaiser Kuo offers the provocative and positive view that pirated materials, especially movie and music CDs, "have penetrated deep into the interior, opening a window into the Western world otherwise inaccessible to the insular Chinese hinterland." See Kuo, "Made in China: Necessary Evil?"

9. All figures come from *Dianying yishu* [*Film Art*], listed at www.asianfilm.org/china.

10. *China Daily*, January 8, 2004.

11. Alice Yan, *South China Morning Post*, November 4, 2003. For more information on the inroads of Hollywood into Chinese movie theaters, see Stanley Rosen, "Hollywood, Globalization, and Film Markets in Asia: Lessons for China?" www.asianfilms.org; and Stanley Rosen, "The Wolf at the Door: Hollywood and the Film Market in China," in *Southern California and the World*, ed. Eric J. Heikkila and Rafael Pizarro (Westport, CT: Praeger, 2002), 60–61.

12. A recent turn of events for Wang is SARFT's decision to clear his *Beijing Bicycle*, which was sent to the Berlin Film Festival before permission had been obtained from SARFT because Wang did not have enough time for the lengthy approval process.

13. Jonathan Noble, "The Trope of the Underground: Politics and Hybridity in New Chinese Cinema" (paper, Symposium on Contemporary Chinese Visual Culture, University of Westminster, February 6, 2004). I would like to thank Jonathan for sharing this essay with me.

14. In an interview with Hong Kong film critic Stephen Teo, Li Yang intimated that his film was based on a novel that won China's highest literary award (the Lao She prize), and hence, the story line itself was not controversial. Li further confessed that he was unsure if *Blind Shaft* was actually banned in China. See Stephen Teo, "There Is No Sixth Generation: Director Li Yang on *Blind Shaft* and His Place in Chinese Cinema," www.senseofcinema.com/contents/03/27/li_yang.html.

15. Ni Zhen, *Memoirs from the Beijing Film Academy: The Genesis of China's Fifth Generation*, trans. Chris Berry (Durham, NC: Duke University Press, 2002), 20.

16. Over the past few years, these directors have begun shifting their attention to aspects of contemporary Chinese society. Chen Kaige's *Big Parade* examines the life of People's Liberation Army (PLA) soldiers, while Zhang Yimou's *Not One Less* portrays the shortage of teachers in a remote village. *Happy Times*, a "comedy," also departs sharply from Zhang Yimou's earlier works on modern Chinese history. Recently Zhang has made forays into historical drama with works set in ancient China such as *Hero* (2002) and *House of Flying Daggers* (2004).

17. Cornelius, *New Chinese Cinema*, 108.

18. Dai Jinhua, "A Scene in the Fog: Reading the Sixth Generation Films," trans. Wang Yiman, in *Cinema and Desire: Feminist Marxism and Cultural Politics in the Work of Dai Jinhua*, ed. Jing Wang and Tani E. Barlow (London: Verso, 2002), 77–78.

19. Ni Zhen, "After *Yellow Earth*," trans. Fu Binbin, in *Film in Contemporary China: Critical Debates, 1979–1989*, ed. George S. Semel, Chen Xihe, and Xia Hong (New York: Praeger, 1993), 31–37.

20. Roger Ebert, "Happy Times," *Chicago Sun-Times*, August 9, 2002, www.suntimes.com/ebert/ebert_reviews/2002/08/080903.html.

21. For some examples, see Mary Ann Farquhar, "The 'Hidden' Gender in *Yellow Earth*," in *Celluloid China: Cinematic Encounters with Culture and Society*, ed. Harry H. Kuoshu (Carbondale: Southern Illinois University Press, 2002), 220–32; Chris Berry and Mary Ann Farquhar, "Post-socialist Strategies: An Analysis of *Yellow Earth* and *Black Cannon Incident*," in *Cinematic Landscapes: Observations on the Visual Arts and Cinema of China and Japan*, ed. Linda C. Ehrlich and David Desser (Austin: University of Texas Press, 1994), 81–116; and Jerome Silbergeld, "Drowning on Dry Land: *Yellow Earth* and the Traditionalism of the 'Avant-garde,'" in *China into Film: Frames of Reference in Contemporary Chinese Cinema* (London: Reaktion, 1999), 15–52.

22. Farquhar, "The 'Hidden' Gender in *Yellow Earth*," 220.

23. George S. Semel, Chen Xihe, and Xia Hong, eds., *Film in Contemporary China: Critical Debates, 1979–1989* (New York: Praeger, 1993), 34.

24. Farquhar, "The 'Hidden' Gender in *Yellow Earth*," 232.

25. Bonnie S. McDougall, *The Yellow Earth* (Hong Kong: Chinese University Press, 1997), 25; quoted in W. K. Cheng, "Imagining the People: 'Yellow Earth' and the Enigma of Nationalist Consciousness," *China Review* 2, no. 2 (Fall 2002): 37–63.

26. Frederic Jameson's idea came under attack shortly after its pronouncement; see for instance, Aijaz Ahmad, "Jameson's Rhetoric of Otherness and the 'National Allegory,'" *Social Text* 17 (Spring 1987): 3–25; and Lydia Liu, *Translingual Practice:*

Literature, National Culture, and Translated Modernity—China, 1900–1937 (Stanford, CA: Stanford University Press, 1995), 185–87. Jameson's view, though problematic and, to some, even bankrupt, is useful in highlighting the fact that Chinese films are often read as allegory for the nation.

27. Richard Corliss, "Bright Lights," *Time Asia*, July 26, 2003, www.time.com/time/asia/arts/printout/0,9788,103002,00.html.

SUGGESTED READINGS

Chris Berry, ed., *Perspectives on Chinese Cinema* (London: British Film Institute, 1991).

———, ed., *Chinese Films in Focus: 25 New Takes* (London: British Film Institute, 2003).

Nick Browne, Paul G. Pickowicz, Vivian Sobchack, and Esther Yau, eds., *New Chinese Cinema: Forms, Identities, Politics* (New York: Cambridge University Press, 1994).

Paul Clark, *Reinventing China: A Generation and Its Films* (Hong Kong: Chinese University Press, 2005).

Sheila Cornelius, with Ian Haydn Smith, *New Chinese Cinema: Challenging Representations* (London: Wallflower Press, 2002).

Shuqin Cui, *Women through the Lens: Gender and Nation in a Century of Chinese Cinema* (Honolulu: University of Hawaii Press, 2003).

Harry H. Kuoshu, *Celluloid China: Cinematic Encounters with Culture and Society* (Carbondale: Southern Illinois University Press, 2002).

Sheldon Hsiao-peng Lu, ed., *Transnational Chinese Cinema: Identity, Nationhood, Gender* (Honolulu: University of Hawaii Press, 1997).

Jerome Silbergeld, *China into Film: Frames of Reference in Contemporary Chinese Cinema* (London: Reaktion, 1999).

Kwok-kan Tam and Wimal Dissanayake, *New Chinese Cinema* (Hong Kong: Oxford University Press, 1998).

Yingjin Zhang, *Screening China: Critical Interventions, Cinematic Reconfigurations, and the Transnational Imaginary in Contemporary Chinese Cinema* (Ann Arbor: University of Michigan Press, 2002).

Film

Yellow Earth (dir. Chen Kaige, 1984)
Red Sorghum (dir. Zhang Yimou, 1987)
Farewell My Concubine (dir. Chen Kaige, 1993)
Suzhou River (dir. Lou Ye, 2000)
Shadow Magic (dir. Ann Hu, 2001)
Springtime in a Small Town (dir. Tian Zhuangzhuang, 2002)
Unknown Pleasure (dir. Jia Zhangke, 2002)
Blind Shaft (dir. Li Yang, 2003)
Kekexili (*Mountain Patrol*) (dir. Lu Chuan, 2004)

II

BACK STAGE

I would like to reiterate here what China stands for. We will continue to hold high the banner of peace, development and cooperation, unswervingly follow the road of peaceful development, firmly pursue the independent foreign policy of peace and dedicate ourselves to developing friendly relations and cooperation with all countries on the basis of the Five Principles of Peaceful Coexistence. Always integrating our development with the common progress of mankind, we take full advantage of the opportunities brought by world peace and development to pursue our own development while going for better promotion of world peace and common development through our successful development. China will, as always, abide by the purposes and principles of the UN Charter, actively participate in international affairs and fulfill its international obligations, and work with other countries in building towards a new international political and economic order that is fair and rational. The Chinese nation loves peace. China's development, instead of hurting or threatening anyone, can only serve peace, stability and common prosperity in the world. Throughout the long history, human communities have never been so closely interconnected in interests and destinies. Our common goals have put us all in the same boat, and the common challenges we face require that we get united. Let us join hands and work together to build a harmonious world with lasting peace and common prosperity.

President Hu Jintao, 2005

8

Fictional China

Howard Goldblatt

Thirty years after China's Cultural Revolution, when "culture" nearly died, two worlds of contemporary Chinese fiction have evolved: the one that in recent years has captured large, sometimes vast, numbers of readers in Chinese, and the one that includes works read by considerably smaller numbers of people outside China in translation.[1] These two worlds, while not mutually exclusive, are radically and increasingly disparate. Obviously, only a tiny fraction of the fiction published in China finds its way into other cultures, and the selection process, guided by such factors as a limited number of translators, publishing agendas, and reader interest, presents an idiosyncratic—some would say skewed—view of Chinese literature and society. Happily, some of the best writing and the most interesting Chinese fiction does get translated, though there is an inevitable time gap, sometimes substantial, that creates a loss of immediacy. Predictably, the fullness of available title lists and the diversity of offerings in China's bookstores (some of which occupy entire city blocks) cannot be accurately gauged by the quantity and nature of those titles published in the West.

For most of the country's history, book publishing in the PRC has been predictably monochromatic: heroes and villains, reforms and back-sliding, paeans and diatribes. But since the dark days of 1989, when untold numbers of Chinese citizens were killed in and around Tiananmen Square,[2] the literary scene has undergone a remarkable "caffeinization." A more differentiated, or even anarchistic, selection of offerings, one that caters to all tastes—high and low, domestic and foreign, licensed and pirated—is available to book buyers. This phenomenon has been greeted by everything from outright glee to head scratching and alarm. Very postmodern, some would say.

Youth, we are told (usually, and stridently, by the young) will be served. That is certainly the case in twenty-first-century China, which, paradoxically, is witnessing an unbalanced aging of its population, thanks largely to the one-child policy. As a mixture of bohemianism and runaway consumerism grips the urban centers, largely escapist, sensational, and all too often slipshod writing from the laptops of twenty-somethings and younger—in some cases, much younger—has flooded the bookstores. That trend is partially reflected in the West, where an uptick in interest in Chinese writing has occurred, in particular in autobiographical, unashamedly confessional, and unaffectedly juvenile novels, mostly by girls and young women. The ranks of Western readers curious about contemporary China in general, and its literature and the arts in particular, are being swelled by more casual readers eager to share vicariously experiences with sex, drugs, punk music, and teenage angst.

As the year 2000 approached its end, *Time Asia* published a special report: "Young China." In it a gaggle of young writers, most under the age of thirty and some still in their teens, whose first novels had shot to the top of bestseller lists, was introduced. Some, including Mian Mian, author of the gritty novel *Candy*,[3] and Wei Hui, who made a splash with *Shanghai Baby*[4] (together they are known as the "shock sisters"), have since had their works translated into many foreign languages, and they appear to have been well received in foreign countries, especially since their publishers can truthfully claim that the novels have been banned in China.[5] Both the bannings and the cachet this lends to foreign-language editions are trends that have continued into the twenty-first century.

But before we consider in greater depth purveyors to an expanding Chinese market in kiddie-lit, glam-lit, and grunge-lit, it may be instructive to see what members of earlier generations of writers, those who experienced the Cultural Revolution firsthand as adults or as children, have accomplished in recent years.

It has been stated before, but certainly bears repeating, that the selection of Gao Xingjian as winner of the 2000 Nobel Prize in Literature came as a surprise to nearly everyone—in China, in the West, just about everywhere. Maybe it shouldn't have.

For years, the Nobel Prize in Literature has been an obsession with Chinese writers, critics, academics, and the general population. Published comments on the subject have run from indignation to despair to outright denial of the likelihood of the prize ever being awarded to a Chinese author. The absence of a Chinese laureate—Pearl Buck, the 1938 winner, and one that many would like to forget, was the closest they'd come—intrigued observers for years. The academy must have had that in mind when they elected Göran Malmqvist, emeritus professor of Stockholm University and a specialist in Chinese literature, to their body. In 1987 Malmqvist himself was quoted in the *New York Times* as saying, "That's one major reason I was elected to the Academy . . . to broaden their linguistic competence. The time will come, and I think it will come very soon, when we have a Chinese." It took thirteen years. But why this particular writer out of the many, including the expatriate poet Bei Dao, the nonagenarian Ba Jin, and Shen Congwen, who had been nominated in the past?

To answer that question, we need to look briefly at the prize itself before turning our attention to Gao and the works for which he was honored. While questions attend the selections in all fields, for sheer controversy the Nobel Prize in Literature is rivaled only by the Nobel Peace Prize. No one believes that the laureate of the year is by definition, even acclamation, the best living writer not yet to have won the prize. Many factors are involved, from cultural diversity to international visibility and, of course, politics.

Politically, it depends upon where one stands. The official Chinese reaction to Gao's award was that the selection of Gao, as a French citizen whose works had been banned in China for years, was a deliberate provocation by the Swedish Academy and undeserved by Gao. The unofficial reaction was more positive, if uninformed, and it should not be held against Gao that the Chinese government and its media organs mounted a vilification campaign against him or that Taiwan and Hong Kong went gaga over a writer hardly anyone in either place had ever heard of, let alone read.

Gao first came to attention in China through his plays of the early 1980s, less than a decade after the end of the Cultural Revolution. Influenced by the European modernists, whom he studied and translated, he sought to capture the suffering caused by and the inanity of the Cultural Revolution and other calamitous political campaigns in China that had stifled the creativity and deadened the spirit of the Chinese people for much of their recent history, if not longer. But it is his fiction that will be the standard by which his selection is evaluated by most people. Gao's novel *Soul Mountain* was hailed by the Swedish Academy as "one of those singular literary creations that seem impossible to compare with anything but themselves." Essentially created out of the author's search for meaning in life following a misdiagnosis of lung cancer and political attacks on his plays, this long novel memorializes a ten-month sojourn in China's southwest outposts, to which he had fled to escape persecution, and it becomes a sort of spiritual voyage.

One of the qualities that place Gao in the ranks of respected Nobel Laureates and differentiate him from many Chinese writers is the universal appeal of his works as distinctively Chinese yet transcending national boundaries—less parochial, less didactic, and much more sexual, which adds to his appeal outside China. Among Gao's favorite themes is the relationship between the individual and the collective entity. That is the case with *Soul Mountain* and with his second novel, *One Man's Bible*, as well.[6] Gao's Nobel

Prize has drawn more attention to Chinese writing; Western publishers, notably large commercial houses, are increasingly inclined to have China on
their lists, in spite of generally anemic sales.

Other writers whose names have been associated with the Nobel Prize
have also been active in recent years, most prominently, Mo Yan, whose
fifth novel, *Big Breasts and Wide Hips*,[7] recreates the historical sweep and
earthy exuberance of his powerful debut novel, *Red Sorghum*.[8] This latest
work, which is mainly about women—their strengths, their trials, and their
ability to endure—is a prodigious novel that relates the story of one family
from the time of the Japanese invasion of China in the mid-1930s up to the
post-Mao era, with an extended flashback to the turn of the twentieth century. Interfamily struggles and intrigues, involving complex and sensitive
historical and political issues, lend the novel an allegorical quality; as such,
it represents Mo Yan's vision of the twentieth century in China. Prior to this
book's publication, Mo Yan had startled his readers with *The Garlic Ballads*,
a political novel that highlighted the plight of China's peasants in the face
of an unfeeling bureaucracy and corrupt officials.[9] After that came a
metafictional novel that attacked China's vaunted epicureanism by linking
it to cannibalism; *The Republic of Wine*[10] is the most incisive, trenchant, and
readable social satire any modern Chinese writer has created. In the view of
one critic,

> Nothing in *Red Sorghum* or *The Garlic Ballads* quite prepares the reader for the
> surprises to be found in *The Republic of Wine*, a veritable cornucopia of com-
> edy, ingenuity, and technical dexterity. Mo Yan's purpose dawns upon us grad-
> ually as we discover a fictional structure unlike anything we are likely to have
> seen before, perhaps Laurence Sterne's *Tristram Shandy* offering the closest par-
> allel, or to a certain extent the fictions of Jorge Luis Borges.[11]

In recent years, Mo Yan has continued to write big, lusty novels that are ce-
menting his reputation as the most prolific of China's serious writers, a constant thorn in the side of the official literary establishment, and still a favorite among readers, domestic and international.

Shanxi province novelist Li Rui, author of *Silver City*,[12] also continues to
impress observers of literary China with his revealing portraits of the impoverished Chinese countryside and the hardscrabble lives of its inhabitants in such novels as *The Windless Tree* and *A Vast Cloudless Sky*.[13] Both Mo
Yan and Li Rui are devoted to the task of unearthing (or creating) alternative versions of China's modern history, viewed through the prism of daily
life in the parts of China that the authors know best. Swimming against a
current of official histories and grand narratives of revolutionary determinism, these authors are squarely in opposition to everything from history
textbooks to TV dramas of heroism and martyrdom; yet they, and others
like them, persist in their quest to recuperate the true essence of China's

past while exploding popular and more comforting views by presenting contrasting tales of ignorance, brutality, complacency, corruption, and willful oppression.

Yet another diehard novelist, and one for whom "experimentalist" may be the most fitting description, is Han Shaogong, whose *A Dictionary of Maqiao*,[14] a novel in the form of a dictionary, "emerges as one grand idiom," according to one reviewer, "a meditation on the trapdoors of language and on the micro-histories buried within words."[15] Like many writers of his generation, Han laments the dilution of culture and language in contemporary, globalized China and worries that language is losing the power "to describe the nuances in life."[16] This stance is sure to keep him and those who share all or part of his concerns off the best-seller lists. Worse yet, given the current emphasis on a market economy, with publishers increasingly concerned about the bottom line and with the tendency of erstwhile readers to search out less-challenging cultural commodities, even seeing their work published has become increasingly difficult for experimental writers. Popular assaults on language, a phenomenon in all cultures, while almost always successful, are at least slowed down and brought to public notice by members of society who live by the word—a Sisyphean yet clearly worthy undertaking.

"Nobody reads anymore," is how Nanjing novelist Su Tong, author of *Raise the Red Lantern* and *Rice*,[17] characterizes the cultural scene during an interview in Singapore. Once part of a cadre of young writers (now entering their middle years) who enjoyed a huge domestic readership, he has witnessed a sea change in the reception of literature among literate Chinese, who now "are all trying to [make] money" and are too busy to read. There are, he concludes, "fewer and fewer paying readers," thanks to this single-minded urge to get rich, as well as to the effects of book piracy and the appeal of television and movies.[18] The reality of there being fewer readers for the likes of Su Tong has thinned the ranks of literary stalwarts, many of whom, like Liu Heng (*Black Snow*; *Green River Daydreams*),[19] have moved into the film industry, some successfully, others not. Their places have been taken by the lean and hungry youngsters whose books either sell in the tens of thousands or are banned and then sell in the hundreds of thousands and often, as a result, find their way into the hands of eager translators.

Of the so-called avant-gardists of the 1980s and 1990s, virtually none remain committed to the edgy, symbolic style of writing that gained popularity in the period before the Tiananmen massacre; a significant drop in general readership has launched a return to gritty realism among large numbers of established and upcoming writers. Su Tong, whose pessimistic musings we have just noted, continues to write, preferring historical settings, as in the recently published *My Life as Emperor*, the tale of a child ruler whose abuse of power nearly brings his nation to ruin and that some have read as political theater.[20] More recent history is at the center of Ye Zhaoyan's *Nanjing, 1937: A Love Story*,[21] set in the days leading up to the infamous Rape of Nanjing. The fact that many if not most Chinese historical novels are set in a time prior to the contemporary era, whether imperial, republican, or merely pre–Jiang Zemin, does not fully blunt the social and political critiques embedded in them.

Another writer, Yu Hua, whose disorienting stories of grotesque brutality and layered symbolism were so popular and influential in the late 1980s, was among the first to move away from modernist writing and back to more accessible language and stories. His novel *To Live*,[22] which Zhang Yimou turned into a highly regarded film, is written in a traditional realistic style, as is the novel that followed, *Chronicle of a Blood Merchant*.[23] In referring to earlier works by the avant-gardists, Ge Fei, one of their number, stated that "the practice of modernism, with its interest centering on ideas and concepts, has inevitably hurt some other essential virtues of the novel, and limited the potential of Chinese writers."[24] Ma Yuan, who wrote elliptical, often other-worldly tales of Tibet, agrees: "[Modernist works] fail to provide the joy of reading . . . A great novel must first be attractive."[25] It should also be marketable these days, a time when, according to Yu Hua, "the popularity machinery has become more and more unpredictable in modern society, where the market interferes more powerfully than ever."[26] Whereas readers were once challenged, if not derided, they are now eagerly sought out by writers who can no longer rely on the "iron rice bowl" of the Writers Association (a state-run cultural apparatus whose primary, if not explicitly acknowledged, function has been to control writers), which issues meager paychecks these days. Readers want to be entertained more than they want to be educated or uplifted, and their desires are being met by writers and publishers throughout the country. Yet some of the major figures of the past few decades manage to produce humanistic novels and stories of sufficient quality to continue to appeal to dedicated readers, foreign and domestic.

The 1990s, a nervous decade after Tiananmen, witnessed the rise of a slew of apocalyptic novels, mostly focusing on corruption. The most famous of these page-turners is a fictional recreation of a corruption scandal involving Chen Xitong, then mayor of Beijing. In real life, Chen's vice mayor committed suicide and Chen himself was sent to prison, the highest-ranking official to be so dealt with since the Cultural Revolution. Yet another explosive novel, *Jueze* [*The choice*], which was turned into a movie, was recommended to every member of the CCP by Jiang Zemin, since it centered on corruption (safely below the highest ranks of party cadres), especially in the countryside.[27]

The late 1990s saw an upswing in urban tales, focusing mostly on Beijing and Shanghai but including other cities caught up in economic reforms,

modernization, and the resultant social problems. Novelist and film director Zhu Wen's *What Is Garbage and What Is Love*, a pseudo-satire set in Beijing, will soon be out in translation. Meanwhile, Shanghai novelist Wang
Anyi continues to write at a frenetic pace. Following the publication in 1995
of *Changhe ge* [*Song of everlasting sorrow*], a hefty, historical, celebratory, and
prize-winning novel of Shanghai, Wang has published several slighter yet
always finely crafted novels that further consolidate her reputation as
Shanghai's finest writer, and one whose character portraits are, in the view
of many, peerless.[28] In an age when story generally trumps style, Wang's
popularity with critics, scholars, and dedicated readers of highly nuanced
writing appears not to be matched, and her graceful style does not easily
translate into foreign languages.

Another renowned writer, probably the oldest among these, manages to
keep writing and selling relatively well, owing largely to his status as minister of culture during the early reform era (in the wake of the disastrous Cultural Revolution). Currently vice chairman of the Chinese Writers Association, Wang Meng, a once-controversial author whose critiques of early
governmental malfeasance landed him in internal exile for over a decade,
writes at a leisurely pace, capturing the spotlight once every several years
with a new novel or by his participation in the latest literary dogfight. The
paradox of his literary offerings has been an experimental and highly sophisticated style of narration in works with a decidedly conservative ideological content. It has often been a case of "love the writing, hate the book"
(or vice versa). His novel *Green Fox* deviates from his earlier work, however,
for it is a story of love and "the need for sex, a motif he seldom touched in
his previous writing, but which gets considerable attention here."[29]

Sex is in. It is really in. As members of the *linglei* (alternative lifestyle)
generation—China's Generation X, I suppose, or beyond—leap into the literary fray, the terms *body writing* and *lower-body literature* have entered the
hip lexicon. The terms come from Wang Shuo, enfant terrible of the late
1980s and early 1990s, whose "hooligan" novels, such as *Playing for Thrills*
(which Stephen King called "perhaps the most brilliantly entertaining
'hardboiled' novel of the 90s . . . China noir") and *Please Don't Call Me Human*, a spoof on China's quest for the Olympics, captivated Chinese readers
for a decade.[30] But by the end of the century, he was passé. Sensational
works that gained considerable appeal in China, owing to the reputedly autobiographical nature of the writing—in particular, graphic, often cavalierly
narrated, and sometimes drug-enhanced sex scenes (glam-lit novelist Mian
Mian once chided her contemporary Wei Hui for not having actually *done*
the things she wrote about)—have created a niche that others have been
happy to occupy, notably represented by the Mu Zimei phenomenon and
one-night-stand confessionals.[31] Mu is a twenty-five-year-old sex columnist
"whose beat is her own bedroom," and whose Internet site, before being

shut down by government censors, attracted 10 million visitors daily.[32] Not only has her writing (a scheduled book was banned before publication) "prompted a raging debate about sex and women among netizens on the Internet, where more people are writing blogs or arguing anonymously about a host of subjects in chat rooms and discussion pages,"[33] but it seems to have had an enabling effect on emerging fiction writers. And the urge to exploit sexuality has not been restricted to the new generation. Like their younger counterparts, established writers such as Chen Ran, Jia Pingwa, and Hong Ying have seen their works labeled salacious and, at other times, too "private . . . [too] individual."

This latter criticism was recently leveled at Chen Ran, whose novel *A Private Life* "challenges, not only the Maoist state's prescription of heterosexual monogamous marriage as the only lawful context for sex, but also the dominance of heterosexual liberation in post-Mao China."[34] Chen explores, in other words, lesbian eroticism and bisexuality,[35] themes that not so many years ago would have been off-limits, except through the most obscure allusions and the like.

Jia Pingwa, who was granted the title of Knight of Arts and Literature by the French Ministry of Culture in 2003, reveals a panoply of male fantasies in his (censored) 1993 novel *The Abandoned Capital*, which "recounts the sexual exploits of its famous author . . . [while commenting] on the impotence of intellectuals in late twentieth-century society,"[36] a frequently visited topos, as we have seen with Mo Yan. It has been cited as "the most explicit sexual writing since Liberation in 1949."[37] One of this rambling, narcissistic novel's subplots involves a libel lawsuit brought by one of the characters against another. But in an example of life imitating art, novelist Hong Ying was taken to court in a real lawsuit following publication of her novel *K: The Art of Love*.[38] A fictionalized account of a purported love affair between Julian Bell, son of Bloomsbury dame Vanessa Bell, and a glamorous Chinese author of the 1920s and 1930s, the novel offers graphic, if overly stylized, scenes of steamy, even kinky sex. Descendants of Ling Shuhua, the real-life model for the female character, sued the author for defamation of character. They won, thereby casting a pall over a community of writers who were intent on testing the morality waters, especially when real-life models were involved. Hong Ying's latest novel, *The Peacock Cries*, dealing with the Three Gorges dam controversy, and a mystery titled *Death in Shanghai* put her back on slightly safer ground.

Members of the younger generation must have assumed that the cautionary lessons they took from the travails of Chen Ran, Hong Ying, and Jia Pingwa were limited to the homosexual, the grandiosely autobiographical, and the historically based and were not a result of sex per se, especially when that sex was grounded in revelations of teenage and young-adult angst, paired with rock 'n' roll—one of many manifestations of urban hedonism.

While Wei Hui and Mian Mian have been relatively quiet in recent years,[39] their younger "sisters" have not been. In 2002, a twenty-year-old *linglei* woman published a highly autobiographical, diary-influenced novel she had written at the age of seventeen. *Beijing Doll*,[40] by Chun Sue (Chun Shu), a high-school dropout, became an instant best-seller because it "bared her sex life and punk fetish . . . [and stayed] away from the grander ideologies such as democracy, freedom and equality that have often motivated her alternative brethren in the West."[41] In some ways reminiscent of the work of Wang Shuo and Wang Anyi, whose evocations of Beijing and Shanghai approach the level of gazetteer, Chun Sue makes her geographical setting (primarily Beijing's Xidan district) come alive, particularly the "bar-hopping, bed-swapping, pill-popping children of the 1970s and 1980s,"[42] foreign and domestic. Despite the absence of political apostasy, her two books,[43] which evoke the lassitude of urban youth, often with too much disposable cash and too few ideals, have been banned in China as "unsuitable and too depressing for young readers.[44]

Another school dropout, Han Han, who writes of campus life, most prominently in *Sanchong men* [*Triple gates*]—which was also written at the age of seventeen[45]—has been the target of government criticism for his attacks on China's hidebound education system. "Han's distaste for the establishment," according to one observer, "is alternately mature and juvenile . . . [He is] a reluctant symbol to those youth in China dreaming of a way off the achievement track."[46]

A sense of disaffection—with school, with society in general, with ideology, with moral rectitude—permeates the work of some of the most popular young Chinese writers, and it sometimes takes the forms of self-revelation, reclusivity, self-destruction, and reckless hedonism, to the horror of the writers' parents. Whatever the form, however, these works resonate with readers throughout the urban landscape in China, especially given the refreshing absence in them of political content and concerns, and they constitute yet another window into contemporary Chinese society for the rest of the world on those few occasions that they are read outside China. That is not to say that politics play no role; politics hang around, most notably in works like Zhang Tiantian's *Song of Lei Feng*, a fictionalized account of the Maoist ideal of ideological purity and martyrdom, and in a dark and quite moving novel of Cultural Revolution romance, Yan Lianke's *Hard as Water* [*Jianying ru shui*], as well as in Yan Lianke's *Serve the People* [*Wei renmin fuwu*], which also deals with the Cultural Revolution, or in works by Tibetans, such as Alai's prize-winning and internationally renowned novel *Red Poppies*,[47] which tells the tale of a warlord family in the first half of the twentieth century. All of these works touch upon China's political scene, although, once again, safely in the past.

Nowhere do sex, political dissidence, and other social "pathologies" play a bigger role in fiction than on the Internet. The anarchy of the Web, the freedom it offers from publishers, and the promise of a large, anonymous, and highly participatory readership make it an irresistible forum for would-be novelists. Homosexuality is among the most popular themes of cyber-fiction from China. So too are crime stories, romances, and science fiction. Some of the writing, after garnering comments online, has been revised and published in print, although most of the work simply drifts off into cyber-space, where it probably belongs.

Not all the purveyors of kiddie-lit in more traditional venues write in condemnation of an educational system that has, by most standards, not served China's youths particularly well; nor are they roaming through sex-ual minefields. That may be because for many of them, barely prepubes-cent, concepts of sexuality can only be off on some far horizon. Young writ-ers I introduced a mere five years ago, today appear as éminences grises alongside the children who are publishing (and selling) today. According to *China Daily*,

> Ever since 16-year-old Yu Xiu debuted with "The Season of Flower and the Sea-son of Rain," writers who have graced headlines have become younger and younger. Wei Ni was 15 when she wrote "Live Again for You," a 130,000-word tome; 12-year-old Gu Likun penned "Legend of Sorcerer"; "Tell You I'm Not Stupid" was the creation of 9-year-old Zhang Mengmeng; Jiang Fangzhou was seven when she published her first novel and 10 when she finished her second; Dou Kou, who chronicled his "wanderings" in a travelogue, was six.[48]

Beyond the obvious assumption that children of those ages most likely re-ceived more than mere encouragement from their parents, and the quite jus-tifiable suspicion that the writing cannot be good, what this phenomenon says about the contemporary publishing scene in China and the standards and demands of the Chinese reading public is not something in which rea-sonable human beings can take pride. Children imitate, children experi-ment, children have a childish view of the world; what they do not have is the maturity and experience to make meaningful contributions to any liter-ary corpus or to expand the horizons of human knowledge. In China, "chil-dren's literature" has taken on a whole new, and worrisome, definition.

For obvious reasons, most of this "literature" will not find its way beyond China's shores; in fact, as I noted above, only a tiny fraction of the vast amount of published Chinese fiction, poetry, and other writing ever does, owing to a dearth of qualified translators, the hesitancy of U.S. and other publishers to take on foreign literature generally, and an only modest in-terest by foreign readers, most of whom learn about China via expatriate Chinese writers who write about their homeland. The novelist Ha Jin, who came to the United States in 1987 and won the 1999 National Book Award for his novel *Waiting*, is the most successful (after Gao Xingjian) of this crowd. A series of finely crafted novels and story collections has made this

Boston University professor a significant figure in American letters and an authoritative voice for pre-Tiananmen, primarily rural China. Other highly regarded expatriate novelists include Anchee Min (*Becoming Madame Mao; Red Azalea*), a one-time actress in revolutionary dramas, whose novels focus on her experiences prior to moving to the United States, where she lives and writes; and Dai Sijie, author of the best-selling *Balzac and the Little Chinese Seamstress*, who, along with teenage Prix Goncourt winner Shan Sa (*The Girl Who Played Go*), has taken up residence in France. All too often, these émigré writers "speak for China" in ways denied their peers back home, though their peers writing in China nonetheless assume that foreigners, particularly citizens of the United States, are vitally interested in their country and culture and should therefore come eagerly to translations of their work.

They are, of course, wrong. There is something about perceived authority and veracity (actually, a perceived lack of both) that keeps U.S. readers, at least, away from translated literature in droves. Expatriates (even non-Chinese) writing about China in English, however far removed from the Central Kingdom they may be, fare far better than novelists who live, work, and absorb the myriad nuances of life in contemporary China but rely upon translators to make their work available to Western readers. Since it would probably be easier to teach all Americans how to read Chinese than to change their views on translation, publishers, editors, and translators in the West will continue to serve up apologies to the writers whose work they—we—introduce to readers. In the end, the China we come to know through them, the one beyond the headlines, will remain enigmatic and woefully incomplete.

NOTES

Some of the material in this chapter has been adapted from my "Border Crossings: Chinese Writing, in Their World and Ours," in *China beyond the Headlines*, ed. Timothy B. Weston and Lionel M. Jensen (Lanham, MD: Rowman & Littlefield, 2000), 327–46; and from the following previously published essays: "Of Silk Purses and Sows' Ears: Features and Prospects of Contemporary Chinese Fiction in the West," *Translation Review* 59 (2000): 21–28; "Forbidden Food: The 'Saturnicon' of Mo Yan," *World Literature Today* 74, no. 3 (Summer 2000): 477–85; "Pushing the (Red) Envelope," *Time Asia*, October 23, 2000, 86–87; "Astute Decision by the Academy or Deliberate Provocation of China?" *Times Higher Education Supplement*, March 16, 2001, 19; and "The Writing Life," *Washington Post*, April 28, 2002. In the discussions in this chapter, I have striven to highlight representative works that are available in English translation.

1. I have resisted the temptation to include extra-literary categories of books published and sold in China—everything from new works on Mao Zedong (nearly one

hundred titles in 2003, the 110th anniversary of his birth) to how-to sex manuals, and a broad range of scholarly, sensational, informative, and otherwise worthy new works in print. Similarly, I cannot possibly deal with the considerable quantity of translated titles that appear on bookshelves in China, many of which, such as President Bill Clinton's and Senator Hillary Rodham Clinton's autobiographies, become huge best-sellers.

Book exhibits, of which the annual Beijing Book Fair is China's largest and most representative (in 2004, more than five hundred publishers displayed books in nearly 1,500 booths, according to *China Daily*, January 15, 2004), have become major international events. A book published in the Twenty-first-Century Greater Shanghai Series, *Shei zai changxiao* [*Who are best-sellers*]? (2003) gives verbal and photographic portraits of nearly fifty fiction and nonfiction authors whose recent works have sold from thirty thousand to 3 million copies. These figures do not include pirated copies, whose numbers cannot be determined but are often considerably higher than publishers' runs. A few of the authors included, though with comparatively modest numbers, are well-established, respected novelists. Not surprisingly, no poets made the list.

2. One of the few literary works to deal with Tiananmen, and the only one available in English translation, is Hong Ying, *Summer of Betrayal*, trans. Martha Avery (New York: Grove, 1997). Terrence Cheng's *Sons of Heaven* (New York: William Morrow, 2002), written in English by a Taiwanese immigrant to the United States, fictionalizes the background and primary characters (soldier and student) in the famous tank standoff near Tiananmen Square on June 4, 1989.

3. Mian Mian, *Candy*, trans. Andrea Lingenfelter (New York: Little, Brown and Company, 2003).

4. Wei Hui, *Shanghai Baby*, trans. Bruce Humes (New York: Pocket Books, 2001).

5. Unlike films, which are frequently canned by censors during production or prior to release, potentially offensive books are usually not banned until they have been published. When the treatment of sex, politics, Tibet, or Taiwan goes beyond acceptable limits, word comes down from one official bureau or another for the book to be pulled from shelves (the author is usually visited by government representatives, and the publisher is often fined); pirated copies then show up in book stalls almost immediately. Many of the books that bear a publishing company imprint are actually printed and distributed privately by entrepreneurs who purchase a *shu hao* (the equivalent of an ISBN) from a publisher, whose name then appears on the spine and the copyright page; it is perfectly legal.

6. Gao Xingjian, *Soul Mountain*, trans. Mabel Lee (New York: HarperCollins, 2000); and Gao Xingjian, *One Man's Bible*, trans. Mabel Lee (New York: HarperCollins, 2002).

7. Mo Yan, *Big Breasts and Wide Hips*, trans. Howard Goldblatt (New York: Arcade, 2004).

8. Mo Yan, *Red Sorghum*, trans. Howard Goldblatt (New York: Viking, 1993).

9. Mo Yan, *The Garlic Ballads*, trans. Howard Goldblatt (New York: Viking, 1995).

10. Mo Yan, *The Republic of Wine*, trans. Howard Goldblatt (New York: Arcade, 2000).

11. M. Thomas Inge, "Mo Yan through Western Eyes," *World Literature Today* 74, no. 3 (Summer 2000): 504.

12. Li Rui, *Silver City*, trans. Howard Goldblatt (New York: Metropolitan, 1997).

13. *Wufeng zhi shu* and *Wanli wuyun*.

14. Han Shaogong, *A Dictionary of Maqiao*, trans. Julia Lovell (New York: Columbia University Press, 2003).

15. *New York Times Book Review*, August 31, 2003, 17. Han's latest work *Anshi* [*Intimations*] continues his exploration into the uses and values of words.

16. *China Daily*, May 8, 2003. The works of Han Shaogong and his fellow experimentalist, Can Xue, are well described and analyzed in Rong Cai, *The Subject in Crisis in Contemporary Chinese Literature* (Honolulu: University of Hawaii Press, 2004).

17. Su Tong, *Raise the Red Lantern*, trans. Michael S. Duke (New York: HarperCollins, 2004); and Su Tong, *Rice*, trans. Howard Goldblatt (New York: HarperCollins, 2004).

18. Alexa Olsen, Associated Press, 2003.

19. Liu Heng, *Black Snow*, trans. Howard Goldblatt (New York: Atlantic Monthly Press, 1993); and Liu Heng, *Green River Daydreams*, trans. Howard Goldblatt (New York: Grove, 2001).

20. See for instance John Updike, "Bitter Bamboo: Two Novels from China," *New Yorker*, May 9, 2005, 84–87. The second novel reviewed is Mo Yan, *Big Breasts and Big Hips*.

21. Ye Zhaoyan, *Nanjing, 1937: A Love Story*, trans. Michael Berry (New York: Columbia University Press, 2002).

22. Yu Hua, *To Live*, trans. Michael Berry (New York: Anchor Books, 2003).

23. Yu Hua, *Chronicle of a Blood Merchant*, trans. Andrew Jones (New York: Pantheon, 2003).

24. Ge Fei, "Avant-garde Writers Take a Step Back," *China Daily*, December 18, 2002.

25. Ge Fei, "Avant-garde Writers Take a Step Back."

26. Ge Fei, "Avant-garde Writers Take a Step Back." Stories focusing on Tibet, including several by Ma Yuan, appear in Herbert J. Batt, ed., *Tales of Tibet: Sky Burials, Prayer Wheels, and Wind Horses* (Lanham, MD: Rowman & Littlefield, 2001). A more recent work, Fan Wen's *Shui ru dadi* [*Land of water and milk*] (2004), focuses on Tibetan religion.

27. A comprehensive study of corruption fiction, by Jeffrey Kinkley, will soon be published.

28. A translation of *Changhen ge* [*Tale of everlasting sorrow*], which won the 1995 Mao Dun Prize, is in progress, as is one for another novel, *Fu ping*, which shared second place in the 2003 Shanghai Novel and Novella Award with Li Rui's *Silver City*.

29. *China Daily*, January 15, 2004. Several of Wang Meng's works are available in English.

30. Wang Shuo, *Playing for Thrills*, trans. Howard Goldblatt (New York: William Morrow, 1997); Wang Shuo, *Please Don't Call Me Human*, trans. Howard Goldblatt (New York: Hyperion, 2000).

31. In 2003, the China Film Publishing House published a series of narrations by nineteen urban women about their one-night stands. That was followed the same year by the tales of fourteen urban women who turned one-night stands into longer relationships (China Workers Publishing House).

32. www.nytimes.com/2003/11/30/international/asia/30CHIN.html.

33. www.nytimes.com/2003/11/30/international/asia/30CHIN.html.

34. Tze-lan Sang, *The Emerging Lesbian: Female Same-Sex Desire in Modern China* (Chicago: University of Chicago Press, 2003), 210.

35. Chen Ran, *A Private Life*, trans. John Howard-Gibbon (New York: Columbia University Press, 2004). Gay and lesbian fiction from the PRC is far less common or popular than that from Taiwan. Twenty-six-year-old novelist Ch'iu Miao-chin (Qiu Miaojin) stunned readers in Taiwan when, after killing off the lesbian heroine of her novel *Letters from Montmarte*, she committed suicide in France.

36. Robin Visser, "Post-Mao Urban Fiction," in *The Columbia Companion to Modern East Asian Literature*, ed. Joshua Mostow (New York: Columbia University Press, 2003), 572. This is an excellent reference for the basics in literary developments, works, and figures in China (including Hong Kong and Taiwan), Japan, and Korea.

37. *China Daily*, "Bodies Melting into Words," December 4, 2003. Variously translated as *Abandoned Capital* or *City in Ruins*, it has not appeared in English.

38. Hong Ying, *K: The Art of Love*, trans. Nicky Harman and Henry Zhao (London: Marion Boyars, 2002).

39. In a San Francisco interview (Anna-Sophie Loewenberg, *SF Gate*, January 28, 2004), Mian Mian announced the imminent publication of a new novel, *Panda Sex*, the first of a series of "more mature" works.

40. Chun Sue, *Beijing Doll*, trans. Howard Goldblatt (New York: Riverhead Books, 2004).

41. *Time Asia*, "The New Radicals," February 2, 2004, 36.

42. In "Pushing the (Red) Envelope," I use this set of terms in reference to Wei Wei and Mian Mian. In fairness, Chun Sue avoids the issue of drugs in her novels.

43. Her second, even more sexually revealing novel, *Changda bantian de huanle* [*Fun and games*], appeared in 2003.

44. *Time Asia*, "The New Radicals," 36.

45. Variously translated as *The Three Gates* or *The Third Way*.

46. Grady A. Epstein, "He's China's Rebel without a Cause," *Boston Globe*, March 30, 2003. Han Han is, as well, in the forefront of a trend toward a more assertive approach to the business end of literary publishing. With his 2005 novel *Yizuo chengshi* [*One city*], he and others, such as Jiang Rong, author of the huge and hugely popular novel *Lang tuteng* [*Wolf totem*], are demanding higher royalty percentages from domestic publishers and are commanding six-figure (US$) advances for translation rights from Western publishers with offices in China, who must then develop more aggressive marketing strategies than with previously published translations.

47. Alai, *Red Poppies*, trans. Howard Goldblatt and Sylvia Li-chün Lin (New York: Houghton Mifflin, 2002). See Michiko Kakutani's review in the *New York Times*, April 19, 2002, B40.

48. *China Daily*, "China's Bards Becoming Younger and Younger," August 29, 2003.

9

Of Rice and Meat

Real Chinese Food

Susan D. Blum

Mann ist was Mann isst [You are what you eat].

If there is anything we are serious about, it is neither religion nor learn-ing, but food.

—Lin Yutang

The world was treated to a frightening peek into Chinese foodways when SARS (sudden acute respiratory syndrome) hit the news in the spring of 2003. SARS is a terrifying respiratory illness, and in this case it killed health workers, spreading throughout entire buildings in Hong Kong and pene-trating all but the most sophisticated facial masks. With a high mortality rate, it began in animal populations and jumped to humans, traveling via planes to North America. SARS was followed by bird flu (avian influenza A [H5N1]), which similarly originated in chickens in Southeast Asia and southern China, forcing the slaughter of millions of apparently healthy fowl in Asia and Europe. In 2005, U.S. senators fought to appear most alarmed about a potential bird flu pandemic, an outbreak that would be reminiscent of the 1918–1919 influenza pandemic that killed between 20 million and 40 million people worldwide and also originated in birds. Sud-denly, the papers filled with stories of the eating in China of civet cats, of Cantonese people dining on endangered species, of the close relationship between animals and humans. What in fact do ill birds and exotic animals have to do with egg rolls and hot-and-sour soup? What is going on with real Chinese food? Are all the widespread, innocuous images of rice and chop-sticks a cover for a macabre cuisine of bestiality and sucking out brains from unwitting monkeys?

In this chapter I introduce basic information about foodways in China, including general patterns and the primary symbolic foci of rice and meat. I describe a food system quite remote from the fried rice and sweet-and-sour chicken that people throughout the world commonly associate with "eating Chinese." I also stress that there are many forms of Chinese food, varying across time, space, social class, ethnic group, and occasion. But in order to understand even Americanized Chinese food, and certainly to understand the contemporary food-related scares noted above, we must plunge further into Chinese society.

TRADITIONS AND IDEALS

Food is obviously a central part of every human society, but it is never mere material for the maintenance of biological existence. People in every society have rules, beliefs, ideas, and taboos about what is eaten, how it is eaten, with whom it is eaten, and about the roles that eating plays in everyday life. We know that China's is among the most elaborate food systems in the world, but the core of the system is very simple, consisting of an opposition between *fan* (starchy staples) and *cai* (other dishes).

Fan

Fan (rhyming with the English word *con*) is the word used (in Mandarin) for both cooked rice and food in general. The common greeting *Ni chi fan le ma?* (Have you eaten yet?) refers to the eating of a meal, not the eating of just anything. Meals center on a starchy staple or grain, which in the iconic view of contemporary China is usually rice, though it can be and has been many other things as well. The traditional Chinese diet includes very little meat—an ecologically sustainable way to eat in an environment that has little room for error. At all meals, except the fanciest banquets, the main food eaten is *fan*.

In earliest times, the principal grain was millet in the North and rice in the South. (Rice has been grown in China, it appears, since around 5000 BCE.) By the Shang period (ca. 1550–1046 BCE), wheat and barley had been introduced from Inner Asia. Much later, sorghum came from Africa. Missionaries introduced New World crops—potatoes, peanuts, corn, and chilies—in the sixteenth century, especially in the mountainous Southwest and in the populous, fertile Sichuan basin. New foods were continually incorporated into the foodstuffs of China; new starchy foods were simply placed into the category of *fan*.

Fan's Partner: *Cai*

Accompanying *fan* except during famines is *cai* or *song* (dishes), the stuff that is put on top of *fan* to make it go down better. As early as the Shang period, there also seemed to be a distinction between vessels for *fan* and *cai*. (There were yet separate types of vessels for serving alcoholic beverages, which were probably made from fermented millet.) Being primarily vegetables, and sometimes grown on precious land using the carefully collected nightsoil (aged human manure, a very rich fertilizer) of nearby residents, the most commonly eaten *cai* are legumes, especially peanuts, beans, and most noteworthy, soybeans. Soybeans were cultivated in the Zhou period (1046–771 BCE), and by the early Han dynasty (208 BCE–221 CE) soybeans were fermented and widespread. Bean curd (*doufu*, or in Japanese, *tofu*) was invented probably in the late Tang dynasty (618–907 CE) or early Song dynasty (960–1279 CE). Soy can be turned into vegetarian "meat" dishes and served to devout, non-meat-eating Buddhists. Soybeans can be roasted or stir fried, and the by-products can be turned into noodles or a kind of sticky, chewy film (like fruit leather); the stalks can be fed to pigs.[1]

While vegetables predominate in the traditional Chinese diet, there is a place in that diet for meat, poultry, fish, and eggs as well. Most Chinese eat seafood if they are anywhere near a coast or a waterway. Chewy dried cuttlefish (squid) is a favorite snack; crabs are beloved seasonal treats. Eggs sometimes provide a little extra protein and are given as gifts to women who have delivered children.

The generic meat (*rou*) is pork (or *zhurou*, in contrast, say, to the meat of cattle, *niurou*, or sheep, *yangrou*). Pigs have the advantage of eating the parts of foods that humans cannot eat, such as the chaff of wheat and corn husks, though feeding pigs is a laborious affair. Pigs are typically slaughtered at the New Year, in the heart of the winter. Some of the meat is then cured and saved as sausage, and some is made into food like *jiaozi*, or meat dumplings. Dumpling preparation is a family event that most people in China recall with nostalgia. In rural China, the midpoint of winter is a time of rest, of family, and of the only meat-eating many Chinese ever had in the past.

Other meats are also desired and accepted. In general, the Chinese have few prejudices about what constitutes appropriate meat, as well as few about what parts of animals are acceptable. In contrast to people in the United States, who tend to be quite squeamish about meats and cuts, in China the inner parts of animals (tripe, organs) and the extremities (e.g., chicken feet) are considered perfectly acceptable and indeed desirable foods. Some of the most common sources of animal protein in China will be familiar to an American diner: pork, chicken, fish, and shellfish. But some will be less familiar: sea slugs, the inner organs of various domesticated animals, and wild animals. Dogs, long regarded by Han Chinese as delicacies, are eaten for warmth in winter and for virility. According to the Animals Asia Foundation, an organization that seeks the humane treatment of animals in Asia, while Hong Kong, Taiwan, and the Philippines have abolished the eating of dogs and cats, in China the desire for dogs and cats is increasing.[2] Further, bears, tigers, and other endangered species are used for their parts (livers, paws, etc.) in medicine. Poachers can earn large sums of money for delivering such animals, and government enforcement of prohibitions against such action has been lax.

Since many of these animals are caught, slaughtered, and sold illegally, there is no official oversight of their living conditions. Animals are often crowded into transport vehicles and cages, as merchants maximize their profits and consumers seek access to once-rare delicacies. The Cantonese are especially known to favor oddities in their diets. Since with increased wealth, consumption of rare animal products also increases, these preferences cannot be attributed to poverty and necessity.

Animals in China live in close proximity to humans even before they go to market. In rural areas, chickens usually roam around courtyards, and pigs live just off the family's house. Among ethnic minorities, such as the Dai of Yunnan province, houses are built on stilts,[3] with the lower level accommodating animals and the upper level housing the family. Nomads in the North and West live close to their herds, relying on them for warmth, milk, and wealth as well as for meat. Boat people live among fish and other products of the sea. But the density of southeastern China is unlike that of most other parts of the world. While Yunnan's minorities, northern nomads, and boat people may spread out with their animals, in places like Guangzhou's core area people are as dense as 50,989 per square kilometer. All these tendencies—enjoyment of rare animals, lack of official supervision of their care, and crowding—help account for the Chinese origin of bird flu and SARS.

Freshness

No matter what kind of animal protein it is, the sources of it are optimally kept alive until just before they are cooked. Large markets feature cages with live chickens and ducks, and tanks with fish, eels, and seafood. Only the very new middle class in China will have ever seen meat products sold the way people in the United States buy them: packaged in plastic and with no resemblance to their original form. Without squeamishness, the Chinese often seem perfectly content to look at animals in their complete forms. One typical ritual offering at a rural funeral is a pig's head, given by daughters who have married and left their natal families.

Animals are also sold live because of technological limitations (refrigerated trucks are rare), the premium placed on freshness, and force of habit.

Chinese shoppers are very discriminating, and will seek to examine animals prior to purchase.

The Limits of the Edible

While it is true that most Chinese are far more accepting than people in the United States of a diverse set of meats, there is one meat that is definitively unacceptable: that of humans. Yet it is also the case that the idea of cannibalism is frequently invoked, if only to be rejected. Stories of cannibalism surface from time to time, whether in a second century BCE account of the historian Sima Qian (the *Shi Ji*), or in Cultural Revolution scandals of a politically divided village that consumed its weakest members. The May Fourth writer Lu Xun drew on the metaphor of *chi ren de ren* (people who eat people) in his brilliant story "Medicine" about buns with human flesh being unable to cure a very ill father. In his novel *The Republic of Wine*, author Mo Yan writes a political satire of privilege, with elements of magical realism, describing a kingdom where infant boys, sold by their desperately poor peasant parents, are served as a delicacy to top officials. These and other common mentions of cannibalism—allegories for various social ills—seem to suggest unease among the Chinese about where to draw the line between what can be eaten and what cannot. Perhaps the reasons for drawing such a line are less clear when so much is permitted.

Everyday Meals

Chinese meals usually consist of *fan*, *cai* of vegetables, meats, or proteins such as *doufu* or eggs, and soup. The same structure holds, whether the *fan* is noodles, rice, sweet potatoes, steamed bread, or porridge. Even *jiaozi* (dumplings) or *hundun* (wontons)—thin wrappers made of dough containing a filling of meat and vegetables—or flatbread with meats and vegetables inserted within, are regarded as a combination of *fan* and *cai*.

Almost every proper meal in China ends with the soup. This can be as simple as hot water splashed into the pot or bowl to get the last of the sauce or as luxurious as shark's fin soup. Typically, drinks do not accompany meals, aside from toasts at banquets, so the soup serves to quench the diner's thirst.

In most of China, shopping is done daily. As late as 2001, only 82 percent of urban households had refrigerators; in poor Western provinces such as Yunnan and Guizhou where there are substantial minority populations, this figure was as low as 5 percent. The national average was 14 percent. Most shopping occurs at markets, some of which consist of farmers setting out baskets of produce from peri-urban farms, and some of which are permanent structures with fixed displays. Prices are almost always negotiable, and since people spend significant portions of their income on food, it is worthwhile to save even tiny amounts. It is usually believed in China that some people—especially middle-aged women—are better at shopping than others. Shoppers inspect the foodstuffs very carefully, looking to see that the beancurd is fresh, the green onions are crisp, the fish eyes are clear. The very act of shopping has a public dimension. The shopper who wants a lower price may very loudly announce that she is going to the next vendor because she knows his price is lower; the spurned vendor may then meet or beat the competitor's price. Sometimes shoppers work together to get the better of vendors; sometimes vendors do the same, going so far as to plant fictitious buyers to raise prices by praising the goods.

The necessities of daily life can usually be bought at these daily markets. This includes oil, salt, pepper and other spices, vegetables and fruits, meats, beancurd and other soy products, noodles, pastries, fish, and poultry. Given the premium placed on freshness, there would be little gained from buying food all at once and storing it. Even people with refrigerators use them primarily for drinks and ice cream, not for the ingredients of daily fare.

Once the foodstuffs are bought, the time-consuming preparation begins. Ordinary-grade grain has to be picked over to remove stones and other foreign matter. These needed preparations can be quite tedious and may be skimped in public contexts. (Many students complain about stones left in the rice in their mess halls.) Vegetables (grown using nightsoil) must be washed carefully, and their outer layers removed. Finally, the foodstuffs are cut into the proper shapes—long, thin, round, or whatever is called for in a particular dish—using the all-purpose cleaver.

Since most cooking is done very quickly, all preparatory work is completed before the actual moment of cooking. The ingredients are placed in porcelain or plastic bowls: peas in one bowl, beancurd in another, cabbage in another, garlic in another. Each ingredient must be cooked just enough. Food that is overcooked is *lan* (rotten, or mushy); food that is just right is *cui* (to the perfect, crispy point). Because timing is critical, some ingredients are cooked briefly, removed from the pan, and added again at the last moment. Some cooking is slow; in some parts of China such as Fujian, stews and long-cooked meats are popular items.

Cooking fuel has been scarce in China for millennia; aspects of Chinese cooking—from the small chunks of foods requiring minimal cooking time to the wok, which maximizes surface area—are often explained as maximally efficient in terms of fuel use. While the rural Chinese still rely on coal and wood, efforts are under way to convert them to cleaner fuels such as liquid or gas fuels.

Rice is cooked by bringing water and rice to a boil, covering the pot, and turning off the heat. *Mantou* (steamed bread), a staple of northern cuisine, is made with a bamboo basket placed in a wok. Traditionally, the Chinese have had no ovens, aside from those of the Hui (Muslim) sellers of bread, so there is no real baking done, though this is changing quickly among a growing middle class that can afford Western-style kitchens.

Needless to say, it is essential for each family to have someone with the time to conduct all the necessary commerce and preparation for meals. Usually it is the retired elders of the family. Those without such help may today resort to buying prepared foods, which are now becoming common, if expensive. Unlike in the United States, where the poor tend to cook very rarely and resort to fast food and snacks, in China the poorest of the poor usually cook tiny amounts of poor ingredients; buying ready-made foods would be too expensive. The exception is instant noodles: the Chinese bought 27.7 billion packets of them in 2004.

Banquets: Hosting and Guesting

Hosting and guesting are widespread and meaning-drenched human practices, with common mutual obligations cemented through the sharing of a meal provided by one of the parties. Throughout China—urban, rural, wealthy, poor—people spend huge amounts to host banquets. And banquets have been recorded for thousands of years in China.

The out-of-the-ordinariness of banquets is usually marked in myriad ways, from table settings to special drinks to special foods. Elaborateness may signal importance or formality, or both. One of the main inversions at banquets is the predominance of *cai* and the superfluity of *fan*. Banquet-goers often comment that they are too full to eat any *fan*, yet a meal is not a meal without it. A compliment for a generous host is that there were so many *cai* that the guests could eat no rice at all. (But the *fan* must at least be present.)

Another banquet inversion is serving food to fellow diners. As in everyday meals, each diner has her or his own bowl, and small amounts of the dishes are placed in them from the main serving platter or bowl. High-ranking people never serve themselves; others vie to fill their bowls for them, giving them the choicest items. If diners do take their own food, it should be of the least value—beancurd rather than shrimp, vegetables rather than meat.

Some foods have symbolic value; the most famous of these is fish as the final course. This is because in Mandarin, the word for "fish" is *yu*, which sounds exactly like the Mandarin word meaning "surplus." The phrase that comes to everyone's lips is *Nian nian chi yu* (May we have fish [surplus] every year). Thus the fish symbolizes abundance. In a very amusing but poignant scene in the film *Yellow Earth* (see chapter 7), the peasants serve wooden fish with sauce at the end of the wedding banquet. One local explains to an outsider, "We don't have fish around here, but we have to serve them anyway, so this is how we manage."

For the less well to do, there are limits to how elaborate banquets can be, but their banquets are still set apart from the quotidian. Certain foods are obligatory at peasant banquets, such as noodles in the North. At rural weddings, where it is not uncommon for all the males of a village to be fed, relatives of the married couple eat more costly food than the other villagers.

At elaborate urban banquets, the *cai* may involve rare ingredients such as civet, and very time-consuming preparation, with foods carved into decorative shapes. Foreigners and officials tend to have banquet after banquet, often to the point of boredom. Chinese officials have complained since the 1980s about gaining weight from constant banqueting.

Banquets are important for the establishment and nurturing of relationships, or *guanxi*, in a cycle of reciprocal gifting that in many ways forms the backbone of Chinese society. Written records are kept of invitations and gifts, especially at life-cycle rituals such as weddings and funerals. There is a competitive dimension to these banquets, since giving is a way of being owed as well as a way of gaining status. One way of upping the ante in the cycle of gifting is to provide unusual meats and ingredients, the so-called *ye wei* (wild tastes).

Seating at banquets is also significant. People with the greatest status are seated in the seat farthest from and facing the door, and closest to the host. Though guests must demur and contest, they will end up where expected. Even in settings where hosts may say *Suibian zuo* (sit anywhere), well-brought-up guests should be able to gauge their own relative status and sit accordingly.

Conversation at banquets is not usually for the purpose of expressing confidences or of doing business but rather is supposed to be public and light-hearted. It is a performance of interaction and is facilitated by toasting.

Drinking

Drinking has until recently been fairly rare in Chinese society and was almost entirely reserved for festive, social occasions. People at banquets do not drink alcohol at whim but in response to toasts. They do not fill their own cups but attentively look to see that their neighbors' cups are filled. A subordinate will eagerly fill a superior's cup constantly. Toasting successively, with fixed expressions such as *Wo jing ni* (I honor you) or *Gan bei* (bottoms up), is the focus of much riotous interaction. People often protest, saying they can't drink any more, but then are urged to do so anyway, for the sake of the honor, reputation, or prestige of the one who proposed the toast. This is known as *gei mianzi* (giving face).

Once I was at a farewell banquet at a university. One of the teachers explained that she had a cold and didn't feel well, but in order to *gei mianzi*, she would drink anyway. I excused her, saying that she certainly shouldn't drink for me, but she insisted and went ahead. Since she sacrificed for this, I felt obliged to reciprocate, protesting all the while.

Ideally, all the participants empty their (small) cups of liquor; foreigners and women are sometimes grudgingly permitted to take sips. Someone who says *Wo buhui hejiu* (I can't drink) may opt out entirely. But it is basically an all-or-nothing endeavor. *The Republic of Wine*, for example, features drinking contests and an entire region saturated with alcohol. Much of the drinking in the book is deployed as a weapon to weaken opponents, who are nonetheless held by the obligation of *gei mianzi* to accept a toast.

Drinks vary but are usually *maotai*, or a similarly strong, distilled drink made of grain. Beer and wine have also become increasingly popular in China, the Germans having introduced pilsner in their treaty-port concession of Qingdao in the late nineteenth century. Grape wine was little known and little liked until the 1990s, aside from a very small class of foreign-influenced cosmopolitans. But China has now entered the world's wine-making ranks, and its wines have improved to the point that some of them are considered quite fine.

Drinking at weddings is a central part of the festivities. The bride and groom, who are often young and embarrassed, go from table to table, in descending order of relationship to them, and toast their guests. If they become slightly drunk, that is a not-unwelcome result.

Coffee and Tea

Tea originated in China and spread to the rest of the world; indeed, all the words for tea throughout the world come from some variant of the Hokkien word *chai*: we have *cha* in Mandarin, *tea* in English (originally pronounced *tay*), *thé* in French, *chai* in Russian, and so forth. By the time of the Southern Song dynasty (1127–1279 CE), a ditty indicated that the seven daily necessities were tea, rice, firewood, oil, vinegar, salt, and soybean sauce.

By the turn of the twentieth century, tea was being served in elaborate rituals for the literati. Not quite as complex as the Japanese tea ceremony, these rituals nonetheless had rules for boiling water, steeping the tea, pouring the tea, and so forth. A seventeenth-century story by Zhang Dai (1597–1689 CE) tells of a visit to a tea connoisseur. In the story, Zhang identifies not only the tea leaves and their style of preparation but the water from a particular spring. The poor mostly drank boiled water.

In China of the 1980s, people carried around jars—most commonly pickle jars—with tea leaves and water. Thermoses of boiled water were everywhere, so tea drinkers could replenish their jars as needed. Ceremony was utterly lacking in such drinking, just as North Americans may keep a mug of coffee or tea at their desk while working. By the 1990s, as consumer goods proliferated, a special type of insulated cup had become very popular in Chinese cities. Since the early 2000s, traditional-style teahouses have provided quiet settings with elegant service and snacks. A few genuine old teahouses endure where retired people smoke and listen to Peking opera or storytellers.

A new phenomenon has recently arisen in China: coffee drinking. Coffee is in many ways a symbol of internationalism and cosmopolitanism in China, and it has become extremely popular in the most urbanized areas. Starbucks is rapidly opening branches in China, and its CEO, Howard Schultz, recently forecast that by 2008 there would a greater number of Starbucks outlets in China than in the United States. Even those who dislike coffee are eager to be seen as modern consumers, and in urban China the place to be seen is Starbucks. There were thirty-nine outlets in Shanghai in 2004—more than in Hong Kong—and over ninety in China as a whole; by 2005 that number had risen above three hundred.

Health and Symbolism

Food maintains and restores health; at the first sign of illness, Chinese people evaluate their diet, eliminating or adding particular foods. They regard the body not as a self-contained unit that needs to go to the mechanic when things break down but rather more like a fine violin that needs constant tuning and swells and shrinks with the weather. Everything in the universe is classified as a combination of *yin* and *yang*, and as *re* (hot) or *liang* (cold), with the goal being proper balance between them. Cucumbers are cold; dog and snake meat are hot; rice is neutral. And though there is some connection between cool foods and acid foods, and between hot foods and calories and fat, these principles cannot be entirely converted to a chemical analysis. For instance, some oranges are cool while others are hot. Balance also depends on season. Dog meat is heating, and during winter, when the body needs to have its heat restored, dog meat is much sought after.

One consequence of the belief that the body exists as a porous and impressionable element within the larger cosmos is the notion that food and environment profoundly affect a person; movement from one environment to another is often seen as dangerous. *Shui tu bu fu* (The water and soil are not appropriate) is an expression that explains travelers' common experience of malaise or worse. It is common for Chinese people to take food from home—often rice—on their journeys.

Foods have symbolic meanings in all cultures, especially on ritual occasions. In China, long noodles stand for long life, and grains of rice left in a bowl are said to indicate the pockmarks on a future spouse's face. Lotus sticks together, and it is eaten at weddings to indicate firmness of relationship. Pork and chicken have been traditional offerings to spirits. Food is offered to gods at temples and to ghosts on certain dangerous days. Chinese people also give their ancestors dishes on birthdays and death days.

VARIATIONS

The Newest Imports

Not all the eating in today's China is of Chinese food. Since the economic reforms of the late 1970s and especially since the economic growth of the 1990s, foreign or foreign-style restaurants and shops that sell imported foods have multiplied in large cities. Rural shops may sell domestic copies of foreign products such as candies and buns, and virtually all urban shops sell Coca-Cola and Pepsi, Colgate and Cadbury. Until recently, most food was bought at small markets, but in the past decade groceries (supermarkets) have begun to offer an assortment of processed goods in a single large shop. In the largest cities, such as Beijing and Shanghai, foreign groceries such as Carrefour sell an astonishing array of foreign goods, including butter-filled croissants and ripe Brie. One shop advertises itself on the Internet, in English, as Beijing's largest vegetable supermarket:

> The Largest Vegetable Supermarket in Beijing

> This vegetable supermarket was built in Beijing on September 2nd in 1999. It has business area of 4000 square meters. All goods on sale are completely numbered and network electronic balances of high accuracy are fixed. Most of the vegetables are picked in that very day; maize flour is grinded and processed in peasants' houses; Living fouls [fowls] are butchered on the spot.

Even in this modern context, with fixed, nonnegotiable prices and Internet advertising, the on-the-spot butchering of fowl is celebrated. Despite the increase in such modern stores, up to 85 percent of food in Beijing is still purchased in small, agricultural markets.

In addition to Starbucks, fast-food restaurants are very popular. Most famous are KFC and McDonald's, as well as their imitators.[4] In Hong Kong, McDonald's serves the desires of children. In the past, Chinese children were never at the center of any celebration between the celebration one hundred days after their birth and their engagement to be married. Since the late 1980s, however, birthday parties at McDonald's have become opportunities for a growing middle class to display its largesse and devotion to its most singular product: its one child. The book *Feeding China's Little Emperors* (the title refers to these spoiled, single children) reminds readers that foodways in China are changing. As advertising permeates China's cities, Chinese children want the products they see on TV or at friends' houses. With increased disposable, middle-class income, these children's desires are often met.

Still, fast-food restaurants—especially foreign ones—remain peripheral to the foodways in China. They are expensive, they do not serve most social purposes (aside from demonstrating status), and they are used mostly for snacking.

On the Streets: Snacking

Street food is one of the great pleasures of Chinese cities; and in rural areas, periodic markets and festivals attract crowds in part through the foods that are available then and only then. A good proportion of the calories consumed daily in China come from snacks. Snacks, in contrast to meals, may be defined by the times they are taken, by the form of the food, or by the context of their consumption. Commonly, snacks occur between proper, recognized meals: at 10 a.m. or 3 p.m., in contrast to breakfast at 7:30 and lunch at 12. The anthropologist Xin Liu describes a poor northern village where people eat twice daily—a common pattern for China throughout history—but neglects to mention whether there is any eating at all between times. Snacks need not consist of *fan-cai* combinations; they can be a bowl of noodles, fruit, melon seeds, or any number of other things. They can be bought at a corner stand and eaten or drunk there, the customer returning the bowl or the glass to the vendor. Snacks might be consumed with others, but not usually at a fixed site with table settings. (Meals may also be eaten this way. I have seen many a family eating scattered around a courtyard, each person sitting alone on a stool with his or her own bowl.) Typical northern street snacks are grilled meat, roasted chestnuts, and sweet potatoes in winter, and popsicles and drinks in summer. Common southern snacks are pineapples and sugar-coated hawthorns.

Snacks are often eaten at *xiaochibu*, little stalls or restaurants equivalent to the trucks that line the streets near many American college campuses. Here for just a few yuan, snackers can buy a bowl of noodles, a quick lunch of a few *cai* and some passable rice, or even a dinner for a special occasion. The floors of the *xiaochibu* are concrete, the tables rudimentary. Some have extremely gifted cooks, and may be very popular and crowded.

Variants: Elite/Folk; North/South; Buddhist; Muslim/Han/Nomad

The expression *Chinese food* oversimplifies China's vast geographic, economic, cultural, religious, ethnic, and linguistic diversity.[5] *Chinese* usually means Han, China's majority ethnic group, constituting approximately 92 percent of the population. The other 8 percent—over 100 million—are themselves quite varied, from pastoralist Mongolians in the North to Thai-speaking Buddhist rice-growers such as the Dai in the Southwest.

The Han Chinese tend to eat according to the principles enumerated above (*fan, cai,* soup), but with significant regional variations. There are clear differences between the wheat, cabbage, garlic, and pork of the North, the seafood, rice, and vinegar of the Southeast, the peppers, potatoes, and corn of the West and Southwest, and the subtle, experimental flavors of the South. People in each region stereotype those of other regions. People from Shandong province—bumpkins, by common perception—are said to be stinky from eating garlic and onions. The Hunanese and Sichuanese are known for their fiery revolutionary spirits, derived from the hot peppers they eat. People from the Southeast are said to be slick and wily, like the crabs they savor. And it is said of the Cantonese that they will eat anything with four legs except a table. But the main difference cited—one that might make a marriage between a Northerner and a Southerner uncomfortable—is in the *fan.* Northerners eat wheat products: steamed buns, noodles, fried bread; Southerners eat rice.

Some ethnic minorities—the ones considered most civilized, such as the Bai, Dai, and Zhuang in the Southwest—like the Han cultivate and eat rice. Other groups cultivate grain but do not use Han techniques; the Wa, for example, use slash-and-burn horticulture, which Chinese social science places in the "primitive" category. In the Northwest, in places like Xinjiang and Tibet, conditions for agriculture are limited. In Tibet, the only grain easily grown is barley; in Xinjiang, wheat can be grown. Some of the best noodles I have ever eaten were made in a small restaurant in Kunming where the proprietor was an ethnic Russian from Xinjiang. She folded flour and water, swung the dough around, and cut it into noodles. Xinjiang also has oases, where grapes for wine and raisins are produced, which are then sold by itinerant vendors throughout China.

In the North and Northeast, pastoral nomads such as Mongols and Uighurs herd their flocks, eating meat rather than grain as their staple and serving the meat in a big slab. Most Han find this "uncivilized," even nauseating, since they cut their meat into small, bite-size pieces. Korean barbecue is also very meat-focused; the Han might eat it as a novelty but would not consider eating it every day.

Ten of China's fifty-five ethnic minority groups, totaling over 20 million people, are Muslim: the Uighurs, Kazakhs, Kyrgyz, Uzbeks, Tatars, and Tajik of Xinjiang; the Salar, Bao'an, and Dongxiang of Qinghai and Gansu; and the Hui, who live throughout China. All these groups adhere to some extent to Muslim dietary prohibitions of pork and alcohol. Given that pork is the quintessential Han Chinese meat and that drinking and toasting are central aspects of banquets, any person who must opt out of the sociality that results from eating and drinking in a group must also be excluded from other important aspects of life in China, including business and political deal making. Thus food can both tie people together and set people apart. Hui restaurants, called *qing zhen* (clean and true), follow strict rules about washing and ingredients. Just as kosher food is bought by many non-Jewish people in the United States as cleaner and purer than ordinary food, so many in China see Hui food as more authentic and pure. Since the 1990s, however, Hui children have learned to lobby their families to eat the same snack foods as their Han counterparts. Future food practices in China are likely to diverge from those of the present.

In most societies, though not all, there is a difference between what the wealthy and the poor eat. Egalitarian societies such as communities of hunters and gatherers (e.g., the !Kung of southern Africa) have no social differentiation. Everyone eats the same foods and in the same ways. In Melanesian societies (Papua New Guinea), status differences are reflected not in consumption but in giving away foodstuffs. In North America and Europe there are enormous differences between the kinds of foods eaten by the elite (caviar, champagne, asparagus, organic greens, wild salmon, expensive lattes) and the poor (white bread, fast food, chips, soda, and coffee from convenience stores). In China, however, the difference is not so much in the things people at different social levels eat but in the care taken with the preparation, the relative amounts of *fan* versus *cai*, and the quality of the foodstuffs. Only the extremely privileged can afford the rare ingredients that go into banquets, such as shark's fin and sea slugs, but these are not everyday items; for everyday consumption, the Chinese people eat grains, greens, and some protein.

The greatest disparities in diet are between urban and rural residents, and coastal and inland provinces. In 2001 in Shanghai, people spent ¥4,022 a year on food per capita, while in Shanxi province they spent only ¥1,413. People in Beijing spent an average of ¥750 per capita on dining out, while in the poor province of Hebei, urban residents spent only ¥90. Food took 48 percent of the living expenses of rural households, and rural households spent from a high of ¥1,539 per capita per year in Shanghai to a low of ¥227 in Guizhou province.[6] Grain consumption ranged from 287 kg per person in Tibet to 134 kg per person in Beijing. Annual per capita consumption of starches and tubers varied only from 12.65 kg to 14.64 kg between the lowest- and highest-income urban households. Similarly, the poorest households bought 4.74 kg per capita of bean curd, while the wealthiest bought 6.4 kg. There are noticeable differences, however, in consumption of meat, vegetables, and fish and shellfish: the poorest bought 12.88 kg of pork per capita each year, while the wealthiest bought 18.35 kg; and the poorest bought 100.74 kg of vegetables per person, while the richest bought 135.14 kg. Shanghai residents spent ¥624 per capita on aquatic products, while urban residents of Shanxi province spent only ¥36.

The elite in China pay great attention to fine and rare ingredients, to the composition of their dinner parties, and to serving pieces. Ordinary people are concerned with filling themselves adequately to survive the next day's work. Even this basic subsistence, however, provides a challenge.

CHALLENGES

Feeding China

Providing food for China's 1.3 billion is the primary challenge of anyone who governs China. Traditional Chinese agriculture relied on locally available seeds, reused resources as fertilizer, and wasted very little. Since animal protein was used sparingly, the entire system would be considered low on the food chain, because soybeans and legumes are very efficient in terms of producing energy and protein. (In contrast, the U.S. system is extremely inefficient. The protein conversion efficiency of beef may be as low as 5 percent.) Even so, the system in China relies on everything going right—rain and snow, monsoon and sunshine. Despite irrigation's being part of the Chinese system from earliest times, disasters were and continue to be a common feature of life in China. Droughts and floods are especially common. A saying has it that in seven out of every ten years there is a drought somewhere. The more that marginal lands are used for agriculture, the greater the tendency for disaster.

For these and other reasons, poverty and hunger have been a reality for a large component of the Chinese population for millennia, and as E. N. Anderson points out in *The Food of China*, knowledge of famine foods has been passed down dutifully from one generation to the next. These foods include the chaff of grain, bark, and wild plants. At truly desperate moments, as I suggested above, rumors of cannibalism circulate; there have been such reports from the time of the Han dynasty through the Cultural Revolution, most notoriously in an event alleged to have occurred in the 1960s in the Guangxi Zhuang Autonomous Region: starving because of politically directed agricultural policies that resulted in paltry harvests, villagers decided to eat the politically weak.

Poverty and starvation can be alleviated through good government. The ideal of the ever-normal granary—a model in which the government buys surplus grain at low prices during years of abundance and sells its stockpiled grain during years of starvation—was proposed during the Wang Mang interregnum (9–23 CE, between the Former and Latter Han dynasties [206 BCE—220 CE]) and was implemented periodically afterward. But even more important than the model's actual implementation was the idea of wise rulers with so much forethought that they could intervene in the otherwise inevitable periods of trouble. Ideal governments are judged by their capacity to feed people; many actual governments have fallen far short.

Recent famines in China have had political consequences (and causes). The hardship of the Great Leap Forward ("The Three Hard Years," 1958–1961) were caused in part by the CCP's attempt to achieve huge leaps of modernization and industrialization overnight. A combination of irrational policies—dictated by politics—and natural disasters (floods and droughts) led to death by starvation of an estimated 30 million people. (Some died from diseases exacerbated by weakness from lack of food.) As Erik Mueggler points out in his book *The Age of Wild Ghosts*, the suffering engendered by that misguided period has been neither forgotten nor eradicated; rather, it lingers, hauntingly, in people's memories and rituals.

One of the great successes claimed for post-reform China is that markets are flourishing and food is now widely available. Poverty eradication is regarded as a measure of the success of the Chinese revolution, despite that revolution's many weaknesses and failures. Official estimates of poverty rates were 270 million in 1978, 90 million in 1996, and 26 million in 2000. (Most outside observers contest these figures.)[7]

In the 1950s and 1960s, China aimed for self-reliance, especially food self-sufficiency. With China's entry into the World Trade Organization (WTO) in 2001, which prohibited barriers to imports, China has begun to import rice from Indonesia and California. The Chinese do not regard rice with quite the same nationalistic fervor that the Japanese do; in Japan, imports of rice have been resisted, sometimes violently, for decades. There have been no such protests in China. Such protests as do occur—illegal though they are—have to do with farmers protesting their huge tax burden or workers protesting payment in IOUs rather than cash.[8] Such farmer protests are increasingly common.

Grain has been at the center of China's agricultural policies for the entire existence of the PRC. "Take grain as the key link" was a slogan often circulated during the mid-1970s. Excess zeal and political overreaching led to insistence that even unviable environments such as Mongolia be planted with rice. Naturally, this led to disaster. During the 1950s, 1960s, and 1970s, farmers (whether individually or collectively) were required to turn over their harvests and then received a certain portion of it back as rations. Beginning in the late 1970s, the *bao chan dao hu* (household responsibility) system changed this requirement: each household was to turn over a certain amount of its harvest to the state, and the surplus could be kept or sold by the producers, though grain was kept at low prices to benefit urban consumers. Suddenly, markets were inundated with fruits, vegetables, and meats, whereas during the earlier decades only the sorriest produce was available. This in turn accounted for the first effects of the reforms: the growing wealth of peri-urban farmers in coastal provinces.

Since the late 1990s, however, there have been two new wrinkles in this otherwise smooth transition to sufficiency: increasing disparities between the wealthy and the poor, and the reluctance of farmers to grow grain.

The income disparity between a wealthy coastal province like Jiangsu and a poor interior province like Guizhou is about sevenfold. In spring 2004, Prime Minister Wen Jiabao announced that at long last the central government was going to address these disparities by abolishing rural taxes and raising prices on foods so that farmers could earn more of a livelihood. If this indeed occurs, it will go a long way toward remedying the long-standing inequality between city and country in China.

The Chinese government's other challenge is to persuade farmers to grow more grain. Since grain earns less than other foods, grain farmers cannot make a living and prefer more lucrative crops. Since spring 2004 the government has attempted to persuade farmers to produce more grain, and in 2004, for the first time in five years, China began importing wheat, mostly from the United States.

Whatever the treatment of the farmers, feeding China is always difficult. In 1995 Lester Brown published an alarming book called *Who Will Feed China?* that detailed the challenges of attempting to feed such a large population (one-fifth of the world's population) with a decreasing amount of farmland (because of urbanization and industrialization) and with increasingly unreliable water sources. Brown argued that no matter how small its population increase is in years to come, China will face serious and potentially disastrous problems. Within twenty-four hours of the publication of Brown's book, the Chinese government had called a press conference to contest his statistics and to challenge his conclusions about China's inability to feed itself.

Everyone agrees that the official Chinese statistics given for almost every category—land, water, fertilizer, consumption, production—are inaccurate. For instance, Vaclav Smil argues that the official estimates of China's available land holdings are low by at least 36 percent.[9] Thus he sees Brown's predictions of disaster as based on faulty assumptions of land scarcity and population increase. While accepting Brown's point that grain production in China stagnated after it reached a peak in 1984, Smil presents a more optimistic picture of China's prospects. He sees increasing efficiency, change of preferred foodstuffs, and better policies as capable of solving the problems.

Still, the magnitude of environmental and economic disasters accompanying food production is overwhelming: China's gross domestic product (GDP) is reduced at least 10 percent because of environmental pollution and ecosystem degradation, and drought and water shortages in the North affect an area larger than France. Further, reliance on chemical fertilizers results in decreasing soil fertility. Even Smil, who contests Brown's gloomy predictions, states clearly that if the difference between China's grain production and grain consumption exceeds 200 million tons a year, the rest of the world will be unable to meet that need.

EATING CHINESE

The study of food in China leads to considerations of agriculture, social relations, the family, the economy, religion, identity, and nationalism. Feeding China, like the feeding of any nation, is a central concern of the governed as well as the governing; a discourse of morality accompanies any claims of being able to support China's large population. While China has been able to subsist on its agricultural base quite adequately for the most part—aside from the inevitable floods and famines, handled with varying degrees of success by different regimes—food has meanings far above those of mere subsistence. As in all societies, food can serve to express significance at almost every level of life.

At its most basic level, food eaten reflects choices people make about the plants and animals in their environment. The Chinese eat a relatively large proportion of available foodstuffs, especially in comparison to people elsewhere who eat a limited selection. At the same time, people rarely eat food in its natural form; it is almost always transformed into a culturally appropriate aspect of edibility. In China, this means quick cooking of vegetables and meats, so that they retain their color and their crispness. It also means that exotic animals are the perfect centerpiece for lavish banquets and that live birds destined for the table live side by side with their keepers.

The fact that expenditures on food remain the greatest part of the average Chinese budget, even with increasing income, shows how central food is to all of Chinese life. Deeply embedded aesthetic, cognitive, and performative principles guide the focus on food. *Min yi shi wei tian* (The people take food as heaven). It is not food alone but its connections to all aspects of meaningful human life that reigns supreme.

When we read and hear news accounts of food scandals, it is important that we keep the entire background in mind. It is true that when China sneezes, the world catches cold, simply because of China's huge population. But the great successes of China's agricultural system should be recalled along with the shocking, the horrific, and even the diseased. At its best, this system can be environmentally and socially harmonious. It is only when it is at its worst that it causes environmental disaster. Let us hope that sanity and imagination reign and that China can be fed and can eat in good health—for all our sakes.

NOTES

1. This summary, and much of this chapter, relies on the rich account of food in China of E. N. Anderson, *The Food of China* (New Haven, CT: Yale University Press, 1988).

2. South Koreans were pressured to refrain from eating dog meat because of the World Cup in 2002. They compromised by attending to the conditions under which the animals were slaughtered but continue to eat dog meat.

3. See Susan D. Blum, "China's Many Faces: Ethnic, Cultural, and Religious Pluralism" in *China beyond the Headlines*, ed. Timothy B. Weston and Lionel M. Jensen (Lanham, MD: Rowman & Littlefield, 2000), 69–95.

4. In *Golden Arches East: McDonald's in East Asia*, James Watson and his students compare the use and understanding of McDonald's in North China with that in Taiwan, Hong Kong, South Korea, and Japan. The varying success of McDonald's foods depended on the context into which they were introduced. In Japan, for instance, great efforts were made to show that eating with the hands could be acceptable and civilized. In China, people pooled their French fries and turned them into a kind of communal *fan*, with the sandwiches the *cai*. In Korea, McDonald's came to be seen as an emblem of Americanness and was regarded as an ideal focus of anti-U.S. political protests.

5. See Blum, "China's Many Faces."

6. By way of contrast, in the United States, lower- and middle-income people spend about 16 percent, and the wealthy might spend as little as 5 percent of their income on food.

7. Robert Benewick and Stephanie Donald, *The State of China Atlas* (London: Penguin Reference, 1999), 25. See Jonathan Unger, *The Transformation of Rural China* (Armonk, NY: M. E. Sharpe, 2002), 173, 173nn7–8. Unger recounts being told that a village party secretary report should increase every family's income by one hundred yuan because doing so would inflate per capita income "so that the officials could claim they had eliminated poverty. In reality, severe poverty remained entrenched in the village, and at the time of my visit in 1988 a third of the families could not afford to purchase matches or salt" (173).

8. See Timothy B. Weston, "China's Labor Woes: Will the Workers Crash the Party?" in *China beyond the Headlines*, ed. Weston and Jensen, 245–72.

9. See Vaclav Smil, *China's Past, China's Future: Energy, Food, Environment* (London: RoutledgeCurzon, 2004), 6–7 on Chinese statistics in general, and 127–130 on estimating China's available land.

SUGGESTED READINGS

E. N. Anderson, *The Food of China* (New Haven, CT: Yale University Press, 1988).
———, *Everyone Eats: Understanding Food and Culture* (New York: New York University Press, 2005).
Francesca Bray, *The Rice Economies: Technology and Development in Asian Societies* (Berkeley: University of California Press, 1986).

Lester Brown, *Who Will Feed China? Wake-Up Call for a Small Planet* (New York: W. W. Norton, 1995).

K. C. Chang, ed., *Food in Chinese Culture: Anthropological and Historical Perspectives* (New Haven, CT: Yale University Press, 1977).

Carole Counihan and Penny Van Esterik, eds., *Food and Culture: A Reader* (London: Routledge, 1997).

Mary Douglas, "Deciphering a Meal," in *Myth, Symbol, and Culture,* ed. Clifford Geertz (New York: W. W. Norton, 1971), 61–81.

Jun Jing, ed., *Feeding China's Little Emperors: Food, Children, and Social Change* (Stanford, CA: Stanford University Press, 2000).

Lin Yutang, *My Country and My People* (Taibei: Ruiguang, 1964).

Richard Sanders, *Prospects for Sustainable Development in the Chinese Countryside: The Political Economy of Chinese Ecological Agriculture* (Aldershot, UK: Ashgate, 2000).

Vaclav Smil, *Feeding the World: A Challenge for the Twenty-first Century* (Cambridge, MA: MIT Press, 2000).

———, *China's Past, China's Future: Energy, Food, Environment* (London: Routledge-Curzon, 2004).

Jonathan Unger, *The Transformation of Rural China* (Armonk, NY: M. E. Sharpe, 2002).

Margaret Visser, *The Rituals of Dinner: The Origins, Evolution, Eccentricities, and Meanings of Table Manners* (New York: Penguin, 1991).

James L. Watson, ed., *Golden Arches East: McDonald's in East Asia,* 2nd ed. (Stanford, CA: Stanford University Press, 2004).

David Y. H. Wu and Tan Chee-beng, eds., *Changing Chinese Foodways in Asia* (Hong Kong: Chinese University Press, 2001).

David Y. H. Wu and Sidney C. H. Cheung, eds., *The Globalization of Chinese Food* (Honolulu: University of Hawai'i Press, 2002).

Yunxiang Yan, *The Flow of Gifts: Reciprocity and Social Networks in a Chinese Village* (Stanford, CA: Stanford University Press, 2000).

Mayfair Mei-hui Yang, *Gifts, Favors, and Banquets: The Art of Social Relationships in China* (Ithaca, NY: Cornell University Press, 1994).

Zheng Yi, *Scarlet Memorial: Tales of Cannibalism in Modern China,* trans. T. P. Sym (Boulder, CO: Westview, 1996).

10

Herding the Masses

Public Opinion and Democracy in Today's China

Tong Lam

> The conscious and intelligent manipulation of the organized habits and
> opinions of the masses is an important element in democratic society.
>
> —Edward Bernays

> The ultimate objective of public opinion surveys is to fortify and
> strengthen the reputation and authority of the government . . . Public re-
> lations and public opinion research are the pivotal tactics for social sur-
> veillance and public relations strategies adjustments.
>
> —Hu Ningsheng

At the dawn of the new millennium, the mainstream U.S. media seem more
optimistic than ever about the inevitable arrival of a democratic China. On
the fifteenth anniversary of the June 1989 Tiananmen Square uprising, *New
York Times* columnist Nicholas D. Kristof declared that the "struggle for
China's soul is over," because even though "political pluralism" has yet to
arrive, "economic, social and cultural pluralism" has paved the way for it.
"No middle class is content with more choices of coffees [at Starbucks] than
of candidates on a ballot," he claimed. Behind this anticipated triumph of
capitalism and democracy lies the United States' "most potent weapons of
mass destruction, like potbellied business executives and bare-bellied Brit-
ney Spears."[1] Kristof, of course, is hardly alone in believing in the transforming power of capitalism. Since the mid-nineteenth century, countless
Western diplomats, merchants, missionaries, and scholars have put their
faith in the efficacy of free trade in "salvaging" China. In a uniquely perverse example of the power of this metaphor, even the forced opium trade

was once regarded as instrumental in integrating China into the world economic system, freeing the Chinese people from their presumably stagnant culture and timelessly tyrannical regimes.

However, this sense of optimism about Western democratic values and global capitalism, as well as their positive transformative effects on the future of China, is difficult to reconcile with the harsh realities of corporate scandals, the erosion of civil liberties, and torture of prisoners overseas that have tarnished the U.S. democratic myth at home and abroad. Thus, as the media stresses the length of China's path to democracy, the United States itself seems to slip farther and farther away from the very democratic ideals it claims to represent. In such a paradoxical context, to insist on the validity of the United States as a model for democratic development is hypocritical. At its worse, this interpretive habit represents a perverse sense of morality wherein the explicit political and social wrongs of the United States, as they were in nineteenth-century Europe, can be legitimately transposed into a matter of Chinese "rights." At the heart of this problem is the unwillingness of many China observers and critics to use the same benchmark to scrutinize their own society.

The media critique of China's political scene is a perfect case in point. In the U.S. news media, especially the more sophisticated newspapers such as the New York Times and Washington Post, there is no shortage of news about China these days. Indeed, from twenty-four-hour cable news to hometown newspapers, China has increasingly overshadowed Japan, becoming the most prominent Asian nation in U.S. news coverage. Moreover, not unlike U.S. news coverage of Japan in the 1980s and 1990s, current journalistic accounts of China focus heavily on issues that are particularly suited to U.S. audiences, such as China's rapid social and economic transformation and its implications for the United States. And when Chinese domestic politics are mentioned, the story tends to concentrate on internal power struggles of the CCP or the lack of political freedom for the ordinary Chinese citizen. In sum, U.S. audiences are presented with a China that is socially and economically vibrant on the one hand, and politically stagnant on the other. What is more, they are left with an impression that there is a widening "gap" between China's socioeconomic development and its political development. It is because of this "gap," journalists and political pundits assure us, that a democratic upheaval—one presumably triggered by economic liberalization—is imminent.

The very idea that China will follow a proper trajectory of political development has unfortunately left many journalists and political pundits handicapped in understanding the complex social and political dynamics in post-socialist China. While there is no doubt that the Chinese government has continued to buttress its authoritarian rule by means of censorship and police brutality, the government has also begun to introduce some forms of local elections, the rule of law, and the use of public opinion polls in the realm of domestic politics. These seeming contradictions, which do not conform to the scenario of imminent democratic upheaval projected by political pundits, and are not measurable with respect to standard political-science models, have put China in a very different place politically and socially than it was a decade ago. How, then, do we understand this new China of global capitalism? Are these simply public relations gestures for softening the totalitarian image of China's one-party dictatorship, or are they indeed new techniques of governance for instituting a new kind of citizens and participatory politics in the newly arrived global economic order?

The U.S. mainstream media, lacking a proper framework within which to explore these paradoxes, are unable to interpret such significant social and political phenomena as the proliferation of Chinese public opinion polls. As for the political pundits and analysts who do pay attention to such emergent phenomena, they opt for simplifying state-controlled public opinion in China as false and differentiating it from "genuine" public opinion in a liberal democracy like that of the United States. Of course, these critics are correct in observing that the U.S. media, by comparison, are far more diverse than China's. However, they have failed to problematize the monolithic and often nonreflective nature of the U.S. media, especially the ways in which the mainstream media airwaves are increasingly dominated by media conglomerates and propaganda machines. After all, even if social and political crises such as health care and war are reported in the United States, they are rarely analyzed and debated in a healthy and productive manner. Little wonder that many Chinese policy experts themselves have been advising their government to model its public opinion management after the practices common in the United States, hoping that the use of a semblance of public participation can substitute for a real democratic politics.

Granted, the Chinese political system is noticeably different from that of the United States, but we should not simply project such a difference onto the realm of public opinion practices in these two societies. Nor should we simply demarcate China from the Western world by idealizing the nature of public opinion in the latter. In this chapter, in addition to examining the rise of public opinion in contemporary China and analyzing the ways it is used and understood by Chinese policymakers, I also juxtapose the Chinese experience with that of the United States. Using cases from both countries to illuminate one another, I argue that public opinion polls, no matter how widespread the sample, do not automatically entail democratization. As such, the novel phenomenon of public opinion in post-socialist China is an opportunity for us to reflect on the nature of public opinion in a world that is increasingly dominated by the logic of global capitalism. Ultimately, by showing how public opinion has become a form of public relations strategy for social control and political manipulation, while also acting as a new kind of mass politics for cultivating patriotic citizens for economic production in these two vastly different political systems, I urge readers to rethink critically the problematic relationship between democracy and public opinion in China as well as in the United States today.

THE RISE OF PUBLIC OPINION IN CHINA

For anyone accustomed to personal computers and the Internet, public opinion polls are common currency. Polls directed at consumers, viewers, or voters pop up on the screen several times a week, and the topics about which U.S. cybercitizens are polled range from celebrities, the economy, newly released films, and the performance of the Congress and the president to the war in Iraq. The polling impulse is no stranger to the Chinese either, and in recent years China has emerged as another society for which public opinion and its polling are considered important. The Chinese fascination with opinion polls is evident in popular cultural media such as newspapers, magazines, television, radio, and cyberspace run by the government and the private sector alike.[2] The government has especially mobilized public opinion to show its interest in forming a more transparent and democratic system, with the hope that such gestures will help the CCP reclaim a legitimacy squandered by rising political discontent, economic disparity, and the mounting social tensions of the past twenty-five years.

Even in the area of foreign policy, the government routinely solicits public opinion to maximize its gains in the arena of international politics. For instance, in spring 2001 the Chinese government used emotionally agitated patriotic sentiment to acquire political leverage against the United States in an orchestrated public reaction to the downing of a Chinese fighter jet after it collided with a U.S. spy plane.[3] And in April 2005, spontaneous public protests against a misrepresentation of World War II history in the rewriting of Japanese textbooks were also used by the government to bolster its domestic popularity (on these student protests and what they reveal about the complexity of Chinese nationalism, see chapter 5). Similarly, when China's president Hu Jintao visited Canada in September 2005, the Chinese Embassy routinely mobilized the Canadian Chinese diaspora to stage large-scale welcoming rallies as a way to showcase the legitimacy of the government.

As the Chinese government uses public opinion to rationalize its domestic and foreign policies, the Chinese media—both official and unofficial—have also grown accustomed to discussing or even celebrating the significance of public opinion. Recently, for example, when the Beijing Municipal Government, due to mounting public pressure, stopped collecting tolls on a city expressway in order to ease traffic congestion, several local newspapers called it a "victory of public opinion" in an era of economic reform.[4] In short, even though the Chinese government itself has stopped short of linking economic reform to political liberalization, the Chinese media seem to suggest that without respecting public opinion, China's modernization project will remain incomplete. As such, they further imply that China's economic progress has finally introduced greater political freedom in the country—an assertion that has been religiously held by many Western observers of China. Although there is much Chinese media hype about these opinion surveys, the hype rarely pays attention to the surveys' critical technicalities, such as issues of sampling, margin of error, and tabulation. After all, many of these are online, instant polls, and their accuracy is highly questionable. Nonetheless, the significance of these opinion polls lies in their perceived sense of representativeness and public participation, not their actual reflection of popular opinion. In a sense, it is the mere soliciting of public opinion, against a backdrop of decades of political repression, that feels like participation.

The following examples will demonstrate just how prevalent, and at times how controversial, public opinion polls have become in Chinese daily life. In mid-November 2003, the Supervision and Evaluation Office of the Beijing Municipal Government launched an online survey asking local residents to rate the performance of the capital's various municipal agencies, such as the Communications Commission and the Urban Planning Commission. In less than a month, an astonishing 130,000 people had participated in the survey, revealing Beijing residents' readiness to take part in an assessment of public affairs that were immediately relevant to their lives. Right away this survey attracted great media attention in China. The official *Renmin ribao* [*People's Daily*], for one, hailed the poll as demonstrative of the government's growing commitment to "open new channels of communication with the public."[5] Public interest in the poll aside, responses to most of the survey questions were conspicuously negative. Except for the Tax Bureau, which enjoys its popularity because of its ineffectiveness in collecting taxes, most municipal agencies received overwhelmingly unfavorable ratings.[6] The range and depth of unsatisfactory sentiment was so disturbing to the city government that the online poll was terminated just three weeks after it was launched.

Also during this period, official and independent Chinese newspapers were racing to report the findings of another survey—conducted by Horizon Research—regarding the performance of top government officials in twenty selected counties and cities. In that survey, the mayors of Beijing and Shanghai reportedly stood out as the most favorably viewed political chiefs, receiving approval ratings of 70.5 percent and 67.4 percent respectively.[7] Significantly, Chinese press coverage of the poll did not simply end with these positive statistics. The report in the *People's Daily* went farther to mention that in none of the other evaluative categories—including performance in policy making, actual achievements, personal image, honesty, and care for the people—had the officials received favorable ratings from more than 50 percent of the public. However, the report stopped short of getting into the specifics of many of the most negative statistics, such as the fact that an overwhelming majority of the public believed that their representatives were vulnerable to corruption. Although admitting that county magistrates often received poorer ratings than city mayors, the *People's Daily* did not seek to elaborate on such obvious discrepancies in the broader context of the ever-worsening internal economic and geopolitical disparities inherent in China's integration into global capitalism.

All evasions notwithstanding, such an acknowledgment of the widespread existence of public dissatisfaction would have been inconceivable just a decade ago. Throughout the history of the PRC, the CCP has always emphasized its solidarity with the masses and downplayed their dissent or even antagonism. In this regard, although an approval rating from approximately two-thirds of the respondents could be interpreted as an admirable mandate from the people, it would have been seen as a scandal in the China of the socialist past, when the party framed its political legitimacy with its ideological role as "the dictatorship of the proletariat," and when no one dared to state publicly the deficiencies of the government.

REPORTING ON CHINESE PUBLIC OPINION

Given the U.S. media's interest in such U.S.-related Chinese news as human rights, trade disputes, and other contentious issues, it should not be surprising that the rise of public opinion in China as a new political phenomenon gets little coverage. But even within the foreign English-language media, China's gradual appreciation of public opinion is often understood simply as an early stage in China's long march toward democracy. Subsequently, the media reaction to such an apparent political relaxation is normally mixed, expressing both hope and reservation toward China's changing political scene. The *South China Morning Post*, for example, a Hong Kong–based English newspaper that is generally more attentive to current affairs in China and still exercises some editorial independence from Beijing, followed quite closely the several political polls mentioned above. As one might expect, the *South China Morning Post* is particularly interested in covering controversies, such as when an opinion poll is shut down or when a poll's negative findings are ignored by or not represented in the Chinese press. One report in the *South China Morning Post* emphasized that the Chinese media coverage of the survey of the performance of government officials had intentionally filtered out the most negative findings, such as the strong public conviction that all government officials are vulnerable to corruption.[8]

Reports like this are of course correct in stating that the Chinese use of public opinion, in terms of how it is solicited, disseminated, and represented, remains rather limited. Yet such criticisms are often articulated at the expense of a more complete description of the extent to which the Chinese media are willing to mention at least some of the negative public opinion. In fact, the *South China Morning Post* article only mentions the Chinese news report on the high approval ratings received by the mayors of Beijing and Shanghai, creating the impression that unfavorable statistics were omitted altogether. This tendency in the Western media as reflected here in Hong Kong's most popular English daily—to accentuate the negative by decontextualization and, in this case, to neglect the Chinese acknowledgment, albeit inadequate, of the negative findings of public opinion polls—is no less problematic than the Chinese reluctance to report and elaborate on the most negative statistics.

Similarly, instead of trying to reconcile China's tightening social control with its apparent democratization, the Western-language mainstream media often deploy the unfit model of linear democratic development to explain these contradictions away. For example, a *Financial Times* piece written around the same time in 2003 as the *South China Morning Post* report bluntly describes China's "democratic model" as a "toothless tiger" because the party-state's interest in public opinion is not "aimed at replacing the communist monopoly on national power but at strengthening it."[9] Meanwhile, a *New York Times* article reports the same impression by depicting Chinese democratization as nothing but a protracted process of becoming just like the West. The title of this article, "Democracy, Chinese style: 2 Steps Forward, 1 Step Back," epitomizes a popular Western conception of the Chinese regime's hesitation to assume the inevitable course of democracy. Implicit in this argument, as in the "toothless tiger" characterization from the *Financial Times*, is the conviction that political reform in China is increasingly being outpaced by China's rapid economic development. "Even as leaders are embracing Western-style capitalism," the article comments, "political change is happening only in tiny steps."[10]

In short, regardless of whether it is optimistic or skeptical about current political developments in China, the Western media, implicitly or explicitly, share a common presumption that China must follow a particular path of democratization, the end point of which is exemplified by the contemporary United States and other Western liberal democracies. Specifically, the skeptics contend that the current manipulative use of public opinion by the Chinese government is essentially a tactic to prolong the CCP's authoritarian rule. This skeptical view is particularly echoed in the routine coverage of Chinese censorship, propaganda campaigns, and human rights abuses as impediments to democracy. As for the optimists who are more hopeful for a democratic China in the near future, they do more than just report the different political realities between China and the West. These commentators highlight shared aspirations for freedom and democracy by marshaling opinions from Western scholars, diplomats, and pundits, as well as from Chinese citizens—intellectuals, teachers, entrepreneurs, and even workers. In particular, by emphasizing Chinese discontent with the current political system and the yearning of the Chinese for a more transparent and democratic system, these reports reinforce a liberal narrative that prizes an open society, free speech, and unchecked public opinion.

As the mainstream media promote the idea of democratic governance through contrast with European-American ideals of economic and political liberalism, the Chinese media have also begun to cite the rise of public opinion in China as evidence of the nation's increasing political openness. With the mainstream and Chinese media proceeding in this manner, it has become very convenient to conclude that citizens of China and the United States share the same belief that public opinion, as the general will of individual citizens, is the foundation for an open and democratic society and that the Chinese government, despite its procrastination and reluctance, is beginning to give in to demands for greater democracy. However, while it is true that the two nations are becoming much more alike in step with the dictates of global capitalism, even the most optimistic Western observers would immediately contend that such a conclusion seems too hasty. After all, from Internet censorship to crackdowns on political dissent, there is plenty of evidence to suggest that at a time when the political process in China appears to have become more open, political control remains as tight as it always has been. And no matter how much some political scientists like to insist that there has to be a direct correspondence between economic growth and political openness, China's steady, virtually undeviating economic success since the brutal political suppression in 1989 has shattered many, if not all, of their arguments. In short, exponential expansion of the economy does not inevitably trigger democratization. As such, this paradox calls for a new way to examine the meaning of public opinion in contemporary democratic politics, one that rejects the outdated, dichotomous framework of "totalitarianism versus democracy" and emphasizes the narrowing distinction between "us" and "them."

PUBLIC OPINION AND DEMOCRACY

One way of undertaking such an alternative analysis is to reexamine, in both historical and contemporary contexts, the concept of public opinion in the United States. After touring this country in 1831–1832, French aristocrat Alexis de Tocqueville (1805–1859), who was drawn to the ever-transforming New World, penned some of the most profound and prophetic remarks on the young republic, many of which continue to be relevant today. Although Tocqueville greatly admired the eminently democratic social condition emerging in the New World, he was equally shocked by the virtual dearth of freedom of opinion. "I know no country in which there is so little true independence of mind and freedom of discussion as in America," he wrote in his celebrated *Democracy in America* (1835). "As long as the majority is still undecided, discussion is carried on," he observed. "But as soon as its decision is irrevocably pronounced, a submissive silence is observed, and the friends, as well as the opponents, of the measure united in assenting to its propriety."[11] Tocqueville's insight, of course, seems to ring even truer in a post–September 11 context, as questioning of the "war on terror" and the legitimacy of the U.S. invasion of Iraq are treated as unpatriotic. In any case, one of the greatest ironies of this democracy for Tocqueville was that even though its citizens seemed to be free, the freedom they enjoyed was physical rather than intellectual. Or to put it differently, while the excessive power of a European monarchy could physically discipline the bodies of its opponents, it could never coerce or capture their souls. In contrast, under the tyranny of the majority opinion, such spiritual incarceration was a fact of life, according to Tocqueville, who lamented, "The body is left free, and the soul is enslaved."[12]

Even in the nineteenth century, the positive relationship between democracy and public opinion that the global media—China's included—take for granted was not immediately obvious. Long before our contemporary social thinkers sought to problematize the idea of public opinion as the basic index of democracy, Tocqueville had already seen from the vantage point of Old Europe both the virtue and vice of this new form of democratic polity. On the contrary, from the standpoint of the planters and landed aristocrats who drafted the Declaration of Independence and the Constitution, public opinion, as the foundation for the new republic, was unequivocally a positive thing. That, of course, was only because their concept of the public was narrowly confined to a small circle of social and political elites, excluding slaves, women, and non–property owners. They envisioned a world in which this small group of private citizens, when acting in the public realm, would be capable of exercising rational thought, making decisions based on private interests that would axiomatically benefit society at large. Insofar as democratic activism was equivalent to nurturing the rational self-interest of the legislating minority, any determination of public opinion would necessarily reflect a diminished range of limited, rather than universal suffrage.

FROM PUBLIC OPINION TO PROPAGANDA

By the early twentieth century, however, the meaning of public opinion had obtained new dimensions more akin to our contemporary conception. Particularly during the interwar years, when industrialization transformed the United States from an elite to a mass society in which public opinion emerged as a new social and political phenomenon, social thinkers were more concerned about public opinion's vices than its virtues, most arguing that the democratic appetites of the industrial masses must be properly managed. In the 1920s, Walter Lippmann (1889–1974), one of the very first to dwell on the subject, argued that the political behavior of the masses must be understood as a response to the outside world, and one based on imaginative fictions rather than observed realities. This elitist and condescending conception of the masses led him to believe that "it is no longer possible to believe in the original dogma of democracy."[13] Rather, the seemingly chaotic and irrational field of public opinion must be scrutinized, mediated, and sanctioned by designated institutions and social experts before crystallizing into a collective will. And in a very curious way, Lippmann's concept resembled one of the CCP's key mass-mobilization paradigms, *qunzhong luxian* (the mass line): "From the masses to the masses." All political action—"to the masses"—was the consequence of the inspired mediation of the party, which distilled "from the masses" the organization and direction of their agency on behalf of *renmin* (the people).

Edward Bernays (1891–1995) joined Lippmann in advocating the manufacture of new institutional tools to manage the democratic appetite of the masses. Bernays was, by far, the foremost advocate of the development of a new science to manage the public. In fact, he believed that manipulating the masses was not merely natural and logical; it was essential to the smooth operation of a pluralist society with a dispersed population and diverse opinions. "The conscious and intelligent manipulation of the organized habits and opinions of the masses is an important element in democratic society," he asserted. Bernays further argued that propaganda is instrumental to the health of an opinion-driven democracy.[14]

It could be said that in responding to the rise of mass society, U.S. social thinkers were seeking new frameworks of governance to cope with an emergent reality: that with widespread suffrage would come the prospect of multiply diverse and contradictory opinion. Instead of regarding their fellow citizens as rational and autonomous individuals capable of making prudent choices, they came to conclude that the masses, in order to become productive citizens for industrial and corporate capitalism, had first to become political subjects. Needless to say, this rather dim and pessimistic view of humanity cast even greater doubt on the meaning of democracy than Alexis de Tocqueville's assertions of the previous century. Whereas Tocqueville suggested that independent thinking and rational debate existed prior to the formation of a majority opinion, early-twentieth-century U.S. public opinion experts argued that the majority opinion must be orchestrated by the elites to herd the masses in a particular direction. For them, there was to be no dialectic, only dictates.

Since World War II, the idea of using public opinion to manage the masses has become quite inseparable from public relations practice. Bernays himself, sometimes known as the "father of public relations," aided in the realization of his theories of mass politics by serving as consultant to numerous U.S. government agencies and corporations. Like other public opinion experts of his generation, he played a central role in shaping the public images of major U.S. corporations in a wide range of industries, such as Columbia Broadcasting System (CBS), the American Tobacco Company, and General Electric (GE). It is obvious from these few items in Bernays's biography that public relations is simply another area where political and commercial practices intersect. For instance, President Ronald Reagan (1911–2004), who was known as "the Great Communicator," was an official public spokesman for GE for nearly a decade in the 1950s.[15] Indeed, the introduction of public relations into democratic politics has substantially enhanced the ability of any democratically elected government to shape public opinion to suit its goals and policies. As the imaginative fictions of the governing overtake the reality of the governed, the already thin line between public opinion and propaganda becomes completely blurred. That line is often very difficult to distinguish in both the United States and China.

PUBLIC RELATIONS AND
GOVERNANCE IN CONTEMPORARY CHINA

If public opinion has emerged as a pivotal public relations technique in the postwar United States, it has taken on a new significance in the context of post–Cold War global capitalism. In the case of China, the extent to which public relations techniques have become an integral component of the art of government is rather striking. As it has in the commercial sector, the government is striving to project a positive image of itself in the minds of a wider domestic and international public. Along with this development, sure enough, is a rapid surge of Chinese and English websites and publications bearing information about China as well as the Chinese government itself, such as xinhua.net and Chinadaily.com. This new trend of conducting government business in an apparently open manner is equally pronounced among the new Chinese leadership, who frequently stage Western-style news conferences and even invite reporters to attend portions of their internal meetings. In fact, government agencies in China, from the State Council to local police departments, are now required to hold routine press conferences in order to present themselves as more accountable, transparent, and people friendly. For a growing number of Chinese public opinion experts who advise the government, the staged appearances of official spokespersons at these conferences are just as important as those of the national leaders, since these press events are regarded as instrumental in swaying public opinion at home and abroad.[16]

Obviously, all these new developments did not occur in a vacuum. The PRC itself has a long history of using propaganda campaigns to direct the masses.[17] Since the 1990s, however, this rich tradition of Communist propaganda has been reconfigured and retooled to serve the neoliberal agenda of market reform and political stabilization. One of the best ways to locate the driving force of this novel development is to examine China's new but highly influential public relations and policy research industry. In a collaborative project carried out by the Central Party School and the Chinese Academy of Social Science with support from various governmental agencies, research institutions, universities, and business corporations, Chinese public relations expert Hu Ningsheng and his associates have laid out a governing formula for the new generation of Chinese leaders. Specifically, in their 1998 publication *Zhongguo zhengfu xingxiang zhanlue yanjiu* [*A study of the image strategies for Chinese government*], these researchers painstakingly illustrate the significance of public relations as a political instrument. As China becomes increasingly integrated into the global capitalist order, "scientific management" of the Chinese government image in the market economy is "a novel concept with significant political implications and social consequences."[18] Hu and his team of policy thinkers, public opinion experts, and image strategists emphasize the need to recognize the importance and applicability of the logic of the market in the field of governance, and they urge governmental agencies to rationalize their activities by adopting the public relations strategies practiced by transnational corporations such as Coca-Cola in order to repackage themselves for public consumption.

Significantly, calls for using marketing strategies to govern imply a redefinition of Chinese citizens as consumer subjects. And it is in this light that public opinion surveys become an important aspect of the emerging governing philosophy in contemporary China. In any major Chinese news or search-engine website, for instance, there are dozens and at times hundreds of reports generated by online and offline opinion surveys, offering information for mass consumption about Chinese society and politics. While many of these Chinese public opinion polls remain quite amateur in conception and application, the public relations and polling industry as a whole in China is fast becoming sophisticated and professional. More importantly, even though many of these reports are generated by traditional government agencies such as the Bureau of Statistics in Beijing, more and more of them are being produced by private research and consultant companies, such as Beijing Social Facts and Public Opinion Survey Center, and Horizon Research.

In fact the Horizon Group, parent company of Horizon Research and one of the leading public relations and consultant firms in China, is a perfect example of this new development. Founded in 1992, the Horizon Group provides market research, public opinion polling, policy analysis, and similar kinds of business- and government-oriented services. The research division of the group, Horizon Research, which conducted the survey mentioned earlier on the performance of government officials, is particularly strong in using "scientific methods to offer and develop full-scale marketing research, management research, and policy analysis."[19] Horizon Research's data collection and analysis involve such methods as phone interviews, online surveys, focus groups, targeted interviews, and onsite monitoring. This intermingling of commercial and governmental practices is further demonstrated in the company's clientele. In addition to Chinese enterprises and multinational corporations, the company has also provided its services to Chinese and foreign governments, the United Nations, and many nongovernmental organizations (NGOs). During the first decade of its existence, Horizon Research reportedly completed over five thousand such projects.

MANUFACTURING PUBLIC OPINION FOR PUBLIC CONSUMPTION

As the mushrooming of consultant firms like Horizon Group confirms the neoliberal trend of privatizing governmental activities in order to achieve greater economic efficiency, it also reveals a more telling aspect of our global economic order. Specifically, neoliberal capitalism requires the establishment of a stable political environment that will not disrupt economic production and consumption. The constitution of some form of rule of law and political legitimacy, therefore, becomes primary for the governing regime. To cultivate such political legitimacy, as the president of Horizon Research, Yuan Yue, has put it, the decision-making process of the government must shift from a "leadership-driven" model to a "public-driven" one, giving the masses a heightened sense of participation.[20] This shift, however, is not an indication of real democratization. Anyone familiar with the politics of public opinion and social statistics will know that surveys are never politically neutral; statistics are always used to substantiate ideological arguments and political powers, not to replace them.[21] Nevertheless, the transition to an "opinion-driven" governing model offers testimony of a novel, twenty-first-century Chinese statecraft. It indicates, among other things, an attempt by the government to tighten its control over the population by fostering greater political legitimacy through the installation of a different kind of participatory politics.

This new way of thinking also resonates clearly in the policy advice given by Hu Ningsheng and his associates. According to them, the combined techniques of "propaganda" and "consultation" are particularly central to public relations strategies in remaking the image of the government. They specify that propaganda, as a form of public relations management, should aim at directing the masses for governmental purposes. In this sense, not unlike Edward Bernays and other U.S. public opinion experts, Chinese policy experts and public relations strategists regard propaganda as a proper and indeed an indispensable means of molding public opinion for the sake of governance and social control. And like the United States, where the government increasingly relies on prepackaged news prepared by public relations consultants, as opposed to journalists, to disseminate information (or rather, disinformation) to the public, Chinese policy experts are becoming more adept at using the mass media to communicate with the public in order to cultivate opinion that is favorable to the government.[22]

Closely associated with the idea of propaganda is what these researchers call *shehui zixun* (social consultation), which fosters greater attentiveness to public opinion through the use of routine public opinion polls and surveys. Thus, as in the United States, where the approval ratings of political leaders and the popularity of public policies are constantly tracked and evaluated by a bevy of news agencies, interest groups, think tanks, political parties, and "talking heads," public opinion experts in China highlight the need to monitor the public's satisfaction with government officials and policies. Indeed, these recommendations are fairly consistent with the social and political experiments that the Chinese government has been carrying out in recent years. Annual tracking polls, for example, have been conducted since at least 1993 on numerous issues such as the government's general effectiveness and efficiency, its reform policies, its anticorruption campaigns, and even the degree to which it complies with the law.[23]

Again, although the main work of these polls is the collection of information, their purposes are more than just public consultation. Like their U.S. counterparts, Chinese public relations strategists emphasize the use of polls and surveys to "manufacture information" for the purpose of communicating with the public and swaying its opinions.[24] A good example of this impulse toward manufacturing public consensus was the government's initial refusal to publish poll results concerning public support for Beijing's bid for the 2008 Olympic Games until after it had achieved overwhelming support of 95 percent following a series of heavy-handed propaganda campaigns.[25] A similar U.S. instance of such conscious manipulation was an attempt by the U.S. government to recast unpopular proposals such as its environmental policies and proposal for Social Security privatization as a Clear Skies Initiative and a choice for personal accounts, respectively, in hope of garnering public support.

In many ways, such attempts at packaging and marketing political symbols, ideologies, and social policies as commodities for public consumption and manipulation have become commonplace in this era of global capitalism. Just as the U.S. government and mainstream media frequently reduce complicated events to sensational spectacle and patriotic celebration, Chinese public relations strategists are also keen to deploy a public relations language that is "simple, precise, lively, and sensational" in order to persuade the public.[26] To elucidate their arguments, Hu and his fellow researchers even explain that the success of Ronald Reagan's presidency was the result of an effective use of image managers, media experts, and public opinion pollsters who, under the watchful eye of Madison Avenue commercial talent Michael Deaver, carefully crafted Reagan's scripts and drew up his itineraries. They also maintain that Bill Clinton defeated his opponent in the 1992 presidential election by imprinting a nonelitist and more approachable image of himself in the public's mind.

At times, however, China's authoritarian, one-party system does set Chinese public relations strategies apart from their U.S. counterparts. Whereas in the United States one can find a contingent of independent media, policy watchdogs, and unions that seeks to unmask and counter the public relations campaigns administered by the government and large corporations, in China no such political friction is allowed. Chinese public opinion polls, regardless of their origins, are normally nonpolitical in nature. As for those that are political, they are mostly geared toward the legitimacy of the party-state, such as its trustworthiness and international status. Others seek to examine the political awareness of the public by surveying its understanding of the latest political doctrines, political symbols such as the national anthem, and even the very idea of patriotism.[27] The underlying purpose of these polls, needless to say, is to foster a sense of national solidarity—a new-age "mass line"—under the leadership of the party.

Citizens of China and the United States alike are constantly reminded of their national identities, patriotic duties, and cultural heritages. Chinese public relations experts, for instance, suggest that public relations should play a critical role in constructing the ideology of the nation. As in the United States, where Republicans and Democrats alike love to use the symbolism of the flag (the "Stars and Stripes") and the rhetoric of "God Bless

America" to instill a sense of patriotism and political belonging, Chinese government image strategists have fully realized the advantage of maximizing the propagandistic value of such political symbols as the Chinese national flag, national anthem, and national emblem. Indeed, they even identify the daily flag-raising ceremony in Tiananmen Square, the government's participation in the anniversary of the Nanjing Massacre, and similar spectacles as proper examples of using public relations techniques for maintaining the legitimacy of the government and cultivating a new sense of national unity.[28] For this reason, the power of public relations techniques and public opinion polls lies not just in their ability to persuade the public, but also in their ability to promote co-optation of the public by the political process. It is this power that transforms highly controlled political participation into the foundation of a government's claims of political representation.

CONCLUSION

Western journalists and political pundits are not entirely incorrect when they assert that China is becoming more like the United States. And the growing similarities between the two countries are certainly not confined to the superficiality of menus at McDonald's and Starbucks. Like the United States, China is increasingly subject to, and subjugated by, the logic and mechanisms of global capitalism. As a result the Chinese government, like the U.S. government, in order to mask political tensions caused by rapidly rising social and economic disparities, frequently resorts to the techniques of cultural identity and nationalism to nurture national pride and solidarity. Not surprisingly, as we have seen, Chinese public policy and opinion experts themselves have urged their government to model itself after the United States by adapting marketing techniques and consumer surveys to the realm of domestic politics in order to cultivate public support for the government's agenda. In this respect, this self-conscious deployment of public opinion defamiliarizes our deep-rooted assumptions about the direct correspondence between public opinion and democracy, while also demonstrating the growing resemblance between China and the United States.

However, having pointed out an increased and increasingly more sophisticated use of public opinion to create a sense of political openness in China and the growing similarity between China and the United States, we must not excuse the Chinese government from its habitual, brutal suppression of political dissents. Nor should we be satisfied with its attempt to orchestrate an approximation of greater democracy by emphasizing its increased reliance on public opinion. Rather, these contradictions remind us of the complications of the shared economic and political conditions that define our existence in the new millennium. And like Chinese citizens, U.S. citizens deserve to have more genuine and more meaningful choices than simply which brand of coffee they'll drink.

NOTES

An earlier version of this chapter was presented at the China's Changing Position in the International Community Conference, University of Vienna, May 2004. Research on this chapter was partially supported by an East Asian Collections Travel Grant provided by the Perkins Library of Duke University. I also thank Lionel Jensen, Timothy Cheek, and two anonymous readers for their insightful comments on earlier drafts.

1. Nicholas D. Kristof, "The Tiananmen Victory," *New York Times*, June 2, 2004, A23.

2. Some of these polls have also been reported in the mainstream Western media. See for instance Matthew Forney, "Beijing's Final Sprint: Thanks to a Savvy Public Relations Campaign, Even Some of China's Critics Are Supporting Its Bid for the 2008 Games," *Time Asia*, July 16, 2001; Joseph Kahn, "Beijing Vows to Aid Poor and Deepen Market Policy," *New York Times*, October 15, 2003, 9; and Mark O'Neill, "Rich List Puts China's Wealthy in a League of Their Own," *South China Morning Post*, April 8, 2003.

3. Significantly, while the Chinese government uses public opinion to justify its foreign policies, U.S. policymakers also deploy the idea of a "China threat" to shape U.S. public opinion toward China. See James A. Nathan and Charles Tien, "The 'China Threat,' National Missile Defense and American Public Opinion," *Defense and Security Analysis* 19, no. 1 (2003): 35–54.

4. Interestingly enough, the Guangzhou-based *Nanfang Daily* cautioned that calculated compromises like this one made by the government represented a strategic adjustment rather than a "victory of public opinion." See Yang Yizhong, "A Cautious Note on the 'Victory of Public Opinion,'" *Nanfang Daily*, January 1, 2004, www.nanfangdaily.com.cn.

5. Jane Cai, "Beijing City Hall Panned in Poll," *South China Morning Post*, December 6, 2003.

6. The least popular municipal departments were the Communications Commission and the Urban Planning Commission, which received 86 percent and 75 percent dissatisfaction ratings, respectively. See Cai, "Beijing City Hall Panned."

7. David Fang, "Pioneering Survey Gives the People a Voice: Public Opinion Is Being Given More Importance, Experts Say," *South China Morning Post*, November 21, 2003.

8. See Fang, "Pioneering Survey Gives the People a Voice"; and Irene Wang, "Negative Response Shuts Opinion Poll," *South China Morning Post*, December 7, 2003.

9. Mure Dickie, "China's Democratic Model May Be Toothless Tiger," *Financial Times*, October 13, 2003.

10. Jim Yardley, "Democracy, Chinese Style: 2 Steps Forward, 1 Step Back," *New York Times*, December 21, 2003.

11. Alexis de Tocqueville, *Democracy in America*, trans. Henry Reeve (New York: D. Appleton, 1904), 280.

12. Tocqueville, *Democracy in America*, 281–82.

13. Walter Lippmann, *Public Opinion* (New York: Harcourt, Brace, 1922), 14–16, 21, 258–49.

14. For Lippmann's discussion of propaganda, see Lippmann, *Public Opinion*, 26, 248. For Bernays's response, see Edward L. Bernays, *Crystallizing Public Opinion* (New York: Liveright, 1961), 122. See also Edward L. Bernays, *Propaganda* (New York: Liveright, 1928).

15. Stuart Ewen, *PR! A Social History of Spin* (New York: Basic Books, 1996), 395.

16. A recent article in the *New York Times* has reported that this new way of conducting government business represents a fundamental shift in the reasoning of the Chinese government rather than the personal style of the new president Hu Jintao and his associates. Yet the article predictably falls back on a conventional argument about China's political openness, wondering whether the Chinese "autocratic system of government can open itself and become flexible enough" to court the intellectuals. See Howard W. French, "China Opens a Window on the Really Big Ideas," *New York Times*, June 2, 2004, A4. See also *Straits Times*, "Chinese Cops Told to Work with Media," January 3, 2004; and *China Daily*, "Info Minister: 'Opening Up' for News, Too," January 5, 2004. For an example of how this method is being articulated by Chinese public opinion experts, see Li Jianming, *Shehui yulun yuanli [Principles of public opinion]* (Beijing: Huaxia chubanshe, 2002), 255.

17. See Timothy Cheek, *Propaganda and Culture in Mao's China: Deng Tuo and the Intelligentsia* (Oxford: Oxford University Press, 1997), ch. 3; and Yuezhi Zhao, *Media, Market, and Democracy in China: Between the Party Line and the Bottom Line* (Urbana: University of Illinois Press, 1998).

18. Hu Ningsheng, ed., *Zhongguo zhengfu xingxiang zhanglue [A study of the image strategies for Chinese government]*, 2 vols. (Beijing: Zhonggong zhongyang dangxiao chubanshe, 1998), 2:1546.

19. See www.horizon-china.com/servlet/Page?Node=8729.

20. Ma Shilong, Zhang Laicheng, and Xing Xing, "Minjian vs. guanfang, nengfou gong ying—lingdian yanjiu zixun jituan dongshichang Yuan Yue zhuanfang [The public vs. the authorities—can they both win? An interview with the president of Horizon Research Yuan Yue]," *Shuju [Data]* (January 2005): 50–53.

21. The current connection between politics and public opinion research is not entirely new. As in many other societies, there is in China a long history of using social survey research for the purpose of social reordering. My own research has indicated that when social science was introduced in China a century ago, it was quickly employed by contending political parties to advance their projects of social engineering and citizen cultivation.

22. David Barstow and Robin Stein, "The Message Machine: How the Government Makes News; Under Bush, a New Age of Prepackaged News," *New York Times*, March 13, 2005, 1. U.S. federal auditors eventually characterized this practice as "covert propaganda." See Robert Pear, "Buying of News by Bush's Aides Is Ruled Illegal," *New York Times*, October 1, 2005.

23. The findings in these polls seem to confirm that public opinion tracking is essential to the success of the government's public relations strategies. While the Chinese public generally has a positive overall impression of the government, it often harbors discontent over some key areas. For instance, polls suggest the public generally views the government as inefficient, unrestrained by the legal system, and plagued by widespread corruption. Similarly, a majority of the Chinese public, including party cadres, holds a negative impression of the CCP. If nothing else, these numbers indicate that the government has a lot of work to do on a number of significant issues. See Hu, *Zhongguo zhengfu xingxiang*, 2:1511–16.

24. See Hu, *Zhongguo zhengfu xingxiang zhanglue*, 2:1359.

25. Forney, "Beijing's Final Sprint."

26. Hu, *Zhongguo zhengfu xingxiang zhanglue*, 2:1360.

27. Hu, *Zhongguo zhengfu xingxiang zhanglue*, 2:1520.

28. Hu, *Zhongguo zhengfu xingxiang zhanglue*, 2:1520–22.

SUGGESTED READINGS

Edward L. Bernays, *Crystallizing Public Opinion* (New York: Liveright, 1961).

Alexis de Tocqueville, *Democracy in America*, trans. Henry Reeve (New York: D. Appleton, 1904).

Thomas de Zengotita, *Mediated: How the Media Shapes Your World and the Way You Live in It* (New York: Bloomsbury, 2005).

Stuart Ewen, *PR! A Social History of Spin* (New York: Basic Books, 1996).

Edward S. Herman and Noam Chomsky, *Manufacturing Consent* (New York: Pantheon, 1988).

John D. Lindau and Timothy Cheek, *Market Economics and Political Change: Comparing China and Mexico* (Lanham, MD: Rowman & Littlefield, 1988).

Daniel C. Lynch, *After the Propaganda State: Media, Politics, and Thought Work in Reformed China* (Stanford, CA: Stanford University Press, 1999).

Wang Hui, *China's New Order: Society, Politics, and Economy in Transition*, ed. and trans. Theodore Huters (Cambridge, MA: Harvard University Press, 2003).

Yuezhi Zhao, *Media, Market, and Democracy in China: Between the Party Line and the Bottom Line* (Urbana: University of Illinois Press, 1998).

11

Sex Tourism and the Lure of the Ethnic Erotic in Southwest China

Sandra Teresa Hyde

On a sweltering afternoon, so hot you can almost hear the sidewalks sizzle, grandmothers fan sleeping grandsons under the palm trees that line South Nationality Road. As night falls, quiet yields to motorcycles and red taxis filled with finely dressed tourists racing to discos and bars blaring Japanese karaoke and American rock and roll. Subtle changes are taking place in the life of the streets. By day, locals go about their daily affairs, and at night the tourists, 2 million of whom flock every year to China's southwest border region of Xishuangbanna Dai Nationality Autonomous Prefecture (hereafter referred to by its Tai name, Sipsongpanna) in southern Yunnan province, emerge from their air-conditioned hotel rooms, looking to slake their thirst for a blend of commerce, capital, and commodity fetishism.

This is the world of China's ethnic margins, a world that has undergone dramatic development in recent years following the government's designation of this region and other ethnic areas of the Southwest as tourist sites and special economic zones (SEZs). Sipsongpanna is important because it is at the crossroads between three countries: China, Laos, and Myanmar (Burma). And for China's growing middle class in the last decade, it also has become a well-known and admired tourist destination. Development here is a story about how a small town on the Lancang River became a city of sex tourism, and of how Han migration and China's state tourism policies transformed a series of large Tai villages into the cosmopolitan city of Jinghong. Over the recent course of this development, the rural villages of Sipsongpanna became urban Jinghong.[1]

The rapidity of this urban transformation owes much to the particular resonance of Jinghong in the popular Chinese imagination—a place where fantasies of sex, travel, and minority ethnicity come together. By exploring

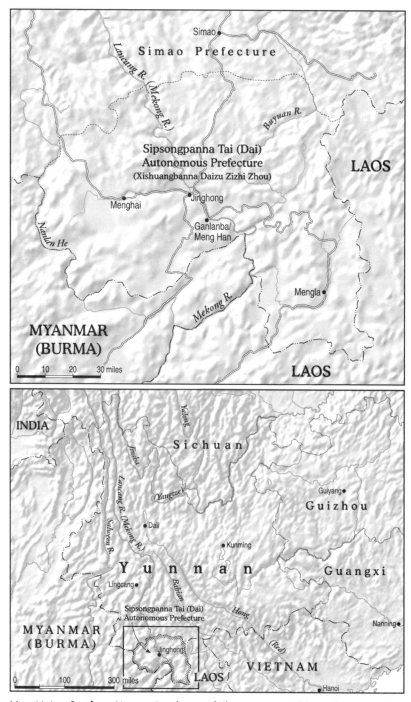

Map 11.1.   Southern Yunnan Province and Sipsongpanna (Xishuangbanna) Prefecture in Relation to Myanmar and Laos

the unique context of Jinghong's development, we discover that sexuality and sexual practices become an important part of what it means to be modern in contemporary China. This notion of modernity, as in much of North America, embraces sexual desire and pleasure as legitimate, while it simultaneously castigates the purveyors of prostitution as dangerous and polluting Others. Understanding how travelers, migrants, and locals negotiate the inevitable differences between their imagination of Sipsongpanna and what they encounter when visiting or living there enriches our general understanding of contemporary Chinese sexual practice and modernity, revealing the excitement and danger of the material transformation of the everyday.

Although the focus of this chapter is the political economy of sex in China's Southwest, the topic opens onto a global panorama of sex trafficking. I begin with a discussion of prostitution as a global phenomenon, followed by a brief social history of Sipsongpanna and the city of Jinghong, because we must know something about the region's past in order to understand why it is now marketed as a sexy tourist destination. I next explore how exoticism in Sipsongpanna is practiced by women of China's majority Han, performing and playing on the cultural characteristics of Tai-Lüe ethnicity. In other words, I explore how fantasies about the exotic Tai are experimented with and fulfilled through prostitution performed by Han women, and how in turn these women imagine and construct fantasies for male tourists through their practices. This eroticization will take on a human face for us through the experiences of two people connected to the New Wind Hair Salon in Jinghong: the madam who owns the salon, and a businessman who is its customer. I then conclude with an analysis of China's changing sexual morality and some of the practices that mark sexuality as intrinsic to modernity in Jinghong. In thinking beyond the headlines, we see a place that is, both by virtue of geography and ethnicity, on the margins of the Chinese nation but that upon closer, local investigation is actually not so marginal or traditional after all.[2]

GLOBAL CONSUMPTION, TOURISM, AND PROSTITUTION

Sex for hire in China is a commercial juggernaut, as evidenced by its massive number of sex workers: some 10 million men and women, according to the World Health Organization (WHO). Experts believe that prostitution accounts for as much as 6–12 percent of the country's annual gross domestic product (GDP). Commercial sex availability is not simply an urban phenomenon—although it is most pronounced in China's major cities like Beijing, Guangzhou, and Shanghai—and its accelerated growth cannot be explained as a sudden escalation of public desire. The burgeoning national market for sex is evident in the offenses listed in the expanding records of police blotters. In an ongoing effort to interdict vice, the Chinese government has conducted several prominent crackdowns, commonly called *yanda* (strike hard) campaigns. Over the past two decades, Chinese police blotters have become swollen with the records of hundreds of thousands of arrests of men and women in these official campaigns, not to mention those of numerous national scandals involving children in the sex trade, solicitations of underage sex (under fourteen years of age), involuntary sexual servitude, and kidnapping.

It is especially the countryside, in the provinces of Guizhou, Sichuan, and Yunnan, that has become the site of a new sexual predation in which girls and young women are abducted and either sold into sexual slavery or bought by men in search of a wife. This phenomenon was the focus of government attention in the late 1980s and early 1990s when an investigation led to the shutting down of a national kidnapping and slavery racket operating in Shandong and Jiangxi provinces. Highly publicized figures from the government's 2000 *yanda* campaign revealed that women drawn into the dark commerce of sexual enslavement by aggressive brokers and kidnappers were conveyed like currency along the backroads of China's drug trade to Myanmar and Thailand, into Malaysia and Singapore, and sometimes as far as Italy, Mexico, and the United States.

Set against this global backdrop, the sexual economy of Sipsongpanna complicates the role of predator and prey and provides sociological clues to the steady growth of sex trafficking in China. According to local folklore and, more importantly, in terms of the local economy, Jinghong is a *piaocheng* or a city of prostitution. It provides Han Chinese male tourists with a sex-oriented tourist destination. Principally, these male tourists come to Jinghong to consume Tai minority women. However, the majority of prostitutes in Jinghong are not Tai but Han women from the nearby regions of Sichuan (the first province to the north of Yunnan) and Guizhou (the first province to the east of Yunnan) who dress in Tai clothing to attract Han male customers. They—just like the men who solicit them—provide an allure that is marketed in tourist brochures.

The market in sex tourism is not unique to China. In many tourist spots around the world, including neighboring Thailand to the west, both foreign and local men and women seek the pleasure and profitability of trading money for sex. In other parts of the globe, like the Caribbean and parts of West Africa, it is female tourists from the global North who seek the pleasures of the global South by consuming sun, sand, surf, and local men. The relationships between these global trafficking poles are complicated and intersected by unequal power and political relations. Furthermore, sex tourism sites can also be found in many large cities in the United States.

In this respect, it is important to note that prostitution is not a monolithic enterprise; its myriad forms are expressed in various ways at different times

in numerous geographic locales. Scholars such as Ronald Weitzer have noted
that the critical details of sex work—what kind of work prostitutes perform,
in what location, and what forms of compensation are provided—are not
well defined or understood.[3] In Jinghong, women who work in places classified as middle-level brothels perform a variety of services ranging from providing *anmo* (sensual massages), *tuiyou* (a hand job, or literally, "pushing out
oil"), or the local euphemism *da feiji* (hit the airplane), to having sex with
men back in their hotel rooms. In some aid circles in Yunnan, for example
at the Women's and Children's Law Project in Jinghong, the western term *sex
worker* (*xing gongzuozhe*) has been appropriated as a term of respect for
women that trade in sex.[4] However, as Marjolein Van der Veen points out, the
term *sex worker* itself also reifies a particular identity, rather than acknowledging that these women have other identities such as mother, sister, and
daughter and often work at other jobs; they are not just sex workers.

A HISTORY OF SIPSONGPANNA

Prior to the thirteenth century, Sipsongpanna (literally in Sipsongpanna
Tai, "twelve rice fields or regions") was a de facto kingdom of Thailand,
with links to the other three major northern kingdoms of Lan Na, Keng
Tung, and Lan Zhang. According to Tai historian Ratanaporn Sethakul, the
Tai-Lüe state was unlike other Tai states, because it remained confederated
and bound by kinship relations of the ruling classes—those that aligned
themselves to form a confederation of a dozen or more *chau* or *panna*. The
Tai-Lüe kingdom was weakened by the interference of its two powerful
neighbors, the Chinese and the Burmese (now Myanmar), because they
both wanted to keep Sipsongpanna as a buffer to ensure peaceful frontiers.
The Sipsongpanna kingdom was renamed Xishuangbanna Dai Nationality
Autonomous Prefecture on January 24, 1953, when the Communists integrated this suzerain territory into mainland China as part of the process of
Sinicizing all regions of China. Muang Jinghong was the capital of the Sipsongpanna kingdom for more than eight hundred years and is now Jinghong, the prefectural capital. It borders the Shan states of Myanmar to the
southwest, the northern tip of Laos to the southeast, and Simao county in
Yunnan province to the north. (See map 11.1.)
    Sipsongpanna has a land base of nineteen thousand square kilometers
and is situated on the Yunnan plateau divided by the Lancang River. The
river winds down from the northwest to the south of the prefecture and
continues into Southeast Asia, where it is known as the Mekong. Sipsongpanna is divided into two counties and one main city: Menghai county to
the southwest, Mengla county to the southeast, and Jinghong city, the regional capital, close to the center. In the early 1950s, the population of Sip-

songpanna was around 60,000 to 75,000, whereas by the end of 2003 the population had grown to 873,694, of which 75 percent were ethnic minorities, the Tai being the largest at 35 percent of the total population. The remarkable population increase in these decades was due to waves of Han Chinese in-migration, and the Han currently make up over 30 percent of the urban population of Jinghong proper (as compared to less than 10 percent in the 1950s).

Historically, Sipsongpanna was not a Han tourist destination. Prior to the 1950s there was virtually no foreign trade with Yunnan province, and so this region lived up to its name as Mysterious Land South of the Clouds. The Han Chinese came to Sipsongpanna in three distinct waves of migration: in the 1950s, to plant rubber; during the Cultural Revolution (1966 to 1976), when educated youths were sent down (*xiaxiang*) to serve the poor minorities; and finally, in the 1990s and after, to develop local state resources like rubber, the largest cash crop in the region, and manganese mines.[5] In the late 1980s and early 1990s, several Tai villages south of Jinghong were demolished as a new economic development zone was built for foreign joint-venture hotels, restaurants, and tourist parks. While market-based economic development was key in this process, according to local rumors in Jinghong, little or no compensation was given to Tai village leaders for repossession of their lands.

Under provincial policies in the late 1980s, Han authorities opened trade routes into the "golden quadrangle" of Laos, northern Thailand, Myanmar, and southwestern China, increasing pathways for future transnational flows and migration. The central Beijing government viewed Sipsongpanna as a critical gateway into Southeast Asia for trade, goods, and tourists. Opening this gateway also meant marketing the region through tourism.[6] In the past few years, a number of tourist websites have appeared bearing descriptions of the pleasures and wonders of this place that retains one-sixth of China's incredible plant diversity and thirteen of Yunnan's twenty-two ethnic minority groups.[7] Sipsongpanna was the launching point for emerging ethnic and ecological tourism to its tropical rain forests, Buddhist temples, and Tai villages in the mid-1980s. In 1993, the UN Educational, Scientific and Cultural Organization (UNESCO) designated Sipsongpanna a world biosphere reserve because of its remarkably varied plant and animal life. Owing to its tropical rain forests, its biodiversity, and its three main nature reserves, by the late 1980s Sipsongpanna had also become a honeymoon spot for Han couples, a place of rest and relaxation for businessmen, and a prime destination for government-sponsored, all-expenses-paid, work-unit meetings.

During this same interval, economic necessity complemented romance in the expanding popularity of Sipsongpanna. China's large *liudong renkou* (floating population), approximately 150 million migrants, has spread out across the country in search of work. While 90 percent of Sipsongpanna's tourists in the late 1990s were newly prosperous Han Chinese from greater China, the working immigrants that powered the tourist industry came from a wider Asian diaspora: for example, the Singaporeans who cut hair in a salon owned by someone from Macao, and the Pakistani who traveled from Myanmar to sell jade. Migrant Chinese workers also came from Sichuan to drive taxicabs, from Hunan to sell imported Korean clothing, and from Guizhou to run the *meirong ting* (beauty salons) that are, in essence, brothels.

In 1995, more than 1.5 million tourists came to Sipsongpanna. Almost ten years later in 2004, the number of tourists had increased to 2.71 million Chinese (99 percent) and around 33,000 foreign nationals (1 percent).[8] The majority of these tourists are middle-class Han Chinese who come to Sipsongpanna for rest and relaxation at the end of their Kunming-based business meetings. But by the early 1990s, a very different kind of tourist had also arrived in Jinghong: middle-aged males with money to spend on brothels, dancing girls, and gambling. In Jinghong, sex tourism is practiced under the guise of such businesses as karaoke bars, hair salons, barber-shops, massage parlors, saunas, and bars, where services extend beyond the karaoke microphone and the blow dryer. Massage parlors not only provide massages but also have on-site escort services where young women may entertain men in the privacy of their hotel rooms.

Jinghong is a forty-five-minute flight, or a twenty-four-hour bus ride, from Kunming. The Regional Development Office now paints what anthropologist Grant Evans calls a "Disney Worldesque" picture of the future, capturing the world beyond China's very real and enforced borders. Sipsongpanna provides a unique case, for although few Chinese have passports to travel overseas, they can go on excursions to Chinese-controlled border towns in both Myanmar and Laos. Once there, these tourists can spend their yuan in Chinese-run businesses, thus benefiting the Chinese on both sides of the border. The Local Development Office now plans to resurrect what was formerly the largest Tai temple, torn down during the Cultural Revolution, as an ethno-religious theme park in order to bring the authentic flavor of Southeast Asia within China's borders. A three-hundred-meter bridge has already been built to connect the industrial district on one side of the river with the commercial center of Jinghong; in addition, Sipsongpanna is becoming part of the Association of Southeast Asian Nations (ASEAN) development projects, including a superhighway under construction between Yunnan and Thailand.

Li, a young man of twenty-nine who works for the provincial Public Security Bureau, pointed out that key leaders of the local police went to a conference in Las Vegas in 1995 and returned with visions of turning Sipsongpanna into the Las Vegas of China.[9] However, the local model for sex tourism is not the United States but rather Thailand, which also mixes elephant rides, rainforest tours, and dancing minority women with sex and sex tourism. As economic development under Deng Xiaoping's dictum "To get rich is glorious" took root in China in the 1980s and 1990s, the Chinese state appropriated collective farmland and redistributed it for private redevelopment. Four-star international hotels (built by Thai-Chinese, Taiwanese-Chinese, and Shanghainese developers) emerged from the fields, and rice cultivation in the two adjacent Tai villages of Manjinglan and Manting was destroyed.[10] Many Tai were critical of this appropriation, but most local Han understood it in terms of progress and development. Xiao Feng, a Han woman of twenty-five, born and raised in Jinghong, who is a school teacher by profession and currently a tour guide and secretary, told me this story:

> Jinghong was very poor prior to economic reforms; everyone was treated the same and served the same, [and] respected one another's spirits. When I was growing up the only large buildings were the prefecture's Communist Party headquarters. The site of Xishuangbanna hotel was a Tai village called Manyun. Now the Tai villagers are landlords, they have become rich subdividing the bottom dirt floors of their houses into rooms for let. Before, the peasants' trade market was just vegetable fields: the road to the Teacher Training School was just dirt. Everything changed with the airport, with planes came new businesses, with new businesses came the *heishehui* [Chinese Mafia], prostitution came in 1992, and gambling in 1994. Jinghong is definitely now a town dependent on *lüyouye* [the tourism industry] . . . We have moved from an idealistic to a realistic society.

For Xiao Feng, China under socialism was very idealistic, but under Deng Xiaoping's striving for market socialism, it had become more realistic: realistic in providing jobs outside the *danwei* (work-unit) system, as well as in the growth of newfound leisure activities. No informant, including Feng, could give me the origins of prostitution in Jinghong; however, many stated that "it came with the airport," as if planes and sex went together. In order to understand this linking of commerce and sexual congress on the margins, we must understand Chinese historical conceptions of race and ethnicity.

RACE AND ETHNICITY IN CHINA

Research on *minzu* (race) in modern China reminds us that racial preferences are common to almost all cultures. In the early 1950s, the CCP sent hundreds of researchers to the border areas to distinguish the Han Chinese from the non-Han groups. Those researchers applied a nineteenth-century evolutionary schema of stages from primitive to civilized, thus identifying the majority Han as the pinnacle of civilization and the minority non-Han as belonging to the lower rungs of the scale. Under Mao Zedong, *minzu* was understood as synonymous with class, and minorities in China were determined in relationship to poverty. The definition of a minority was based on Stalin's four criteria for a common nationality: territory, language, economy, and nature. The results created fifty-five officially recognized minority groups that then constituted 8 percent of the Chinese population, while the remaining 92 percent was the Han majority. The largest minority groups in China are the Zhuang, the Hui, the Miao, and the Uighurs; the Tai, discussed here, are actually only the seventeenth-largest group, with a population of just over 1 million.[11]

In late 1990s Sipsongpanna, ethnic groups were divided by economic class and occupation and with specific reference to the lands they inhabited.[12] The landscape in Sipsongpanna is subtropical: the Tai minority control the lowland, wet-rice fields and therefore the richest agricultural land; the Bulang minority, the middle hillsides; the Akha, the mountaintops; and the Han Chinese, the townships of Mengla, Menghai, and Jinghong. In order to market Sipsongpanna to Greater China and the Han Chinese, the notion of a peripheral space, a space outside the norms of urban living in Shanghai, Guangzhou, Beijing, or even Kunming must be maintained. Sipsongpanna is marketed as a rural paradise complete with an urban center that coordinates, manages, and filters such rural pleasures as elephant riding and Tai women bathing in a river.

PERFORMING ETHNICITY

In exploring the social construction of ethnicity, it is important to recognize the distinction between social representations of the Tai and actual Tai cultural practices.[13] In Jinghong, because Han migrants and tourists both claim to appropriate authentic images of Tai culture, ethnicity becomes an especially malleable category. However, even the fluidity of ethnic boundaries has its limits. Louisa Schein has noted that the Han often construct the non-Han as feminized minority Others, and in Sipsongpanna this is evident in the local market economy for sex tourism. The consumers in this market, Han men, drive the market for ethnic women, who are in fact Han women who mimic Tai culture for profit. But money is not the only desired profit here: what these Han women can do away from home, away from watchful eyes, is also important. Over and over again, people remarked to me that Sipsongpanna is the land of freedom, unbounded cultural limits, and promiscuous sex—things not identified with or obtainable in Han society.

Among other ethnic groups in Sipsongpanna, there is a prevalent belief that the Tai are the most intelligent, clever, and enterprising of the minority peoples. It is said of them, *Tamen you wenhua* (They have culture), unlike the Bulang or the Lahu peoples, because the Tai possess a written language based on ancient Pali-Hindu texts and are practicing Theravada Buddhists who continue to train young male monks in the old traditions. Such veneration is contested by Han Chinese entrepreneurs, who remark on how *bendiren* (or "locals," an epithet for the Tai) are stupid because they do not have a clue about how to run a business: *Bendiren bu hui chiku* (Locals don't know how to eat bitterness). The expression *eating bitterness* asks further explanation. *To eat bitterness* in China has multiple meanings, but here it means that one must work hard and suffer in order to reap the benefits of one's labors at a later time. When outsiders say the locals don't know how to eat bitterness, they mean that they are unable to delay gratification.

The Tai, although economically and socially marginalized in urban Jinghong by not selling sex, are relatively rich compared to other minorities like the Bulang and the Akha. Local Tai explain their uninvolvement in the sex industry by linking it to their strength in maintaining cultural values and traditions. Here the local Tai see themselves as superior to the Han, who have forgotten traditional notions of fidelity. While Tai villagers uphold notions of traditional culture that militate against images of sexual promiscuity, in the city of Jinghong, the local Tai often express their own feelings of inferiority. Many local Tai entrepreneurs who are engaged in business mention how their friends and family members do not like or know how to work hard. When I asked Ai Yang, the young owner of an appliance store, how he could call his Tai compatriots "lazy, unable to eat bitterness," if he was successful, he shrugged his shoulders and said, "I am different, not like other Tai."

In Jinghong, Tai villagers no longer grow as much rice as they once did because they have become landlords for the local Han immigrants who live beneath Tai homes in the spaces formerly reserved for farm machinery and pigs. While many of the locals joke about the Han living in livestock quarters, the situation of these locals is very precarious because the government may crack down on illegally registered tenants at any time. These tenants are often migrant youths who come to Jinghong from China's hinterland in search of employment. Another consequence of the "Hanification" of Sipsongpanna is the replacement of Tai businesses with Han businesses. In 1995 on Manting Street, there were three or four restaurants run by local Tais, but by 1996 there were almost no Tai businesses. Han businessmen had bought most of the Tai-owned restaurants and turned them into clubs replete with pseudo-Tai dancing, dinner-table massages, and pseudo-Tai food. By 2002, all of the street signs and message boards that were once bilingual in Mandarin and Tai were now only Mandarin.

One local teacher, Ai Lao, a man of thirty-four, complained bitterly that the breakdown in Tai culture was evident in the decline of Tai farming methods and traditional customs. Ai Lao was involved in several projects intended to revive Tai culture: playing in a local all-Tai rock band, teaching at a local temple school, and organizing cross-border exchanges with Tai-Lüe in Myanmar, Laos, and Thailand. For Ai Yang and Ai Lao, the city of Jinghong embraced both a promotion of Tai culture (it brought in money and capital) and a revulsion toward and destruction of that culture (it sanitized Tai practices and paved over village farm plots). The consequences of this promotion and destruction of Tai culture means Sipsongpanna Tai are now looking to the former borders of the Tai nation, which crisscross contemporary Southeast Asia. There they seek support and capital for such endeavors as training young monks, preserving the Buddhist palm-leaf scriptures, and investing in Tai businesses.

Tai women are often depicted as exotic and sexually alluring, whether in films about sent-down Han youth during the Cultural Revolution, in images on clothes, or in the native portraits of the *Yunnan huapai* (Yunnan school of painting). Beginning in the late 1980s, the Yunnan school focused predominantly on Han artists depicting minority subjects. Much of the work of the Yunnan school was focused on the eroticization of minority women, and Tai women in particular. If one examines a catalog featuring paintings of the Yunnan school, one notices that the images all resemble abstract, eroticized pinups. These portraits dramatize the sexuality of Tai women, displaying them with large, uncovered breasts, thin waists, and tightly wrapped sarongs. Paintings of the Yunnan school have obtained international notoriety and are immensely popular among Han buyers in Beijing.

In Sipsongpanna, the Han represent and perform "Tai-ness" for a Han audience in order to achieve gains in their own economic status, personal freedom, desires, and amusements. In Jinghong, what is Tai sells, and therefore one merely "becomes Tai" in order to profit. This applies most readily to Han women, who dress in Tai clothing to attract Han male sex customers. Local Han female entertainment workers—including tour guides, restaurant servers, dancers, and some prostitutes—dress in Tai women's ethnic clothing, which is a close-fitting, floor-length sarong and a short-cropped, long-sleeved top. Because the Han Chinese women from Sichuan and Guizhou who work in the brothels, nightclubs, and karaoke bars all dress in the traditional clothing of the Tai minority, they are often at first glance perceived as local Tai by Han tourists. But all one has to do is speak with these women to know they are not from Jinghong, for they speak with the accent of outsiders.

There are other outsiders present within this confusing, sexualized complex in which Han and Tai are commingled: white women. What is being marketed in Jinghong is not just beautiful minority women but also Westernized representations of them. While white women are not notably pres-

Figure 11.1.   Sexualized Western models on a billboard in Guangzhou. (Photo: Peter H. Jaynes)

ent in Yunnan school paintings, they are present in depictions of sexual promiscuity and in places of sexual consumption. In the hair salons in Jinghong, posters of white women line the walls, and these images carry over to popular magazines, and to the photo-novella comic books used for HIV/AIDS prevention (see figure 11.1). The white woman also appears as the ethnographer.

As a white, Western-educated woman and as an AIDS activist, I came to China and to Yunnan because it was ground zero of the Chinese AIDS epidemic. After not receiving permission to study Tai village life in a high-prevalence county, I was redirected to Jinghong and Sipsongpanna. This particular assignment permitted me to follow earlier speculation that because the Tai in one place had high rates of AIDS, so might the Tai in

Sipsongpanna. Reaching out to an illegal industry as a foreign white woman provided both challenges and opportunities. The male clients often eagerly accepted me, while the women, at first, did not. I had easier access to the higher-class, more-visible salons than to the lower-class, low-income brothels. In the low-income brothels, the owners were only interested in pimping me, rather than in me studying them. If defining oneself as proper requires defining oneself against a racially contrived Other, then it stands to reason that the Han might perceive the non-Han as a repository of pleasure, as marked by sex as they are by race. But to put a human face on this sex industry and on how the eroticization of ethnicity operates, I turn now to two people at the New Wind Hair Salon: Madam Liu and Manager Zhou.

FEMALE FANTASIES OF WORK: MADAM LIU'S HAIR SALON

Madam Liu operates a hair salon that is also a brothel.[14] Her story provides a canvas on which to sketch the larger issues of how tourism in a border region operates by creating and selling a kind of fantasy community. As I mentioned above, prostitution functions here as a quasi-legal business under the gaze of the state. Prostitution is quasi-legal because it commonly occurs in the otherwise legitimate shops of barbers and hair stylists. The sex industry's hair-salon guise has a distinct architecture of task: the outer storefronts are hair salons; the middle rooms are massage parlors; and the inner sanctums, the small rooms with raised beds, are the brothels. Whereas the front room of the salon, the one most visible from the street, is legal, the back rooms are the sites of illegal sexual exchanges. There is a complicated but often cohesive and cordial relationship between legitimate businesses, businesses on the legal periphery such as hair salons that are also brothels, and the local police, who represent the Chinese state. Local policemen warn their favorite brothel owners when a nationwide government *yanda* campaign begins.

Liu, a Rubenesque Han woman in her late thirties, is divorced from her husband, who lives in Guizhou province. Liu has been a resident of Jinghong since 1994, and she and her lover, Tan, a bus driver, own the New Wind Hair Salon. In our conversations, Liu said she was glad when she came to Jinghong because it meant an escape from drudgery and her miserable marriage. She regularly works from one in the afternoon to one in the morning, beginning with haircuts in the afternoon and at night dispatching her staff on calls. The majority of the sex conducted through the salon consists of hand jobs and massages in the back room. Sex acts that require condoms are conducted on calls. Men negotiate these encounters by driving or walking up to the salon, and discussing the price and place with Liu. She then yells to a woman to come over and accompany the man to his hotel. When I met Liu, she had four women working in her salon: Wang and Yue from Ruili, a border town in northwestern Yunnan, and Gu and Ling from rural villages in Sichuan—all ethnically Han, but presented as Tai.

When I first met Yue she was twenty-three years old. She had come to Jinghong from Ruili only one month earlier because work opportunities were better. She said, "In Ruili the hair salons employing prostitutes only operate for local businessmen not tourists and you cannot make as much money. Local businessmen are not interested in paying local women for their services, but in Xishuangbanna you become something special." Wang, also twenty-three and from Ruili, came to Sipsongpanna to visit her sister, who worked in one of the gambling salons. Her sister made good money. Although Wang wasn't making as much as her sister, she preferred Jinghong to Ruili. Yue, Wang, Gu, and Ling all said they could make ¥200 to ¥300 per day (US$25 to $38), 70 percent of which they gave to Liu. On good days they took home ¥100, meaning that they could clear ¥1,000 to ¥2,000 a month, or four to six times what shop assistants or restaurant workers make. While Yue and her sister spent most of their earnings on fancy clothing, perfumes, and jewelry, Gu, a twenty-seven-year-old married woman from Sichuan, sent a portion home to her family. Gu told me that her parents were peasants and she had not told them what kind of work she did in Jinghong. Her biggest frustration was that she missed her six-year-old son terribly. She only got to see him once a year at Spring Festival. But there was no work in her hometown.

Wang and Yue were the most popular women in the salon, perhaps because they often dressed in Tai clothing: beautiful batiks that were closely cropped to fit their figures. Regarding her dress, Yue explained that the men who came to Xishuangbanna really liked the Tai look, and so to attract customers and keep Liu happy, she often dressed that way. While she laughed at the idea that anyone could mistake her for a Tai woman, she said that Tai clothes were so beautiful that men came in just to look, and that brought more customers into the salon.

In 1997 there were more than one hundred hair salons throughout Jinghong that resembled Liu's place. Some were genuine beauty salons that only cut hair. Others cut hair and conducted prostitution on the side (like Liu's), and still others were complete frauds. For Liu, Yue, Gu, and Wang, Sipsongpanna was a land of opportunity, but an opportunity that had to be masked, for they could not be honest about their professions to their families in their natal homes. Because hair salons have become synonymous with prostitution, even mentioning that they worked in a salon could be dangerous. Gu would have preferred to stay on her family's land in Sichuan, for working the fields would have maintained her sense of family and grounding in what she called her roots in the soil. Just as prostitution has

Figure 11.2.   Sex sells: An advertisement for a spa. (Photo: Peter H. Jaynes)

to be hidden behind the facades of beauty parlors, so too, these women had to lie to their families about what they did.

Several of my informants countered the view, espoused by several members of the *Fulian* (Women's Federation), that "Women are just being exploited again . . . We are back to pre-liberation China and what have we gained? One step forward and two steps back." (See figure 11.2.) What appears as a marker of difference between the pre-liberation sex industry and its contemporary renaissance is the fact that a number of young women consider prostitution a viable occupation rather than a form of servitude. Other informants remarked, "It is much easier to get a job, a good job, as a female than a male. There are just many more opportunities." When asked about the differences in salary between prostitutes and female tour guides (key tour guides are all young women under the age of thirty), one informant explained it this way: "While there is not a big monetary difference, prostitutes don't get to admire their work." These prostitutes make more per month than tour guides, but then they must pay for clothing, makeup, and the madam's commission. As a tour guide, a young woman makes around ¥1,000 to ¥3,000 a month ($120 to $370) and everything is hers to keep. The tour company even provides the uniforms.

While women prostitutes capitalize on their beauty and mimic Tai ethnicity, thereby seeking freedom and profit, the question remains, why do men come to Sipsongpanna? I turn now to the story of one of the many men who come to Jinghong.

MALE FANTASIES OF PLACE: MANAGER ZHOU

Head counts on each flight from which I disembarked in Jinghong revealed that most planes were full of men. On some flights of two hundred passengers, I was one of only two or three females. A few times, all-female work-unit tour groups skewed the balance to around 60 percent males and 40 percent females. Several of my informants mentioned there is a saying in Sipsongpanna, *chi qingchun fan*, which means "eating spring rice." "Eating spring rice" is a play on the socialist-era metaphor of the *tiefanwan* (iron rice bowl). Having an iron rice bowl meant that the Chinese people would always have a guarantee of sufficient food to eat, because their rice bowls would never break. "Eating spring rice" plays on the earlier saying as a way to say that rice bowls do not last forever—that young girls fade into older women, and they cannot live off their beauty forever.[15]

As China becomes part of the global economy, new products must be consumed to denote the increasing prosperity of its citizenry. Therefore, sex and buying sex have become part of what it means to have a modern identity in northern Chinese cities. Wealthy men down bottles of XO Cognac, luxuriate in fancy hotel rooms, and consume dinners as well as the women of their ethnic fantasy in Jinghong. Sipsongpanna's sexual pleasures carry connotations far beyond intrinsic physical satisfaction. Here it is precisely these nouveau riche, male tourists who come for sex and women. And while the provincial government condones neither prostitution nor gambling, several of my male informants described Jinghong as one of the most popular places in China to seek both.[16] A wealthy Hong Kong businessman sitting in a friend's cafe asked a local businessman what he should invest in. The local man told him, "Why, prostitution and gambling, that's where the money is." Workers like Liu, Yue, Ling, Gu, and Wang have varied relationships to the city of Jinghong; however, the tourists are the ones who ultimately drive this local economy of pleasure and reinforce the popular image of the ethnic erotic. Their relationship with the place provides another picture of Jinghong. In Manager Zhou, an assistant manager of a trading company in Jiangxi province, and who was in Sipsongpanna for an extended business meeting and vacation, we can observe the drive to sexualize this special place.

After numerous requests from Liu's customers to join them in the nightclubs, one night I acquiesced and went out with Zhou, who frequented the hair salon for massages. I decided it would be an ethnographic exchange: he wanted to discuss U.S. politics as we gambled and danced, and I wanted to find out why he came to Sipsongpanna. After several hours of gambling at the New Elephant Hotel, I finally got my nerve up to talk about Liu. I almost fell off my chair when he posed the rhetorical question "Of course, you know she is not a hairdresser?" I replied that I most certainly did. When I asked him why he and his colleagues came to engage in massages, he laughed: "I'm on vacation. Away from my wife, of course, I want some relaxation accompanied by beautiful women." Another informant distinguished his feelings about infidelity this way: "Sex is like eating. If I eat cabbage every day, I may want some fancy seafood once in a while. If you eat seafood every day, you want cabbage. For one cannot live by eating the same thing all the time. It gets boring."

Manager Zhou did not discuss with his wife his trips to Sipsongpanna but said that going to Sipsongpanna was a frequent treat for him. He didn't consider gambling out of the ordinary, and he told me that the slot machines in Sipsongpanna were rigged. The owners of the hotels were not honest gamblers: they cheated him. For Manager Zhou, Sipsongpanna was a place where fantasies came true. It was also, more simply, a break in his routine, a chance to both work and play in a freer environment. He repeated, like a mantra, that in Sipsongpanna the women were more open because of the influences of Tai culture, and their sexual promiscuity made this place desirable to him.

CONTEMPORARY NOTIONS OF
PROSTITUTION, SEX, AND MODERNITY

Many studies of prostitution are built on a framework of sexual division: the exploited (prostitutes) and the exploiters (customers). Such static, binary oppositions are not appropriate to the fluid medium of ethnicity and entertainment in Sipsongpanna, where exploitation is very complicated. Here we have more than the exploited and exploiters; in fact, there are several groups. If we only see Han wives (the ones living in China's hinterland) as virtuous and Tai girls as uncivilized in their rural paradise, we miss the fact that there are also Han women who are prostitutes (the unvirtuous) and Han men who are buying sex (another unvirtuous category). While I do not intend to dismiss the very real exploitation that exists within the sex industry, one needs to determine who is exploiting whom, at what time, in what place, and perhaps out of what assumptions about ethnicity.

The resurgence of prostitution as an occupation for women in contemporary China is only one facet of the proliferation of places in that country where sexuality seeks expression. Sex is considered essential for the rebirth of the Chinese nation, and the state repeatedly proclaims that if a conjugal couple is happy, then so is the nation. Contemporary versions of sexuality in China have been shaped by and have responded to earlier understandings of sex and sexuality. From my own experiences and in comparing China in 1985 to China in 2005, I am struck by a burgeoning rise of brash and copious images of sex and sexuality. Long gone are the days when men and women looked and dressed alike in shapeless dark-blue, tan, or gray pants with matching, button-down Mao jackets. However, accompanying these changes in fashion and behavior is the commercialization of women's bodies and a rampant increase in sexually transmitted infections (STIs) and, now, HIV/AIDS. Here once again, the meaning of sex and sexuality has shifted.

To understand sexual modernity in China, one needs more than scientific facts and statistical reports. This is because preventing the spread of STIs is complicated by moral judgments about which sexual acts are morally unacceptable and also dangerous. Chinese sociologist Pan Suiming points out that the notion that all Chinese female sex workers are at high risk for STIs may be erroneous because many of them, such as some of the women I describe here, are in the business of non-penetrative sex.[17] Even so, Dr. Shen Jie, director of China's National Center for AIDS Prevention and Control, noted in May 2004 that heterosexual transmission of HIV/AIDS would become the next major route of infection in China over the next decade.[18] China's AIDS crisis has been unfolding now for over a decade, and is growing worse. In 2003 the Chinese government acknowledged that 840,000 persons were infected with HIV, and said that the largest at-risk groups were former plasma donors from central China and intravenous drug users from Yunnan. Nevertheless, China's overall infection rate is still less than 1 percent of the population. However, WHO officials estimate that there are probably between 1.5 million and 2 million Chinese who have HIV/AIDS. What makes this circumstance particularly frightening is that infection rates are increasing at 30 percent a year. In Yunnan in 2003, the majority of HIV-positive persons were twenty- to thirty-year-old males who were intravenous drug users, Han Chinese, and unemployed peasants.[19] Jinghong still remains a place with low rates of reported HIV incidence.

Despite the rise in STIs, many of my informants (both Han and Tai) fervidly asserted that they, unlike promiscuous Westerners, are very cautious and conservative in the ways of sex. Yet at other times I saw them engage in all kinds of sexual activities that completely contradicted the way they talked about themselves. Here sex and the sex industry were not about Han repression and Tai promiscuity but about how sex as a commodity is circulated. Representations of sex are everywhere here in a plethora of sex-toy advertisements and products, condom packages, videos and films, anti-HIV/AIDS campaigns, hair salons that are in fact brothels, sexy clothing, and even stories in the news about sex. As a result, the desire to consume new-fangled

leisure amusements—among tourists and locals alike—includes the enjoyment of these sexual commodities, often without a proper understanding of
the consequences.

For a sex tourism site to be successful, it is critical to manage the image of
the place rather than develop strict moral imperatives regarding sex. What often gets repressed in Jinghong is the will to know and to openly acknowledge
what is being practiced. One informant in her thirties, in speaking about
taboo acts, said, "In China we just do . . . We act. We never speak about what
we have done." Thus in almost every Chinese city, one sees street posters advertising fly-by-night pseudo-physicians who claim to cure STIs, male impotence, and AIDS, yet such cures are not openly discussed. In Jinghong, these
posters are prominent only in the alleyways where locals venture; they are
torn down where tourists are apt to view them. The idea that dangerous sex
must be concealed in order to promote tourism fits with the notion of competing moral universes: a modern sexual morality promotes sex tourism
while a parochial one hides the consequences of unprotected sex.

Nonetheless, despite a rather rudimentary understanding of STIs, several
of my female informants alluded to their sex work as a sign of modernity,
and to the idea that modern China embraces sexual liberation and affords
them the freedom to capitalize on their sexuality. Xiao Feng, a young
woman quoted earlier, explained prostitution this way:

> Prostitutes make quick money . . . They think about the impressions of mar-
> riage and the lights of the city . . . Most are from the countryside and outside
> the province, and it [sex] is just a fashion for society . . . There are so many sin-
> gle women in Jinghong, the women who make up the sex industry are in
> highly paid occupations, and that is why prostitutes are plentiful. There is a
> saying in Jinghong, *yang xiao bai lian*, which means "to raise a small group of
> young handsome men." If women can keep a gaggle of handsome men around
> and just work [exchanging sex for money] . . . cultivate this group . . . just take
> care of these elegant boys, the boys will take care of their girlfriends in return.
> To have a nice-looking man to look at and take care of you while you are pro-
> vided with money is pleasing.

For local Han women like Xiao Feng, prostitution signifies the numerous
opportunities women in Jinghong have to make money and become
wealthy. Here the practice of selling one's body for money completely
trumps older notions of proper gender hierarchies. Sexuality in today's
China shapes and is shaped by the dynamics of human social life that
brings the rural into the city of Jinghong (through representations of Tai
culture) and the globalized urban cosmopolitan into rural Sipsongpanna
(via the sex trade). What these competing sexual mores pivot around is the
eroticization of the Tai, for it is upon this that the entire sex tourism industry in Sipsongpanna depends and thrives.

BEYOND THE "DISNEYESQUE"

If the contemporary sex industry as I have described it in Jinghong stands for liberation from the bonds of sexual convention (and the rise of modern, urban pleasures) wherein market forces revolutionize certain social practices, it has also become an object in itself to be acquired by the consumer. The meaning of sex in this context entails more than just a biological need to reproduce, and more than a fact of life. Sex here has taken on a life of its own as a kind of fetish. The linking of market reform and sexuality within modernity has meant a rise in numerous occupations and activities on the periphery: prostitution, karaoke girls, and gambling, each obsessively quasi-sanctioned by the state in urban and semi-urban centers. Newly blossoming work opportunities encompass occupations that span from the legal to the illegal, and all of the people working in them help create a modern vision of Sipsongpanna that bolsters its reputation as a fantasyland. Other locals, such as the police, have developed even grander visions of Sipsongpanna beyond that of it as a "Disneyesque" pleasure ground, based on their own international travels to places like Las Vegas and Bangkok.

In China, market forces have revolutionized social practices, including sexuality. Sex and the sex industry, unlike the discourse of national liberation, are laden with references to the rise of moral decay and crime, especially because they are associated with Tai women and now with HIV/AIDS. Several of the women I spoke with see themselves as part and parcel of a larger project that embraces sexual liberation, and maintain the freedom to capitalize on their sexuality. Where is the exploitation in this? If taking care of "elegant boys" means providing for oneself and one's family, then these Chinese women today are not returning to pre-liberation gender roles (concubine and mistress), but neither do they embody the trope of self-actualized, strong women from the Maoist era. Although labor migration may be a giant step toward economic liberalization, it has not always been a step forward for migrant women. Moreover, the promise of economic gain implicit in the great migration presently under way in China is, as we have seen in the Southwest, portentous for the nation and the world, as it acts as an engine of wealth and a conduit for HIV/AIDS.

NOTES

My heartfelt gratitude goes to my informants, for without them this fieldwork could never have been done. Original research was generously supported by a Fulbright-Hays Doctoral Research Abroad Fellowship, the Wenner-Gren Foundation, the Center for HIV/AIDS Prevention Studies at the University of California, San Francisco, and from the University of California, Berkeley, two Foreign Language and Area Studies grants, a Regent's Fellowship from the Center for Chinese Studies, and an Anthropology Department Lowie Award. Writing time was made possible by a National Institute of Mental Health Postdoctoral Training Fellowship at Harvard Medical School and by grants from the Social Science Research Council of Canada. Many people have commented on this chapter in a previous version that was published in Nancy N. Chen et al., eds., *China Urban* (2001), and a longer version is forthcoming in my book *Eating Spring Rice: The Cultural Politics of AIDS in Southwest China.* For this version, I thank Tim Weston, Lionel Jensen, Angela Davies, and two anonymous reviewers for providing close readings of the text and invaluable suggestions for revision.

1. The Han are the most common and thus rhetorically and ideologically dominant of China's fifty-six official *shaoshu minzu* (ethnic peoples). This somewhat fungible category is now fully conflated with the identity of the Chinese nation. For the purposes of reference, *Han* may be taken on sociological analogy with *white* in U.S. society.

2. During twenty months of ethnographic fieldwork between 1996 and 2000 on a larger project on the emergence of the HIV/AIDS epidemic in Yunnan province, I conducted twenty interviews with men and women of diverse occupations ranging from prostitute to tour guide. In my original dissertation research on HIV/AIDS in Yunnan, Jinghong was selected as a field site because of cultural assumptions about the Tai being *luanjiao* (loose, sexually uninhibited people), and thus I was to find out what risky sexual practices might predispose them to HIV/AIDS.

3. Ronald Weitzer, ed., *Sex for Sale: Prostitution, Pornography, and the Sex Industry* (New York: Routledge, 2000).

4. See Sandra Teresa Hyde, "Selling Sex and Sidestepping the State: Prostitutes, Condoms, and HIV/AIDS Prevention in Southwest China," *East Asia* 18, no. 4 (Winter 2000). The label *sex worker* reveals a tendency to view prostitution as either work, or as essentially dehumanizing. Taking into consideration these critical perspectives, I switch here between *prostitutes* (mimicking my informants' literal use of the term *jinu*), *sex workers* (when talking about them as a general category of worker), and *female entertainment workers* (covering a broader category than just women who exchange sex for money).

5. Rubber first came in the 1950s, somewhat informally with the Chinese returning from Thailand, then in the form of official state research on rubber. The state began to lower the price of rubber during the 1990s as it became clearer that China would be accepted into the WTO. However, rubber remains the premier cash crop in the region, and farmers plant trees with the assumption that the price will go up again (Janet Sturgeon, personal communication, June 30, 2004).

6. Recently, several scholars have done research on tourism and its impact on ethnic groups in China. Three of the pioneers in this area of scholarship are Margaret Byrne Swain, Tim Oakes, and Grant Evans.

7. For example, see www.echinaromance.com.

8. Information obtained from www.bndaily.com.cn (March 29, 2005).

9. I have used pseudonyms for all the informants in this chapter. In most cases where confidentiality is key, I have also disguised identities and added characteristics that would make it difficult to identify them. I found this was crucial given the sensitive nature of HIV/AIDS as a topic of inquiry and the legal issues involved in

working with people who are ostensibly outside the law and potentially subject to prosecution.

10. Sara Davis, *Song and Silence: Ethnic Revival on China's Southwest Borders* (New York: Columbia University Press, 2005). Davis notes that the contemporary Mandarin term *man* is an inaccurate translation of the Tai term *ban*; thus these Tai names are *Banjinglan* and *Banting*, the old township names.

11. Li Dexi et al., *Zhongguo minzu gongzuo nianjin* [*China's yearbook of ethnic works*] (Beijing: Editorial Committee of China's Yearbook of Ethnic Works, 2003). Rey Chow (2002) points out the difficulty with such expressions and the slippage between race as associated with sociobiology and physical determinism, versus ethnicity as a cultural category. In China, this slippage is more apparent in language because the word *minzu* means "nationality," but it is often translated as "ethnicity," as in *shaoshu minzu*, or "minority ethnicities."

12. In Sipsongpanna, a popular Han folk notion classifies the Tai into three subgroups: the floral Tai, the water Tai, and the black Tai. This cultural characterization of the Tai follows an established pattern of Han/minority relations that is documented in Susan D. Blum, *Portraits of "Primitives": Ordering Human Kinds in the Chinese Nation* (Lanham, MD: Rowman & Littlefield, 2001), 68–91. The Tai language has undergone changes similar to Kazak in Xinjiang. There, as in Sipsongpanna, three generations often cannot communicate through one writing system. In Sipsongpanna, what is called *lao Dai wen*, or "old Dai," is now the official language. However, from 1961 to 1986 a script called *xin Dai wen*, or "new Dai," was used. This renaissance in Tai culture can be attributed to links with Southeast Asia, where several other countries' minority groups use old script. Professor Gao Lishi, a Tai linguist at Yunnan Minorities Institute, says that ethnologists classify the Tai into ten groups that speak at least three mutually unintelligible languages (personal communication, January 1996).

13. Historians note that this southern frontier historically was perceived as a desolate wasteland of malarial and leprosy-infested jungles. Today the perception is that malaria and leprosy have only recently been eradicated, and not completely from Sipsongpanna (see Wang Lianfang 1993 and Yin Shaoting 1986:69–74).

14. This ethnography privileges the female sex worker because that is the one to whom I had access. There were rumors about the presence of *mianshou* (gigolos) in Jinghong; however, I did not come into contact with any of them.

15. I would like to thank Mayfair Yang for pointing this out.

16. Brothel owning was one of the crimes punishable by death under China's legal code when I was conducting fieldwork.

17. Pan Suiming, *Cunzai yu huangmiu: Zhongguo dixia xingchanye kaocha* [*Existing in falsehoods: An investigation of China's underground sex industry*] (Beijing: Qunyan, 1999).

18. Shen Jie, "Presentation on China's AIDS Epidemic" (paper, Third Annual Asia Public Policy Workshop, John F. Kennedy School of Government, Harvard University, 2004).

19. Manhong Jia, Luo Hongbing, Zhang Xiaobo, and Ren Lijuan, "Yunnansheng shoulun jingmaixidu renqun aizibing ganran xingwei jiance jieguo fenxi [Data analysis of the first pools of AIDS transmission through intravenous drug users in Yunnan Province]," *Jibing jiance* [*Disease Monitoring*] 18, no. 7 (2003): 249–52.

SUGGESTED READINGS

Ai Kham Ngeun, "Xishuangbanna: The Challenges of Cultural Survival and Preservation." Paper read at *Culture at the Crossroads: The Challenge of Preservation and Development in Sipsongpanna, Yunnan,* Chiang Mai University, Thailand, 2002.

Susan D. Blum, *Portraits of "Primitives": Ordering Human Kinds in the Chinese Nation* (Lanham, MD: Rowman & Littlefield, 2001).

Rey Chow, *The Protestant Ethnic and the Spirit of Capitalism* (New York: Columbia University Press, 2002).

Sara Davis, *Song and Silence: Ethnic Revival on China's Southwest Borders* (New York: Columbia University Press, 2005).

Grant Evans, *Where China Meets Southeast Asia: Social and Cultural Change in the Border Regions,* ed. Grant Evans, Chris Hutton, and Kuah Khun-eng (Singapore: ISEAS, 2000).

Judith Farquhar, *Appetites: Food and Sex in Post-Socialist China* (Durham, NC: Duke University Press, 2002).

Steven Gregory, "Men in Paradise: Sex Tourism and the Political Economy of Masculinity," in *Race, Nature, and the Politics of Difference,* ed. Donald Moore, Jake Kosek, and Anand Padian (Durham, NC: Duke University Press, 2003).

Hsieh Shih-chung, "On the Dynamics of Tai/Tai-Lue Ethnicity," in *Cultural Encounters on China's Ethnic Frontiers,* ed. Stevan Harell (Seattle: University of Washington Press, 1995), 301–28.

Sandra Teresa Hyde, "Selling Sex and Sidestepping the State: Prostitutes, Condoms, and HIV/AIDS Prevention in Southwest China," *East Asia* 18, no. 4 (Winter 2000).

———, "When Riding a Tiger It Is Difficult to Dismount: STIs and HIV/AIDS in Contemporary China," *Yale-China Health Journal* 2 (Autumn 2003): 72–82.

———, "Eating Spring Rice: Transactional Sex in the Age of Epidemics," *China Review* 5, no. 1 (Spring 2004).

Jia Manhong, Luo Hongbing, Zhang Xiaobo, and Ren Lijuan, "Yunnansheng shoulun jingmaixidu renqun aizibing ganran xingwei jiance jieguo fenxi [Data analysis of the first pools of AIDS transmission through intravenous drug users in Yunnan Province]," *Jibing jiance [Disease Monitoring]* 18, no. 7 (2003): 249–52.

Joan Kaufman, Anthony Saich, and Arthur Kleinman, "Social Policy and HIV/AIDS in China." Paper read at the Third Annual Asia Public Policy Workshop, Kennedy School of Government, Harvard University, 2004.

Li Dexi et al., *Zhongguo minzu gongzuo nianjin [China's yearbook of ethnic works]* (Beijing: Editorial Committee of China's Yearbook of Ethnic Works, 2003).

Tim Oakes, *Tourism and Modernity in China,* China in Transition Series (New York: Routledge, 1998).

Pan Suiming, *Cunzai yu huangmiu: Zhongguo dixia xingchanye kaocha [Existing in falsehoods: An investigation of China's underground sex industry]* (Beijing: Qunyan, 1999).

Louisa Schein, "The Consumption of Color and the Politics of White Skin in Post-Mao China," *Social Text* 41 (1994): 141–64.

———, *Minority Rules: The Miao and the Feminine in China's Cultural Politics* (Durham, NC: Duke University Press, 2000).

Ratanaporn Sethakul, "Community Rights of the Lüü in China, Laos, and Thailand," *Tai Culture* 5, no. 2 (2000): 69–103.

Shen Jie, "Presentation on China's AIDS Epidemic." Paper read at the Third Annual Asia Public Policy Workshop, Kennedy School of Government, Harvard University, 2004.

Sun Tairen, *Sun Tairen huaji* [*Sun Tairen's collection of paintings*] (Kunming, China: Yunnan yishu chubanshe, 1995).

Margaret Byrn Swain and Janet Henshall Momsen, *Gender/Tourism/Fun (Tourism Dynamics)* (Elmsford, NY: Cognizant Communications, 2002).

Marjolein Van der Veen, "Rethinking Commodification and Prostitution: An Effort at Peacemaking in the Battles over Prostitution," *Rethinking Marxism* 13 no. 2 (2001): 30–51.

Wang Lianfang, *Yunnan minzu gongzuo huiyi lu* [*A Memoir and Record of Work among Yunnan's Minorities*], *Yunnan wenshi ziliao xuanze, di sishiwu zhang* [*Yunnan Cultural History Data Collections*], vol. 45 (Kunming: Yunnan People's Publishing House, 1993).

Ronald Weitzer, ed., *Sex for Sale: Prostitution, Pornography, and the Sex Industry* (New York: Routledge, 2000).

Yin Shaoting, "Shuo zhang [Speaking of Miasma]," *Yunnan difangzhi tongxun* [*The communication annals of places in Yunnan* 4 (1986): 69–74.

Zhang Li, *Strangers in the City: Reconfigurations of Space, Power, and Social Networks within China's Floating Population* (Stanford, CA: Stanford University Press, 2001).

Zheng Lan, *Travels through Xishuangbanna: China's Subtropical Home of Many Nationalities* (Beijing: Foreign Languages Press, 1981).

12

Welcome to Paradise!

A Sino-U.S. Joint-Venture Project

Tim Oakes

> The vastness of China's west makes it impossible not to think of the American west. America's west has the rugged cowboy; China's west has the rugged Tibetan. America's west has [the] majestic Sierra Nevada, China's west has the world's most majestic Himalayas. And wealth in resources? China's west has an even richer future than America's![1]
>
> —Zhang Guangming and Wang Shaoyi

When China launched its campaign to "Open Up the West" (*xibu dakaifa*) late in 1999, comparisons to the experience of the United States were inevitable. This one, however, gave me pause. Rugged Tibetans? It first struck me as odd that such an image could be conjured to express the promise of China's western regions. Tibetans were, after all, a prime target of the campaign's efforts to "civilize" China's frontiers. The very ruggedness of the Tibetan was, for the most part, a problem that the campaign set out to solve. Li Dezhu, minister of China's State Nationalities Affairs Commission, had said so himself. The western region's "traditional cultures," Li argued, were "deep seated" and "relatively backward."[2] Because of this, Li continued, it was important to recognize that while traditions that are "suitable" to development should be recognized, "we must also be adept at assimilating the cultural traditions of the Han nationality and all other advanced nationalities." China's campaign to Open Up the West, in other words, asserted that "backward nationalities" (like Tibetans) would have to adapt to the ways of the "advanced nationalities" (like the Han). As one observer puts it, this approach treats Tibetan culture as "a problem to be overcome" rather than "a feature to be protected and nourished."[3]

240

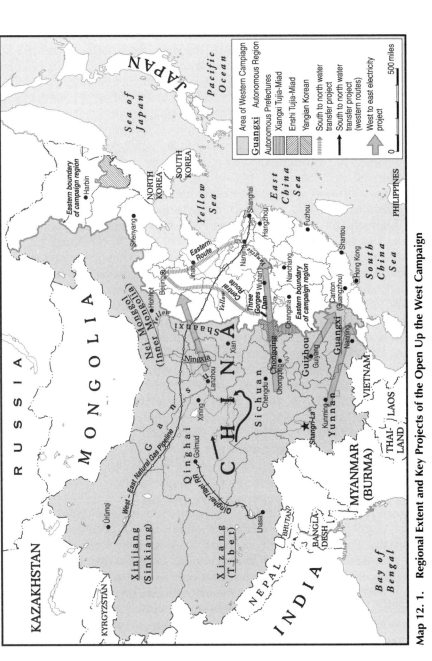

Map 12. 1.   Regional Extent and Key Projects of the Open Up the West Campaign

How strange, then, that the decidedly cowboyish qualities of the "rugged Tibetan" should be drawn upon to shed a favorable light on China's western development campaign in comparison to the history of America's westward expansion. After all, the Tenth Five-Year Plan for Tibet—coinciding with the initiation of Open Up the West—called the nomadic Tibetan herdsman "out-dated." The Tibetan cowboy could "neither take full advantage of pasture or cope with natural disasters, nor facilitate the modernization drive of social lives." Accordingly, Qinghai province called upon Tibetans and Mongols (the Chinese West's other cowboys) to slaughter their animals and settle down, thereby raising their "quality of life" and increasing their wealth.[4] Furthermore, Open Up the West would help improve the "quality" of the Tibetans by introducing them to more Han people. The campaign's promotion of westward Han migration from China proper was likened by Li Dezhu to "a peacock flying west," with the assumption that the "higher quality" Han would provide a healthy example from which the rugged Tibetan could learn.[5]

Like the American cowboy, the rugged Tibetan cowboy is a myth that obscures a much more disturbing reality. Put this way, there was nothing odd about Zhang and Wang's comparison at all. For at the same time that Open Up the West sought to resurrect China's colonial designs on its western borderlands, it professed to solidify China's national identity. In this respect, the campaign was self-consciously modeled on the U.S. precedent. What Zhang and Wang saw in the U.S. experience of westward expansion is a successful example of national mythmaking. The U.S. frontier cowboy was in fact underpaid, overworked, and in most other respects quite unromantic. And the U.S. frontier, far from being the virgin land of opportunity that it has been mythologized to be, was a land of conquest, a land whose indigenous population was eliminated with such systematic deceit and violence that the United States would easily have been indicted for genocide were it happening today. Indeed, Beijing has not passed up opportunities in the recent past to point this out, whenever it issues its inevitable rebuttals to U.S. dispersions of China's human rights record. This bickering is predictable between two imperial powers who share the same basic geopolitical ambitions. At any rate, the more accurate comparison would be between the Tibetan and the Native American. But this would have landed Zhang and Wang in some hot water that they no doubt sought to avoid. Criticism of America's imperial past was no longer appropriate, now that it was the model for China's development strategies in the twenty-first century.

But it is more than the geopolitics of empire that China's campaign has in common with the United States. The two countries share a much deeper cultural fascination with their western frontiers. Discourses of the western frontier have been fundamental to shaping the imperial and national imaginations of both China and the United States. There are vast differences in these discourses, to be sure. The western frontier has been a defining aspect of Chinese identity for several thousand years, making the U.S. version a mere blip in history by comparison. Likewise, the settling of the western United States was played out in extremely different historical and geographical contexts, not least of which is the fact that the U.S. West has a coastline, which China's interior obviously lacks. But China's West has—like America's—inspired myths that have become fundamental to the telling of the nation's history. China's West has also—like America's—inspired alternative narratives of national identity, some utopian, some radically unorthodox. By launching a campaign of western development, China has also initiated a new era of mythmaking.

And here the U.S. experience suggests yet another model. For the settling of the western United States is not simply a myth of national identity. It is also a commercial product. The myth of the West sells. It sells books, paintings, clothes, children's birthday party themes, and, most importantly, tourism. The U.S. model of western development offers not only the rugged cowboy but a theme park in which to play the cowboy. And the theme park model is certainly one that China has taken to heart. If California was singled out by the campaign's framers as the model par excellence of nineteenth-century land development and twentieth-century high-tech industrialization, then Disneyland's Frontierland in Anaheim, California, surely marks the apogee of America's ability to turn myths into money.[6] The theme park's alchemic magic, churning the ephemera of myth into hard cash, is something that the U.S. West has also bequeathed to China.

This chapter is about the growing commercial power of the frontier myth in China. My focus will be on the reconstruction of the myth of the western frontier as a product of the campaign to Open Up the West as well as a broader pattern of intercultural exchange between China and the United States, and my argument shall be that the myth of the frontier serves to recentralize state power in China's western regions. By mythologizing the western frontier, the campaign to Open Up the West packages itself as a new civilizing mission, and one to which commercial tourism development in particular is contributing.

LAYING THE FOUNDATION FOR NEW MYTHS

When China officially launched its western development campaign in 2000, national mythmaking was not part of the official agenda. In fact, the official agenda was ambiguous at best. Premier Zhu Rongji saw the new impetus for western development as

> crucial to the efforts to boost domestic demand, promote sustained national economic growth and bring about coordinated development of regional economies

for eventual common prosperity as well as to strengthen national unity, safe-
guard social stability and consolidate border defense.[7]

Zhu's shopping-list approach to characterizing the campaign to Open Up
the West reflects the basic features of what has been called a soft policy, or
a campaign designed with sufficient ambiguity to allow—in its various local implementations—for a broad spectrum of competing, shifting, and
even contradictory agendas "producing a diverse array of goals and measures."[8] There is no single policy document that summarizes the campaign
to Open Up the West. Indeed, the campaign has been something of a work
in progress since at least the early 1990s, and the various official announcements—throughout 1999—of its imminent launch indicate more
the culmination of a set of longer-term trends than a bold or innovative reorientation in state regional-development policies.

The most readily identified of these long-term trends is the CCP's repeated
promises throughout the 1990s to eventually redress growing inequalities associated with market-oriented reforms and economic decentralization. Thus,
official pronouncements of the campaign to Open Up the West characterize
it as the party's promised response to decades of festering inequality between
China's rapidly growing eastern provinces and its stagnating western regions.
Western leaders had been grumbling for some time about the state of things,
pointing out with increasing urgency that China's uneven growth was resting
on an ever-flimsy scaffold of social discontent. As early as the mid-1980s,
western leaders had been forming alliances to do for themselves what Beijing
was at the time unwilling to do. Officials and scholars from Sichuan, Yunnan, and Guizhou provinces, for instance, formed the Research Forum for the
Strategy to Open Up the Southwest, while leaders from Xinjiang, Gansu, and
Ningxia Huizu did the same—albeit with less success—for the Northwest.
When Deng Xiaoping made his well-known Southern Tour in 1992, he addressed these growing concerns by noting that by the end of the century,
China would have attained a "moderately high standard of living" and would
by then be able to more directly address its income disparities.[9] In the subsequent years leading up to 2000, the extent of those disparities was subject
to increasingly vocal academic criticism within China. Probably the most influential of these critical voices came from Hu Angang, director of the State
Council's Research Institute on National Conditions, who wrote that China's
pattern of development was not only unsustainable but could well result in
state failure and territorial devolution similar to that experienced by Yugoslavia.[10] With this intellectual urgency added to the CCP's standing promise to appease China's discontented western provinces, the stage was thus set
for a major campaign to kick off the new century.

One of the greatest initial difficulties was to simply define which "West"
the campaign's planners were targeting. Getting it right was of crucial im-

portance, of course, for immediate and very practical political reasons. But it was also important because, as will be discussed in greater detail later, the western region has always been fundamental to Chinese constructions of political, social, and cultural identity. To proclaim a campaign of rapid development for such a region was to invite a complicated and perhaps even disquieting discussion about how certain localities have historically fit into the broader narrative of "Chineseness." But by far the most important question at the outset of the campaign was simply who was in and who was out—which regions were to be bestowed with the promised flows of cash and favorable policies?

Beijing has a well-established history of carving China up into regions to help determine the distribution of resources and favors. During the Seventh Five-Year Plan, which covered the second half of the 1980s, a tripartite regionalization scheme was conceived that identified a coastal belt of provinces that would benefit first from reform policies featuring modernization and liberalized trade and investment policies, and central and western regions that would supply energy and other raw materials, as well as labor, to the "coastal front" in China's engagement with the global economy. The western region identified under this scheme—which had explicitly been given the role of little more than a support base for eastern economic growth—was the same western region initially defined in the campaign to Open Up the West in 1999. By late 2000, however, two additional provincial units, one previously central (Inner Mongolia), and one previously eastern (Guangxi), had been added. This was most likely due to their status as autonomous regions, which complemented the campaign's goal of building solidarity among nationalities. Not only were they autonomous regions, but they were autonomous regions where the Han were a clear majority and where the dominant minority were relatively assimilated to the "advanced" ways of the Han.

This expansion was followed, probably for similar reasons, by the further addition of three autonomous prefectures, in Hubei, Hunan, and Jilin. These latter additions stretched the concept of a Western Interior quite thin. Guangxi, after all, is a coastal region, while Inner Mongolia and Jilin stretch far into China's Northeast. However, it is best to understand the West of the campaign in metaphorical, rather than territorial, terms.[11] The campaign's West is a frontier region of poverty, ethnic minorities, and poor economic infrastructure. It is a place, in other words, in need of a civilizing boost from the East. To be sure, the region is also home to great concentrations of wealth (for instance, in its major urban centers of Xi'an, Chongqing, Chengdu, and Kunming), a vast majority of Han Chinese, and some of the most sophisticated technological infrastructure in China. Many parts of this region thus compare favorably with the rest of China in a whole range of socioeconomic categories.

Given such a vast and diverse region, it seems impossible that the campaign would not seek to address a broad range of concerns. According to one analysis, five agendas addressed by the campaign can be identified: (1) regional equality, (2) private investment, (3) infrastructure investment, (4) integration and assimilation of nationalities, and (5) environmentally sustainable development.[12] These five agendas also suggest a chronology of the campaign's gradual design. Regional equality (agenda 1) had, rhetorically at least, been on the CCP's long-term agenda for some time and, as suggested above, formed the primary impulse for the campaign's gradual formulation in the late 1990s. The party's initial answer to inequality was infrastructural investment (agenda 3), and it was this kind of development that dominated official announcements associated with the campaign in 1999 and 2000. Thus, several massive projects that had been planned during the 1990s were officially unveiled to coincide with the campaign's launch in 2000. These included, at a combined estimated cost of over US$90 billion, a South–North water diversion project, a West–East natural gas transfer project, a West–East electricity transfer project, and the Qinghai–Tibet railway.[13] To these could be added, for an additional $25 billion, what many regarded as the infrastructural lynchpin of the whole campaign: the Three Gorges dam. Significant as they were in terms of absolute investments, these high-profile projects carried perhaps even more symbolic weight as markers of the state's commitment to developing the West. Certainly they were promoted in the media as such, even though China's overall pattern of investments continued to overwhelmingly favor the eastern coastal provinces. The campaign's key projects, in other words, cannot really be seen as a significant departure from established state regional-development expenditures.

The other component of the campaign's economic development agenda—the encouragement of private investment (agenda 2)—can therefore be seen as an implicit acknowledgement of the state's inability or unwillingness to fundamentally transform its investment priorities in regional terms. The private sector is expected to fill in the gap. But here the campaign has offered much more in terms of rhetoric than capital, and there have been many concerns voiced by scholars of the western provinces that the campaign in fact offers very little for improving the climate for private investment in the western region. This was, for instance, the message of a 2001 conference held in Guizhou in which participants—mostly scholars and officials from various western provinces—complained that instead of improving conditions for the expansion of the nonstate sector locally, the campaign was little more than an intensification of eastern exploitation of western resources.[14] This was, to be sure, a criticism directed as much toward conservative and protectionist local governments as toward the campaign's central designers. But it suggests that the campaign's implementation has emphasized high-profile infrastructure projects (all of which focus on natural resource extraction) at the expense of more basic and smaller-scale concerns such as education and local state capacity.

Indeed, to view the campaign from the perspective of a poor province like Guizhou is to see an unprecedented intensification of resource extraction that brings western provinces and their resources into Beijing's orbit as never before.[15] For some, the campaign was reminiscent of the center's previous power over resource allocation and distribution during the planned economy of the Mao era.[16] As was noted in the *South China Morning Post*'s coverage of the Sixteenth Party Congress in 2002, whenever talk turned to western development, "officials barely touched on fashionable subjects such as private investments and entrepreneurs. Just as the rest of China is accelerating the move towards a market economy, the western region appears to be a throwback to the planned economy of an earlier era."[17] Potential investors in Hong Kong seemed to agree. A high-profile delegation of seventy-one Hong Kong businessmen toured the Chinese West in 2000 and managed to cough up only $30 million. An editorial in the *South China Morning Post* at the time argued that the needs of western development and the expertise that Hong Kong was able to provide were a "poor match."[18]

The center's apparent reluctance to see the campaign as an opportunity to shift paradigms in terms of economic development brings us to another agenda that emerged from the initial concern with inequality. Hu Angang's dire warnings of China becoming another Yugoslavia put nation building and ethnic solidarity (agenda 4) front and center in the eyes of many in the CCP. In this sense, the large-scale infrastructure projects heralded by the campaign may be more about the recentralization of state power in the western regions than about basic development. This is an aspect of the campaign that has attracted less attention in the Western media. Articles on the campaign in the *New York Times* and *Fortune*, for example, have focused on evaluating the success of privatization and foreign investment but have had little to say regarding broader political implications.[19] In an article about Chongqing, *Fortune* writer Richard Tomlinson emphasized the growing role of the private sector in the city's exploding economy as an indicator of an emerging class of independent entrepreneurs. Tomlinson, in other words, looked to the campaign to produce the kind of class that a publication like *Fortune* could relate to. Yet further analysis makes clear that, to the contrary, Chongqing's massive infrastructure investments associated with the campaign to Open Up the West will only make it more beholden to the bureaucratic directives of the center.[20] This is because private-sector development has remained stagnant in Chongqing while the city's $23 billion infrastructural spending spree—including eight highways, a monorail network, a sewage system, a new airport, and a container port—is incurring a vast debt that municipal revenues, let alone the private sector, will not come close to covering. One analyst's conservative estimate that the center will be expected to carry the city's nearly ¥600 billion shortfall during the Tenth Five-Year Plan is an illustration of the way the campaign will entrench the role of the center in western development more broadly.[21] While *Fortune* scouts the streets of Chongqing for evidence of a rising middle class founded on private enterprise, state control is being redefined and rearticulated in more fundamental ways.

Thus, rather than heralding the rise of a region where the free market will reign, the campaign can be read as a response to the problems wrought by two decades of decentralization and localism. A clear statement in this regard was not simply the center's carving off Chongqing from Sichuan in 1997 (in response to Sichuan's reluctance to bear the costs of the Three Gorges project) but more tellingly, its humiliating removal of Chongqing's home-grown leadership in 1999, to be replaced with outsiders from Hunan and Jiangsu.[22] Elsewhere, China's provinces had been acting like little fiefdoms, engaging in "cabbage wars" and "cotton wars" and needlessly duplicating themselves in everything from oranges to electricity.[23] In this respect, Beijing saw the campaign as an opportunity to recentralize its control before the situation got entirely out of hand.[24] Clearly the West would have to develop so that incomes in Xinjiang caught up to those in Guangdong, which in 2000 were already twice as high. But if in acquiring Guangdong's level of wealth Xinjiang also acquired that province's sense of uppity autonomy from Beijing, it could mean serious trouble for China's sensitive borderlands. Equality would have to be achieved by strengthening the center's control, rather than relinquishing it, for example, to market forces. Equality would, in short, be a colonial project. The *kaifa* (opening) of the West, then, connotes more the exploitation of resources than a new kind of liberalism. True, the campaign professes to open the Chinese West to the global marketplace of investment capital, but Beijing is keeping both hands firmly on the door.

But it is perhaps in the area of ethnic relations that this centralizing aspect of the campaign achieved its most significant expression: that of a civilizing mission. As noted at the outset of this chapter, the campaign to Open Up the West was accompanied by a rhetoric encouraging a new generation of pioneers to leave the comforts of their eastern cities and head West. This rhetoric illustrates the CCP's desire to reverse the dominant West–East direction of mobility witnessed during the reform era. But it also marks what one Xinjiang observer called a "radical alteration" of the state's nationalities policy.[25] Li Dezhu's likening of this new migration to "a peacock flying west" was accompanied by the acknowledgement that what was being promoted in the campaign was in fact the *ningjuhua* (homogenization) of the western population. Before Li's article came out in *Seeking Truth*, the party had never before hinted that the dilution of western minority nationality groups with an influx of Han immigrants was even remotely connected to state policy. Li's advocacy of Han immigration marked not so much the departure from a trend—such dilution had, after all, been going on all along anyway—but the party's willingness to finally break the taboo of publicly acknowledging that trend. Li thus admitted that some "conflicts and clashes" should be expected as western minority groups found their world increasingly dominated by the Han. It was all for their own good in the long run, Li said, but the transition might be difficult for some.

It is here that comparisons with America's westward expansion achieve their most significant symbolic power. Li Dezhu's article perhaps marks the beginning of a rhetorical reconstruction of China's western frontier as a virgin land, a clean slate. America's development had never been hindered by an explicit policy professing tolerance for and recognition of different nationalities. Native Americans weren't a nationality group. They weren't even citizens. They were simply in the way. Li's article suggests that the CCP feels the time has come for China to adopt a similar attitude. "America is West and the wind blowing," wrote the poet Archibald MacLeish in 1930.[26] China's promoters of western development saw the same America that MacLeish saw; they saw an America that drew its strength from its (empty) frontier. Economists Tang Songan and Li Yongtai, for instance, write that "the American west is a region of incredible resources and wealth, but its most important resource is that which is *undeveloped*. America's west is America's *hopes*. The west preserves the hopes of the American nation [italics mine]."[27] They also note that the idea of a boundless frontier continues to invigorate and strengthen the United States today, remarking, for instance, on the continuing relevance of Frederick Jackson Turner's well-known frontier thesis. At Chicago's 1893 Columbia Exposition, Turner famously proclaimed that "the existence of an area of free land, its continuous recession, and the advance of American settlement westward explain American development."[28] But while the frontier's wealth of "free land" was, for Turner, responsible for nurturing a distinctly North American form of republicanism, Beijing's western frontier is called upon to reestablish the authority of the central government.

It is in the campaign's function as a recentralization and entrenchment of central power in the West that the associated myths of the frontier serve their most immediate purpose. The myth of China's western regions as a frontier enables a new kind of spatial imaginary, one that symbolically underpins the authority of the center. This spatial imaginary also underpins a growing tourism industry throughout the region, one that is beginning to be an economic force in its own right. In fact, in some parts of the western region, tourism is just about the only industry in which the private sector has begun to play a significant role in regional development. The call for Han migrants to go west is echoed by a call for eastern tourists to do the same. Moreover, tourism development has been singled out in campaign announcements as a key component of the drive to develop the western regions economically.

Tourism is significant not only because it represents the leading edge of economic restructuring in many of the western region's most remote places, but also because it thrives on the civilizing myths of the frontier. While western China's dramatic scenery makes tourism an obvious target for promotion, frontier imagery and mythology have also become increasingly visible in tourism promotion. In Guizhou, a history of early Ming frontier warfare and colonization has become central to the province's incipient heritage-tourism industry, while local histories of Han penetration into the region—previously dominated by minority groups such as the Miao and Buyei—have become packaged in various ways as return-to-the-past tourism for urban Chinese seeking to return to China's wild frontiers for a day.[29] In these cases, tourism development has tended to play on the imagery of a barbarian frontier becoming civilized under gradual Han influence, and this is an image in which local governments are increasingly finding commercial potential.

A significant feature of Guizhou's frontier tourism, however, is not simply the commercial replaying for tourists of China's deep-seated civilizing mission but the reconstruction of a place once lost. The heritage villages being promoted in Guizhou, so the story goes, have preserved a unique, frontier way of life because the past centuries of chaos, warfare, socialism, and most recently, reform and modernization have largely passed them by. Preserved in isolation, they are now promoted as "living fossils" of a way of life long forgotten in China's bustling eastern metropolises. Planeloads of tourists from Nanjing now come to Guizhou to "search for their roots" on the frontier.

The most spectacular example of tourism development along China's frontiers, however, is found in Yunnan. Tourism has grown in recent years to become Yunnan's largest foreign-exchange earner. Already in 1999, before the official launch of the campaign to Open Up the West, Yunnan was earning $350 million from tourism, or 25 percent of the entire western region's tourism income that year. This represented an astonishing twenty-two-fold increase over the province's 1990 earnings. And the region of Yunnan that has grown most rapidly has been the province's northwestern frontier with Tibet. In Diqing Tibetan Autonomous Prefecture, tourism grew from some fifty thousand visitors in 1998 to well over 1 million just two years later.[30] This growth preceded Diqing's official recognition and name change, in 2001, to Shangri-La (see figure 12.1).While the relationship between Shangri-La and the frontier mythologizing of the campaign to Open Up the West will be discussed later, here we may simply note that, as in Guizhou, tourists have been flocking to Yunnan to discover a paradise that was once lost but has now been found anew.

Figure 12.1.   Hillside sign for Shangri-La, a province that decided to change its name to attract tourists. (Photo: Tim Oakes)

PARADISE LOST: THE ROLE OF THE FRONTIER
IN NATIONAL AND TOURIST IMAGINATIONS

Turner's claim that the successive westward settling of a receding frontier
created a distinctly U.S. kind of individualism and democracy is well
known. Turner's claim that a vast expanse of free land was responsible for
nurturing a unique American republicanism was, clearly, mythmaking of
the first order. For it was not just the land that helped build America but a
frontier connoting an open, progressive future toward which Americans
equally strived. What made Turner's mythmaking particularly brilliant was
the fact that he couched it as a nostalgic look back on something that had
disappeared as soon as our gaze turned its way. Turner's thesis was, after all,
delivered on the occasion of the "closing" of the frontier. In this sense, the
frontier was a kind of utopia, a place that could only be appreciated once it
was lost forever. Turner's lament of its closing was what, more than anything, solidified the frontier as a core myth of U.S. national identity.

In closing the frontier, Turner assured us that it would, paradoxically, stay open, as a metaphor, forever lodged in the North American collective imagination. The frontier is alive and well in the United States today as a metaphor for technological innovation, progress, and "the edge of exciting possibilities."[31] Far from closing, the frontier is again and again invoked in any number of "openings." It just keeps forever receding—like the shooting stars on the screen of the starship USS *Enterprise* in the television series and movie *Star Trek*—into the infinity of "Space: The final frontier." At the same time, however, this closing of the frontier managed to freeze in perpetuity an ideal, the kernel of the myth, of utopian possibility. The Jeffersonian yeoman invoked by Turner was a plea against an inevitable corrupting of the dream, now that the West had been definitively "settled."[32] And as if either to confirm Turner's worst nightmare or to realize his ultimate dream (depending on your perspective), the frontier can now be visited again and again, all for the price of admission to Disneyland. The necessity of this closing, and of a nostalgic look back, made possible the conversion of myth into capital: the frontier's resurrection as Frontierland in Anaheim, California. If Turner created a paradise only by closing its doors forever, Disney promises the impossible: a return to this paradise lost. This is, after all, what theme parks do; they knit together fiction and reality for those of us willing to suspend disbelief for a few hours.

But if a few hours of suspended disbelief is all a theme park asks of us, a nation asks a great deal more. The problem with Turner's thesis is that it has inspired the suspension of disbelief for much more than a few hours. The dominant narrative of U.S. history has required the suspension of disbelief for well over a century. This was a frontier less of democratic progress than imperialism and colonialism.[33] The land wasn't free, it was taken. And this is the history upon which Guizhou's frontier heritage villages rest as well. Remarkably well preserved, the villages display a frozen landscape of conquest and warfare, established as they were six centuries ago by Chinese soldiers sent from the eastern heartland to take the land from indigenous groups that had been there long before them. Today, tourists can visit their colonizing settlements as they would a theme park and relive—Frontierland-style—the myth of the frontier.

Of course, the myth of China's frontier, like that of America's, has required vigilant management and control by the state. Frontier archaeology, for example, has been subject to strict state control.[34] Thus, the possibility that the frontier could be an open zone where Chinese civilization acquired foreign influences was deemed unpatriotic and worse, politically suspect during the Mao era. The suggestion, for instance, that copper and bronze metallurgy might have emerged first in western Asia and then brought to China somewhat later was once denounced as the "clamor" of "imperialists and the so-called archaeologists of the revisionist Soviet Union."[35] The state's sense of control over interpretations of frontier history has been so haunted by the possibilities of an open frontier that for decades foreign archaeologists were simply banned from fieldwork in China. And when the China Borderlands Research Center was established in the 1990s to promote modern Chinese frontier studies, things hadn't really changed that much. The key themes of frontier research in China were still identified as national unity, ethnic solidarity, and social stability. Frontier studies, the center declared, would help develop patriotism among Han Chinese and minority nationalities. As one historian pointed out, "The rigid boundaries of territory and identity implied by [China's] nationality policy require fixed historical interpretation and ideological reinforcement. Frontier studies in China reflect the center's fear of losing its grip on the definition of national essences."[36]

Yet this orthodoxy has also contributed to the occasional idealization of the frontier in China as a space to which the nation could always return if a crisis of integrity were to befall it. And this is precisely what has happened again and again throughout Chinese history. Indeed, the campaign to open up the West can also be interpreted in this way. If nationalism in China, as one historian has argued, has "gone south," then Beijing's call to "go west" can be read as a campaign of return to the frontiers to recentralize an increasingly chaotic and open discourse of national identity.[37] If the frontier, in other words, was where "Chineseness" was originally forged, then the frontier needs to be found again so that such an identity can always be recovered if need be. Confucius was only the first in a line of scholars to recognize this. The *Han Shu* records the Great Sage saying, "Lost rites can be recovered from the remote peripheries."[38] He is also said to have declared that it was on the frontiers that his philosophy was most likely to be realized.[39]

More recently, many intellectuals of the early twentieth century looked to China's frontiers as spaces where the nation might recover a lost vitality in the face of foreign subjugation.[40] China shared with Europe and the United States a tendency to idealize "the savage" in times of social or cultural crisis, attributing to the Other all those qualities that its own society had lost.[41] The frontier continues to provide this kind of alternative space for the resolution of social and cultural crises of identity. Hui writer Zhang Chengzhi's historical novel *Xinlingshi* [*A history of the soul*] narrates the history of the Jahriyya sect of Islam in Gansu, and the rise of Ma Mingxin, who gathered a large group of followers and whose religious movement was violently suppressed by the Qing in 1781. Zhang "depicts an open frontier that offers opportunity for creative spiritual development . . . For him, the frontier becomes the source of an alternative history, a support for a private quest utterly divorced from the imperatives of imperial or national politics."[42] Zhang's frontier is less the poor and barren region subject to the civilizing force of Beijing's Open Up the West campaign than a "seedbed for China's only truly humane community."

This idea of the frontier as salvation has inevitably spread from these intellectual projects to contemporary popular culture. The growing popularity of cultural geography in China reflects this trend of repackaging the frontier to fit the needs of China's current reforms. In the volumes *Renwen Zhongguo* [*Human China*] and *Diyu Zhongguo* [*Regional China*], for example, traditional frontier provinces are described as either lost regions now rediscovered (thereby maintaining their purity and vitality) or as cradles of Chinese civilization, places where China can rediscover a history appropriate for the times. The Tang capital Chang'an (today's Xi'an, capital of Shaanxi province) is thus recalled not only as a frontier city but as one of the first "world cities." In fact, Chang'an's place at the hub of the silk road trade network is said to have inspired China's global sojourners to name each of their communities *Tangrenjie* (or "Tang neighborhood," commonly translated as "Chinatown").[43] This revision replaces the conventional explanation for the name *Tangrenjie*—that they were founded by Tang people from China's southern coastal regions—with one linked to the myth of the frontier. It is further claimed that Shaanxi people, in their walled-off isolation, have preserved the "winds of reform" that started blowing as early as the Western Han dynasty but are only now reaching the rest of China.[44] Pastoral Mongols are said to embody a freedom that compares favorably to stiff Han Confucianism in this day of openness and reform, while Xinjiang is said to retain the ancient Silk Road spirit of openness that China proper needs to learn anew.[45]

Inevitably, these mythical reinventions have been absorbed and reproduced by the tourism industry. Back in Guizhou, Miao villagers are reminded by industry officials that they are "the Chinese of the Tang Dynasty."[46] As such, they are responsible not simply for maintaining Miao customs for outsiders to appreciate and purchase but for recalling what Chinese culture once was. This role of the frontier Miao as keepers of tradition recalls an earlier time, when a local Qing magistrate referred, in 1727, to the *Miaojiang* (Miao borderlands) in Guizhou as a *taohuayuan*, a "utopia."[47] After a year of the region's violent subjugation at the hands of the Qing army, the magistrate was inspired to praise the noble Miao for their "self-sufficiency," "lack of want for anything," and their "courtesy." But while the magistrate's view of a lost paradise of noble savages was only possible once the destruction of that paradise was finally assured, tourism in Guizhou and throughout the western region is promising a return to this lost frontier paradise so that the roots of the nation may once again be discovered.

THE WESTERN FRONTIER AS COMMERCIAL UTOPIA—
WELCOME BACK TO PARADISE

This reminds us, again, that shadowing China's dominant narrative of strict frontier control and management as the forward-looking key to good state-craft is a narrative of nostalgia for a purer past, an ideal world lost. Ma-hayana Buddhism had already predisposed Chinese popular culture to look west for paradise, for the "pure land" where true enlightenment could be achieved. Wu Cheng'en's sixteenth-century romance *Xiyou ji* [*Journey to the West*] further helped solidify the association of the West with a fantasy land. Indeed, Wu's romance was canonized by the CCP under Mao as a metaphor for China's own journey toward a Communist utopia.[48] Elite Chinese cosmology also reinforced the West as paradise by locating there the sacred Kunlun Mountain, the pivot between heaven and earth. The most iconic symbol of paradise, however, is the classic *Taohuayuan* [*Peach blossom spring*] by fifth-century poet Tao Qian, a work the title of which has become synonymous with utopia. *Taohuayuan* is a brief prose poem about a fisherman who stumbles upon an orderly land of happy people wearing foreign-looking clothes. They tell the fisherman that they are descendants of refugees who themselves stumbled on the place to avoid the chaos of the Qin unification. Since then they have been completely cut off from the world. After much wining and dining, the fisherman bids them farewell but is told to keep his mouth shut about the place. He fails to do this, however, and announces his discovery as soon as he reaches the nearest prefecture town. This weakness on his part makes return to the orderly land impossible. The local magistrate sends someone with him to find the place again, but they get lost along the way and never find it. The narrative ends on a curious note: "Liu Ziji of Nanyang was a person of noble character. When he heard this story he was happy and planned to visit the place, but before he could make the trip, he died of illness. Since then, no one has ever looked for the place." Tao thus constructs a myth of paradise as an ever-present possibility, a place that could perhaps be stumbled upon again.

Tao Qian did not explicitly situate *Taohuayuan* in the West. But, as the example from Guizhou's *Miaojiang* indicates, the name has been invoked at times to capture the utopic qualities of China's frontiers. The word *utopia* means, literally, "nonplace." A utopia is inherently impossible, an ideal that can never be actualized. This theme of impossibility resonates not only in the Western myth of Eden and other versions of paradise lost but also with Tao's fisherman and his inability to return to Taohuayuan. Utopia can only be discovered when we are not looking for it, and once found, it can never be left. This sensibility has found much appeal in both Chinese and European-American traditions. It is a sensibility that, it turns out, was destined for cross-fertilization between these traditions, and such cross-fertilization was most spectacularly initiated by James Hilton's 1933 novel *Lost Horizon*.

Lost Horizon's resemblances to Tao Qian's prose poem deserve noting. Like Tao's fisherman, Hilton's protagonist, Robert Conway, does not purposefully stumble onto paradise. He is hardly searching for utopia, but once there, he is quickly entranced by its beauty, calm, and orderliness in juxtaposition to the chaos of the outside world. Shangri-La is, like Taohuayuan, a place where everyone is happy and where everyone wears foreign-looking clothes (at least from the perspective of Conway and his marooned companions). Like Taohuayuan, Shangri-La is a place inhabited by refugees from the chaos of the outside world. And like the fisherman, Conway voluntarily leaves. These similarities are not meant to suggest a set of universal qualities to which all utopias must subscribe—for there are also a great many differences between the visions of Tao and Hilton—but rather to suggest one possible explanation for the obvious resonance *Lost Horizon* has had in China. It is telling, then, that when Frank Capra's film version of the novel was released in Shanghai in the late 1930s, it carried the Chinese title *Taohuayuan yanji* [*Romance of the peach blossom spring*]. A few years later, another film produced a theme song that would help cement the name *Shangri-La* in Chinese popular culture. "This Beautiful Shangri-La" was very popular in the late 1940s, and according to one cultural critic, "Many educated Chinese of the pre-1949 generation still remember the tune, if not the entire lyric."[49] More recently, the term *Shangri-La* conjures associations with a Singapore-based luxury hotel chain and with a new tourism destination along China's Tibetan frontier.

Shangri-La is a term that has its own social history, one that bridges China, the United States, Tibet, Britain, and probably a few other places like Singapore and Dharmasala as well. Its remarkable currency in China speaks to a frontier fascination that is particularly shared by China and the United States alike. Only now, China's frontier has expanded and merged with America's. The frontiers of China and America meet and converge in Shangri-La, and it is the commercial dimension of the frontier idea that has enabled this.

China has been a kind of frontier for U.S. travelers for some time now. Under Mao, China was a mysterious yet highly desired frontier for many U.S. radicals looking for an alternative to the debacle of the Vietnam War. For post-Vietnam-era students like me, China was the newly opened frontier of culturally authentic otherness. And for travelers from all over the world, China has been on the frontiers of cultural tourism since the early 1980s. A curious book was recently published, in English, by a U.S. business consultant who, tired of the money-making rat-race that Beijing has become, heads west to find Shangri-La.[50] Lawrence Brahm's "alternative philosophy travelogue" makes clear that America's western frontier didn't simply stop at the California coast but reemerged in China, first in places like Beijing where opportunities were fresh and fortunes could once again be made. But as Beijing soon came to resemble the worst urban nightmare of many U.S. residents, the frontier kept heading west, to ultimately find in Zhang and Wang's "rugged Tibetan" the cowboy spirit of the western United States born again.

Brahm tells a friend in Beijing about his dream to go west in search of a truer frontier, and this friend tells him that this West sounds like Shangri-La, "a place she had heard about once, maybe twice." She adds that "people talk of Shangri-la, but there are many controversies over where it really is. If you want to search for it, I think it must be in the west. Take a road and follow it, just go without any direction."[51] The journey leads Brahm to initiate a multimedia project, "Searching for Shangri-La," to record the "still uncontaminated" cultures of the Qinghai-Tibet plateau before they are lost "due to overdevelopment, careless tourism, and short-sightedness." Thus like Turner before him, along with all good frontier mythmaking more generally, Brahm drives his project forward by invoking the ever-eminent closing of a frontier as he attempts to "document the 'lost horizon' before it is lost."[52]

As a product of intercultural exchange, then, the myth of Shangri-La derives much of its power from a mutual fascination with the frontier and, increasingly, a desire to translate that fascination into political power (Beijing's civilizing project) or capital (tourism development). *Lost Horizon* itself, scholars have argued, did not appear in a cultural vacuum but was the result of a unique historical moment (the 1920s and 1930s) of intercultural exchange between Tibet and the West.[53] Indeed, it has been argued that Tibetans, particularly those in exile, have gradually succumbed to Hilton's fantasy of a Western utopia in Tibet. This is a succumbing that reveals not only a desire among Tibetans to see their country as a kind of paradise valued by Westerners but also the growing impossibility of return for most of them.[54]

The fact that Brahm heads west to search for something that, by definition, is impossible to find alerts us to an important shift that has occurred in the development of the Shangri-La myth. That shift is first seen in Frank Capra's film version of Hilton's novel: in the Hollywood *Lost Horizon*, Conway gets to come back to Shangri-La. It is this return to paradise that puts a tourist's spin on the search for an authentic paradise. Unlike Tao Qian's fisherman, Capra's Conway finds his way back, even after he tells everyone about it. And this is exactly what commercial tourism promises: a return, again and again, to paradise. While the promise of everlasting return is a cornerstone of the international tourism industry in all its multifaceted guises, it reaches its zenith in the theme park, especially in the zenith of theme parks, Disneyland. Frontierland is always open.

What tourism does with the equation is insist that paradise be located in a specific place. Without a location, paradise cannot be sold. Hilton's riddle of Shangri-La's true location would have to be solved if tourists, like Capra's

Conway, were to have the opportunity to themselves achieve the impossible. There have been many claims made by would-be Shangri-Las throughout China's Tibetan frontier regions, but Yunnan's Zhongdian county in Diqing Tibetan Autonomous Prefecture was the quickest to grasp the commercial potential of branding itself as paradise. The county also legitimized its claims with scholarly accounts that served to transform Shangri-La from an external, imported idea, to an indigenous one by claiming it, in effect, for China and Tibet. In so doing, the county also implicitly linked Shangri-La to the broader mythmaking project associated with the Open Up the West campaign. The commerce of tourism development would naturally reinforce that project and allow a place like Diqing to reinvent itself not just as a tourist's paradise but as a region faithfully leading the Open Up the West campaign's charge to integrate and colonize the frontier and turn the "rugged Tibetan" into a servant of national myths. And this was the role played by Hilton's Tibetans as well; they helped Shangri-La become a vault for the treasures of civilization.

Zhongdian's panel of scholars set out to prove beyond a doubt that Zhongdian was not just the place that Hilton had in mind when he wrote *Lost Horizon* but that Zhongdian was Shangri-La before Hilton himself came up with the name *Shangri-La*. In other words, it was not enough to accept that Hilton invented the name—even if he had an actual place in mind—the name itself had to be Tibetan. Thus, *xiang ge li la* is said to derive from the Tibetan *Shambhala*, which in the dialect spoken in Diqing supposedly means "The sun and moon of the heart." Indeed, it is likely that Hilton derived his term from *Shambhala*.[55] But in Zhongdian, the claim is that Hilton derived it precisely from the Diqing version of *Shambhala*. At any rate, there is no corroborating evidence to even remotely suggest any truth to this claim that *Shangri-La* is derived from a Diqing dialect word for *paradise*.[56] The real issue for Zhongdian is not so much the Hilton connection but the nailing down of a free-floating, cultural idea and the actualization of a fantasy. Shangri-La needed to be pinned down and located so its tremendous commercial power could be unleashed. The claims of Zhongdian's experts are really about preparing a place for commoditization.

Visitors may now fly directly to Diqing, and one of their first sights upon disembarking is a huge, white, Hollywood-style message written into the side of a nearby mountain: Shangri-La. In other words, welcome to paradise, Hollywood-style. Western tourists have told me that the sign makes them feel like they're arriving at a theme park. But for the local government, the theme-park allusion also serves to mark Diqing as a civilized place, a leading prefecture.

The myth of Shangri-La contributes to civilizing Diqing in two ways: as a frontier repository for "lost rites" and "spiritual vitality" (of the type that contributes to national strength) and as an advanced and innovative place on the cutting-edge of change. That cutting edge represents the frontiers of commoditization in China—a new economy of cultural symbols and exotic images—and this is precisely what the Open Up the West campaign promises to bring to China's remote western frontier. "Local government officials often speak of Shangri-la as a 'leading' Tibetan area in China—an area that can set an example for others in terms of social stability and economic progress."[57] This progress comes about by the materializing and locating of myths and fantasies. Diqing's Shangri-La is like a theme park because it marries fantasy with reality; it locates a nonplace and enables one to visit and enjoy this place at will. But it does more than simply traffic in the profitability of a powerful myth authored by a British novelist. It actualizes a frontier myth that already had much power in China but that has become a product of intercultural exchange.

It should also be noted that such neat and tidy myths are naturally quite difficult to sustain, despite the power they may hold over a nation's collective imagination. The intercultural exchanges that helped produce Shangri-La as a viable myth of western development in China are also capable of producing unforeseen outcomes as well as opening new spaces capable of challenging the center's hegemony of frontier mythmaking. The myth of Shangri-La is part of a much larger process of exchange in which China's frontier regions become globalized spaces. Northwest Yunnan has been the setting for new environmental and cultural politics in which international agents, such as the Nature Conservancy, actively contribute. The result has been new articulations of Tibetan cultural politics as seen, for instance, in a debate over using the Tibetan name (Kawegabo) or the Chinese name (Meilixue) for Diqing's highest mountain, an unexpected decision to ban mountaineering on the same peak in deference to its sacredness, and in a rise of alternative tourism in the region, a tourism that deliberately challenges the Shangri-La myth.[58] Similarly, in Guizhou, minority Chinese have made known their displeasure with the government's promotion as heritage of a landscape of Han colonization and conquest. While a civilizing message may dominate the rhetoric of western development emanating from the government, intercultural exchanges are both capable of reinforcing and subverting this rhetoric. In the United States, the idea of a frontier has become so politically charged that some historians can barely bring themselves to utter the word *frontier*, at least without scare quotes.[59] And perhaps this too will be an unexpected outcome of China's Open Up the West campaign.

CONCLUSION

In her film *Shangri-La*, New York–based artist Patty Chang makes the point that a lot of work goes into the construction of a nonplace. Shangri-La may be an ephemeral destination, but its myth requires very real fabrication, nails, and hammers. Chang journeys to Diqing and films the building of several installations that materialize the myth of paradise: a mountain made of plywood and mirrors and driven around the dusty streets on the back of an old pickup; a decorated cake shaped like the mountain in *Lost Horizon* and displayed on the shelves of a cake shop. In one scene, she films a group of local monks climbing a rocky mountain. We quickly realize, however, that the mountain is fabricated and that, in fact, it is inside the large, glassed-in atrium of a hotel. The hotel, it turns out, is the Paradise Hotel with real monks climbing a fake mountain under a glass ceiling in Paradise. The film is full of plays on the arbitrariness of the divide between the real and the fake, giving us the sense that fakery is a necessary part of utopia, that the facade is crucial to authenticity. Chang's point is that the contrived fake, the whole commercial project, the theme park itself, not only cannot be avoided but is essential to the building paradise on earth.

The campaign to Open Up the West has set the stage upon which this façade of paradise is now being built in Diqing. And while the exoticism of Tibet sets the scene and provides the drama, Chang reminds us that paradise is a construction project like any other, with workers, dust, plywood, and glass. Paradise is a commercial venture on the frontier, where the false-fronted shops suggest the unlimited possibilities of a civilized future, and where "rugged Tibetans" become lucrative symbols of the new leisure economy that continues to transform China. The myth of a frontier paradise now informs a national identity of leisure and consumption in China today. The myth imagines a shiny future for the nation—like Chang's mountain of mirrors—that will emerge out of the vast construction project of Open Up the West.

NOTES

Thanks to Ralph Litzinger and Emily Yeh for their generosity in contributing their ideas and resources to this chapter, as well as for their critical comments and suggestions. Thanks to Tim Weston and Lionel Jensen for their helpful comments, and to the participants of the workshop "Opening Up the West: China's Regional Development Policy" in Hamburg, Germany, May 2003, which inspired my thinking on this subject. Thanks also to Ed Mestre for supplying the photograph of Shangri-La.

1. Zhang Guangming and Wang Shaoyi, eds., *Xibu dakaifa* [*Open up the West*] (Tianjin, China: Tianjin shehui kexueyuan chubanshe, 2000), 1.

2. Li Dezhu, "Large-Scale Development of Western China and China's Nationality Problems," *Qiushi* [*Seeking Truth*] (June 1, 2000), Foreign Broadcast Information Service, June 15, 2000.

3. Susette Cooke, "Great Western Development in the Tibet Autonomous Region: Merging Tibetan Culture into the Chinese Economic Fast-Lane" (paper, China Quar-

terly, Institute of Asian Affairs, and Institute for International Studies workshop, "Opening Up the West: China's Regional Development Policy," Hamburg, Germany, May 8–10, 2003).

4. David S. G. Goodman, "The Politics of the West: Equality, Nation-Building, and Colonization," *Provincial China* 7, no. 2 (2002): 137.

5. Li Dezhu, "Large-Scale Development of Western China"; Emily Yeh, "Is Lhasa Urban? Migration, Tourism, and Competing Chinese Imaginaries of Tibet" (paper, UTS-UNSW Centre for Research on Provincial China, "Place Imaginaries, Mobilities, and the Limits of Representation," Hunter Valley, New South Wales, June 7–9, 2004).

6. Goodman, "The Politics of the West," 135.

7. Zhu Rongji, "Premier Zhu Rongji's Government Work Report for 2000 to the Third Session of the Ninth National People's Congress, 5 March 2000," *China Daily*, March 6, 2000, cited in Goodman, "The Politics of the West," 132.

8. Heike Holbig, "The Emergence of the Campaign to Open Up the West: Ideological Formation, Central Decision-Making, and the Role of the Provinces," *China Quarterly* 178 (June 2004): 335–36.

9. Holbig, "The Emergence of the Campaign to Open Up the West," 337.

10. Hu Angang, "Too Large Regional Income Inequality Is Risky," *Chinese Economic Studies* 29, no. 6 (1996): 72–75; Hu Angang, Wang Shaoguang, and Kang Xiaoguang, *Zhongguo diqu chaju baogao* [*Report on regional inequality in China*] (Shenyang, China: Liaoning renmin chubanshe, 1995).

11. Goodman, "The Politics of the West," 128–29.

12. Holbig, "The Emergence of the Campaign to Open Up the West," 355–56.

13. Joseph Kahn, "China Gambles on Big Projects for Its Stability," *New York Times*, January 13, 2003.

14. Fu Tao, "Chinese Scholars Call for Privatization in the West," *China Development Brief* 4, no. 1 (Summer 2001), www.chinadevelopmentbrief.com/prtarticle.asp?sec=19&sub=1&art=356.

15. Tim Oakes, "Building a Southern Dynamo: Guizhou and State Power," *China Quarterly* 178 (June 2004): 467–87.

16. Throughout this chapter, *center* refers to China's central government in Beijing and is meant to distinguish central from local government in China. I prefer this term to the more general *Chinese government* in order to highlight the fact that China's vast and sprawling state is a highly decentered one and that there are often tensions, contradictions, and disagreements between the central government in Beijing and local governments at the provincial and municipal levels.

17. Nailene Chou Weist, "More Spending to Close Wealth Gap in Western Region," *South China Morning Post*, November 13, 2002.

18. See Elizabeth Economy, "China's Go West Campaign: Ecological Construction or Ecological Exploitation," *China Environment Series* 5 (2002): 5.

19. Craig Smith, "Taming the Chinese Hinterland," *New York Times*, November 7, 2000; Richard Tomlinson, "The New Wild West: China Makes a High-Stakes Bet on Developing Its Heartland," *Fortune*, October 4, 2004, 200–210.

20. Lijian Hong, "Chongqing: Opportunities and Risks," *China Quarterly* 178 (June 2004): 448–66.

21. Hong, "Chongqing: Opportunities and Risks."

22. Hong, "Chongqing: Opportunities and Risks."

23. Scott Rozelle, "Stagnation without Equity: Patterns of Growth and Inequality in China's Rural Economy," *China Journal* 35 (1996): 63–92; Andrew Watson, "Conflict over Cabbages: The Reform of Wholesale Marketing," in *The Third Revolution in China's Countryside*, ed. R. Garnaut, S. Guo, and G. Ma (Cambridge: Cambridge University Press, 1996), 144–63.

24. Oakes, "Building a Southern Dynamo."

25. Nicholas Bequelin, "Staged Development in Xinjiang," *China Quarterly* 178 (June 2004): 358–78.

26. Archibald MacLeish, "American Letter," in *New Found Land: Fourteen Poems* (Boston: Houghton Mifflin, 1930).

27. Tang Songan and Li Yongtai, *Xibudakaifa: Xibu de ziyuan, zhengce yu jiyun* [*Open up the West: Western resources, policies, and prospects*] (Haikou, China: Nanfang chubanshe, 2000), 420–21.

28. Frederick Jackson Turner, "The Significance of the Frontier in American History," *Annual Report of the American Historical Association for the Year 1893* (Washington, D.C.: Government Printing Office), 199. The essence of Turner's frontier thesis was that the successive westward settling of a receding frontier created a distinctly American kind of individualism and democracy. From a virgin wilderness, Turner believed, hearty pioneers wrested a Jeffersonian republic. In the process, Europeans became Americans. For Turner, America's unique form of democracy emerged because an ever-receding frontier had provided the free land necessary for the equality of all citizens. The frontier was thus an important safety valve for poverty relief, which promoted democracy. For critical essays on the legacy of Turner's frontier thesis, see J. R. Grossman, ed., *The Frontier in American Culture* (Berkeley: University of California Press, 1994).

29. Tim Oakes, "Eating the Food of the Ancestors: Place, Tradition, and Tourism in a Chinese Frontier River Town, *Ecumene* 6, no. 2 (1999): 123–45; Tim Oakes, "Land of Living Fossils: Scaling Cultural Prestige in China's Periphery," in *Locating China: Space, Place, and Popular Culture*, ed. J. Wang (London: Routledge, 2005).

30. Ralph Litzinger, "The Mobilization of 'Nature': Perspectives from Northwest Yunnan," *China Quarterly* 178 (June 2004): 488–504.

31. Patricia Limerick, "The Adventures of the Frontier in the 20th Century," in *The Frontier in American Culture*, ed. J. R. Grossman (Berkeley: University of California Press, 1994), 66–102.

32. Richard White, "Frederick Jackson Turner and Buffalo Bill," in *The Frontier in American Culture*, ed. J. R. Grossman (Berkeley: University of California Press, 1994), 6–65.

33. Patricia Limerick, *The Legacy of Conquest: The Unbroken Past of the American West* (New York: W.W. Norton, 1987).

34. Robert Thorp, "'Let the Past Serve the Present': The Ideological Claims of Cultural Relics Work," *China Exchange News* 20, no. 2 (1992): 16–19; Tong Enzheng, "Thirty Years of Chinese Archaeology (1949–1979)," in *Nationalism, Politics, and the Practice of Archaeology*, ed. P. Kohl and C. Fawcett (Cambridge: Cambridge University Press, 1995), 177–97.

35. Tong Enzheng, "Thirty Years of Chinese Archaeology," 187.

36. Peter Purdue, "Identifying China's Northwest, for Nation and Empire," in *Locating China: Space, Place, and Popular Culture*, ed. J. Wang (London: Routledge, 2005), 94–114.

37. Edward Friedman, "Reconstructing China's National Identity: A Southern Alternative to Mao-Era Anti-imperialist Nationalism," *Journal of Asian Studies* 53, no. 1 (1994): 67–91.

38. Cited in Weng Naiqun, "Naxi Cultural Reproduction and Tourism Development" (paper, annual meeting of the Association for Asian Studies, Chicago, IL, March 2001).

39. Thomas Heberer, "Old Tibet a Hell on Earth? The Myth of Tibet and Tibetans in Chinese Art and Propaganda," in *Imagining Tibet: Perceptions, Projections, and Fantasies*, ed. T. Dodin and H. Rather (Boston: Wisdom Publications, 2001), 119.

40. Jeffrey Kinkley, *The Odyssey of Shen Congwen* (Stanford, CA: Stanford University Press, 1987); David Der-wei Wang, *Fictional Realism in Twentieth-century China: Mao Dun, Lao She, Shen Congwen* (New York: Columbia University Press, 1992); Tim Oakes, "Shen Congwen's Literary Regionalism and the Gendered Landscape of Chinese Modernity," *Geografiska Annaler* B 77, no. 2 (1995): 93–107.

41. Heberer, "Old Tibet a Hell on Earth?" 119–20.

42. Purdue, "Identifying China's Northwest."

43. Chen Jinchuan, ed., *Diyu Zhongguo: Quyu wenhua jingshen yu guomin diyu xingge* [*Regional China: Regional ethos and the national character of localities*] (Beijing: Dang'an chubanshe, 1998), 23–30.

44. Xin Xiangyang et al., eds., *Renwen Zhongguo: Zhongguo de nanbei qingmao yu renwen jingshen* [*Human China: Humanism and the character of South and North China*] (Beijing: Zhongguo shehui chubanshe, 1996), 984–90.

45. Chen Jinchuan, *Diyu Zhongguo*, 271–74, 318–30.

46. Tim Oakes, "China's Provincial Identities: Reviving Regionalism and Reinventing 'Chineseness,'" *Journal of Asian Studies* 59, no. 3 (2000): 681.

47. *Taijiang xianzhi* [*Taijiang county gazetteer*] (Guiyang, China: Guizhou renmin chubanshe, 1994), 1.

48. Rudolf Wagner, "Reading the Chairman Mao Memorial Hall in Peking: The Tribulations of the Implied Pilgrim," in *Pilgrims and Sacred Sites in China*, ed. S. Naquin and C.-f. Yü (Berkeley: University of California Press, 1992), 379.

49. Gang Yue, "From Shambhala to Shangri-La: A Traveling Sign in the Era of Global Tourism," in *Cultural Studies in China*, ed. Y. Jin and D. Tao (Singapore: Times Media Academic, 2004), 165–83.

50. Lawrence Brahm, *Searching for Shangri-la: An Alternative Philosophy Travelogue* (Beijing: Higher Education Press, 2004).

51. Brahm, *Searching for Shangri-La*, 7.

52. Brahm, *Searching for Shangri-La*, 172–73.

53. Peter Hansen, "Tibetan Horizon: Tibet and Cinema in the Early Twentieth Century," in *Imagining Tibet: Perceptions, Projections, and Fantasies*, ed. T. Dodin and H. Rather (Boston: Wisdom Publications, 2001), 91–110.

54. Jamyang Norbu, "Behind the Lost Horizon: Demystifying Tibet," in *Imagining Tibet: Perceptions, Projections, and Fantasies*, ed. T. Dodin and H. Rather (Boston: Wisdom Publications, 2001), 373–78.

55. Donald Lopez Jr., *Prisoners of Shangri-La: Tibetan Buddhism and the West* (Chicago: University of Chicago Press, 1998); Ben Hillman, "Paradise under Construction: Minorities, Myths, and Modernity in Northwest Yunnan," *Asian Ethnicity* 4, no. 2 (June 2003): 175–88.

56. Emily Yeh, personal communication, September 1, 2004; Hillman, "Paradise under Construction."

57. Hillman, "Paradise under Construction," 181.

58. Litzinger, "Mobilization of 'Nature'"; Hillman, "Paradise under Construction"; Caroline Liou, "A Sustainable Future for Shangri-la," www.khampacaravan .com/news_detail.php?id=37.

59. Limerick, "Adventures of the Frontier."

SUGGESTED READINGS

Pamela K. Crossley, Helen Siu, and Donald Sutton, eds., *Empire at the Margins: Culture, Ethnicity, and Frontier in Early Modern China* (Berkeley: University of California Press, 2006).

David S. G. Goodman, ed., *China's Campaign to "Open Up the West": National, Provincial, and Local Perspectives* (Cambridge: Cambridge University Press, 2004).

James R. Grossman, ed., *The Frontier in American Culture* (Berkeley: University of California Press, 1994).

Mette Halskov Hansen, *Frontier People: Han Settlers in Minority Areas of China* (Vancouver: University of British Columbia Press, 2005).

Owen Lattimore, *Inner Asian Frontiers of China* (New York: American Geographical Society, 1951).

Donald Lopez Jr., *Prisoners of Shangri-La: Tibetan Buddhism and the West* (Chicago: University of Chicago Press, 1998).

Peter C. Perdue, *China Marches West: The Qing Conquest of Central Eurasia* (Cambridge, MA: Harvard University Press, 2005).

13

The New Chinese Intellectual

Globalized, Disoriented, Reoriented

Timothy Cheek

I fear no social group has had such ups and downs as intellectuals have, experiencing such a dramatic fate in a century of profound changes: from heroes of creation to objects of remolding, from subjects of discourse to marginal mayflies. . . . They created myths and were shattered by those myths; they led the currents and were engulfed by those currents. They were paragons of excellence and they were thoroughly degraded; they cherished the ideal nation, yet created a spiritual prison. They appear to be the critics, but seem unable to escape their original sin.

—Zhu Yong, *What Should Intellectuals Do?*

This passage, from a 1999 collection of essays on Chinese intellectuals published in Beijing, reflects a concern uppermost in the minds of China's thinkers and writers today: What should intellectuals do? It also alludes to a question that could not be more alien to Western media reports. For what is the original sin of these intellectuals? China's intellectuals have been and continue to be presented in the *New York Times* and *Le Monde* as anti-Communist heroes. Yet this gap between Chinese experience and Western image—between Zhu Yong's self-doubt and the constant parade of "democratic dissidents" from China in the *New York Times*—has closed in scholarly writing. Not only have the questions that animate those born and raised in Western societies changed, but many Chinese intellectuals have also joined the ranks of Western university professors and academic writers. Thus, the global characteristics of China's intellectuals today describe not only the increasing impact of transnational market forces and media interests in China but also the impact of Chinese scholars now active in Western universities.

Zhu Yong's book has not been translated into English, but today thousands of pages and dozens of books by Chinese intellectuals are available in English.[1] While this is good news, the fact remains that how we read those translations and which ones we choose to translate are strongly shaped by our assumptions. And our assumptions are not only shaped by the press and Hollywood movies but also by the academic specialists upon whom we rely to give us "the full story." If this book seeks to criticize and correct the views of China offered in the Western media and to offer some surer footing for understanding China, then the first step to that more solid ground is an appreciation of the strengths and weaknesses of the scholarship that has shaped our knowledge of this increasingly important place.

This chapter reviews the changing stories that authoritative translators—scholars, serious journalists, and literary translators—have told about China's intellectuals over the past twenty-five years in order to provide the reader with the tools to make intelligent use not only of media reports on China, but also of scholarly works. This will not be a case of listing who is right and who is wrong but more an introduction to the tools China specialists use and how they have used them differently over time. The goal is to put those tools in your toolbox, along with some idea of how you might want to use them.

Scholarship is no longer only *by* Westerners *about* China. Increased contact between Chinese and foreign scholars has transformed studies of contemporary China, so that they have become a global phenomenon. The mutual influence resulting from these revived contacts since about 1980 is still developing.[2] Especially for Western scholars interested in studying China's educated elite, this contact has occasioned a shift from imagining intellectuals in a vastly different social context to meeting them, discussing issues face-to-face, and, increasingly, working with them. In fact, the distinction between "Chinese" scholars and "Western" scholars has become blurred as more and more Chinese born in Asia train, work, and publish in the United States and other Western societies. Nonetheless, these new voices build on practices and approaches laid down by previous generations of scholars.

FIGHTING THREE WARS:
WHY WE STUDY CHINESE INTELLECTUALS

Educated people in China have long held top positions in government. China's traditional governments selected officials through state-run academic examinations, a famous system that only ended in 1905. After that, Chinese scholars and writers increasing became known as *zhishifenzi* (intellectuals). China's major twentieth-century leaders, Sun Yat-sen (1866–1925;

a Western-educated physician), Chiang Kai-shek (1888–1975), Mao Zedong (1893–1976), and Deng Xiaoping (1904–1997), each produced extensive scholarly writings to guide his respective revolution. Intellectual participation in Chinese politics has also included prominent dissidents and critics. The fact is, in China intellectuals have been central to modern politics and society.

Western studies have approached modern Chinese intellectuals as a window into understanding how China works and how other countries should best interact with the Chinese state, various Chinese people, and various aspects of Chinese culture.[3] Naturally, these purposes have been shaped by the historical and social context in which scholars in both China and Western societies have found themselves over the past half-century. We can characterize the changing political-intellectual context, particularly for scholars working in the West, by inspecting the changes over the course of three wars: World War II, the Cold War, and the "war on terror." Each war defined a dominant enemy and a (contested) array of core issues.

World War II in Asia was for Westerners part of the world war against fascism. Anyone against imperial Japan was a friend of the Allies; so China, including Mao Zedong and the CCP, was seen by Westerners as an ally. Chinese intellectuals, left-wing as well as independent, were seen as progressive if they opposed Japan and deplored the Chinese Nationalist government's corruption and ineptitude in fighting Japan.

The Cold War abruptly, and without embarrassment, saw a change in alignment. For the West, the enemy shifted from fascism and Japan to Communism and China. But it was a divided China, to be sure. The Korean War in June 1950 settled the case: Mao and the PRC were bad, and the corrupt Nationalist regime of Chiang Kai-shek might yet be redeemable as anti-Communist allies on Formosa (Taiwan). Chinese intellectuals who were soft on Communism were dismissed as propagandists acting under duress or simply deluded. Any Chinese intellectual who had suffered under Communism or had bad things to say about the CCP was good and worthy of study. This clear divide became muddied in the 1960s and 1970s with the Vietnam War as U.S and European scholars divided over the United States' involvement in Southeast Asia and, thus, on their assessment of "Mao's revolution" as an alternative to American military activism in Asia. Some scholars maintained a consistent anti-Communist stand; others, notably those of the Committee of Concerned Asian Scholars (in the United States), took Cultural Revolution pronouncements in the late 1960s as signs of a better alternative to militaristic anti-Communism.[4] Thus, the wholesale negative image of Communist China was blurred. Additionally, since real access to the PRC was profoundly limited for all Westerners—and utterly barred to Americans, the largest cohort of Western researchers—many scholars studied the Chinese language and did field research from the late

1950s to the mid-1970s in Taiwan and Hong Kong. While the realities of life in the PRC remained somewhat misty (and negative reports by U.S. government spy agencies were increasingly doubted during the polemics of the Vietnam War), the dictatorship in Taiwan and social problems in Hong Kong were all too vivid to Western scholars.

This blurring of the Cold War divide took a new twist in the 1970s as the United States and China found political détente against the Soviet Union, marked by the Shanghai Communiqué in 1972. The PRC had taken up China's seat in the UN in 1971, and soon dozens of European, Canadian, Australian, and other non-U.S. scholars started studying in the PRC, bringing a clearer picture of life on the ground in what we now call late Cultural Revolution China.[5] By the 1980s the floodgates of scholarly exchange had opened (and included American researchers, particularly after normalization of U.S.-China relations in 1979, as well as thousands of undergraduate students), bringing hopes of new partnerships. These hopes reached a crescendo in 1989 and were brutally dashed by the military suppression of student and citizen demonstrators around Tiananmen Square on June 4, 1989.

The Cold War between the West and China revived after 1989, even as the Soviet empire disintegrated. Differences over domestic PRC human rights, the fate of Taiwan or Tibet, and U.S. military activities (from the bombing of China's embassy in Belgrade in 1999 to a spy plane incident over the South China Sea in 2001) provoked popular nationalism on both sides.[6] However, a predictable demonization of China as the enemy did not take root. Some journalists played that game, but tellingly, the body of Western (even purely American) scholarship rejected such jingoism, and the conservative Bush administration, not to mention practical-minded European governments, has not been willing to jeopardize the financial interests of large corporations that demand an open and stable global market that includes China.

The "war on terror," launched in reaction to attacks on the United States on September 11, 2001, has cemented this market pragmatism. It has once again changed the enemies and friends list. Now China, even the PRC government, is a friend that frequently votes for U.S. and British resolutions in the UN Security Council, shares information on radical Islamic groups, and cooperates in Central Asia. China is a "strategic partner in the war on terror" and also a very important trading partner for all concerned. It is now a major player in the new world order as a member of the World Trade Organization (WTO) and a major investor in U.S. government bonds. It is more often depicted as a U.S. partner in globalization than as a foe to democratization.

Thus, contemporary research by scholars based in both China and the West is shaped by a shared world order dominated by the interests of financial conglomerates, which soften the geopolitical divides of nation-states and promote the massive exchange of cultural products. This is generally known as *globalization*. As Richard Madsen notes in his excellent study *China and the American Dream*, "Members of both societies are now fatefully becoming engaged with vast, divergent global politico-economic trends that benefit some, disadvantage others, and confuse almost all."[7] Madsen characterizes this new world that we have no choice but to inhabit as defined by three trends: the internationalization of capital, the professionalization of management, and the resulting reaction to these through a "global trend toward particularism—a search for particular communities that give people an identity and a home in the midst of a vast, bewildering, impersonal, and competitive world."[8] Despite their many real differences, one thing China's intellectuals and scholars in Western societies share is this sense of confusion in the face of these global forces. We are all trying to make sense of the post–Cold War world.

China's intellectuals, like their counterparts in every society, are increasingly globalized—subject to the same international market forces, watching similar media outlets and Hollywood movies, and trying to find a way for themselves and their communities in a time of prosperity and terrorism. Chinese intellectuals answer Zhu Yong's question, What should intellectuals do? increasingly with the tools of globalized culture: concepts such as liberalism or postmodernism, technologies such as the Internet and international conferences, and financial support from international companies or agencies (the UN, the Ford Foundation, various national aid agencies). Still, the question of what it means to be Chinese remains a hot topic in China. And as we will see, shared problems and shared tools do not make for shared answers: China's intellectuals make sense of globalization based on their own cultural and historical experience. We would be foolish to expect that they simply wish to become just like us.

THE GOLDMAN SCHOOL AND THE COLD WAR WORLD

What then are the stories Western studies of China's intellectuals have told?[9] The broad lines of Western research on modern China, including specific chapters on Chinese intellectual life and the activities of China's leading intellectuals, are recorded in the volumes of the *Cambridge History of China* covering the Qing dynasty (1644–1911), the Republic (1912–1949), and the PRC (1949–).[10] These volumes follow the image of China's intellectuals made famous by China scholar Merle Goldman.

No scholar stands out to match Merle Goldman's influence among Western scholars writing on China's intellectuals. Not only has she consistently produced well-researched scholarship for forty years (beginning in the mid-1960s), but her approach, tone, and interpretations were broadly accepted by the Cold War generation of Western scholars. Younger scholars have seen fit to criticize Goldman's work but have nonetheless ceded to her the power to define the questions. It is only the post–Cold War generation (which also includes so many Chinese writing in the West today and exhibits a strong postmodernist mood) that has sought to change fundamentally the questions we ask and the knowledge we produce about China's intellectuals.

Goldman's signature work is *Literary Dissent in Communist China* (1967).[11] This work captured the tone for Western research on intellectuals in the Cold War. Covering the activities of major dissident intelligentsia from Lu Xun (1881–1936; China's most famous modern writer) and colleagues in Shanghai in the 1930s to the independent intellectuals struggling in wartime Chongqing, and continuing from the Communist thought-reform campaigns of the 1940s in Yan'an and of the early 1950s throughout the new PRC to the Hundred Flowers debacle of 1957, Goldman's story in *Literary Dissent* sets the terms and the chronology for our understanding of China's intellectuals. I call her model "Russian refuseniks with Chinese characteristics." That is, the intellectuals who turn up on Goldman's radar screen and are the heroes of her narrative were those who were "speaking truth to power," men and women who criticized the government of the day, such as Lu Xun, Wang Shiwei (1906–1947), Hu Feng (1903–1985), Chu Anping (1909–1966), and Ding Ling (1904–1986). The field they fought upon was a political one; their enduring problem was the relationship between intellectuals and the party-state.

Goldman's colleagues largely believed her. Major historical surveys and political-science texts all cited Goldman when they referred to the plight of intellectuals under Mao.[12] Naturally, not everyone agreed. Among mainstream Western academics, it was Mark Selden who took the contrary view, in his justly famous study *The Yenan Way in Revolutionary China* (1971). Selden's approach was, essentially, to ignore Goldman in the accepted academic fashion: politely cite her work and then dismiss it (in this instance, the case of Mao Zedong's 1942 critic, Wang Shiwei) as unrepresentative.[13] Even so, in the heyday of Western euphoria about the claims of the Cultural Revolution, Goldman's approach appealed to most scholars. She read and cited original works in Chinese, she argued clearly and rationally, and her readers were only too aware of the Soviet Russian case. It all made sense at the time.

Goldman became the Elvis Presley of Western scholarship on China's intellectuals. She wasn't the first, and there were many other stars in the business,[14] but she captured the spirit of the time and continued to produce scholarly hits, not only in her series of monographs carrying the story forward over the past twenty-five years but also through nearly a dozen edited volumes with a range of colleagues and rising junior scholars.[15] Through these collaborative efforts Goldman has kept her scholarship lively, promoted and given "air time" to younger scholars, and incorporated and responded to the challenges of other scholars. And in all she has remained true to her original vision—an emphatic focus on the public and political role of humanities intellectuals and the vocation of the intellectual to speak truth to power.

The work of many other scholars found resonance with Goldman's approach.[16] These efforts did not fall simply into Goldman's school or any other but were read according to the shared assumption of both Goldman and her colleagues that the key question was the relationship of China's intellectuals to the state. But beginning in the 1980s, research began to appear that took Goldman's narrative to task. The challenge came through the methods of individual biography and close textual reading—something Goldman and other surveyors of the intellectual field could not afford to do in their broader surveys. Carol Lee Hamrin, a student of Maurice Meisner at the University of Wisconsin, engaged and rethought the meaning of Chinese Leninism through the unappealing case of Yang Xianzhen (1896–1992). A stolid Leninist theorist and one-time head of the central party school, Yang had come to Goldman's attention because he was denounced by the Maoist state in 1964, but Yang did not fit Goldman's refusenik model, because he was a loyal Communist who had simply fallen foul of Chairman Mao. Further studies followed suit, documenting "establishment intellectuals" rather than democratic dissidents in Mao's China and even into the reform era of the 1980s.[17] Others working on intellectuals started from a more critical vision of the Goldman school. Bonnie S. McDougall distinguished "politically active intellectuals" from professional writers and artists as her subject.[18]

The "intellectuals versus the state" narrative that underwrites Goldman's school continued to unravel in further studies—and to be fair, we should note that these changing perspectives are reflected in Goldman's own more recent work.[19] However, this change did not take root (or gain acceptance in the academic and general public) until after the end of the Cold War, with the emergence of the post-Soviet world that we know today. The Cold War era models for understanding China's intellectuals—whether they are seen as Goldman's "refuseniks" or "politically active intellectuals" or "establishment intellectuals"—no longer help us understand the changes in the employment and public activities of Chinese intellectuals today. By the late 1990s, many of China's intellectuals had been disestablished from the CCP or the state and had set up as professionals in universities or as experts in the open market. The question today is less the simple one of intellectuals versus the state and more the open-ended and confusing one of "What should intellectuals do?"

THE GLOBALIZATION OF
RESEARCH ON CHINESE INTELLECTUALS

Merle Goldman's model of Chinese intellectuals as refuseniks made sense to Western readers during the Cold War because, as Richard Madsen has suggested in the case of the United States, public discussion and most influential scholarship about China in the West has been animated by the role of China as a "secondary common reference point"—that is, China studies have served as a metaphor for public debates over the meaning of democracy and identity.[20] Goldman's binary model of China in which intellectuals wore the white hats and the CCP wore the black hats was a useful metaphor for U.S. discussions about democracy during the Cold War standoff between the United States and the Soviet Union. But it does not fit the realities of a post–Cold War world with its internationalized businesses, professionalized management of work (including intellectual life), and revived local pride. It does not help us make sense of globalization and of China's place in this new order.

The experiences of 1989 brought the end of the Cold War and created a dividing line between earlier generations of Western scholars on China's intellectuals and the state and today's generation of scholars. For Western societies, and thus for the audience of Western information about China, the fall of Communism in the Soviet Union and Eastern Europe marked the end of the bipolar Cold War world, an end that lessened the appeal of the bipolar, intellectuals-versus-the-state version of China's intellectuals made famous by Goldman. For scholars in the West, the authors of Western information about China, it was Tiananmen Square that changed everything. The great hopefulness many felt—both in China and in Western society—in the mid-1980s that the CCP might actually make a peaceful transition from Stalinism to something better was shattered by the harsh military crackdown of June 4.[21] The intellectual impact on Western scholars of this unaccountable tragedy cannot be overestimated. It was the end of innocence for yet another generation of China scholars in the West who had projected too many hopes (per Richard Madsen's analysis above) onto China.[22] The result was a continuation of the *disaggregation* of China's intellectuals begun by Hamrin and Cheek, McDougall, and others in the 1980s and a further emphasis on academic disciplinary perspectives that balkanized Western scholarship on China's intellectuals. Today, scholars studying China, as well as China's intellectuals themselves, ask, Do China's intellectuals matter?

A NEW HISTORICAL PERIOD OF CHINA SCHOLARSHIP

These three trends—the disaggregation of intellectuals, an emphasis on academic disciplinary perspectives, and a questioning of the public role of intellectuals in China—have all built upon what can be understood as a new historiographical period in China studies that began in the 1980s but came to fruition in the 1990s. We have seen how Goldman's picture of "good" Chinese refuseniks versus "bad" Communists began to break down on the basis of new research in the 1970s and 1980s. Equally important in influencing Western scholarly perspectives on China in this new historiographical period was personal access to Chinese scholars and surviving participants of the events and issues Western scholars study. A classic early example is Guy Alitto's meeting with Liang Shu-ming (1893–1988) in the early 1980s, at which Dr. Alitto gave Liang his recently completed biography *The Last Confucian: Liang Shu-ming and the Chinese Dilemma of Modernity*. Liang said, "But I am not a Confucian!" As we Western scholars not only met and talked with Chinese intellectuals but lived something of their lives on the campuses and in the cities where they worked, we developed a more complex picture of these intellectuals and the state than the refusenik model allowed.

Fallout from the popular protests and official repression around Tiananmen Square in 1989 shut these contacts down for a couple of years. When relations picked up again in the early 1990s, a new circumstance had emerged: China was globalizing. The single channel of official exchanges and work-unit–based intellectual life began to erode. China's "directed public sphere" that had made the articles that Chinese intellectuals published in *Guangming Daily* or *Renmin ribao* [*People's Daily*] in the 1980s events on the national stage broke open: hundreds of new publishing outlets and considerably more lax enforcement of party censorship gave a much greater scope to China's intellectuals. But it came at the cost of a dilution of their political message. Chinese intellectuals in the 1980s had to watch every word they published in the national press, but what got past the censors made it into a truly national forum. By the 1990s, there was no longer any media outlet both nationally distributed and respected among intellectuals that could match the immense distribution of, say, *Guangming Daily* in the 1980s.[23] At the same time, national academic-exchange organizations were joined and then overtaken by private and university exchange programs not only of scholars but of graduate students both beginning and advanced, and by an increasing flow of undergraduate and even some high-school exchange students and teachers of English. In short, Western scholars had sufficient contacts to help them make friends on an individual basis and hatch cooperative research programs.

The net result of these changes has been the sea change in perspective suggested above—no topic looks monolithic once you get close to it. It really is a case of *duoyuanhua* (pluralization) of our conception of Chinese intellectuals, of our analytical frameworks and disciplinary presentation of our research, and of our sense of why we are doing this, our ideology (in Clifford Geertz's cultural sense), our "So what?" These are the changes and challenges that underscore the three trends of scholarly research that can be seen over the past decade and that define the shift from looking at Chinese intellectuals as heroes in a Cold War fight against tyranny to potential and actual allies today facing shared intellectual, social, and environmental problems that span the globe.

THE DISCIPLINARY DISPERSAL OF WESTERN STUDIES OF CHINESE INTELLECTUALS

We can identify three major lines of research in English-language (and mostly American) scholarship on Chinese intellectuals. Scholars in these three lines of research can be distinguished by the key questions or concerns that motivate their research and organize their work and writing. These more specialized studies represent an improvement on the more general studies of Chinese intellectuals carried out during the 1970s and 1980s, because they are based on extensive new data and contacts in China from the new historiographical period, but they come at a cost: they are balkanized. The political-science studies generally do not draw from the literary or historical studies, or vice versa; the proverbial forest often gets lost in a wealth of trees. To achieve a comprehensive picture of China's intellectuals we need to draw from all lines of research. These three main lines of research concern (1) democratic transitions and state analysis, (2) postmodernism and the critique of capitalism and globalization, and (3) China-centered historical and contextual studies.

Democratic Transitions and State Analysis

The key question for this line of research is "Will China democratize?" It is based on traditional Western political-science methodologies and draws from studies by Lintz, Przeworski, and others who recently have focused on Latin American and East European experience. The strengths of this line of research are its practical focus and its clear, analytical frameworks. Its weaknesses are a lack of critical reflection on some of its assumptions and often a limited empirical basis. Scholars working in this line of research tend to be political scientists, and they work in or assume an audience in government and policy circles, as well as in academia. Good examples of this work include Joseph Fewsmith's *China since Tiananmen* (2001) and David Lynch's *After the Propaganda State* (1999).[24]

Postmodernism and the Critique of Capitalism and Globalization

The key question for this line of research is "Can China survive globalization?" It is based on new methodologies of literary criticism and cultural studies and draws from French theorists like Foucault, Derrida, and Bourdieu (among many others) and an evolving theoretical literature in Western cultural studies, such as work by Stanley Fish. The strengths of this line of research are its challenge to Western cultural assumptions, its call to social justice, and its focus on issues of power and repression. Its weaknesses are a lack of practicality, a certain analytical looseness or abstraction, and often a limited empirical basis. Additionally, this line of research has a problematic relationship to previous radical scholarship in North America. That is, it inherits the radical critique of American values and foreign policy made by Marxist-inspired scholarship of the 1960s and 1970s, but because of the critique of state socialism today (and the terrors of Stalinism and Maoism), it fails to make an explicit acknowledgement of this heritage or to engage it seriously. Thus, there are still other Western scholars of the "old Western Left" who engage the same issues and criticisms as the postmodernists today, but with a different vocabulary.[25] Scholars working in this line of research tend to be academics in literature or cultural studies programs and assume an audience of fellow academics and students. Good examples include Geremie Barmé's *In the Red* (1999), Xudong Zhang's *Whither China?* (2001), Gloria Davies's *Voicing Concerns* (2001), and Tani Barlow's *New Asian Marxisms* (2002).[26]

China-Centered Historical and Contextual Studies

The key question for this line of research is "What is Chinese experience?" It is founded on the methodologies of text-based Sinology, social history, and especially Ming-Qing social and economic historical studies. It draws from a diverse group of empirical-historical studies ranging from the pioneering work of John King Fairbank (1907–1991) to that of Frederic Wakeman (1937–2006) and Philip Kuhn. The strengths of this line of research are its detailed and rich factual base, its strong tradition of source criticism, and its ability to evoke the life of the Other. Its weaknesses are its distance from practical concerns and often its lack of critique of Western assumptions in its analytical approach. For example, Fairbank could maintain what today looks like an astonishingly paternalistic, missionary point of view despite his careful scholarship. Scholars working in this line of research tend to be academics in history or Asian studies departments and assume an audience of fellow academics and students. A very few—such as Jonathan Spence—manage to reach a broader reading public.

This is an extremely large literature that features biographies, and studies of communities, institutions, literature, and thought, and also increasingly includes sociological and anthropological studies of intellectuals (not a feature of Western scholarship on intellectuals before the 1990s). Examples of studies include biographies of revolutionary intellectuals like Shen Dingyi

(1883–1928) and of artists and writers like Feng Zikai (1898–1975), as well as studies of generations among intellectual activists;[27] institutional studies of colleges and universities in Republican China and of Beijing University;[28] studies of literature and society by Perry Link and sets of studies of communities and cultural practices that loom large for intellectuals in two collections Link and colleagues compiled, *Unofficial China* and *Popular China*;[29] and studies on thought and ideology and on the erosion of official ideology, as well as excellent reviews of recent ideology squabbles among "New Left" and "Liberal" intellectuals.[30] Most exciting has been the application of new disciplines to the study of intellectuals, as in sociological studies of teachers in Shanghai and an excellent comprehensive sociology of contemporary Chinese intellectuals, as well as an ethnography of Chinese archaeology professors (provocatively called *Obedient Autonomy*), and a revival of cross-cultural philosophical reflections.[31]

While it is not possible to find a single author or study today that describes China's intellectuals the way Merle Goldman could in previous decades, even this brief listing of recent studies from the three main lines of research shows both the rich trove of knowledge awaiting the serious reader and the need to read research from more than one discipline.

THE GLOBALIZATION OF CHINA'S INTELLECTUALS

The most important impact of globalization for China's intellectuals has been the disestablishment (or de-linking) of China's intellectuals from the party-state and the opening of a confusing array of overlapping alternative roles to play. As the CCP has withdrawn from its totalitarian goal to control all of society, which it did under Mao, and has, instead, embraced "market socialism," it has ended the intellectual's role as public official. The price of today's relative autonomy for China's intellectuals has been a loss of public influence and the birth of the self-doubt and questioning we saw in Zhu Yong's quotation at the beginning of the chapter. We have seen a disaggregation of intellectuals in China—no longer will a Liu Binyan (1925–2005) or a Fang Lizhi (1936–), heroes both of reform in the 1980s, stand for all China's intellectuals. We now regularly see a range of intellectual roles: creative writer, artist, journalist, academic, scientist, technical government or business advisor, and so forth. This has paralleled the disaggregation of the establishment. The state, that is, the party-state under the CCP, is still very much with us. Just ask any Chinese academic. Nonetheless, the authority of the state is more than matched, on a day-to-day level, by the requirements of profession (universities, institutes, businesses) and the financial inducements of commercial publishing.

Profession, the party, and the public are the three masters to whom Chinese intellectuals must attend if they are to survive and to be effective in their chosen goals. A few examples will give us a sense of Chinese intellectuals with global characteristics.

Consider the plight of Liu Dong, editor of *Zhongguo xueshu* [*China Academics*] and professor of comparative literature at Beijing University. Unlike intellectuals under Mao who had to please their party secretary and keep on the right side of the Great Helmsman while pursuing their ideals of socialist service, Professor Liu faces a more complex world. He must not only demonstrate his academic abilities in front of his peers (at Harvard, the copublisher of his journal, as well as his own university), but he must also satisfy market forces, or his journal will go under. Nonetheless, he must still keep on the right side of his party secretary, pay for his cell phone, and take care of his kids' education costs. How does he get his funding? How does he get published? What can he hope his writings will achieve in political or public influence? How will he balance the specialist demands of his academic peers with the commercial interests of an emerging, middle-class readership? He has, of course, new tools: the Internet, Harvard-Yenching funding, that cell phone. But new tools aside, the pressures Professor Liu Dong faces will be familiar to academics in the West, although Liu Dong's conditions are meaningfully different: the party still rules, and China's economic reforms have brought social ills of rural poverty, urban homelessness, and pollution that are everywhere far more intense and urgent than in Western societies. In all, we can see that both Goldman's intellectuals-versus-the-state model and the simple dichotomy of life in China versus life in the West no longer usefully apply.

What does Professor Liu Dong do with his international resources? He declares the fundamental power of *place* (or location) in scholarship. He denounces Chinese scholars who ape Western ways as "pidgin scholarship."[32] He is a most interesting character: a cosmopolitan academic with strong international connections who specializes in German literary history and theory but who yet accepts that his place—living and working in China— defines what he should do: serve China according to his best lights as an intellectual.

Meanwhile, in Shanghai, Xu Jilin, professor of history at East China Normal University, has built a reputation as one of the most prolific, public intellectual-academics in China today. He has published nearly a dozen books, appears regularly in the tony PRC intellectual press such as *Dushu* [*Reading*], or in influential Web journals such as *Ershiyi shiji* [*Twenty-first Century*] and on intellectual Web pages such as *Shiji Zhongguo* [*Century China*],[33] is much more interested in Western ideas for China, particularly in the political philosophy of liberalism—which he takes to be social democracy—than is Liu

Dong. Yet he has traveled and studied in the West much less than Liu. This has not stopped Professor Xu from spending six months as a visiting scholar at Harvard-Yenching in 2001 or from organizing conferences with Western colleagues.[34]

Xu wants to write a history of contemporary Chinese thought in the twentieth century that fulfills the twin requirements of professional scholarship and public impact. It's a tall order, but his many books in Chinese are widely available and sell well in China.[35] His basic goal is to mine China's recent history for solutions to the problems Zhu Yong enumerated above.

Xu Jilin is an interesting case because he is studying what academics in Western societies study: Chinese intellectuals, that is, people like him. For example, Xu puts China's intellectuals of the 1990s into four categories:

1. Pedants—whom he calls *sixiang* (scholars without thought).
2. Pundits—whom he considers neither scholarly nor thoughtful (his example is the popular young commentator Yu Jie, author of *Fire and Ice* [1998] and much loved by less-exalted intellectuals).
3. Public intellectuals—or scholarly thinkers (Gu Zhun is a well-known example).
4. Professionals—or thoughtful scholars (Chen Yinke is a well-known example).

Xu Jilin is himself counted as a public intellectual in China. Yet the Chinese government has recently criticized such public intellectuals for "splitting the people from the party." China's intellectual world has certainly changed since Merle Goldman first started studying literary dissent in the 1960s, but it is not the same world that Western intellectuals live in.

Xu Jilin's four categories and examples give us another sense of the disaggregation of Chinese intellectuals today, but they also raise a question: When is the Chinese intellectual the subject of the study or the researcher of the subject? This is part of the globalization that confounds scholars in China and in Western societies. This confusion goes farther when Chinese scholars receive graduate training in the West, then take up academic posts in America or Europe and publish in English, fully engaging the scholarly discourse in Western academia that we have reviewed here. Thousands of Chinese students have joined the academy in the West, and among them, several study China's intellectuals.

A good example of this globalized hybrid is Professor Zhang Xudong. He is a very important example of contemporary Chinese life because he is a professor of literature and Asian studies at New York University. He is also an adjunct professor at East China Normal University in Shanghai. He is a PRC native with a PhD from Duke University in the United States, and he writes extensively in both English and Chinese. His case raises two interesting issues about the realities of contemporary Chinese intellectual life. First, despite his good scholarship, in recent years Professor Zhang has discovered that one of his important audiences has not been paying much attention to him. Despite the de facto essentialism of North American China studies that accords Zhang Xudong authority to speak on behalf of PRC intellectuals and Chinese people in general, this is demonstrably not the view of his PRC colleagues. PRC academics, such as Professor Liu Dong, have dismissed him as "a foreign scholar," because he can live and work free of the constraints that face scholars working inside China. Indeed, one major reason Zhang Xudong took an adjunct professorship at a major Chinese university was in order to be taken seriously by his Chinese peers again.

Further, with scholars like Zhang Xudong now holding jobs throughout Western universities, who is the Western scholar and who the Chinese subject of study? On almost every topic we have reviewed, from political science to literary studies to historical research, there are PRC natives trained in Western graduate schools who have published books in English. Yet their voice is not uniform. Some (such as Zhang Xudong) embrace postmodernist approaches associated with Foucault or Derrida, while others maintain formal, Western social-science models (as does Tong Yanqi) or attempt to blend them (as do Zhao Yuezhi and Zhao Suisheng).[36] While their childhood experiences in China and recent adventures as immigrants and visible minorities in Western societies surely shape their thinking, nonetheless their social experience as academics in the United States, Canada, and Europe increasingly defines their outlook. At the same time, however, globalizing forces of professionalism bring many of the same forces (tenure review, peer-review academic publishing) to bear on academics like Liu Dong and Xu Jilin inside China.

MAKING SENSE: THE CHALLENGE OF GLOBALIZED INTELLECTUALS

The distance between Chinese intellectuals and Western scholars has decreased over the past twenty years, and the distinction between Chinese intellectuals and scholars of Chinese intellectuals has blurred, even though life under the CCP in reform China and life in Western democracies are not the same—as we can see in the cases of Liu Dong and Xu Jilin. These developments have grown from relaxed international relations for China and rely upon the extensive exchange of people and ideas between China and other societies in recent decades.

This increased contact has come at a cost: Cold War scholarship's clear picture of China's intellectuals (and indeed, of China in general) is a thing of the past. The key image for the twenty-first century is the overwhelming abundance of information we experience through the Internet. As I noted above, Richard Madsen points out that Chinese intellectuals and scholars who study China confront "vast, divergent global politico-economic trends that benefit some, disadvantage others, and confuse almost all." The short answer to Zhu Yong's question for China's intellectuals applies to Western scholars—and to you the general reader as well: our task is to make sense of the confusing trends of globalization and to make sensible use of this rich but balkanized scholarly research on China and China's intellectuals. In this way we can more accurately understand what China, as well as China's intellectuals, faces, how it and they will respond to the challenges of globalization, and where we can all work together.

NOTES

The epigraph to this chapter is taken from Zhu Yong, ed., *Zhishifenzi yinggai gan-shenma?* [*What should intellectuals do?*] (Beijing: Shishi chubanshe, 1999), 1. Zhu Yong is a younger (born in 1968) and noted essay writer and editor in Beijing who reflects on intellectual issues and changes. See also his collection *Liushiniandai jiyi* [*Recollections of the 60s*] (Beijing: Zhongguo wenlian chubanshe, 2002).

1. For example, Wang Hui's book *China's New Order: Society, Politics, and Economy in Transition*, ed. and trans. Theodore Huters (Cambridge, MA: Harvard University Press, 2003). Similar writings appear in the major translation journal *Contemporary Chinese Thought*, ed. Carine Defoort. See also titles marked with an asterisk in the bibliography at the end of this chapter.

2. For example, compare David Shambaugh, ed., *American Studies of Contemporary China* (Armonk, NY: M.E. Sharpe, 1993) and Gloria Davies, ed., *Voicing Concerns: Contemporary Chinese Critical Inquiry* (Lanham, MD: Rowman & Littlefield, 2001).

3. Studies of Chinese intellectuals by scholars inside China focus on what Chinese intellectuals can do to help China now. Wang Hui, *China's New Order* provides an English edition of the views of one of China's notable contemporary intellectuals.

4. The *Bulletin of Concerned Asian Scholars* has served as an important left-of-center voice in American Asian studies since the 1970s; the journal became *Critical Asian Studies* in 2001. The journal's founding statement, for example, states: "We are concerned about the present unwillingness of specialists to speak out against the implications of an Asian policy committed to ensuring American domination of much of Asia." *Critical Asian Studies*, "Committee of Concerned Asian Scholars Statement of Purpose: BCAS Founding Statement," www.bcasnet.org/ccas-sop.htm (July 1, 2006).

5. Timothy Brook and Rene Wagner, "The Teaching of History to Foreign Students at Peking University," *China Quarterly* 71 (September 1977): 598–607.

6. Richard Bernstein and Ross H. Munro, *The Coming Conflict with China* (New York: Knopf, 1997); Ezra Vogel, ed., *Living with China: U.S./China Relations in the Twenty-First Century* (New York: W.W. Norton, 1997).

7. Richard Madsen, *China and the American Dream: A Moral Inquiry* (Los Angeles: University of California Press, 1995), 216.

8. Madsen, *China and the American Dream*, 218.

9. For a lengthy account and detailed bibliography of these studies, see Timothy Cheek, "Studying Our Friends/Befriending Our Studies: Western Scholarship on Chinese Intellectuals and the State in the PRC" (paper, "Historical Thinking and Contemporary Chinese Humanities Studies" conference, University of California, Berkeley, January 2004).

10. Chapters on intellectuals from the relevant volumes of *The Cambridge History of China* have been collected in Merle Goldman and Leo Ou-fan Lee, eds., *An Intellectual History of Modern China* (Cambridge: Cambridge University Press, 2002).

11. Merle Goldman, *Literary Dissent in Communist China* (Cambridge, MA: Harvard University Press, 1967).

12. John King Fairbank, *The United States and China*, 4th ed (Cambridge, MA: Harvard University Press, 1983); Maurice Meisner, *Mao's China and After: A History of the People's Republic* (New York: Free Press, 1999).

13. Mark Selden, *The Yenan Way in Revolutionary China* (Cambridge, MA: Harvard University Press, 1971), 196.

14. Roderick MacFarquhar, *The Hundred Flowers Campaign and the Chinese Intellectuals* (New York: Praeger, 1960); D. W. Fokkema, *Literary Doctrine in China and Soviet Influence 1956–1960* (The Hague: Mouton, 1965); Peter R. Moody, *Opposition and Dissent in Contemporary China* (Stanford, CA: Hoover Institution Press, 1977).

15. Merle Goldman, *China's Intellectuals: Advise and Dissent* (Cambridge, MA: Harvard University Press, 1981); Merle Goldman, *Sowing the Seeds of Democracy in China* (Cambridge, MA: Harvard University Press, 1994); Denis Fred Simon and Merle Goldman, eds., *Science and Technology in Post-Mao China* (Cambridge, MA: Harvard Council on East Asian Studies, 1989); Merle Goldman and Elizabeth J. Perry, *The Changing Meanings of Citizenship in Modern China* (Cambridge, MA: Harvard University Press, 2002).

16. Liu Binyan [Pin-yen Liu], *People and Monsters? And Other Stories and Reportage from China after Mao*, ed. Perry Link (Bloomington: University of Indiana Press, 1983); Michael Duke, *Blooming and Contending: Chinese Literature in the Post-Mao Era* (Bloomington: Indiana University Press, 1985); Michael Duke, ed., *Contemporary Chinese Literature: An Anthology of Post-Mao Fiction and Poetry* (Armonk, NY: M.E. Sharpe, 1985); Jiang Yang, *Chapters from My Life "Downunder,"* trans. Howard Goldblatt (Hong Kong: Chinese University Press, 1984).

17. See chapters on Deng Tuo, Wu Han, Bai Hua, Jian Bozan, Wang Ruowang, and Wang Ruoshui in Carol Lee Hamrin and Timothy Cheek, eds., *China's Establishment Intellectuals* (Armonk, NY: M.E. Sharpe, 1986); and Merle Goldman, ed., with Timothy Cheek and Carol Lee Hamrin, *China's Intellectuals and the State: In Search of a New Relationship* (Cambridge, MA: Council on East Asian Studies, Harvard University, 1987).

18. Bonnie S. McDougall, ed., *Popular Chinese Literature and Performing Arts in the People's Republic of China, 1949–1979* (Berkeley: University of California Press, 1984), 271.

19. Edward Gu and Merle Goldman, *China's Intellectuals between State and Market* (London: Routledge, 2004); Merle Goldman, *From Comrade to Citizen: The Struggle for Political Rights in China* (Cambridge, MA: Harvard University Press, 2005).

20. Madsen, *China and the American Dream*, 211ff. Madsen's book extends this analysis to scholarship by Chinese scholars in the PRC as well, but that aspect is beyond the scope of this chapter.

21. Literally dozens of books by these scholars came out in the aftermath of the June 4 crackdown in China, for example Tony Saich, ed., *The Chinese People's Movement: Perspectives on Spring 1989* (Armonk, NY: M.E. Sharpe, 1990); Brantly Womack, ed., *Contemporary Chinese Politics in Historical Perspective* (New York: Cambridge University Press, 1991); Timothy Brook, *Quelling the People: The Military Suppression of the Beijing Democracy Movement* (New York: Oxford University Press, 1992); and Jeffrey N. Wasserstrom and Elizabeth J. Perry, eds., *Popular Protest and Political Culture in Modern China: Learning from 1989* (Boulder, CO: Westview, 1992).

22. In fact, the history of Western interest in China shows such cycles of hope and crushed expectations going back at least to the sixteenth century. See Jonathan Spence, *The Chan's Great Empire: China in Western Minds* (New York: W.W. Norton, 1998).

23. The public, ideological work in the 1980s is well analyzed in Bill Brugger and David Kelly, *Chinese Marxism in the Post-Mao Era, 1978–94* (Stanford, CA: Stanford University Press, 1990). The break-up of the unified media in China is documented in David Lynch, *After the Propaganda State: Media, Politics, and "Thought Work" in Reformed China* (Stanford, CA: Stanford University Press, 1999).

24. Joseph Fewsmith, *China since Tiananmen: The Politics of Transition* (New York: Cambridge University Press, 2001); Lynch, *After the Propaganda State*.

25. Edward Friedman, Paul G. Pickowicz, Mark Selden, and Kay Ann Johnson, *Chinese Village, Socialist State* (New Haven, CT: Yale University Press, 1991); Arif Dirlik and Maurice Meisner, eds., *Marxism and the Chinese Experience: Issues in Contemporary Socialism* (Armonk, NY: M.E. Sharpe, 1989).

26. Geremie Barmé, *In the Red: On Contemporary Chinese Culture* (New York: Columbia University Press, 1999); Xudong Zhang, ed., *Whither China? Intellectual Politics in Contemporary China* (Durham, NC: Duke University Press, 2001); Davies, *Voicing Concerns*; Tani Barlow, ed., *New Asian Marxisms* (Durham, NC: Duke University Press, 2002).

27. R. Keith Schoppa, *Blood Road: The Mystery of Shen Dingyi in Revolutionary China* (Berkeley: University of California Press, 1995); Geremie Barmé, *An Artist Exile: A Life of Feng Zikai* (Berkeley: University of California Press, 2002); Nora Sausmikat, "Generations, Legitimacy, and Political Ideas in China," *Asian Survey* 43, no. 2 (2003): 352–84.

28. Wen-hsin Yeh, *The Alienated Academy: Culture and Politics in Republican China, 1919–1937* (Cambridge, MA: Harvard Council on East Asian Studies, 1990); Timothy B. Weston, *The Power of Position: Beijing University, Intellectuals, and Chinese Political Culture, 1898–1929* (Berkeley: University of California Press, 2004).

29. Perry Link, *The Uses of Literature: Life in the Socialist Chinese Literary System* (Princeton, NJ: Princeton University Press, 2002); Perry Link, Richard Madsen, and Paul Pickowicz, eds., *Unofficial China: Popular Culture and Thought in the People's Republic of China* (Boulder, CO: Westview, 1989); Perry Link, Richard Madsen, and

Paul Pickowicz, eds., *Popular China: Unofficial Culture in a Globalizing Society* (Lanham, MD: Rowman & Littlefield, 2002).

30. Brugger and Kelly, *Chinese Marxism in the Post-Mao Era*; Kalpana Misra, *From Post-Maoism to Post-Marxism: The Erosion of Official Ideology in Deng's China* (New York: Routledge, 1998); Geremie Barmé, "The Revolution of Resistance," in *Chinese Society: Change, Conflict and Resistance*, ed. Elizabeth J. Perry and Mark Selden (London: Routledge, 2000), 198–220; Xudong Zhang, "Chinese Post-Modernism," *New Left Review* (October 1999).

31. Eddy U, "The Making of *Zhishifenzi*: The Critical Impact of the Registration of Unemployed Intellectuals in the Early PRC," *China Quarterly* 173 (March 2003); Zhidong Hao, *Intellectuals at a Crossroads: The Changing Politics of China's Knowledge Workers* (Albany: State University of New York Press, 2003); Erica E. S. Evasdottir, *Obedient Autonomy: Chinese Intellectuals and the Achievement of Orderly Life* (Vancouver: University of British Columbia Press, 2004); Kim-chong Chong, Sor-hoon Tan, and C. L. Ten, eds., *The Moral Circle and the Self: Chinese and Western Approaches* (Chicago: Open Court, 2003).

32. See Liu Dong, "Jingti renweide 'Yangjingbang xuefeng,'" *Ershiyi shiji* 32 (December 1995): 4–13, translated by Gloria Davies and Li Kaiyu, with a new prefatory section by Liu Dong, as "Revisiting the Perils of 'Designer Pidgin Scholarship,'" in Gloria Davies, ed., *Voicing Concerns: Contemporary Chinese Critical Inquiry* (Lanham, MD: Rowman & Littlefield, 2001), 87–108; and my interview with Liu Dong, Vancouver, British Columbia, October 2003. Chinese text appears in Liu, *Lilun yu xinzhi*, 16–40.

33. "Century China," www.cc.org.cn (July 1, 2006). In July of 2006 Century China and its associated chat forum, China Salon, were shut down by the Communication Administration Bureau of Beijing.

34. Professor Xu and I coorganized a conference titled "Public Intellectuals in China" in December 2002.

35. Xu Jilin, *Ling yizhong qimeng* [*Another kind of enlightenment*] (Guangzhou: Huacheng chubanshe, 1999); Xu Jilin, ed., *Ershi shiji Zhongguo sixiang shi* [*Essays on the history of twentieth-century Chinese thought*] (Shanghai: Dongfang chubanshe, 2000); Jilin Xu, *Xinshiji de sixiang ditu* [*An intellectual map of the new century*] (Tianjin: Tianjin renmin chubanshe, 2002).

36. Yanqi Tong, *Transitions from State Socialism: Economic and Political Change in Hungary and China* (Lanham, MD: Rowman & Littlefield, 1997); Yuezhi Zhao, *Media, Market, and Democracy in China: Between the Party Line and the Bottom Line* (Urbana: University of Illinois Press, 1998); Suisheng Zhao, ed., *China and Democracy* (London: Routledge, 2000).

SUGGESTED READINGS

*Titles marked with an asterisk include, in addition to thoughtful commentary by the editors and chapters by Western scholars, a number of translations of essays by major contemporary Chinese intellectuals.

Geremie Barmé, *In the Red: On Contemporary Chinese Culture* (New York: Columbia University Press, 1999).

*Gloria Davies, _Voicing Concerns: Critical Voices from China_ (Lanham, MD: Rowman & Littlefield, 2001).

Joseph Fewsmith, _China since Tiananmen: The Politics of Transition_ (New York: Cambridge University Press, 2001).

Merle Goldman and Leo Ou-fan Lee, eds., _An Intellectual History of Modern China_ (Cambridge: Cambridge University Press, 2002).

*Edward Gu and Merle Goldman, eds., _China's Intellectuals between State and Market_ (London: Routledge, 2004).

Zhidong Hao, _Intellectuals at a Crossroads: The Changing Politics of China's Knowledge Workers_ (Albany: State University of New York Press, 2003).

Richard Madsen, _China and the American Dream: A Moral Inquiry_ (Los Angeles: University of California Press, 1995).

Kalpana Misra, _From Post-Maoism to Post-Marxism: The Erosion of Official Ideology in Deng's China_ (New York: Routledge, 1998).

Elizabeth J. Perry and Mark Selden, eds., _Chinese Society: Change, Conflict and Resistance_, 2nd ed. (London: RoutledgeCurzon, 2003).

*Chaohua Wang, _One China, Many Paths_ (London: Verso, 2003).

*Hui Wang, _China's New Order: Society, Politics, and Economy in Transition_, ed. and trans. Theodore Huters (Cambridge, MA: Harvard University Press, 2003).

Sang Ye, _China Candid: The People's Republic_, ed. Geremie R. Barmé, with Miriam Lang (Berkeley: University of California Press, 2005).

*Xudong Zhang, ed., _Whither China? Intellectual Politics in Contemporary China_ (Durham, NC: Duke University Press, 2001).

14

Reporting China since the 1960s

John Gittings

Fascinated by China since I was a child, I took my degree in Oriental studies at Oxford and then spent my adult life working in this field as an academic and journalist. I first set eyes on China in 1968—from across the border in Hong Kong where I was writing for the *Far Eastern Economic Review*. I made my first visits in 1971 and 1976 and then traveled regularly to China over the next two decades. I joined the staff of the *Guardian* in 1983 (though I had contributed to it as a freelancer since 1970) and covered most major events including the Beijing massacre in 1989.[1] That newspaper, which for non-British readers can be broadly labeled as center-left, was regarded in Beijing as relatively balanced, although this did not earn any special favors.

I concluded my time at the *Guardian* by setting up the paper's first staff bureau on the mainland in Shanghai in 2001–2003. While doing so, I began to research the work of my distant predecessors who had reported for what was then the *Manchester Guardian* during the anti-Japanese war. They included Harold Timperley, who wrote the first book on the Nanjing Massacre, and Agnes Smedley, who sent a series of brilliant dispatches from the fighting front.[2] Their experiences led me to reflect more seriously upon the complexities of reporting from China. During my time reporting on China, Western opinion on that country has changed dramatically, yet it has always been polarized. In the 1960s and 1970s, it was largely polarized between those who regarded the Maoist approach as an admirable socialist experiment, and the Cold War view that China was the world's first evil empire. In post-Mao China, the polarized views have centered on the question whether a resurgent China is a shining example of the triumph of the market or a looming threat to Western domination. For most of the time in my case during a more recent (cold) war, I have come to reflect on the pressures

285

and constraints under which reportorial work is done and on its partial and often flawed results. This is the theme that, from a largely personal perspective, I will explore. Drawing from my experience of reporting over several decades, in this chapter I discuss the complex interplay between China's historical narrative and our own changing perceptions. And through it all I have found that the question "Whither China?" raised so often over the past century remains as hard to answer as ever.

FIRST REPORTS AND READINGS

On my first visit to China in 1971, I traveled in a group from the UK-based Society for Anglo-Chinese Understanding (SACU) as a "friend of China," not as a journalist, although I had already spent a decade writing on Chinese affairs. After five years of the Cultural Revolution, visas for visiting Western journalists were unobtainable. Nevertheless, the Western appetite then for even the most slender glimpse of China was enormous: I wrote a series of five articles for the *Guardian* that were run in full.

I still have my notes from that first train journey, heading inland, across the bridge at Lowu to Guangzhou, when everything was fresh and new. I recorded the couplet from Mao Zedong on my tea mug and the view of green rice paddies, lychee trees, and cabbages outside. At a station halt we saw conscripts wearing gym shoes, with matting, quilt, and water bottle strapped to their backs. That evening in Guangzhou, our host from the Chinese Committee for Friendship with Foreign Countries told us that the situation was getting better at home and abroad. More and more countries were recognizing China—he groped for the name of Kuwait and had to be prompted. In the streets outside, the slogans of the Cultural Revolution had been painted out—even "The working-class must lead everything"—but its spirit was still thriving. On our first full day we were taken to a school for deaf and mute children. Here there was another slogan: "Liu Shaoqi was a bad egg; he harmed the spirit of revolution; he made us deaf and dumb, we shall smash him to pieces." The children were told they would be cured by Mao Zedong thought, though they were actually being given acupuncture and speech therapy.

By this time I had already been working for a number of years as a China specialist, first at the Royal Institute of International Affairs in London and then for the *Far Eastern Economic Review.* The notion that one might write about mainland China without having visited the mainland was not considered unusual. Only a small number of European students, mostly from Scandinavian countries, had the opportunity to study in China: students from the United States were limited to Taiwan or Hong Kong. Most of the material available for research existed in written form and often in English translation. In a curious way, the study of China then was approached in a way not dissimilar to the study of classical China. There was a limited corpus of available material, and textual analysis was carried to a fine art. Chinese officials clung to orthodox forms of expression, "rectifying the names" in proper Confucian style. As outside observers, we developed a keen eye for any variation that might reveal a heterodox trend, and the sometimes baffling inconsistencies of policy and rhetoric in the Cultural Revolution carried this obsession with verbal form to new heights. Many Chinese too read the official pronouncements for hints of political significance with as much attention as if they were deciphering oracle bones.

These problems of access and interpretation did not exist in a vacuum. To the contrary, China scholarship was set in the highly politicized context of a cold—sometimes hot—war between the so-called free and Communist worlds in which the Beijing government was assigned, as time went on, a particularly demonic role. As in other areas of contemporary studies, the funding and agenda were often linked, openly or covertly, to U.S. government agencies and their requirements. Conversely, direct access to the top Chinese leadership and, during the Cultural Revolution, to the mainland itself was largely confined to a very small number of visitors whose sympathies were manifest. The difference was that these "friends of China" never hid their allegiance, whereas apparently objective scholarship in the West might be tarnished by unseen connections. The revolving door between academia and government, particularly in the United States, was a further complication.

I do not intend to write here in detail about the skein of links between government and the rapidly expanding field of area studies that did so much to set the agenda for scholarship and journalism in the 1960s. The extent of this operation in the United States came under attack during the Vietnam War from dissenting scholars such as the Committee of Concerned Asian Scholars, who organized around the *Bulletin of Concerned Asian Scholars*.[3] The driving force for these area studies came from the U.S. government and its agencies, whose superior purchasing power also dictated the direction of research in Europe, and especially in Britain. My own first research post at the Royal Institute of International Affairs was funded by the Ford Foundation.

With or without these covert institutional links, the Cold War climate of the time influenced the questions asked about China, and the topics chosen for research, to an extent that it is hard to fully appreciate now. Whereas in most disciplines it is taken for granted that scholars and journalists are likely to function better if they have some sympathy for their subject, here it was the reverse. Indeed, China was an object—not a subject—for investigation.

It was often argued that direct exposure to Mao's China was, or could be, harmful to academic or journalistic integrity. The term *brainwashed* was used, not always in jest, about those who had experienced the mainland at first hand. There was a tendency to ridicule rather than to try to understand the specifics of Chinese political culture. I recall a high-level academic conference on China where the U.S. participants—some of the best-known names in the field—rocked with laughter at a showing of the celebratory official Chinese film *The East Is Red* rather than trying to analyze the spirit it conveyed.

Meanwhile at meetings of the SACU, the same film was greeted with respectful applause. It was in this polarized atmosphere that I paid my first visit to China—as a member of a SACU delegation, after having been vetted by a SACU subcommittee to ensure that I would not "upset our Chinese friends." I would, half-literally, be wearing two caps. One was that of journalist: I had already worked for nearly two years in Hong Kong as the *Far Eastern Economic Review*'s China-watcher, and had previously published books on the Chinese army and on Sino-Soviet relations for the Royal Institute of International Affairs. The other cap I would be wearing was a Mao cap that I bought in the Shanghai No. 1 department store and wore not only while traveling around the country but for some time after my return to England.

It has been instructive for me in preparing this chapter to reread both what I had previously written for the *Far Eastern Economic Review* and the five articles I wrote for the *Guardian* after my first visit to China.[4] The conclusion that I reach, with some regret, is that I was better able in Hong Kong to resist the absolutes of the Cold War than during my firsthand experience of visiting China. The circumstances in both cases were very special, though that does not absolve me from critical responsibility. In 1968–1969, the written sources available for understanding China had been greatly enriched by a flood of so-called Red Guard material. This material was not confined to the accounts of bloody battles, often but not always exaggerated, that were headlined outside China. It also included unexpurgated texts of speeches by Mao, transcripts or summaries of internal leadership discussion and conflict, and a good deal of serious political thought and argument. It was as if we journalists were watching, from Hong Kong, a vast stage on which several plays were being acted out at the same time. Given the highly theatrical and declamatory nature of the political culture and lexis of the time, we may have been better able to discern an overall sense and pattern in the drama if we were in the audience than if we were behind the scenes and unable to see the whole stage.

In addition, the information brought by refugees and by travelers from China (though often spiced up by Western intelligence services) provided a degree of corroboration. A number of younger China scholars, mostly using the facilities of the Universities' Service Center in Hong Kong, and some of them *Bulletin of Concerned Asian Scholars* members, helped generate a debate on the Cultural Revolution (often hotly argued) that drew on all these sources. In this stimulating atmosphere, I came to the following conclusion in February 1969 when the Cultural Revolution, in the more limited sense of the period of Red Guard struggle, appeared to have come to an end:

> Neither sweet nor sour, the picture of the Chinese people which has now emerged from the Cultural Revolution assumes for the first time since 1949 something of a three-dimensional character. The mixture of idealism and op-portunism which it has revealed, the remarkable variety of regional, cultural and occupational differences, the wide range of human activities and emo-tions, all add up to a much more complex picture which resists pigeon-holing to the last.[5]

This "three-dimensional" picture that I and other China-watchers sought to convey embraced both the violence and the idealism of the Cultural Revo-lution. We saw the bodies that had floated into the harbor all the way from Guangxi's extreme factional violence. We also read documents such as the Shengwulian manifesto, from an iconoclastic group in Hunan that criti-cized both the CCP and the armed forces and called for the creation of a People's Commune of China.

Reviewing what I wrote for the *Guardian* three years later, after several weeks actually spent in China, I have to admit that the picture I conveyed was more often two- than three-dimensional. Certainly I had been able to observe the everyday detail of life in China in a way that was impossible from afar. Yet in judgment I focused on the idealism of it without acknowl-edging the warping effect of violence and the cult of Mao. I quote again, less happily, from my first article in the *Guardian*.

> It is the sense of a collective spirit which is perhaps, most impressive in educa-tion as it is in the rest of Chinese life. And the Thought of Mao Zedong, itself a rather off-putting concept for eclectically minded visiting Western intellectu-als, begins to make sense as the cement which holds the whole system together. It is not so much a cult of personality but more a collective way of life, which provides the moral imperatives for the youth of China who will inherit Mao's revolution.[6]

The balance could have been corrected if I had written a sixth article in which I listed, without comment, the incidents I had witnessed that hinted at a more troubled reality beneath the surface—and which I still vividly re-call. There was the visit I received early one morning from a village store-keeper (the village was some distance away) who had sold me a couple of books the day before. Escorted by two officials and looking shaken, he ex-plained that regulations did not allow the sale of "provincial titles" to for-eigners: he thrust into my hands the exact sum I had paid in return for the books. Then there was the attempt some of us made to go by bus into

Hangzhou one evening from the hotel where we were staying. We were pursued by our minders, who forced the bus to stop while they explained their concern that we might "get lost." And there was the army commander who joined his men in hoeing a field to demonstrate how "the army and the people are one." Either inexperienced or impatient with the performance, he pushed too vigorously and the tool snapped in his hands.

I shall always regret I did not write that sixth article for the *Guardian*.

AFTER THE CULTURAL REVOLUTION

No one imagined in the early to mid-1970s that within little more than a decade the feature of Maoist socialism that had seemed most distinctive— the People's communes with their systems of collective distribution— would have been jettisoned all over China. Even after the factional struggles of 1975–1976 between Deng Xiaoping and the ultra-left, followed by the death of Mao Zedong and arrest of the Gang of Four, the extent of impending change was not easily foreseen. Foreign observers tended to look for continuity (and foreign diplomats had a vested interest in predicting it): the Chinese who had lived through the upheavals of the past two decades were more realistic. Urged on by one clear-sighted Chinese intellectual in 1978, I predicted that the Cultural Revolution would soon be repudiated. This seemed a bold and even shocking forecast, as was my report on the return of meritocratic selection and the revival of elite "key schools."

The 1980s were a golden time for reporting from China. The upheaval following Mao's death ensured that editorial interest remained high. There was a real desire to know in which direction the Chinese would now move and how far along the chosen road. Even the smallest details were revealing: the new magazines with titles like *World Cinema* and *Modern Living*, the three-piece suits carried home on pedicabs, the notices pinned to lampposts advertising private English lessons, domestic maids for hire, burial plots for sale in the countryside, and the lists of bonus rates on factory blackboards.

As I wrote in October 1978,

> If there was one thing of which most observers outside China were thoroughly convinced during the Cultural Revolution, it was that bonuses had died a decisive death . . . The Shanghai dockers had surely got it right when, rejecting a proposed bonus scheme in 1974, they proclaimed that "We shall be masters of the wharf, not of tonnage!"

How wrong, I now had to admit, we all had been.[7]

Yet it was not yet taken for granted that China had entirely forsaken Mao's road to socialism, and there was still talk of the need to maintain a balance between public and private interest. As I was told in the Fujian countryside in 1983 and on the authority (it was claimed) of Deng Xiaoping himself, "We have to create a new spirit of enthusiasm and a new form of collective."[8] Questions of the "Whither China?" variety, which had been raised at intervals throughout the twentieth century ever since the 1919 student movement, were still worth asking in the 1980s. Already raised by the Shengwulian in Hunan and other radical groups or individuals, they were posed in new ways by the authors of the pamphlets and wall newspapers of the Democracy Wall (1978–1980) who had been politicized by the Cultural Revolution.

It was not only Western academics and journalists who sought an answer to "Whither China?" The itineraries of many tour groups—a fast-expanding business—continued to feature didactic visits to school, factories, or communes, just as they had under the more limited conditions of "friendship travel." Of course, they now included more visits to carpet factories, because these were the classic destinations to which every tourist was taken, willingly or otherwise, by guides who hoped for a percentage compensation or "kickback." However, it was only in the 1990s that tourism in China (except for a very small number of specialized tours) would be reduced to visiting famous sites, staying in four-star hotels, and shopping endlessly.

The political scene grew increasingly lively in the 1980s with the officially sponsored reforms of Deng Xiaoping and those of Party Secretary-General Hu Yaobang, who encouraged a number of reform-minded scholars such as Su Shaozhi and Li Yining to take the debate farther. These reformers were opposed by those who resisted changes that challenged the basis of Mao's socialist vision (and threatened to diminish their own prerogatives). Regrettably though, this lively intellectual ferment was often disparaged at the time by Western diplomats and businesspeople. For them, the most important changes were taking place in foreign policy, where China had formed an opportunistic entente with the West against the Soviet Union, and in the new opportunities for foreign business offered by special economic zones (SEZs) and joint ventures. The significance of the student movement at the time was also talked down, and its protagonists were often dismissed as politically immature. In May 1989, as students were massing in Tiananmen Square and the party leadership split over how to deal with them, the British embassy in Beijing advised the Foreign Office in London not to expect a great upheaval. What was happening was merely part of "the cyclical process of Chinese politics." Indeed, none of us foresaw the truly seismic nature of this event.

REPORTING THE MASSACRE

The Beijing massacre changed the terms of reference under which China was reported in the West and—to a lesser extent—the way in which the ruling regime was viewed by Western governments. After the relative optimism of the 1980s, the reactionary backlash of the old guard in the leadership was a dismal shock. What happened on the night of June 3–4, 1989 (and on subsequent days when the random killings continued), and the repression of the next several years seemed to present a definitively negative answer to all those questions about whether the CCP could accommodate itself to peaceful political change. Many journalists (including me) felt fully entitled to editorialize on the party's illegitimacy, which many of our Chinese friends now took for granted. During those heady weeks of May 1989 in Beijing, we had seen a new force emerge in the streets—not just the students who poured in from all over the country but the people of Beijing themselves, reproaching the confused young soldiers who had been ordered in, staffing the citizens' checkpoints that sought to keep the army away from the city center, and displaying a sense of comradeship that recalled the early years after 1949. The apparently terminal opposition between the party and popular values was dramatized in the contrast between the tired, old, official slogan "Long live the Communist Party of China"—now confined to official statements on press and television—and the newly revived mass slogan "Long live the People" that was carried on banners in Tiananmen Square and shouted by the students with thanks to the people of Beijing.

The inhumanity of a regime that, in the view of so many ordinary Beijingers (and of the *Guardian*'s front page on June 4), had "declared war on its own people" was exposed after the massacre in endless replays on global television. As Eastern Europe began to stir restlessly (in part—especially in Czechoslovakia—because of the Chinese example), we were not so naïve as to postulate that the CCP might crumble or be overthrown. At best, as I suggested three weeks after the massacre, there was a chance that a "responsible leadership" would regain control and put those who had authorized the bloodshed (I included Deng Xiaoping among them) on trial.

It was also hard to dissent from the oversimplified picture of what had actually happened during those terrible nights and days. A ruthless army, it was said, had blasted its way into Beijing under orders from party conservatives; thousands had been killed in the process, including large numbers of students mown down in Tiananmen Square—some of them still sleeping in their tents. But in reality, and however dreadful the event, it was more complicated than that. Massacres tend to get overreported, particularly when those who do the reporting are committed to one side and lack previous experience of such situations.

Most of those killed by the soldiers in fact were nonstudent citizens of Beijing who had sought to bar the soldiers' way, with remarkable and mostly unarmed heroism. Others were bystanders or even spectators who had flocked to the center to join the excitement. Body counts are notoriously inaccurate in such situations. The army did not kill several thousands, nor did it mow down hundreds in the square itself or burn their bodies. These subsequent rumors distracted reporters such as me from extrapolating a more accurate body count from the numbers seen in hospitals. The reality was bad enough.

The massacre and its aftermath largely swept away memory of the Western media's collective misjudgment in generally concluding that such a thing could not happen. Before the massacre, the mood had been so exhilarating that I and most of my colleagues had no time or patience for the chore of traditional China watching. Yet a daily reading of official messages of loyalty in the press would have shown us that a reluctant army was being brought inexorably into line. We were also confused because a section of the Chinese media, having broken away from central control, was printing its own overoptimistic assessment of the popular movement.

The nature of the power struggle at the center was also imperfectly understood, not only by us but by a great majority of the student demonstrators. Optimism should have been dispelled when moderate leader Zhao Ziyang was ousted just before martial law was declared. Instead we and the demonstrators believed that the victors in the struggle, Premier Li Peng and President Yang Shangkun, could somehow be evicted by an obscure constitutional process involving the National People's Congress. This was defective logic. The students were demonstrating in order to bring about a constitutionality that did not yet exist. It could hardly now materialize to save them. The error was compounded just days before the massacre when hundreds of thousands marched to the single slogan "Down with Li Peng"—a futile demand, since he had already been victorious in the internal power struggle.

The death toll resulting from these events is still unclear and will remain so until a proper enquiry is carried out in Beijing. Only a very few correspondents (not including me) remained in the center of the square where thousands of students waited quietly around the Martyrs' Memorial. There they witnessed the final retreat of most of the students through the southeast corner several hours later, after negotiations with the army and a voice vote in favor of withdrawing. There was a horrific incident when a tank ploughed through a line of students at Liubukou, to the west of the square, after they had marched away, yet the official claim that "no one died in the square" was probably true.

Who then were the victims of what we are still justified in calling the Beijing massacre? The army had orders to spare the students if possible but had been authorized to use all necessary means to reach and then defend the square. Most of the attested deaths took place on the approach roads to the square—the vast majority on and around the western section of Chang'an-jie (Chang'an Avenue). Some of those shot were targeted because they were throwing missiles, others were part of crowds seeking to block the way, and quite a number were killed by ricochet shots—including some in their apartments overlooking the avenue. On the next day, several dozen people were shot as they attempted to approach the army lines around the square to remonstrate. In the next few days, there were cases where soldiers shot at isolated groups of civilians, either fearing hostile intent or out of panic or indiscipline. The overall total was, I believe, in the hundreds, not thousands. (The routine formula used to this day by the Associated Press seeks to avoid judgment by saying that "hundreds, if not thousands, died.") However many actually died, it remains of course an entirely unacceptable action for a government to take against its own people.[9]

RETHINKING IN THE 1990S

For some time after the Beijing massacre, it seemed reasonable to suppose that the days—or at least the years—of the CCP were numbered. The examples of the collapse of the Soviet Union and the Eastern European regimes were close at hand. In Beijing, the sense of the Chinese people being stifled by an arid as well as repressive reaction was overwhelming. Nothing much might be happening, but as one dissident writer described it, the democracy movement was like "a bamboo shoot crushed beneath a stone [and] the Chinese people are waiting for the spring rain to fall" so that the bamboo would start growing and push the stone aside.[10]

Yet depression, even despair, does not necessarily lead to rebellion. A few activists continued to bravely challenge the authorities; many others concluded that only (in the words of one analysis produced by a Beijing group) "economic development will guarantee the pursuit of democracy." The changes set in motion, deliberately or otherwise, by the reforms of the 1980s continued to gather pace: there was more social mobility and more entrepreneurial activity, as well as more crime and corruption. Those former students who put economic development first joined the migratory flow heading for the SEZs on the coast. After Deng Xiaoping had embarked on his Southern Tour and kick-started the economic revolution back to life in 1992—and in a higher gear, too—the tentative political revolution that had made a faltering start during the late 1980s began to appear dated and, as a new urban boom developed, irrelevant.

It was about this time that I detected a significant waning of media interest in the sort of "Whither China?" query that had attracted such lively debate in the previous decade. Deng Xiaoping's tour confirmed beyond doubt that China was taking the capitalist road: no one talked any longer about a return to genuine socialist alternatives, and there were no longer any open question about China's destination. The speed of Chinese economic progress swept all before it: as British prime minister John Major remarked when told that China's progress was generating significant social problems, "There can't be much wrong with eight percent GDP growth." A new set of images began to appear on the front covers of Western news magazines, embodying a mixture of admiration and fear at the Chinese advance. To quote from a few in the early months of 1996:

"'China': A Billion Consumers" (*Economist*)
"The Twenty-first Century Starts Here: China Booms; the World Holds Its Breath" (*New York Times Magazine*)
"China on the Move" (*Newsweek*)

The subheading of the *Newsweek* cover story indicates the question that predominated in the U.S. media (the British media were temporarily more interested in the fate of Hong Kong):

After 500 years of humiliation, a surging China is about to reclaim its historical position as one of the world's great powers. But will the reborn China be a friend to the West? or a daunting foe?[11]

These threatening images of China's putative menace often came close to re-evoking the old myth of the "yellow peril." Bizarrely, the notion that China might become a dangerous threat to the Western world existed alongside an entirely opposed set of images focused on the decline and even collapse of the Chinese state. These were no longer related to the suggestion that the Chinese people would become impatient for democracy, which they had been denied in 1989. The argument rather was that rapid economic and social change was creating new tensions, which could not be contained indefinitely. Certainly there were grounds for this view in the growth of urban unemployment, the failure of the regime to check corruption, the creation of a new underclass of migrant workers, and the emergence of new cults such as Falun Gong to fill an ethical void left by the collapse of most of the earlier socialist values.

Yet the metaphors of swirling disintegration were also more seductive, because they helped to maintain interest—not least among media editors—in a story that seemed to have otherwise no end in sight. Thus when the death of Deng Xiaoping appeared imminent, it was almost obligatory to ask, "Will China collapse?" because the idea that post-Deng China would probably get by under the post-Deng leadership that Deng himself had approved was much less arresting. Hong Kong's handover in the same year (1997) prompted widespread speculation that Hong Kong's freedoms would disappear almost overnight. The entry of People's Liberation Army units into the territory, crossing the border within hours of the handover, was widely reported as a symbolic turning point. When these stark predictions proved groundless, much of the Western media overlooked the more gradual erosion of Hong Kong's autonomy in the coming years. The dispute over "right of abode," which led to a "reinterpretation" of the Basic Law by Beijing to the detriment of the powers of Hong Kong's Court of Final Appeal, seemed too complex and legalistic. Beijing's sponsorship of the unpopular chief executive Tung Chee-hwa for a second term was also underreported. My own newspaper, the *Guardian*, did not think it worthwhile to send me from Shanghai to Hong Kong to cover the fifth anniversary of the handover. Media interest only revived in 2003, when public unhappiness over a new security law (the Article 23 controversy) brought a million people into the streets of Hong Kong on the sixth anniversary of the handover.

CONSTRAINTS AND BIAS

Coverage of China in the late 1990s included some excellent reporting, particularly by a number of energetic journalists from the United States, where interest in China, and therefore space, was more sustained. The best of U.S. journalism, I have to admit, outstripped our own British efforts, which sometimes seemed casual and underresearched. (French reporting, notably in *Le Monde* and *Liberation*, was often more thoughtful than either.) The main U.S. bureaus based in China were better resourced and staffed: they often had superior access to the Chinese authorities, who were and are particularly sensitive to their media image in the country they love best, or hate worst. Serious reporting also benefited from U.S. reporters' being given more space in which to do so: the *Washington Post* or *Los Angeles Times* could often spare 1,500–2,000 words on a story to which the *Guardian* or *Daily Telegraph* could only assign 700–800 words. Two examples of effective reporting by the U.S. media at the end of the decade were the *Wall Street Journal*'s coverage of the suppression of Falun Gong, and the *New York Times* exposé of the HIV/AIDS epidemic in Henan province (caused by contaminated blood collection).

Many young Chinese journalists admired (and continue to admire) such reporting and looked forward to the day when they too would be able to tackle sensitive social issues without government constraint. Yet it was also true that many of the Chinese who had lived and worked abroad, however critical of their own government, often complained of unbalanced foreign-media coverage, especially that of the U.S. media. They said that while it was absolutely correct for the foreign media to focus on human rights abuses and China's lack of political freedom, there was an overall lack of balance—a failure to report positively—which to them often appeared to reflect deliberate bias.

One reason for this was restrictive regulations covering the activities of foreign journalists in China, which encouraged an antagonistic relationship between foreign journalists and the authorities who imposed the regulations (see chapter 1, where a similar conclusion is reached). Anyone who sought to report on a sensitive story without permission (which would not be granted—or at least, not in time to satisfy impatient news editors at home) risked a reprimand for "unauthorized news gathering." The stories written by those who did break the rules were necessarily written without official cooperation and relied on informants whose evidence was usually difficult to check and whose own safety might be compromised (and sometimes was, with disastrous effects) by having "given unauthorized information" or even for having "revealed state secrets." Many of these stories thus lacked the minimum balance that would be thought essential elsewhere. If a dissident claimed to have been tortured in prison, there was rarely a formal denial, let alone the opportunity to investigate the claim. Inevitably, some of this reporting suffered from one-sidedness or exaggeration, which then gave ammunition to conservative elements in the Beijing control apparatus who argued against a more open policy.

More information became available from Western and Chinese academics as time went on, or from nongovernmental organizations (NGOs), which could communicate more fruitfully with their Chinese counterparts and to some extent with Chinese government sources. By the late 1990s, a growing number of Chinese newspapers, led by *Nanfang Zhoumo* [*Southern Weekend*], were developing skills in investigative journalism in spite of intermittent government harassment or shut-downs. The most successful reporting from China drew from all these sources to provide a more balanced picture, but on high-profile issues the correspondent might have difficulty in overcoming an editorial desire to produce a black-and-white account.

Another problem was the persistence of a simplistic view, with its origins in the Cold War era, that regarded Chinese Communism as both uniquely reprehensible and incapable of improvement. The dominance of the U.S. media ensured that the view from Washington, D.C., often set the context for Western news reporting of the major stories from China, even though the official parameters might shift abruptly. This became particularly noticeable in coverage of U.S.-China relations in the late 1990s and early 2000s when these were complicated by the transition from the Clinton to the Bush administration.

During Bill Clinton's visit to China in June 1998, the U.S. media first focused upon the plight of Chinese political dissidents, but many reporters took a more complacent view after President Clinton was allowed to call for democracy in an address broadcast live on Chinese television. The White House's simplistic view that President Clinton had established a special rapport with President Jiang Zemin was widely echoed: in fact, President Jiang clamped down within months upon the fledgling Chinese Democracy Party. However a year later, after the United States had bombed the Chinese embassy in Belgrade during the Kosovo war, there was little sympathy for China, which was frequently accused of overreacting. The stage-managed character of the resulting anti-U.S. demonstrations in China received more attention than the genuine anger that they reflected—and that the Chinese government's control measures sought partly to contain.

Western coverage tended to miss the real point that in spite of this provocation, the Jiang regime was determined to maintain, if at all possible, good relations with the United States. (While there were "ups and downs" in U.S.-China relations, said *Renmin ribao* [*People's Daily*], friendly ties between the two countries were "of great importance to the whole world.")[12] Official and popular Chinese reaction in April 2001 to an incident in which a U.S. spy plane made a forced landing on Hainan Island after a collision with a Chinese fighter was also often looked at through a critical U.S. lens. Chinese reaction to the September 11 terrorist attacks on the United States was also subject to misinterpretation. Compared to its usual standards, the Chinese media reported the attack with unusual speed, and official condolences were quickly sent. Popular opinion on the street and in Chinese Internet chat rooms, however, was more varied, with some expressing the view that the United States had only got what it deserved. Yet Western commentators were quick to reproach Beijing for an alleged lack of sympathy: the *Wall Street Journal* even accused "an isolated China [of] seek[ing] friends among the rogue nations of the world."

The reality is that Beijing wanted to maintain the momentum of improved U.S.-China relations in spite of the spy plane crisis and that it had its own domestic reasons for supporting an international war against terror. There was also satisfaction in Beijing that the Bush administration now had a "real enemy" on which to focus instead of demonizing China, as several leading neoconservative figures in Washington had done since the inauguration of George W. Bush. September 11 was described by the *People's Daily* as "a turning-point in the post–Cold War pattern,"[13] and Beijing took advantage of it to step up repression, with tacit U.S. approval, of its own (mostly peaceful) Muslim separatists in Northwest China.

CONCLUSION

In the long term, Western journalists' ability to report China accurately depends above all on the further improvement of mainland journalism. Foreign reporters in all countries rely heavily (whether they admit it or not) on the work of their domestic colleagues, and China is already no exception. As I've indicated, a small but growing number of newspapers in China have acquired a reputation for investigative journalism. More critical writing, including theoretical arguments that implicitly criticize the CCP, can be found on the Internet. Some websites also carry material that originates among critical scholars in Hong Kong or even Taiwan and the United States. Finally, open criticism of the party both from Right (liberal) and Left (neo-Maoist) perspectives is aired on popular Web discussion groups, though the most outspoken contributions will be censored by website monitors.

A *Nanfang Zhoumo* issue in October 2001 gives us an idea of the range of material that astute editors have been able to publish. The front-page article headlined "Will Growing Chinese Soya Beans Infringe American 'Rights'?" was a detailed critique of U.S. agribusiness Monsanto's attempts to secure a broad species patent based upon work it had done with wild soybeans originating from South China. The article, based on briefings from Greenpeace and Chinese environmentalists, was sensitive at the time because China was about to enter the World Trade Organization (WTO) to a fanfare of self-congratulation; Monsanto's case against Chinese growers, the article warned, would be strengthened by the application of WTO rules.

In the same issue, an inside, full-page exposé of illegal timber felling in a county in southwestern Hunan revealed how strict government restrictions had been regularly flouted for the past ten years. It made it clear that this was being done with the complicity of the local Forestry Bureau. While Beijing in principle approves of such exposés, this one came at an awkward time because the government was at the time officially claiming that logging restrictions (tightened up in the previous three years) were now working well. Another short but devastating piece, with grim pictures, took the reader into a privately owned Shaanxi gold mine where poor peasants worked without masks in filthy conditions (several peasants had already died in the same mine). The reporter who wrote the article masqueraded as a miner in order to obtain firsthand information. Chinese journalists who investigate abuses of this kind, I should note, may be beaten or harassed if their identities are discovered. Again, the article raised a serious question about the laxity of government controls.

The use of modern communications—particularly the Internet and mobile technology—to break down the walls of official secrecy in China was illustrated powerfully by the SARS (severe acute respiratory syndrome) crisis in 2003. While Beijing sought to minimize news of the spread of the virus, many thousands of Chinese accessed foreign reports and circulated information by e-mail. As *Caijing* (another outspoken magazine) commented, the choice was between "listening to backstreet gossip and going on the Web." Later the government issued regulations banning the circulation of "electronic rumors," but to no effect. This was the latest round in an ongoing struggle between the regime and civil society, which intensified in the early 2000s when more than twenty journalists and civil rights campaigners were jailed for using the Internet to disseminate "subversive" material. Yet the traffic in electronic news and comment continues to grow, with a wealth of material appearing on sensitive social issues such as the widening gap between rich and poor in China, official corruption, discrimination against migrant workers, and HIV/AIDS. Many of the arguments openly made in these materials would in the past have been denounced as "counter-revolutionary" or "poisonous weeds."

Press freedom in China remains a patchy field in which the mood relaxes and then tightens, where editors who "go too far" may be demoted, and where publications and websites may be censured or closed down. However, many younger Chinese journalists feel that the system is improving slowly and are poised to seize any opportunity that arises. Foreign journalists who complain about restrictions on their own freedom should give full credit to the determination of their Chinese counterparts. We foreign journalists should also be prepared to admit that such restrictions are not an acceptable excuse for shoddy or biased reporting. Unglamorous as it may sound to Western news desks, especially in this new world of high-pressure, round-the-clock coverage, reporting from China still needs balance and consideration—and the foreign media does not have a monopoly on the truth.

Looking back over nearly four decades of writing about China, mostly in a journalistic frame, I have to concur with the judgment of a very senior Chinese official who once said to me, "You have written many articles about our country: some are comparatively correct; others are not so correct." To the obstacles placed in reporters' way by Chinese officials' own bureaucracy must be added the barriers imposed by Cold War politics, which have not yet been wholly demolished, and by more long-standing cultural misconceptions about China in the West. The sheer gap between our societies—including differences in class structure, style of life, and expectations—also play a significant part. On my first visit to Beijing with the SACU delegation, we stayed at the Beijing Hotel, which at that time, we were told, possessed the only automatic entrance and exit doors in the country. Crowds of fascinated Chinese, mostly from outside the capital, gathered beyond the security guards on the pavement to watch foreigners emerge through this amazing device. It is an appropriate metaphor for our partial vision of those spectators (and theirs of us): much later when I published a collection of my reports over the years, I gave it the title "China through the Sliding Door." Nowadays, when there are probably as many sliding doors in Beijing or Shanghai as in London or New York, the gap in perception has significantly narrowed, but there is still a long way to go.

NOTES

1. I've chosen the term *Beijing massacre* over the more commonly used *Tiananmen massacre* because there is little evidence that any killing occurred within Tiananmen

Square. Rather, the first rage of violent repression in the days of June 3–4 and the subsequent sporadic street shooting killed a great many in Beijing streets such as Chang'anjie (Chang'an Avenue) off the square.

2. See John Gittings, "Japanese Rewrite *Guardian* History," *Guardian*, October 4, 2002; and John Gittings, "Agnes Smedley and the *Manchester Guardian*," www .johngittings.com (July 1, 2006).

3. The subject was very usefully revisited by the *Bulletin of Concerned Asian Scholars* in a 1996 conference. See Mark Selden, ed., "Asia, Asian Studies and the National Security State," *Bulletin of Concerned Asian Scholars* 29:1.

4. Extracts from both in John Gittings, *China through the Sliding Door* (London: Simon and Schuster, 1999), chs. 1–2.

5. Gittings, *China through the Sliding Door*, 29.

6. Gittings, *China through the Sliding Door*, 40.

7. Gittings, *China through the Sliding Door*, 63.

8. Gittings, *China through the Sliding Door*, 88–89.

9. This account of media coverage of the Beijing massacre is based upon my essay "Accuracy and Chaos: Reporting Tiananmen," in *Reporting the News from China*, ed. Robin Porter (London: Royal Institute of International Affairs, 1992).

10. *Guardian*, "Chinese Spirit Begins to Stir after Blood and Fire," May 31, 1990.

11. *Newsweek*, "China on the Move," April 1, 1996.

12. *People's Daily* editorial, June 3, 1999.

13. *People's Daily* website, September 17, 2001.

SUGGESTED READINGS

Mobo C. F. Gao, *Gao Village: Rural Life in Modern China* (London: Hurst, 1999).

John Gittings, *Real China: From Cannibalism to Karaoke* (London: Simon and Schuster, 1996).

Colin Mackerras, *Western Images of China*, rev. ed. (Oxford: Oxford University Press, 1999).

Wang Chaohua, ed., *One China, Many Paths* (London: Verso, 2003).

Zhang Lijia and Calum Macleod, eds., *China Remembers* (Hong Kong: Oxford University Press, 1999).

Afterword

China, the United States, and the Fragile Planet

Lionel M. Jensen

The American way of life is not up for negotiation.

—President George H. W. Bush, 1989

No rich person in China was born to be rich, except maybe the chairman of the Communist Party. All the Mercs [Mercedes] you see driving around Beijing today are the product of people learning the tricks of the trade and working hard these last few years.

—anonymous Chinese millionaire, 1999

The essays that make up this volume provide evidence for why we must understand China and also why such understanding is difficult—perhaps even impossible—to come by. Even within the confined context of a collection of chapters, the picture of China we've painted here is so diverse that it might be seen as more a Rauschenberg collage rather than a traditional Chinese landscape. China has always defied simple characterization, but today its complexity challenges, as never before, any observer's comprehension. However, viewing this complexity through the critical eyes of an engaged self-scrutiny enables the viewer to understand contemporary conditions in both China and the United States.

I would like to focus here on two aspects deserving further consideration: first, the environmental consequences of rapid economic expansion, and second, the West's increasingly apprehensive interpretation of China's recent growth. My concern is to urge the reader to think beyond the conventional framework of nation-states and bilateral relations by considering the fragile ecology of growth in the political condition of competitive superpowers.

Here I wish to write not of China's transformations—about which the reader has already learned much—but of the ways the United States and China must reconsider their worldviews as the principal forces of global economic and political might. Estimates that by 2040 the world's total production of carbon gases will exceed 530 gigatons, that the global temperature will have increased by two degrees centigrade, and that catastrophic climate change will ensue make it imperative that we reconcile our demands for material wealth with the earth's finite resources. However, the politics of neither the United States nor China favors such a reckoning, so it is toward this tipping point that these two grand developers rush headlong.

Contrary to government leaders' assertions in an earlier era that "China will never be a superpower,"[1] China has certainly attained the status of an economic superpower. When measured in terms of purchasing power parity, it is now the second-largest economy in the world, having overcome France, Germany, Italy, Japan, Russia, and the United Kingdom in 2004. At the very least, it will before long take its place alongside the United States as a superpower. Whether in actual size, accomplishment, or aspiration, there are no other contenders.[2] Since the 2002 U.S. National Security Strategy call for preemptive war against potential international adversaries, the "rise of China" can only betoken security difficulties for the United States. And for this reason the U.S. Department of Defense has issued statements in support of additional military expenditures to underwrite the production of weapons with long-range strike capability in order to cope with anticipated security threats from China. The Quadrennial Defense Review released in early 2006 found that "of the major emerging powers, China has the greatest potential to compete militarily with the United States and field disruptive military technologies that could over time offset traditional U.S. military advantages absent U.S. counter strategies."[3] Such reports can be expected from military minds trained to recognize other nations as potential enemies, and they reflect policy orientations that have been operant throughout the long history of post–World War II U.S.-China relations. However, China offers little credible evidence of military threat, spending dramatically less on defense than the United States (which expends more annually on defense than all of the Group of 8 [G8] powers combined). It is really the more immediate threat posed by China's gargantuan demand for energy that is the source of U.S. disquiet, as was revealed in a political flap in summer 2005 over the attempted purchase of Unocal Corporation by state-owned Chinese National Offshore Oil Corporation.[4]

The reader must remember that China is still a poor country, and one of the world's most successful newly industrializing economies (NIEs), even as it lends the United States billions of dollars to sustain a deeply indebted U.S. national economy (see figure A.1). China is a nation of contradictions every bit as confounding as those of the United States, but it is clearly on an upward

Figure A.1.   The old and new side by side in a mountain village. (Photo: Peter H. Jaynes)

global political trajectory, while the United States, still prominent, is in decline. China is a twenty-first-century nation with twenty-first-century problems and prospects, having surpassed the United States as the world's greatest
consumer of basic commodities (with the exception of oil).[5] The epigraphs
that opened this chapter highlight the stubborn commitment to materialist
aspirations that inspired both countries' success and portend their failure. The
first statement, from former U.S. president George H. W. Bush, is a simple declaration of noncompromise in advance of the 1989 meetings that resulted in
the Kyoto Protocol. All items were on the table save those that would imperil
the U.S. national standard of living. The second is an anecdote, a statement of
social fact offered by one of China's roughly 240,000 millionaires, that conveys the pride of accomplishment of a material standard of affluence familiar

to anyone in the United States. What does this shift mean for each nation and, more importantly, for the planet? Getting at this question requires some context on my own role as an observer of China's transformations.

For more than three decades I have been a student of China, its art, civilization, culture, history, politics, and religion. As well, in the course of graduate study I have been a foreign student resident in China and Taiwan. My advanced graduate study of China began before there were official relations between it and the United States, so it was fortunate—or was it inevitable?—that my scholarly interest was in premodern intellectual history, a body of research that is textual rather than human. However, I have come of professional age as a Sinologist in the era of China's great transformation. This transformation is every bit as significant as the popular revolution that brought the Communists to power and drew so many admiring Western students from their bourgeois lives to the cause of Chinese Marxism and the promise of erasing economic inequality and political oppression. These ideas, ideas we believed we saw at work in the voluntaristic programs of the utopian socialist reforms of the 1950s, 1960s, and 1970s, especially the Cultural Revolution, stoked the fire of our admiration for Chinese accomplishments.

Because we could not go to China before 1979, we saw China through an opaque prism of surmise and second-hand sources. The context we lacked—and we lacked much—was made up for by obsessive reading of the *Peking Review* and *China Reconstructs* (both published in China in English for the foreign reader), *Modern China*, the *Bulletin of Concerned Asian Scholars*, and the *Survey of China Mainland Press* (a collection of articles from Chinese newspapers translated for the CIA's Joint Publications Research Service), and investigations into the documents of the Asia Research Centre at the Chinese University of Hong Kong. What we couldn't see, we imagined, and always with an air of radical romance, as was revealed in the earliest published reports of the first encounters between Western scholars and the real China, such as the Committee of Concerned Asian Scholars' *China! Inside the People's Republic* and Orville Schell's *In the People's Republic*.[6] Like intellectuals in the time of the Weimar Republic (1918–1933) or those in the streets of Paris in the heady days of the 1968 student uprisings, aspiring "China hands" desperately sought alignment with the working people, believing with fierce intensity that the pen pushed the plow. For this sense of purpose, we found in Mao Zedong's concepts of practice, struggle, uninterrupted revolution, and will an answer of which we were proud. We were all Maoists wearing black-cotton shoes with tire-tread soles, olive-green Mao caps emblazoned with red stars, and sometimes even carrying the Little Red Book.

What we admired, in the style of any generational rebellion, was the bold, nihilistic thrust of Mao as the Great Helmsman damning all caution, casting himself and the CCP into the void in the service of a larger human transformation to remake a society in revolution. As well, we were enthralled with Mao's dogged insistence on a political economy governed by a philosophy of working with the poorest rather than investing in the wealthiest classes in society. This philosophy stood in dramatic contrast to our own society and government in the 1960s and 1970s—disabled by contradiction internally, viscerally divided by an illegitimate foreign war of U.S. occupation in Vietnam, Cambodia, and Laos and by racist domestic politics, and with an unquestioned commitment to the enduring middle-class suburban everyday. It is no wonder that China, its people, its compelling recent history, and its visionary leadership were so admired. Our idealistic fervor felt for the grand Chinese experiment and our lack of reliable empirical knowledge of its tragic human consequences—mass starvation in the Great Leap Forward, the pathological aggression of the Cultural Revolution—troublingly compromised our understanding. We were the holders of a very passionate, purely idealistic admiration that had yet to be reconciled with reality.

The admiration we have today is of a different quality. To my mind it is less profound, because it is less visceral. Knowing of China's recent past of poverty and suffering, Sinologists admire what China has become and is becoming so quickly. Our esteem is measured in the economic transformation of the countryside and in an elevated standard of living, but more dramatically in the hyper-modernization of China's urban landscape and in the glaring familiarity of the global commercial imprint of Louis Vuitton, Gap, Starbucks, Motorola, Ritz Carlton, McDonalds, and other corporate entities, in partnership with Sohu.com and Sina.com, the principal Internet service providers (ISPs) and Internet content providers (ICPs) for the Chinese people. Looking at this commercial excess now, pleasure and astonishment greet the realization that China has made its mark on the world in a way that the world is willing and able to acknowledge.

For those of my Sinological generation in particular, there is in the global embrace of China's transformation an uncommon sense of the heightened *use-value*, as Marx would deem it, of our knowledge of a language and place once seen as strange and forbidding but now in sharp demand. Intellectuals, especially those devoted to the study of China in that earlier political time of remoteness, were an exaggerated *surplus-value*: self-supporting or federally sponsored students of a distant country that was a virtual enemy. If knowledge is power, there was then little popular-culture premium for Sinological wisdom. Today it is obvious how powerful knowledge of China has become; yet its application in the offering of professional opinion or tailoring of intelligence for a China-hungry foreign affairs establishment and an equally ravenous popular media brings little real satisfaction, because it is so easy. As well, it raises sharp questions about the public responsibilities of the China scholar.

In these few reflections on the state of contemporary China, I defer to this public responsibility and confide my subjective inclination to focus on deficiencies in the face of exuberance and achievement. This is naturally a reflection of my temperament, an optimism wounded by the cost of China's contemporary transformation, the militantly arrogant overextension of U.S. power across the globe, and the astonishing resurrection of the Cold War international political frame that yielded so much grief and so little gain. Even in an age of globalization, where one might hope that a fledgling cosmopolitanism would emerge, the din of profit making and the urgency of the struggle for resources to produce more wealth that cannot, because it will not, be equitably distributed are so overwhelming that they impair reflection. In this light, U.S. and Chinese economic aspirations reveal folly, not fortune—two of the largest economies in the world, both dedicated to a philosophy of thoroughly unsustainable growth. Not one nation laying claim against another for the same needs but a convergence of peoples led by governments ill equipped to train them for the very hard choices that are upon them. In January 2006, General Motors (GM) was proud to announce that in 2005 it had sold 665,390 vehicles in China, a 35.2 percent increase over the previous year and enough to make it the number-one seller of cars to the Chinese, having secured 11.2 percent of China's automobile market.[7] Over that same interval, the United States' trade deficit with China exceeded US$200 billion. Securing a dominant market share, one of the keys to profit making, does not bring economic security, at least not in a globalized world where the largest debtor and the largest manufacturer meet as equals.

GLOBALIZATION, SUSTAINABILITY, MORAL CRISIS

Globalization is not an expression of progressive values; moreover, it is unlikely to provide a foundation for action on behalf of greater social justice. Heralded in its favored camps as a "rising tide that lifts all boats," globalization has been the engine of China's aggressive economic expansion. But more to the point, the Chinese government's often skillful management of the currents of global capital has sustained the nation's economic revolution. This adept manipulation is well illustrated in the government's collaboration with private developers in the transformation of the Beijing urban landscape. Aggressively asserting its corporate right to repossess property deemed dangerous or in violation of building codes, the government sees to it that property so confiscated is then sold to developers at a handsome price. The government and its functionaries operate as free agents, cynically marketing the privileged space between command and competitive economies. But it should not be axiomatic that the flow of commerce and communication across the globe is good. And given the volatile protests that greeted the

December 2005 meeting of the World Trade Organization (WTO) in Hong Kong it is clear that globalization has its detractors, some of them quite vociferous, even violent.

This is the instinctively coherent frame for a narrative of China as actor on the world stage. However, given the widespread yet little-represented destructiveness of this model of inevitable progress, the frame must be questioned. Rather than accept the astonishment with which China's annual growth figures are cited, one should ask, Why wouldn't the economy grow at more than 9 percent per year for the last fifteen years? The government relaxed decades-old legal constraints and ideological obstructions to profit making and private property. State-owned enterprises (SOEs) had to privatize, and the household registration system (*hukou*) that had bound rural residents to their village, in effect, was abolished, thereby releasing millions for labor on the enterprise of China's modern future. The social complexes of human labor in China were rearranged, and in this large-scale adjustment, a voluminous national energy of economic self-aggrandizement was released (much as Mao had said would occur in revolutionary praxis). The same utopian blandishments of Promethean agency—"A fall in the pit is a leap in your wit"—that inspired the Great Leap Forward and the Cultural Revolution underwrote the economic reforms of the 1980s and 1990s, when Deng Xiaoping's phrase "to get rich is glorious" inspired a national wealth revolution. So, colossal expansion, expansion without compromise with nature or man, is what one might expect to see and what we have seen with the Three Gorges dam and the proposed damming of the Nu river in western Yunnan province.

Acknowledging this does not detract from China's accomplishments, for in this context of hypergrowth there is much to admire and to celebrate. The Chinese should be proud of what they have achieved in the last two decades as hundreds of millions have been brought out of poverty and the average per capita income has increased fivefold. This growth feeds itself, however, promoted feverishly by a government intent on sustaining its political control through a grisly calculus of economic gain the application of which ravages the landscape in generating profit. The consequences are as evident as they are documented, particularly by the country's State Environmental Protection Agency and a scattering of new environmental groups opposed to unlimited development: China has the worst air and water pollution in Asia and a purported average of six thousand deaths per year in a scarcely regulated coal industry, the most dangerous in the world.

The statistical graffiti of China's rise, the ominous and the exhilarating, are just that—numbers. What is the comprehensive political significance of these numbers? What are the risks run by the accumulation of these statistics? Are these risks necessary to the greater well-being of the Chinese people? Western media attention to politics, to the activities of Beijing's leadership, and to the economic transformation of China comes at the expense of so many other dimensions of significance. For example, China is in the throes of a massive banking crisis, largely a consequence of the requisite privatization and closing of SOEs. Also, the country's pell-mell growth has created an energy shortage; there is simply not enough power to sustain the economy's expansion. Consequently, the government has underwritten massive investment in hydroelectric plants, which in turn has led to the construction of a staggering number of dams. As the reader has learned in this volume, China's energy deficit is complemented by a lack of water so substantial that it requires massive hydro-engineering intervention to redirect the course of southern rivers to divert water to an increasingly dry North.[8] These are necessary adjustments to current exigency, but they offer little promise of achieving a balance between the needs of nature and the commercial impulses of humankind. Sustainability and violent destruction fight like two parties in a civil war.

As this war rages and as Chinese banks increasingly underwrite the U.S. occupation of Iraq and a U.S. domestic housing bubble, the challenging complexity and fearfulness of the present lie beyond our reach because they are hidden, in plain sight, in our headlines. The chapters of this book have made more salient this complexity and given the reader the intellectual and analytical tools necessary to make sense of today's China. A recurring theme in these chapters has been the commercial confluence of globalization, and it is fitting here at the close of the volume to give consideration to this topic, and particularly to consider the misfortune that results from a persistent tendency in Beijing and Washington, D.C., to focus narrowly on the specific national advantages of markets and competition in the pursuit of profit.

GLOBALIZATION AND THE END OF POLARITY

With the convulsive international phenomena of production and distribution we call globalization, the movements of market forces might tend to mitigate the intensity of the bilateral national frameworks according to which the United States and China interpret their relations. Through the global commercial interrelatedness enshrined in the agreements of the WTO, national friction may be overcome by cultural fusion. But what does it mean if polarities dissolve, especially when so much of our political consciousness was made from them? Actually, the question should be put differently: What is the consequence of the collapse of the dichotomous paradigms of security, economic growth, and political expansion to which these two nations have long cleaved? Is this evidence of postmodernity, a world in which the strain of global alliance and interchange (perhaps caused by the urgent pursuit of global capital) negates the reflex for national distinction? One cannot help but wonder if this post–September 11 world has fomented disequilibrium without a name, a moment uncaptured or uncapturable. It is difficult to imagine a time in our modern history in which popular consciousness of change, specifically salient change, was so endemic in the popular imagination. Nevertheless, the habits of mind bred of a half-century of a theory of international politics governed by laws of action and reaction persist. This is an orientation that is responsible for both conflict and imitation.

In a visit to the United States, the editor of a Chinese newspaper offered an astute analysis of the electoral demographics of the country and a searing reflection on the advantageous consequences for China of the demotion of the U.S. moral stature in the world. Commenting on the Chinese leadership's thoughts on the 2004 U.S. presidential election, he said that they favored George W. Bush because of the damage Bush had wrought to the international perception of the United States. One important consequence of the decline in respect for the United States, he pointed out, was the elevation of China's standing in global public opinion.[9] Now the United States, rather than China, was perceived as a significant threat to world peace.

My ardent hope is that we abandon this ideology of scarcity in which one nation's gain is the other's loss and explore alternative paradigms for our relations, paradigms that foster the projection of very different, but compatible, national goals. One area rich with prospects for the collaborative exploration of alternative conceptions of bilateral relations is economic growth and environmental destruction. And in the pursuit of effective maintenance of this delicate equipoise, there is a greater, and for both countries a more sobering, challenge: security.

In the face of mounting concerns about the threat of terrorism, the presumption of mutual security in a global commonweal is difficult to maintain. Furthermore, this habit of bipolar scarcity is a common theme of the media in its efforts to represent the "rise of China," another infelicitous phrase.

CONFLICT OR CONFLUENCE:
THE FUTURE OF SUPERPOWERS

If you were paying attention to the news in spring of 2005, whether reading it online or in a newspaper (but probably not watching television), there were a few items that, taken individually or, better, together, might be viewed as landmarks along a path of involvement in China and as a message of alarm to the two largest world powers. I am not referring in this instance to recurring, apprehensive commentary on China's military expansion, the stubborn pegging of China's national currency to the dollar, escalating tensions between Japan and China, or querulous exchanges between the United

States and China on the role the latter must play in the six-party talks with North Korea. The stories to which I wish to call the reader's attention did not enjoy such prominence. Merely blips on the media radar, they were distress signals that may be viewed as international public facts of a brief on behalf of collaboration for environmental recovery.

Item 1: On May 10, 2005, Jeffrey Immelt, the chief executive officer of General Electric (GE), defied U.S. environmental policy and stated that mandatory controls on carbon dioxide (CO_2) emissions were necessary and said that his company would double its investment in energy and environmental technologies to help other countries such as China reduce greenhouse gases. The political significance of Immelt's statement was his admission that the reduction of emissions from the burning of fossil fuels was a critical global priority on which both the United States and China must focus. The sense of shared responsibility stated in GE's commitment to the transfer and application of key technologies suggests a way toward a credible response to global climate change, wherein the corporation, rather than the government, assumes the responsibility to act.[10]

Item 2: On May 17, 2005, the Xinhua News Agency, an official press outlet of the Chinese government, quoted Chinese scientists conducting research on Mount Everest who reported dangerously accelerated glacial melting on the mountain. The melting point of one glacier had risen about 165 feet in two years—a pace more than twice as fast as normal. This alarming finding is perfectly consistent with reports of melting glaciers and the substantive thinning of the polar icecaps that have been presented for more than a decade. Several months later, in the fall of 2005, the Chinese government announced that automobiles produced in China would have to meet higher fuel efficiency standards, higher than those currently imposed in the United States.

Item 3: On May 19, 2005, B15G, a thirty-one-mile-long iceberg that had calved off the Ross Ice Shelf in 2000, drifted to within sight of Australia's Casey Station near Vicennes Bay, Antarctica. Comprising more than 220 cubic kilometers of ice—equivalent to 200 trillion liters of water—B15G was the first such massive iceberg to travel over 150 kilometers south over the continental shelf.

Dramatic evidence of the scope of climate change far from the shores of the United States and China casts in relief the consequences of development. Science urgently needs to generate appropriate policy guidelines and responses to these developments. It is also critical that the United States and China, the world's largest polluters, assume the leadership necessary to develop alternative, environmentally responsible energies and that they encourage their citizens to conserve and to see in the salvation of the planet an opportunity to advance their national economies.

Global warming is so widely reported in the united States that it has become the stuff of jokes, particularly in the upper Midwest, New England,

and the East, where winter temperatures since 2000 have been ten to sixteen degrees Fahrenheit above normal.[11] Ecology is our planetary dilemma; there is no way around it, because we are surrounded by it, implicated in, and affected by its fate. Global warming, far more than the market, is the great equalizer, and after more than twenty-five years of findings, inquiries, observations, research, and published results (the National Academy of Sciences alone has published more than two hundred reports on this topic), we know that expanding human habitat has caused dramatic climate change: all the world's glaciers are melting—those in Glacier National Park, for example will vanish entirely by 2030; the perennial sea ice that once covered 1.7 billion acres of the Arctic has shrunk by 250 million acres (roughly the area of New York, Georgia, and Texas combined); the oceans have warmed, risen in volume, and grown more acidic; and the range of day and nighttime temperatures is narrowing. Other signs cannot be overlooked, but they may be disregarded if our attention to explicit detail is absorbed by regard for the phantasmagoria of the globalized economy and its prospects for profit and loss. It is this inevitability of increased and substantial risk to human survival that one can hope will bring a reckoning of China and the United States with the pathology of unconstrained development. In China there is hope for action, for as we pointed out in the introduction to this book, China also has a great amount of popular political protest in defense of the environment.

In April 2005, as many as fifty thousand peasants from Huaxi Village in Zhejiang Province rioted in protest against local industrial pollution, destroying police cars and fighting with police officers (see chapter 2).[12] This is certainly one way of focusing the minds of policymakers on the urgency of the environmental problem. And ecology is but one of the unexpected avenues of wider democratic expression available to the common people, at least in China. In the United States, it is less clear that citizens have connected the dots of economy, environment, and politics, because most of them cannot see and feel the consequence of the hazards. The Kyoto Protocol, now aggressively pushed by the United States' European and Asian allies, who are keenly aware of the larger security implications of CO_2 emissions, remains too abstract and unread to foment activity among U.S. citizens and is unknown to most people in China.

A MORAL VALEDICTORY

The matter of *second-generation rights* has been raised in each of the international discussions surrounding the Kyoto Protocol. Because the degeneration of the ozone layer is occurring now more rapidly, this demonstrably raises questions about responsibility and reaction. What should be done, and how should it be carried out? The Chinese argue that as a developing nation with pockets of profound poverty, they should be permitted the ecological freedom to develop with haste—to generate the energy and economic opportunities they require to satisfy the needs of the world's largest population. It is for this reason that the Kyoto Protocol, which went into effect in February of 2005, does not require China, India, or other newly developing nations to reduce their CO_2 emissions in the first phase of the treaty, from 2005 to 2011. The argument in support of international indulgence for China's pollution extends farther in the minds of many Chinese, as readers will note from other chapters in this book, to the right to obtain material comforts equivalent to those enjoyed by U.S. citizens. The consequences of this reasoning are most obvious at the multiplying sites of environmental protest in China and in Hong Kong, and in the cities of Japan and Taiwan, where air pollution and acid rain from China imperil the daily quality of life.

The United States and other developed nations contend that China cannot be given such license to pollute, because the current levels of China's CO_2 production and sulfur dioxide (SO_2) effluent are unsustainable. Focusing on the current rapid pace of global environmental degradation, the United States, believing that the accords demand too much of it and at too great an economic cost, has refused to endorse the Kyoto Protocol. The Chinese contend, as do other less-gargantuan investors in development, that the ozone layer's decline that we presently document was caused by more than two centuries of industrial pollution by Western developing, and now developed, nations. The only way I can imagine transcending the pendulum-like claim and counterclaim of this perspective on environmental right is to compel our two most prominent citizen nations of the globe to think in the context of planetary commonweal and reconcile the good of national economic growth with the globalization of environmental poverty.

My thoughts are given over to the mutual responsibility of China and the United States and the particular global burden that each must bear in reconciling the demands of its citizens with the expectations of the world.[13] It has never been clearer that the fate of both nations is interconnected, although this may not be immediately evident to U.S. citizens, whose broader political consciousness is obscured by "the fog of war" and a vision foreshortened by a narrow and often uncompromising self-interest. China seems now the better prepared for this transition, because it is investing heavily in alternative, cleaner technologies for energy production even as it continues to generate an inhospitable volume of CO_2 gas. The United States is not so inclined; conservation and energy alternatives are explicitly outside the "unvarnished" and undisclosed recommendations of U.S. vice president Dick Cheney's "secret energy task force." Although in his 2006 State of the Union Address President George W. Bush candidly asserted that the United States is "addicted to foreign oil," his administration has not shown strong leadership on this issue and has provided precious little funding to explore "greener" solutions to this problem.

Under its present political leadership, the United States is ill equipped, it seems, to accept the obvious, so it denies it—we do not torture, we are bringing democracy to Iraq, we do not eavesdrop on U.S. citizens without obtaining a court order, the war in Iraq will cost no more than $50 billion. This recitation of untruth is offered not to provoke anger but only to point out how difficult it has become to believe that the U.S. government can act prudently and appropriately in any context of political cost. Consequently, it is unlikely that it can lead its citizens to grapple with the extinction of the planet's resources.[14] Instead, against the ominous projections of its own climate scientists, loudly echoed in the halls of world environmental summits, the United States defends its right to pollute beyond all reasonable constraint on the grounds of economic viability. It is an impulsive defense built on a false dichotomy: economic growth versus environmental stewardship.

The Chinese government is certainly no more courageous in its calculation of national economic gain against ecological adversity. China, like the United States, argues in a similar vein for its national right to burn grand volumes of fossil fuels. Moreover, because the prospect for substantial economic betterment underwrites the CCP's legitimacy, limitless economic growth and political stability are profoundly intertwined. Dr. Song Jian, chairman of the State Science and Technology Commission at the closing ceremony of the China Council for International Co-operation on Environment and Development on October 5, 1997, articulated the fatal nationalist bind of this dilemma in saying,

We fully understand the worldwide campaign to battle the climate change spearheaded by the European Union and Nordic Countries. The voice of small island states also brooks no ignorance. According to the United Nations Framework Convention on Climate Change (UNFCCC) and the Berlin Mandate, China bears no responsibility for reducing greenhouse gas emissions. When we ask the opinions of people from all circles, many people, in particular the scientists think that the emissions control standard should be formulated on a per capita basis. According to the UN Charter, everybody is born equal, and has inalienable rights to enjoy modern technological civilization. Today the per capita consumption is just one tenth of that of the developed countries, one eighth of that of medium developed countries. It is estimated 30–40 years would be needed for China to catch up with the level of medium developed countries. No one is entitled to prohibit families from using refrigerators or those who live or work in such a high temperature of 40 degrees Celsius from enjoying air-conditioning. However the Chinese people and government do [*sic*] have realized their due responsibilities for the global climate change and committed to make efforts to lower down the increase rate of greenhouse gas emissions.[15]

The Chinese government is more mindful of the downside of its Faustian bargain with development, as reflected in its increased demand for higher fuel efficiency standards for all new automobiles and by a call by President Hu Jintao for cleaner energy production facilities. Nonetheless, with a $1.65 trillion economy that expands at 10 percent per year, environment is the first casualty in China.

Again, these two nations meet at a fault line, and both mirror the investment policies of the other, to their own detriment and to the destruction of the earth. The United States burns 600 million metric tons of coal per year while China burns 800 million metric tons, and China currently plans to build as many as five hundred more coal-fired electricity generating plants by 2030. Although the incineration of coal is the greatest source of CO_2 production, the oil needs of these two national powers and a rapidly developing India will also dramatically affect annual global oil consumption, increasing it from 80 million barrels to 119 barrels a day by 2025. The International Energy Agency's World Energy Outlook for 2004 projected that without change in the energy consumption habits of China, India, and the United States, CO_2 emissions in 2030 will be 62 percent greater than today. Economic expansion, sustained by the exhaustion of nonrenewable resources, is justified by national, legally defined right. Yet in light of mounting global environmental disaster, it is necessary that we discuss the limitations of the national right to pursue prosperity at the expense of others.

Apropos of a new mode of, say, global partnership, there is the disturbing fact that China and the United States have balked at international cooperation in the preservation of biodiversity. The recent publication by the Asia-Pacific Partnership on Clean Development and Climate (also known as the AP6, and made up of Australia, China, India, Japan, South Korea, and the United States) of a communiqué intended to address the immediate challenges of the Kyoto Protocol, affirms as a premise that "fossil fuels underpin our economies and will be an enduring reality for our lifetimes and beyond."[16] There could be no more eloquent and tragic testament to the shortsightedness of current policy initiatives of politicians. These nations may be "entitled" by dint of national interest to depend on unclean and unrenewable sources of energy, yet we must insist that such interest is trumped by the needs of the international community. Environmental issues can no longer be separated from issues of world politics and national sovereignty, territorial integrity, and so forth. And it is the environment that will bring the United States and China to their knees. This more than military security, because there will be little security of any sort when there is no environmental health and no energy security.

As observers of China engaged in our own domestic politics, it is important that while acknowledging the constructive direction of China's national agenda, we question respectfully the mechanisms of that agenda's realization. No one nation has the norm of norms, and yet the historical experience of the United States as a twentieth-century democratic, industrial power has led to an exceptionalist ethic buried in the bowels of its being: the world's sole superpower, the greatest country in the world—claims all belied by the more compelling truth of progressive impoverishment. A nationalist ideology when questioned can harden into preferential blindness, such that the most evident and disturbing facts are banished from consciousness or at least frozen in a moment in which the chasm between awareness and action becomes a canyon of resigned quietude.

It is now more necessary than at any other time in their shared histories for these two great nations to obey the flows of their global currents of common predicament and advantage and arrive at a port of conjoined fates, national and international. By understanding more about China and the Chinese, who already know a very great deal about the United States and its citizens, we are more likely to transcend the headlines of our national reactions and find the headwaters of our global cooperation. For this we will need to create appropriate models of multilateral, strategic cooperation on common environmental urgency. China and the United States must devote their future endeavors to addressing these concerns.

Readers would do well to obtain a firm grasp of the complexities of environmental and energy security while not losing sight of the actions and the global disposition of their native countries. In the end these two "most-favored nations" must be able to conceive and ultimately act on what their citizens in their hearts secretly know: that without the earth and its resources, there is no security. Moreover, in this new and very curious circumstance of global indeterminacy and national threat, they will have to rely on the work of future generations of students, among Chinese and U.S. citizens, and on the Chinese and U.S. studies that will shape those students as the leaders who will finally bring clarity to misapprehension through wider understanding of the shared jeopardy of our two nations' exceptionalist pursuit of grander transformations. There is much to be done, and frighteningly little time.

NOTES

1. Joint Communiqué of the United States of America and the People's Republic of China (Shanghai Communiqué), February 28, 1972.

2. In all fairness, I must note that since 2003, India has assumed the role of another possible contender for the status of superpower, and there is an expanding

journalistic and scholarly literature on the race between China and India to become the next economic superpower. See Carl J. Dahlman and Anuja Utz, *India and the Knowledge Economy: Leveraging Strengths and Opportunities* (Washington, D.C.: World Bank, 2005); Raj Kapila and Uma Kapila, *India's Economy in the 21st Century* (New York: Academic Foundation, 2005); and Edward Friedman and Bruce Gilley, *Asia's Giants: Comparing China and India* (New York: Palgrave MacMillan, 2005).

3. Will Durham and Jim Wolf, "Pentagon Plans New Arms to Meet Rivals like China," Reuters News Service, February 3, 2006. The Quadrennial Defense Review comes on the heels of an earlier, vaguely ominous report from the Pentagon titled *The Military Power of the People's Republic of China* (July 2005), which tendentiously portrays an accelerated expansion of the Chinese military intended to conduct campaigns throughout Asia.

4. Michael T. Klare, "Revving Up the China Threat," *The Nation*, October 24, 2005, 28–32.

5. According to Lester R. Brown ("A New World Order," *Guardian*, January 25, 2006, www.guardian.co.uk/china/story/0,,1694346,00.html), China now consumes twice as much meat and more than twice as much steel as the United States.

6. Committee of Concerned Asian Scholars, *China! Inside the People's Republic* (New York: Bantam, 1972); Orville Schell, *In the People's Republic: An American's First-Hand View of Living and Working in China* (New York: Vintage, 1978).

7. *Detroit Free Press*, January 6, 2006, A1.

8. Water scarcity in China is an enormous problem (see chapter 2). According to the Chinese government's Ministry of Water Resources, 60 percent of China's 660 cities face water shortages, and 110 of these cities, including Beijing and Tianjin, face "extreme shortages." So far the multiple strategies involving conservation measures advanced by the government—diverting river flow and liberally seeding clouds— have had little effect. Stocks of potable water are frighteningly low because China is the leading producer of organic water pollution, more than India, Japan, and the United States combined. Nathan Nankivell, "China's Mounting Water Crisis and the Implications for the Chinese Communist Party" (paper, Twelfth Annual CANCAPS Conference, Quebec City, Quebec, December 3–5, 2004).

9. Galal Walker, personal communication, September 6, 2005.

10. The private urge to advance initiatives to develop environmentally sustainable alternatives in energy production is already in evidence in the comprehensive plans of Matsushita (Panasonic) to reclaim polluted sites, reduce CO_2 emissions, enhance energy conservation, and, in concert with the European Union (EU), provide low-cost, high-efficiency recycling while eliminating the use of chemical substances such as lead, mercury, cadmium, and hexavalent chromium, all severely restricted under the EU's Regulation of Hazardous Substances Directive.

11. *New York Times*, "(Barely) Winter '06: Buttercups Are in Bloom," February 3, 2006, A18. According to the National Weather Service, January 2006 was one of the warmest on record throughout the United States. From December 2005 through January 2006, it was so warm that buttercups poked through the soil in Montana and people in Maine played golf in shorts. At the same time, Europe and Russia experienced unusually frigid temperatures.

12. There is additional examination of this case in chapter 3.

13. A 2005 study produced by the National Center for Atmospheric Research at the University of Colorado, Boulder, found that the increase in Chinese imports to the U.S. economy increased the total CO_2 emissions from both countries by 720 million metric tons between 1997 and 2003. The 2003 U.S. emissions of CO_2 would have been 6 percent higher if the United States had manufactured the products it imported from China. Moreover, China's 2003 emissions would have been 14 percent lower had it not produced goods for the U.S. market.

14. Even more astounding in this context is the Bush administration's explicit rejection of conservation and its discouragement of the institution of higher CAFE (corporate average fuel economy) standards for vehicles. During the period of the first oil embargo from 1973 to 1974, the new conservation habits of U.S. consumers resulted in roughly a 30-percent decrease in oil consumption.

15. Song Jian, "China Calls for Equal Per Capita Emissions: Extract from a Speech by Dr. Song Jian," www.gci.org.uk/cop3/songjian.html.

16. As quoted in Wendy Frew, "A Do-Nothing Way of Saving Us All," *Sydney Morning Herald*, January 13, 2006.

Index

AIDS (*aize bing*). *See* HIV/AIDS.
All China Federation of Trade Unions
(ACFTU), 76, 83, 85. *See also* labor
agriculture: farmer rights, 83; farm
taxes, 83
anti-Japanese: sentiment, 9, 123–24,
140–41; protests, 9, 112–14, 121–22,
124
Asian Cup (2004), 112, 124
Asia-Pacific Partnership on Clean
Development, 316

beauty salons (brothels), 228–32; New
Wind Hair Salon, 218, 228–30. *See
also* prostitution
Beijing: 2008 Olympics, 63–65; Beijing
bureau, 34; Beijing Office of
Environmental Defense, 77; Beijing
University, 59; Center for Legal
Assistance to the Victims of
Pollution, 57; central government,
74; energy needs, 78; compared to
the rest of the country, 69; and
foreign journalists, 35; Global
Village of, 56; and political strength,
27
Beijing massacre, 285, 291–94,
300–301n1; confusion surrounding,

292–93; death toll of, 292–94;
explanation of, 300–301n1; power
struggle behind, 293; reporting of,
293. *See also* Tiananmen Square
Berkeley China Internet Project, 130–31
Bernays, Edward (propaganda
advocate), 206–7, 210
bird flu (avian influenza, H5N1), 25,
177, 180
Boxer Rebellion. *See* Century of
Humiliation
Bush, George H. W. (41st president),
303, 305; Bush, George W. (43rd
president), 305, 311; and 2006 State
of the Union Address, 314

capitalism: in China, 68–69, 85, 119;
global capitalism, 9; and
globalization, 304–5, 310–11
cellular phones, 8, 130; and
journalists, 42; and popular protest,
140–41
censorship: American corporations and,
131–32; Chinese Internet police
and, 131; Great Firewall, 8–9, 106,
132–33; history of, 133; keyword
filtering software, 131; and literature,
174n5; and news media, 204; and

About the Contributors

Susan D. Blum is associate professor of cultural and linguistic anthropology and director of the Center for Asian Studies at the University of Notre Dame. Her favorite class to teach is Food and Culture. She is the author of *Portrait of "Primitives": Ordering Human Kinds in the Chinese Nation* (2000) and *Lies That Bind: Chinese Truth, Other Truths* (2007) and the coeditor of *China Off Center: Mapping the Margins of the Middle Kingdom* (2002).

Bei Dao (Zhao Zhenkai) is an honorary member of the American Academy of Arts and Letters and visiting professor of creative writing and East Asian languages and literatures at the University of Notre Dame. He is also co-founder and editor of China's first postrevolution, unofficial literary journal, *Today* [*Jintian*]. His work has been translated into thirty languages and includes five volumes of poetry in English: *Unlock* (2000), *Landscape over Zero* (1996), *Forms of Distance* (1994), *Old Snow* (1992), and *The August Sleepwalker* (1990); a collection of stories, *Waves* (1990); and the essay collections *Blue House* (2000) and *Midnight's Gate* (2005). He has won numerous awards and honors, including the Jeanette Schocken Literary Prize (2005).

Timothy Cheek holds the Louis Cha Chair in Chinese Research at the Institute of Asian Research, University of British Columbia. He is also editor of the journal *Pacific Affairs*. His research, teaching, and translating focus on the recent history of China, especially the role of Chinese intellectuals in the twentieth century and the history of the Chinese Communist Party. His books include *Mao Zedong and China's Revolutions* (2002) and *Propaganda and Culture in Mao's China* (1997), as well as *New Perspectives on State*

Socialism in China (1997), with Tony Saich, and *The Secret Speeches of Chairman Mao* (1989), with Roderick MacFarquhar and Eugene Wu.

Martin Fackler is currently based in Tokyo for the *New York Times*, covering the economies of Japan and South Korea. He was a correspondent in Beijing and Shanghai for The Associated Press from 2000 to 2003. Since 1996 he has written about East Asia for several publications and news services. In 2005 he was part of a team of reporters at the *Wall Street Journal* who won an award from the Society of Publishers in Asia for coverage of the Indian Ocean tsunami.

John Gittings first visited China in 1971 and later taught at the University of Westminster. He was for many years East Asia editor and foreign leader-writer at the *Guardian* and in 2001 opened the paper's first staff bureau in Shanghai. He is now a research associate at the School of Oriental and African Studies Centre of Chinese Studies, University of London, where he is working on peace issues and nuclear proliferation. His most recent book is *The Changing Face of China: From Mao to Market* (2005).

Howard Goldblatt is research professor of Chinese at the University of Notre Dame. He has translated dozens of Chinese-language novels and story collections into English. His translation of *Notes of a Desolate Man* (with Sylvia Li-chün Lin) was selected as the American Literary Translators Association's Translation of the Year for 1999.

Peter Hays Gries is the Harold J. and Ruth Newman Chair in U.S.-China Issues and director of the Institute of U.S.-China Security Studies at the University of Oklahoma. He is the author of *China's New Nationalism: Pride, Politics, and Diplomacy* (2005) and coeditor with Stanley Rosen of *State and Society in 21st Century China: Crisis, Contention, and Legitimation* (2004) and has written over twenty journal articles and book chapters.

Sandra Teresa Hyde is assistant professor in the departments of Anthropology and Social Studies of Medicine at McGill University in Montréal. She is the author of *Eating Spring Rice: The Cultural Politics of AIDS in Southwest China* (2006). Her current research focuses on the prevention and treatment of injection drug use in Yunnan province, in addition to continuing research in North America on how scientists and physicians have reconfigured notions of gender through the endocrinological treatment of the intersexed infant.

Lionel M. Jensen is associate professor and chair of the Department of East Asian Languages and Literatures at the University of Notre Dame, where he also serves as faculty fellow in the Helen Kellogg Institute of International Studies and the Joan B. Kroc Institute for International Peace Studies. He is the author of *Manufacturing Confucianism: Chinese Traditions and Universal Civilization* (1997) and coeditor with Susan D. Blum of *China Off Center: Mapping the Margins of the Middle Kingdom* (2002).

Tong Lam is assistant professor of history at the University of Toronto. He has previously written on Chinese ultranationalism, and his current research project is a book-length study of the role of social science in the making of the Chinese nation-state in the early twentieth century.

Sylvia Li-chün Lin is an assistant professor of Chinese at the University of Notre Dame, and she has written on modern and contemporary Chinese literature and culture. She has also translated fiction from Chinese into English. Her current book project is *Representing Atrocity in Taiwan: The 2/28 Incident and White Terror in Fiction and Film*.

Jonathan S. Noble has taught Chinese language, culture, media, and film at the University of Notre Dame, The Ohio State University, and the College of William and Mary. In addition to publishing a wide assortment of scholarly articles and translations, he has translated over thirty Chinese dramas and films, and he is editing a collection of Meng Jinghui's experimental dramas. He is a member of the National Committee on United States–China Relations (NCUSCR) Public Intellectuals Program.

Tim Oakes is associate professor of geography at the University of Colorado, Boulder. His recently published books include *Translocal China: Linkages, Identities, and the Reimagining of Space* (2006), *Travels in Paradox: Remapping Tourism* (2006), and *Reinventing Tunpu: Cultural Tourism and Social Change in Guizhou* (published in Chinese). He is currently writing an ethnography of Guizhou's Tunpu people.

David Ownby is professor of history and director of the Center for East Asian Studies at the University of Montréal. He has written extensively on the history of secret societies and popular religion in China and has just completed *Falun Gong and China's Future* (2007).

Judith Shapiro is the author of *Mao's War against Nature: Politics and the Environment in Revolutionary China* (2001) and coauthor with Liang Heng of *Son of the Revolution* (1983) and *After the Nightmare* (1987). She directs American University's global environmental politics programs at the School of International Service in Washington, D.C.

Timothy B. Weston is associate professor of history at the University of Colorado, Boulder. He is coeditor of *China beyond the Headlines* (2000) and author of *The Power of Position: Beijing University, Intellectuals, and Chinese Political Culture, 1898–1929* (2004). He recently guest-edited an issue of *Twentieth Century China* focused on newspaper journalism in Republican-era China, which is also the subject of his current book project.

Xiao Qiang is director of the China Internet Project at the Graduate School of Journalism, University of California, Berkeley. He was founding executive director (1991–2002) of the New York–based nongovernmental organization Human Rights in China and was a recipient of a MacArthur Fellowship in 2001.